Heart of the City

A Mark Tatulli Comic

Heart of the City

Andrews McMeel
Publishing

Kansas City

Heart of the City is distributed internationally by Universal Press Syndicate.

00 01 02 03 04 BAH 10 9 8 7 6 5 4 3 2 1

ISBN: 0-7407-0576-8

Library of Congress Catalog Card Number: 99-68670

Heart of the City may be viewed on the Internet at:
www.uexpress.com

E-mail Mark Tatulli at heartofthecity@hotmail.com

TO DONNA –

THE LOVE OF
MY LIFE;
THE SOUL
OF MY WORK

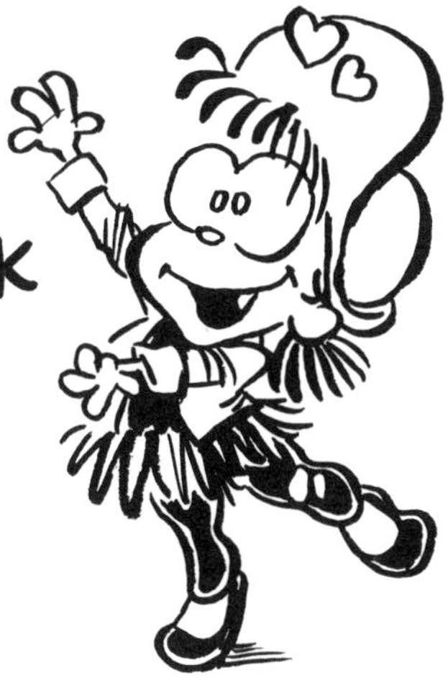

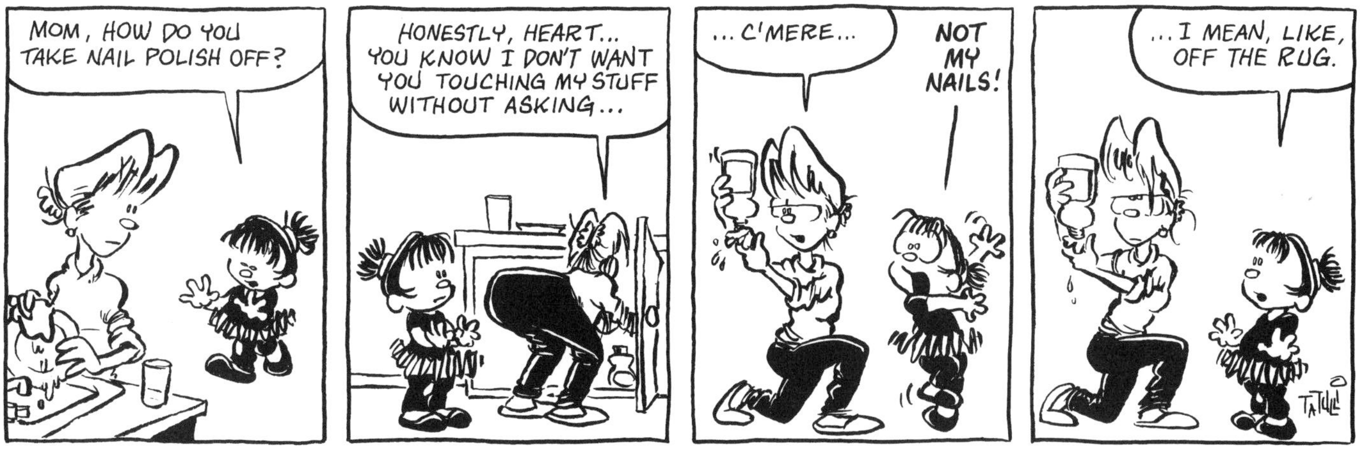
MOM, HOW DO YOU TAKE NAIL POLISH OFF?
HONESTLY, HEART... YOU KNOW I DON'T WANT YOU TOUCHING MY STUFF WITHOUT ASKING...
... C'MERE...
NOT MY NAILS!
... I MEAN, LIKE, OFF THE RUG.

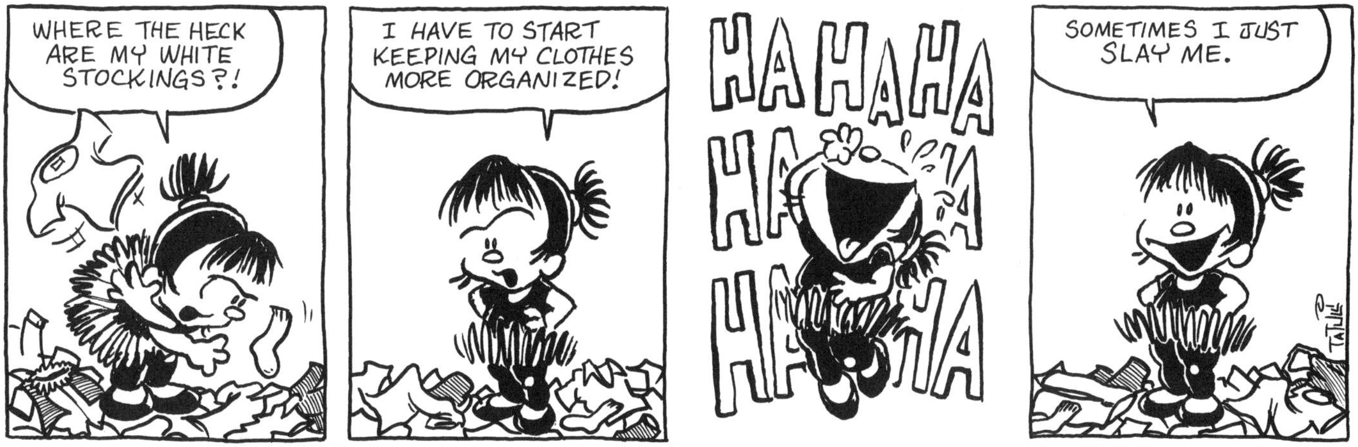
WHERE THE HECK ARE MY WHITE STOCKINGS?!
I HAVE TO START KEEPING MY CLOTHES MORE ORGANIZED!
HAHAHA HA HA HA
SOMETIMES I JUST SLAY ME.

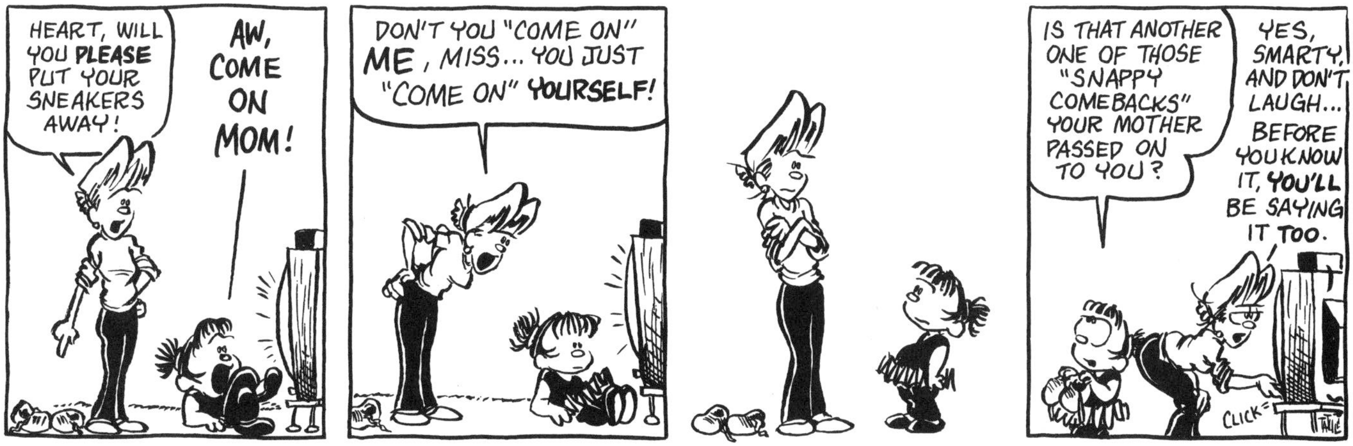
HEART, WILL YOU PLEASE PUT YOUR SNEAKERS AWAY!
AW, COME ON MOM!
DON'T YOU "COME ON" ME, MISS... YOU JUST "COME ON" YOURSELF!
IS THAT ANOTHER ONE OF THOSE "SNAPPY COMEBACKS" YOUR MOTHER PASSED ON TO YOU?
YES, SMARTY, AND DON'T LAUGH... BEFORE YOU KNOW IT, YOU'LL BE SAYING IT TOO.
CLICK

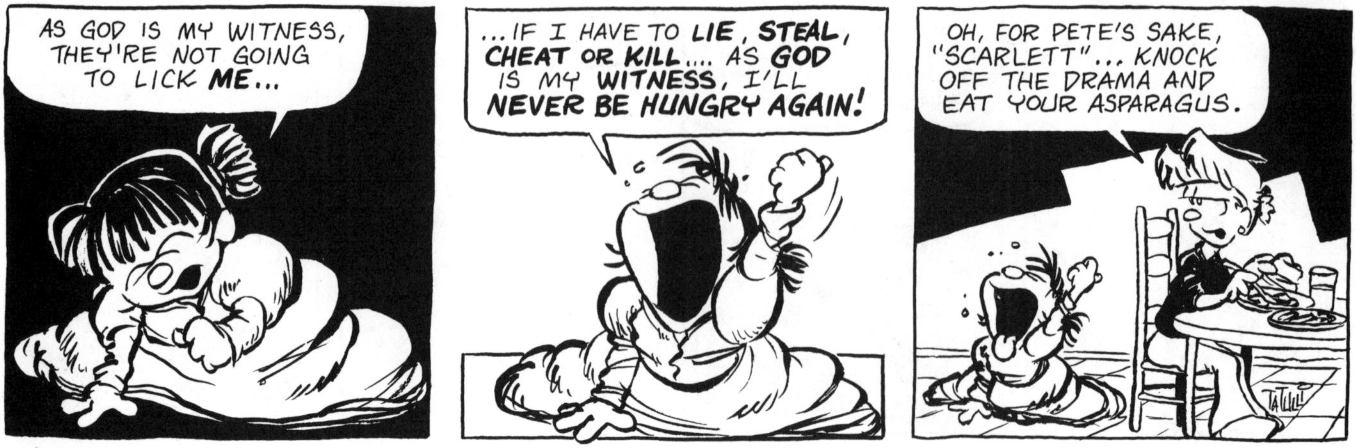
AS GOD IS MY WITNESS, THEY'RE NOT GOING TO LICK **ME**...
...IF I HAVE TO **LIE**, **STEAL**, **CHEAT OR KILL**.... AS **GOD** IS MY **WITNESS**, I'LL **NEVER BE HUNGRY AGAIN!**
OH, FOR PETE'S SAKE, "SCARLETT"... KNOCK OFF THE DRAMA AND EAT YOUR ASPARAGUS.

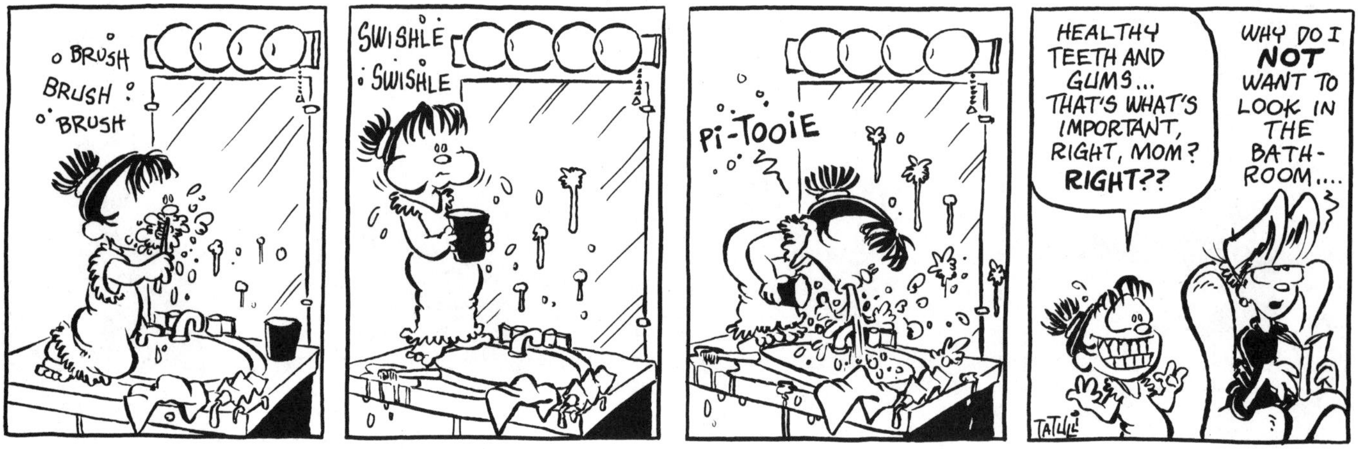
BRUSH
BRUSH
BRUSH
SWISHLE
SWISHLE
PI-TOOIE
HEALTHY TEETH AND GUMS... THAT'S WHAT'S IMPORTANT, RIGHT, MOM? **RIGHT??**
WHY DO I **NOT** WANT TO LOOK IN THE BATH-ROOM....

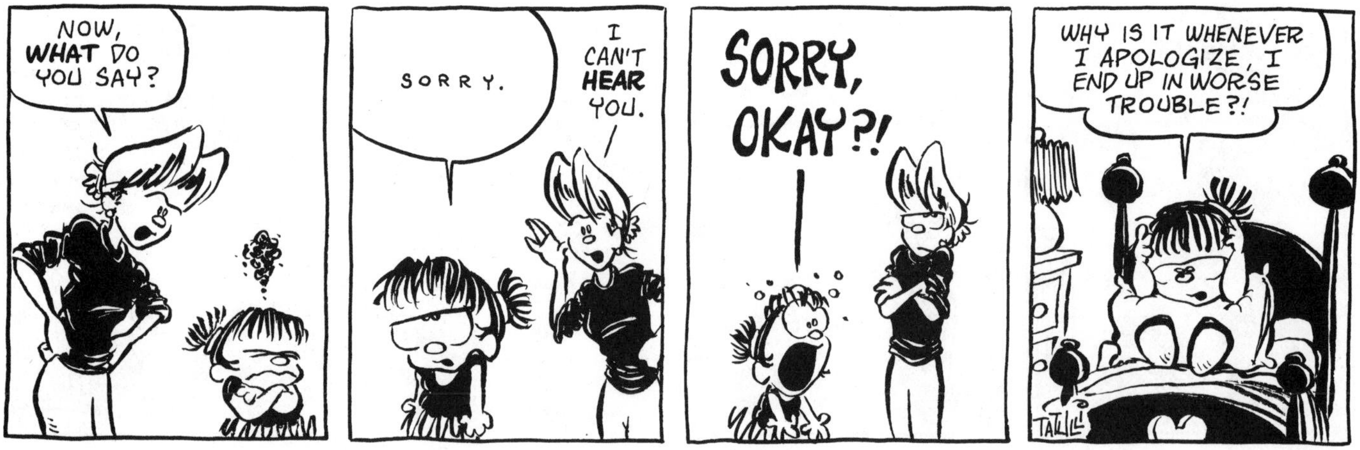
NOW, **WHAT** DO YOU SAY?
SORRY.
I CAN'T **HEAR** YOU.
SORRY, OKAY?!
WHY IS IT WHENEVER I APOLOGIZE, I END UP IN WORSE TROUBLE?!

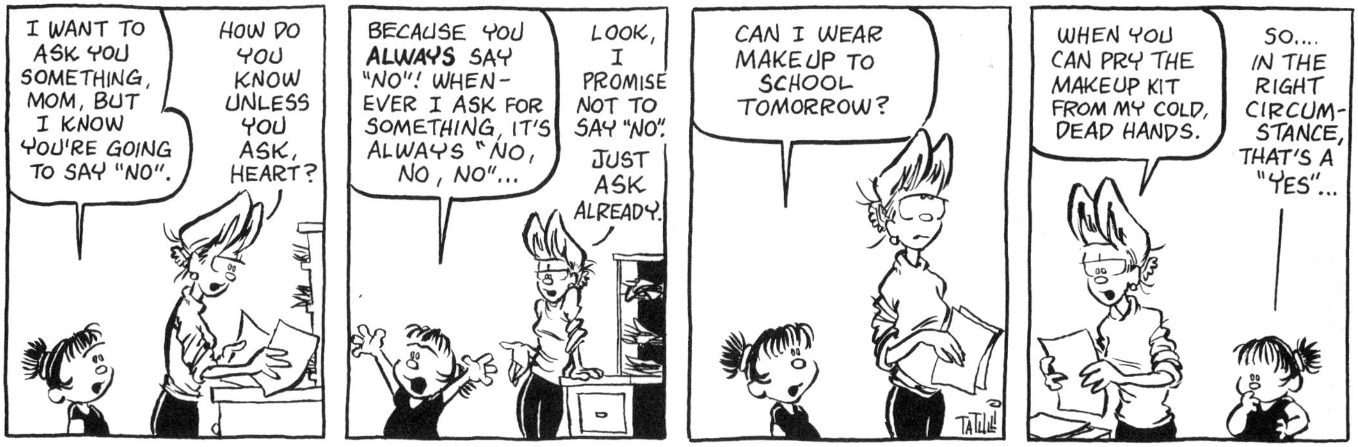
I WANT TO ASK YOU SOMETHING, MOM, BUT I KNOW YOU'RE GOING TO SAY "NO".
HOW DO YOU KNOW UNLESS YOU ASK, HEART?
BECAUSE YOU **ALWAYS** SAY "NO"! WHENEVER I ASK FOR SOMETHING, IT'S ALWAYS "NO, NO, NO"...
LOOK, I PROMISE NOT TO SAY "NO". JUST ASK ALREADY.
CAN I WEAR MAKEUP TO SCHOOL TOMORROW?
TATULLI
WHEN YOU CAN PRY THE MAKEUP KIT FROM MY COLD, DEAD HANDS.
SO.... IN THE RIGHT CIRCUMSTANCE, THAT'S A "YES"...

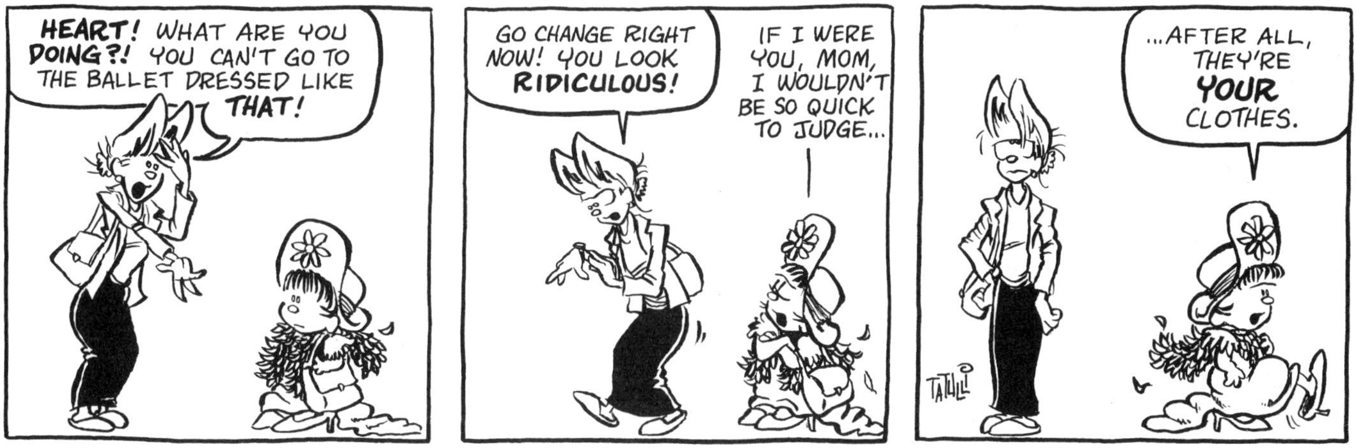
HEART! WHAT ARE YOU **DOING?!** YOU CAN'T GO TO THE BALLET DRESSED LIKE **THAT!**
GO CHANGE RIGHT NOW! YOU LOOK **RIDICULOUS!**
IF I WERE YOU, MOM, I WOULDN'T BE SO QUICK TO JUDGE...
...AFTER ALL, THEY'RE **YOUR** CLOTHES.
TATULLI

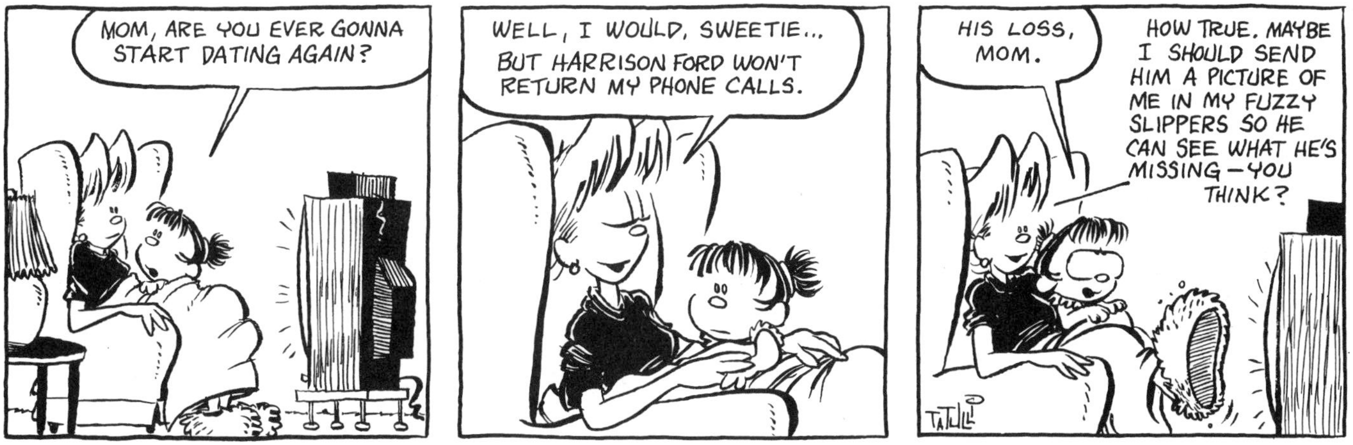
MOM, ARE YOU EVER GONNA START DATING AGAIN?
WELL, I WOULD, SWEETIE... BUT HARRISON FORD WON'T RETURN MY PHONE CALLS.
HIS LOSS, MOM.
HOW TRUE. MAYBE I SHOULD SEND HIM A PICTURE OF ME IN MY FUZZY SLIPPERS SO HE CAN SEE WHAT HE'S MISSING—YOU THINK?
TATULLI

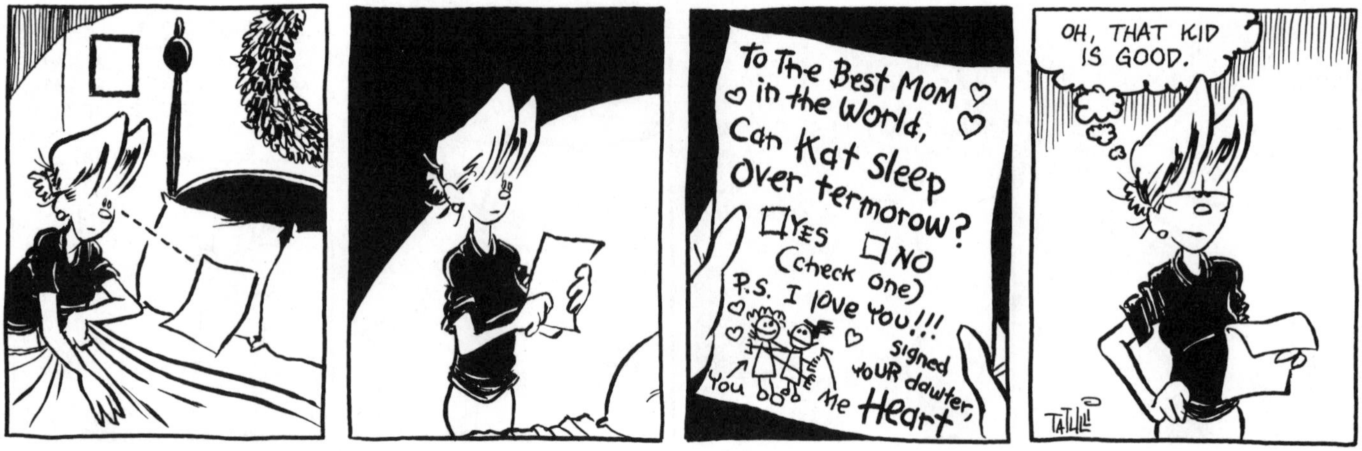
To The Best Mom in the World,
Can Kat Sleep Over termorow?
YES NO
(check one)
P.S. I love You!!!
signed your dawter, Heart
You
Me
OH, THAT KID IS GOOD.
TATULLI

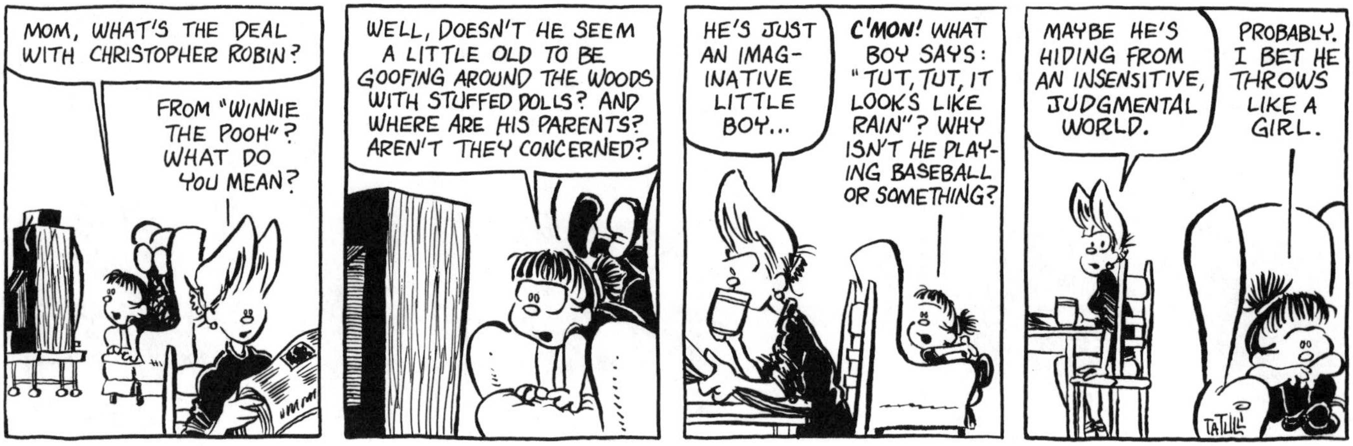
MOM, WHAT'S THE DEAL WITH CHRISTOPHER ROBIN?
FROM "WINNIE THE POOH"? WHAT DO YOU MEAN?
WELL, DOESN'T HE SEEM A LITTLE OLD TO BE GOOFING AROUND THE WOODS WITH STUFFED DOLLS? AND WHERE ARE HIS PARENTS? AREN'T THEY CONCERNED?
HE'S JUST AN IMAGINATIVE LITTLE BOY...
C'MON! WHAT BOY SAYS: "TUT, TUT, IT LOOKS LIKE RAIN"? WHY ISN'T HE PLAYING BASEBALL OR SOMETHING?
MAYBE HE'S HIDING FROM AN INSENSITIVE, JUDGMENTAL WORLD.
PROBABLY. I BET HE THROWS LIKE A GIRL.
TATULLI

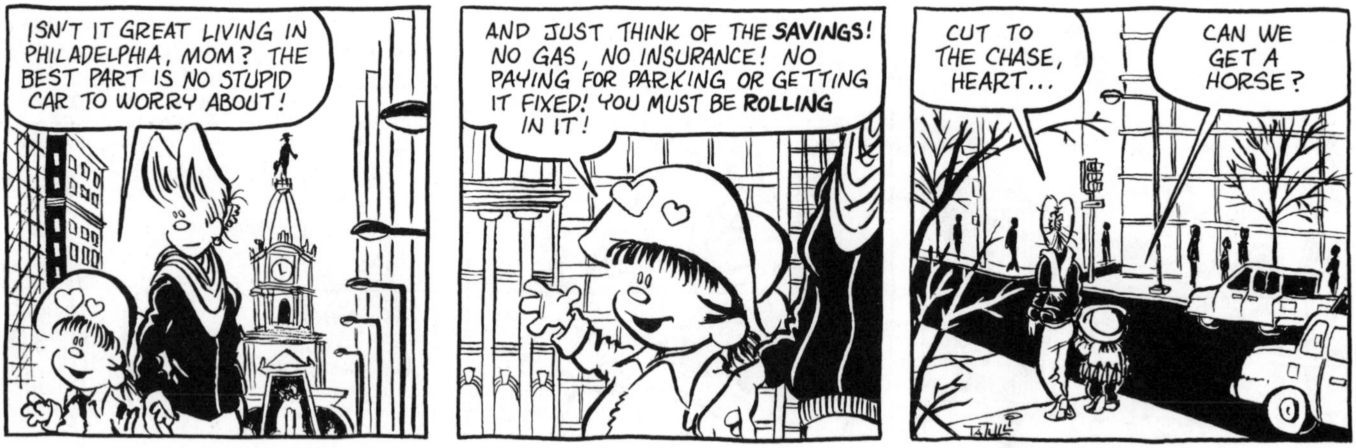
ISN'T IT GREAT LIVING IN PHILADELPHIA, MOM? THE BEST PART IS NO STUPID CAR TO WORRY ABOUT!
AND JUST THINK OF THE SAVINGS! NO GAS, NO INSURANCE! NO PAYING FOR PARKING OR GETTING IT FIXED! YOU MUST BE ROLLING IN IT!
CUT TO THE CHASE, HEART...
CAN WE GET A HORSE?
TATULLI

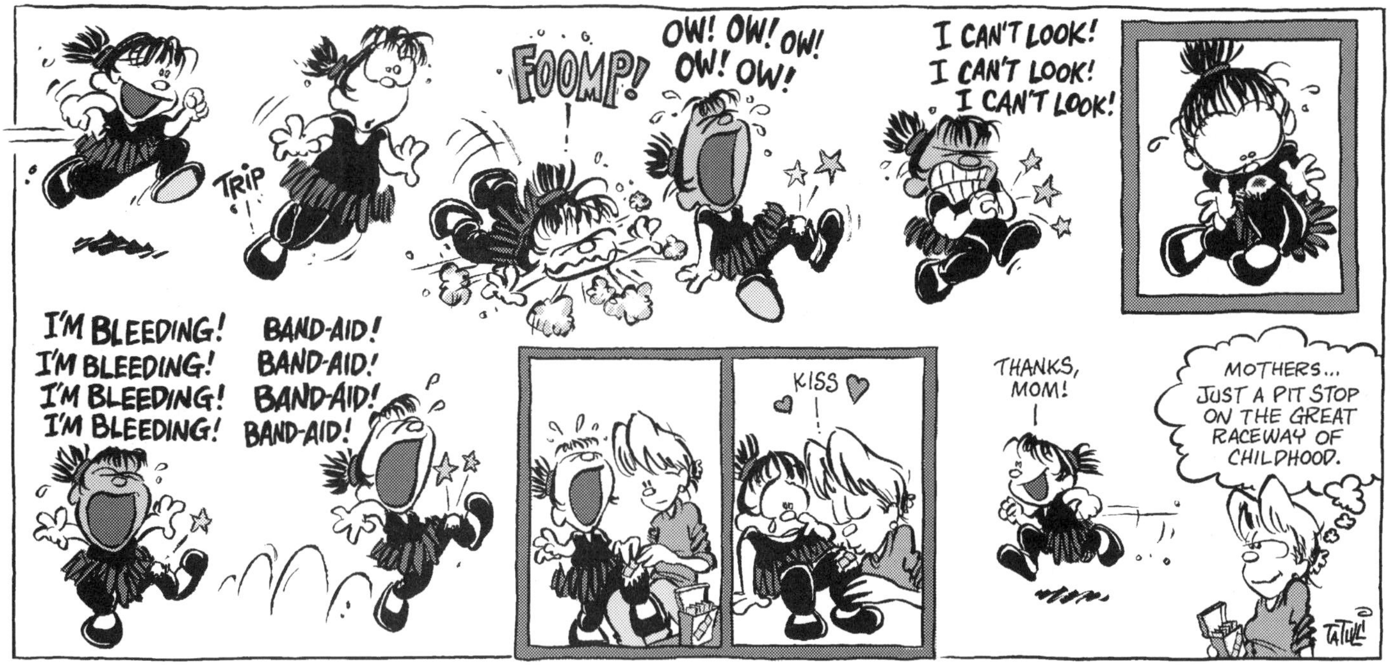
TRIP
FOOMP!
OW! OW! OW! OW! OW!
I CAN'T LOOK! I CAN'T LOOK! I CAN'T LOOK!
I'M BLEEDING! I'M BLEEDING! I'M BLEEDING! I'M BLEEDING!
BAND-AID! BAND-AID! BAND-AID! BAND-AID!
KISS
THANKS, MOM!
MOTHERS... JUST A PIT STOP ON THE GREAT RACEWAY OF CHILDHOOD.
TATULLI

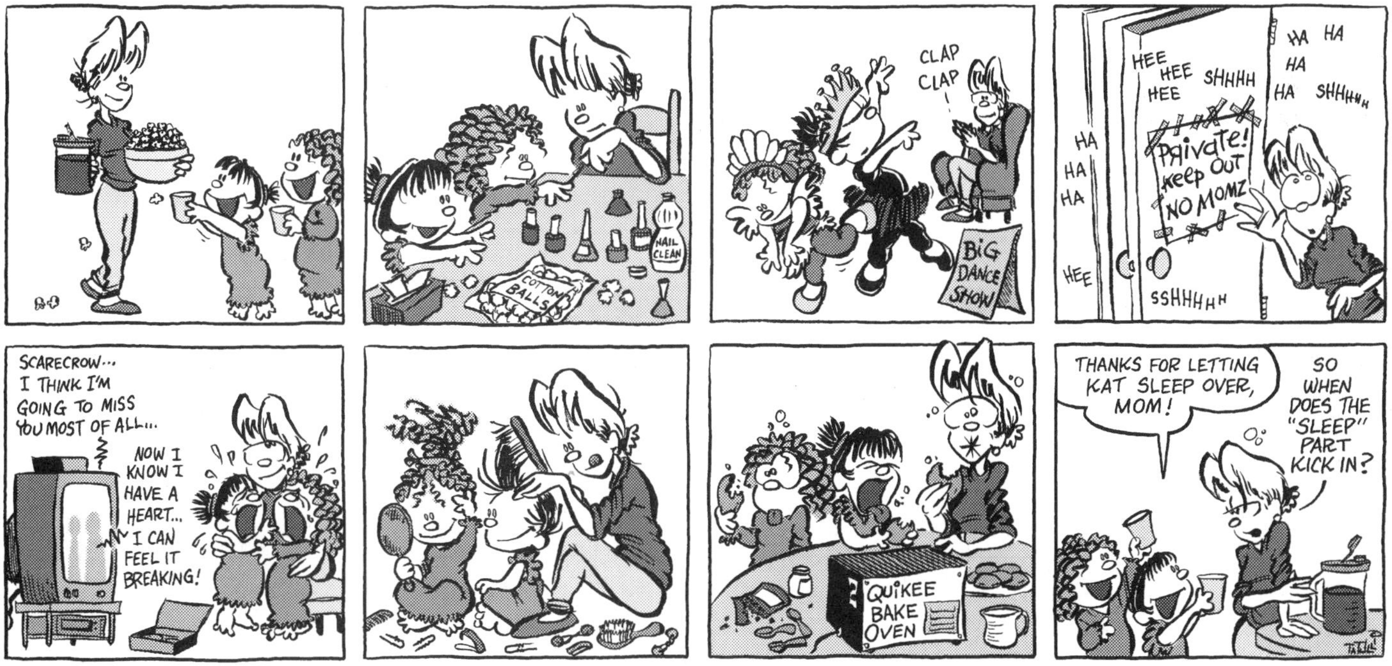
NAIL CLEAN
COTTON BALLS
CLAP CLAP
BIG DANCE SHOW
HEE HEE HEE SHHHH
HA HA HA HA SHHHHH
HA HA HA
HEE
SSHHHHH
PRIVATE! KEEP OUT NO MOMZ
SCARECROW... I THINK I'M GOING TO MISS YOU MOST OF ALL...
NOW I KNOW I HAVE A HEART... I CAN FEEL IT BREAKING!
QUIKEE BAKE OVEN
THANKS FOR LETTING KAT SLEEP OVER, MOM!
SO WHEN DOES THE "SLEEP" PART KICK IN?
TATULLI

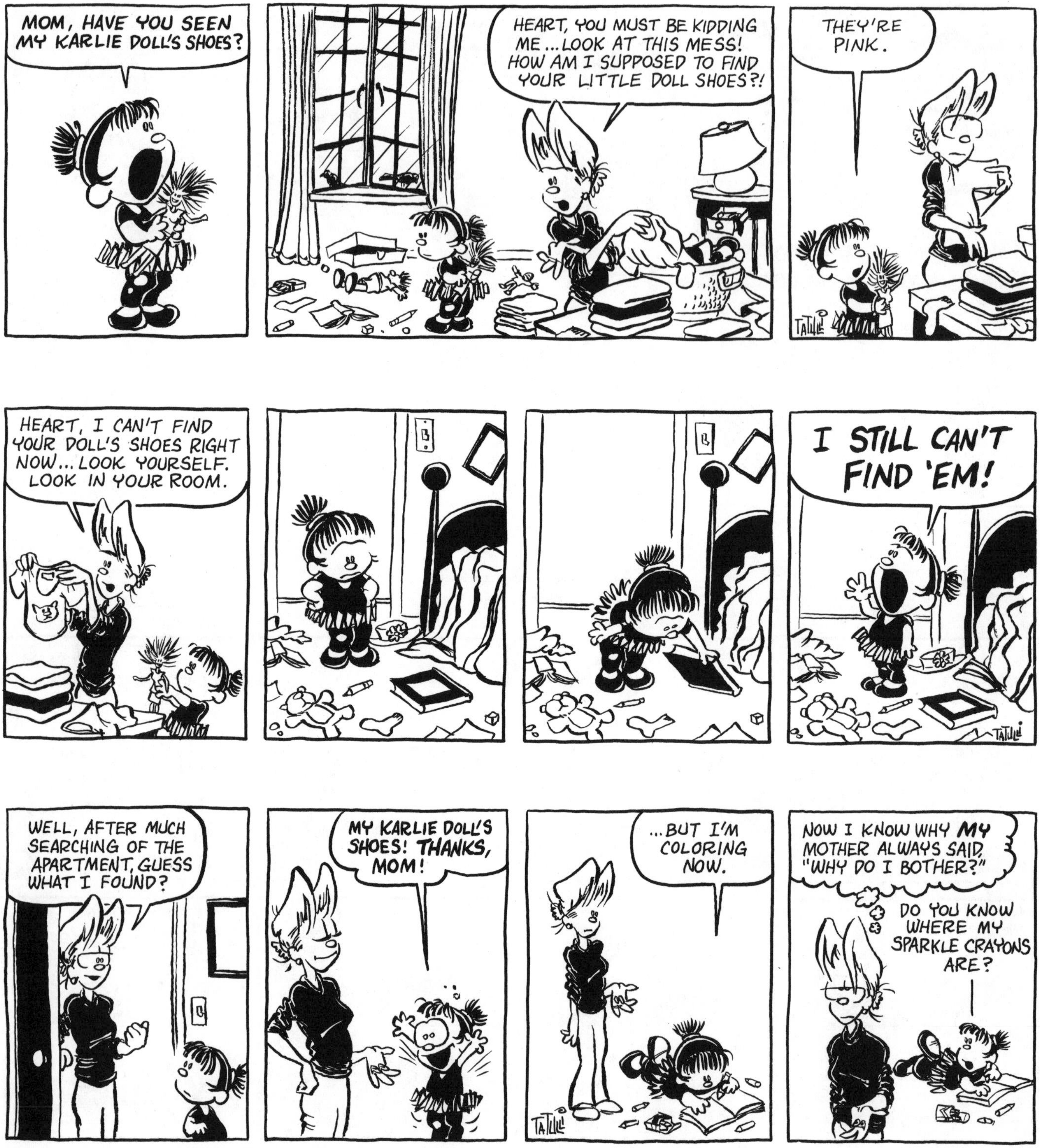
MOM, HAVE YOU SEEN MY KARLIE DOLL'S SHOES?
HEART, YOU MUST BE KIDDING ME...LOOK AT THIS MESS! HOW AM I SUPPOSED TO FIND YOUR LITTLE DOLL SHOES?!
THEY'RE PINK.
TATULLI
HEART, I CAN'T FIND YOUR DOLL'S SHOES RIGHT NOW...LOOK YOURSELF. LOOK IN YOUR ROOM.
I STILL CAN'T FIND 'EM!
TATULLI
WELL, AFTER MUCH SEARCHING OF THE APARTMENT, GUESS WHAT I FOUND?
MY KARLIE DOLL'S SHOES! THANKS, MOM!
...BUT I'M COLORING NOW.
TATULLI
NOW I KNOW WHY MY MOTHER ALWAYS SAID, "WHY DO I BOTHER?"
DO YOU KNOW WHERE MY SPARKLE CRAYONS ARE?

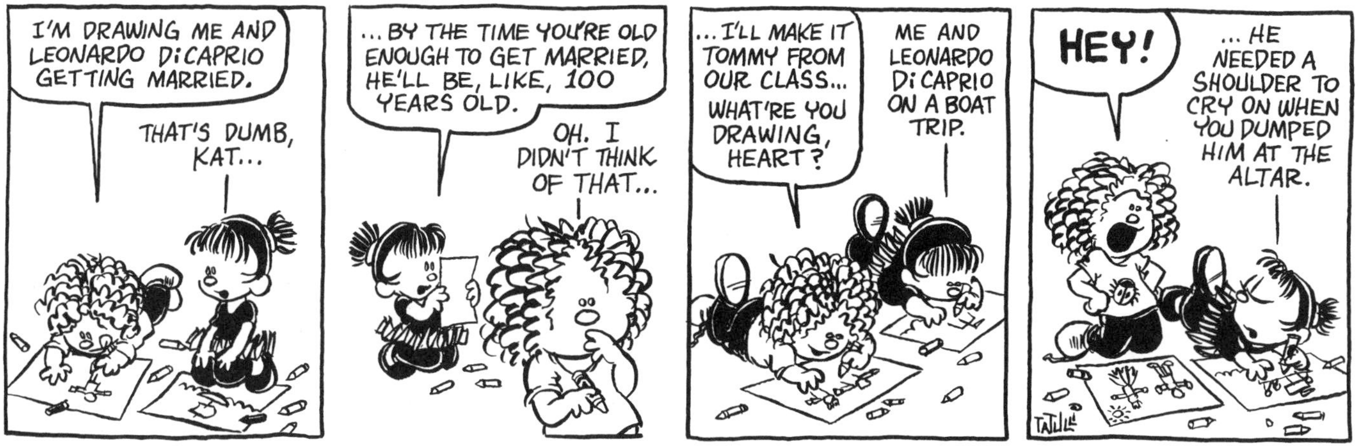

I'M DRAWING ME AND LEONARDO DiCAPRIO GETTING MARRIED.
THAT'S DUMB, KAT...
...BY THE TIME YOU'RE OLD ENOUGH TO GET MARRIED, HE'LL BE, LIKE, 100 YEARS OLD.
OH. I DIDN'T THINK OF THAT...
...I'LL MAKE IT TOMMY FROM OUR CLASS...
WHAT'RE YOU DRAWING, HEART?
ME AND LEONARDO DiCAPRIO ON A BOAT TRIP.
HEY!
...HE NEEDED A SHOULDER TO CRY ON WHEN YOU DUMPED HIM AT THE ALTAR.

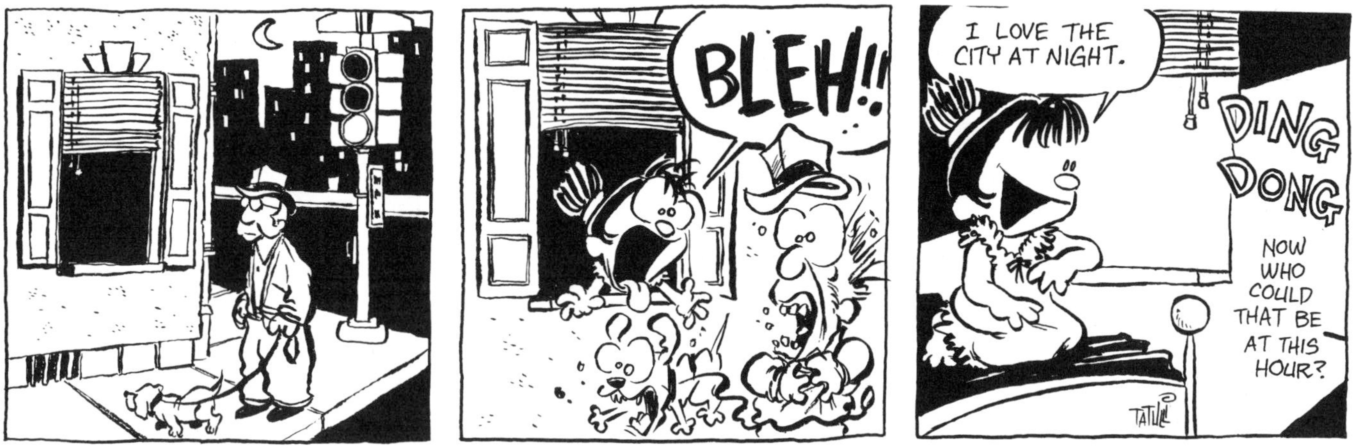

BLEH!!
I LOVE THE CITY AT NIGHT.
DING DONG
NOW WHO COULD THAT BE AT THIS HOUR?

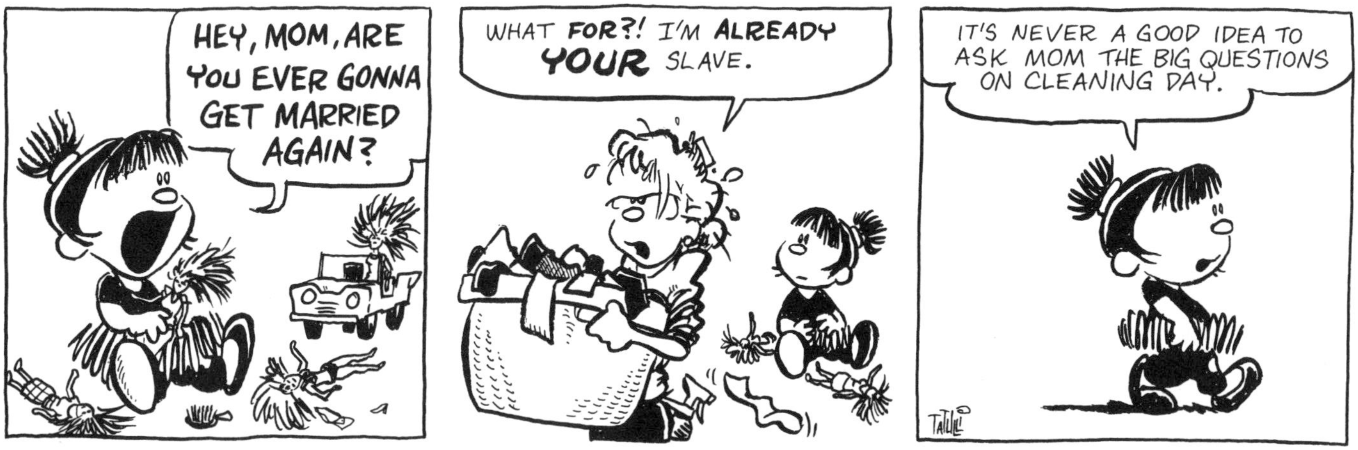

HEY, MOM, ARE YOU EVER GONNA GET MARRIED AGAIN?
WHAT FOR?! I'M ALREADY YOUR SLAVE.
IT'S NEVER A GOOD IDEA TO ASK MOM THE BIG QUESTIONS ON CLEANING DAY.

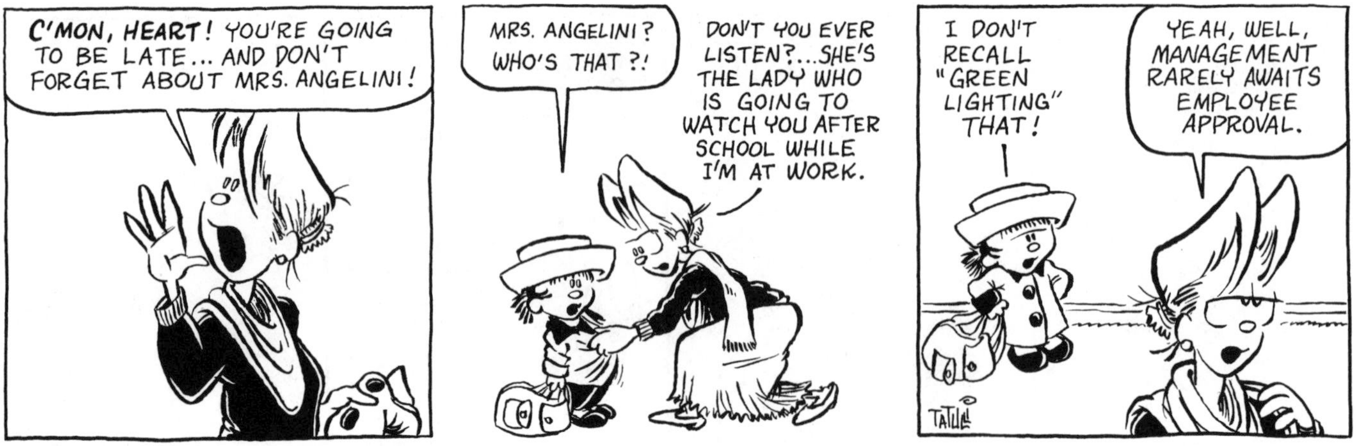
C'MON, HEART! YOU'RE GOING TO BE LATE... AND DON'T FORGET ABOUT MRS. ANGELINI!
MRS. ANGELINI? WHO'S THAT?!
DON'T YOU EVER LISTEN?...SHE'S THE LADY WHO IS GOING TO WATCH YOU AFTER SCHOOL WHILE I'M AT WORK.
I DON'T RECALL "GREEN LIGHTING" THAT!
YEAH, WELL, MANAGEMENT RARELY AWAITS EMPLOYEE APPROVAL.
TATULLI

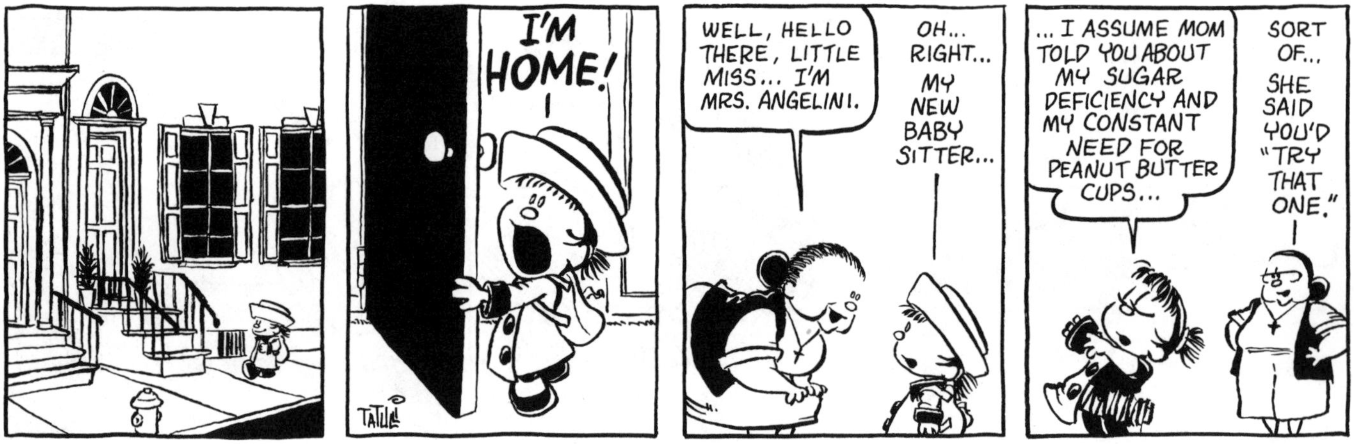
I'M HOME!
TATULLI
WELL, HELLO THERE, LITTLE MISS... I'M MRS. ANGELINI.
OH... RIGHT... MY NEW BABY SITTER...
...I ASSUME MOM TOLD YOU ABOUT MY SUGAR DEFICIENCY AND MY CONSTANT NEED FOR PEANUT BUTTER CUPS...
SORT OF... SHE SAID YOU'D "TRY THAT ONE."

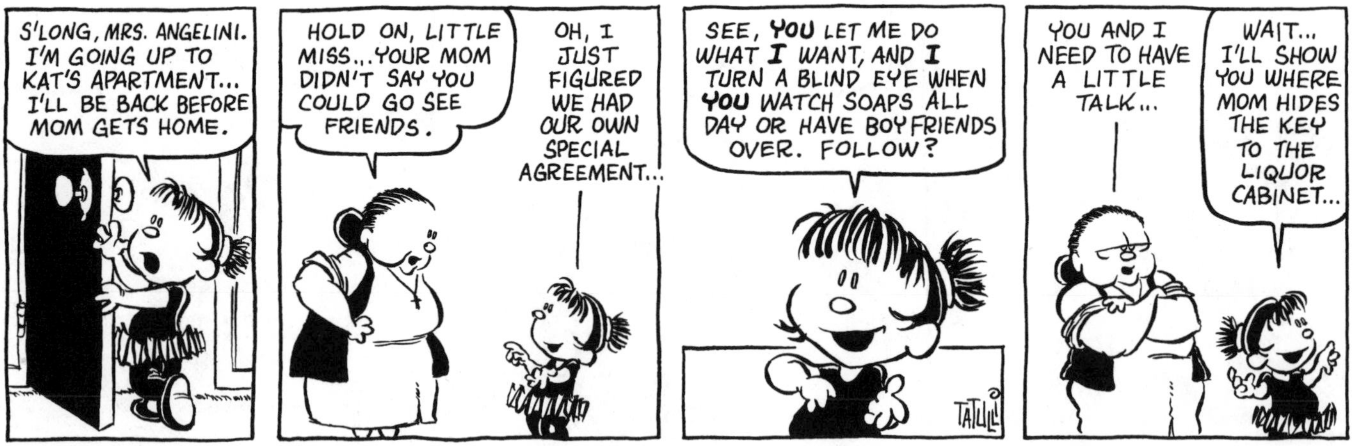
S'LONG, MRS. ANGELINI. I'M GOING UP TO KAT'S APARTMENT... I'LL BE BACK BEFORE MOM GETS HOME.
HOLD ON, LITTLE MISS...YOUR MOM DIDN'T SAY YOU COULD GO SEE FRIENDS.
OH, I JUST FIGURED WE HAD OUR OWN SPECIAL AGREEMENT...
SEE, YOU LET ME DO WHAT I WANT, AND I TURN A BLIND EYE WHEN YOU WATCH SOAPS ALL DAY OR HAVE BOYFRIENDS OVER. FOLLOW?
TATULLI
YOU AND I NEED TO HAVE A LITTLE TALK...
WAIT... I'LL SHOW YOU WHERE MOM HIDES THE KEY TO THE LIQUOR CABINET...

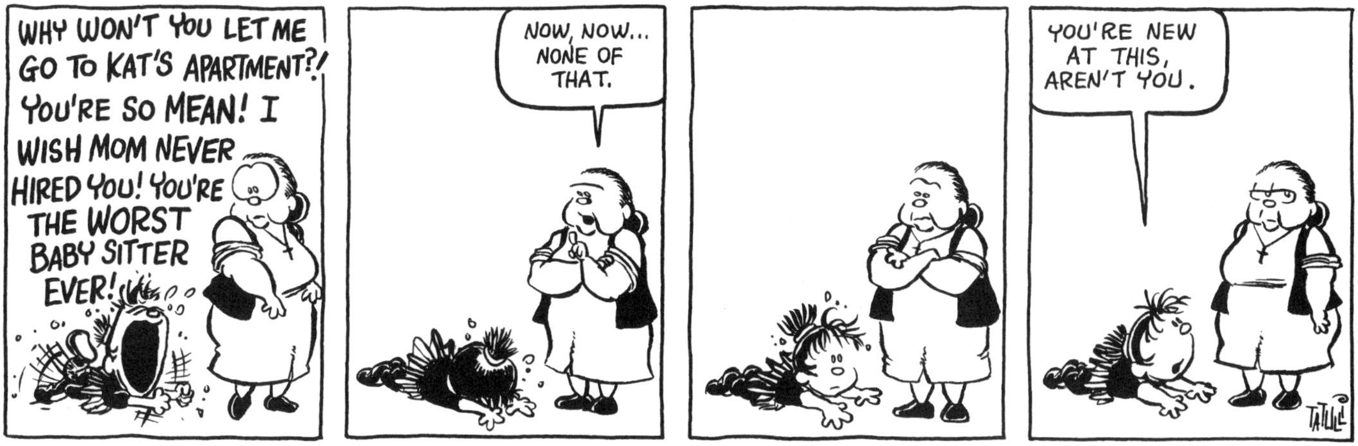
WHY WON'T YOU LET ME GO TO KAT'S APARTMENT?! YOU'RE SO MEAN! I WISH MOM NEVER HIRED YOU! YOU'RE THE WORST BABY SITTER EVER!
NOW, NOW... NONE OF THAT.
YOU'RE NEW AT THIS, AREN'T YOU.

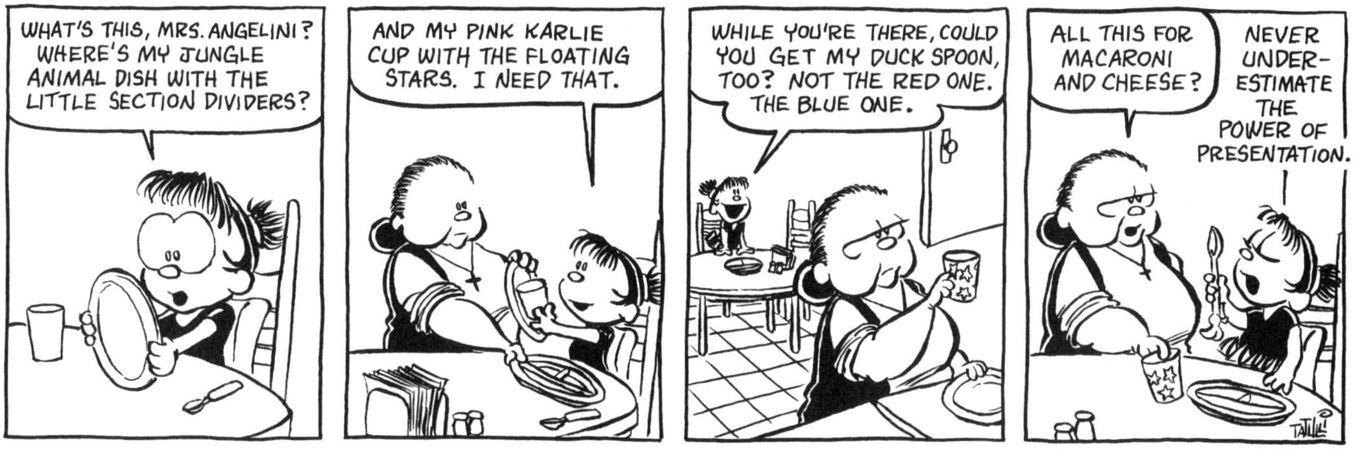
WHAT'S THIS, MRS. ANGELINI? WHERE'S MY JUNGLE ANIMAL DISH WITH THE LITTLE SECTION DIVIDERS?
AND MY PINK KARLIE CUP WITH THE FLOATING STARS. I NEED THAT.
WHILE YOU'RE THERE, COULD YOU GET MY DUCK SPOON, TOO? NOT THE RED ONE. THE BLUE ONE.
ALL THIS FOR MACARONI AND CHEESE?
NEVER UNDER-ESTIMATE THE POWER OF PRESENTATION.

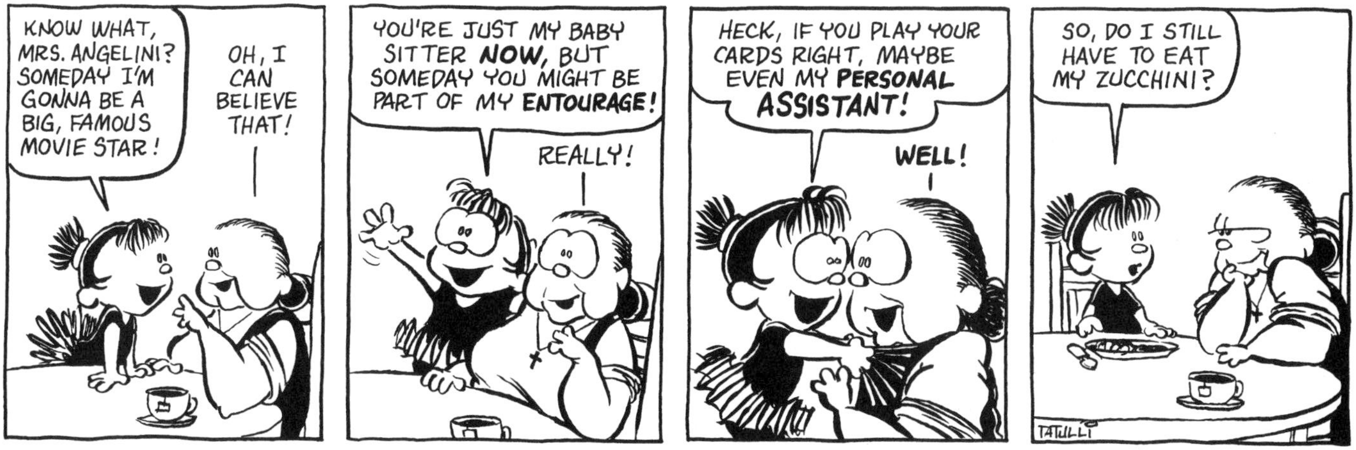
KNOW WHAT, MRS. ANGELINI? SOMEDAY I'M GONNA BE A BIG, FAMOUS MOVIE STAR!
OH, I CAN BELIEVE THAT!
YOU'RE JUST MY BABY SITTER NOW, BUT SOMEDAY YOU MIGHT BE PART OF MY ENTOURAGE!
REALLY!
HECK, IF YOU PLAY YOUR CARDS RIGHT, MAYBE EVEN MY PERSONAL ASSISTANT!
WELL!
SO, DO I STILL HAVE TO EAT MY ZUCCHINI?

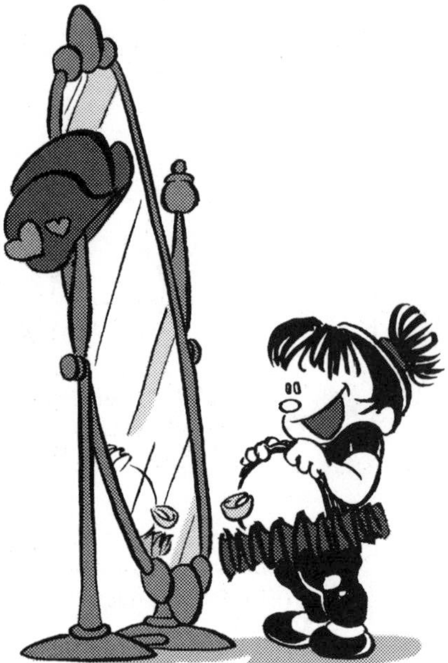

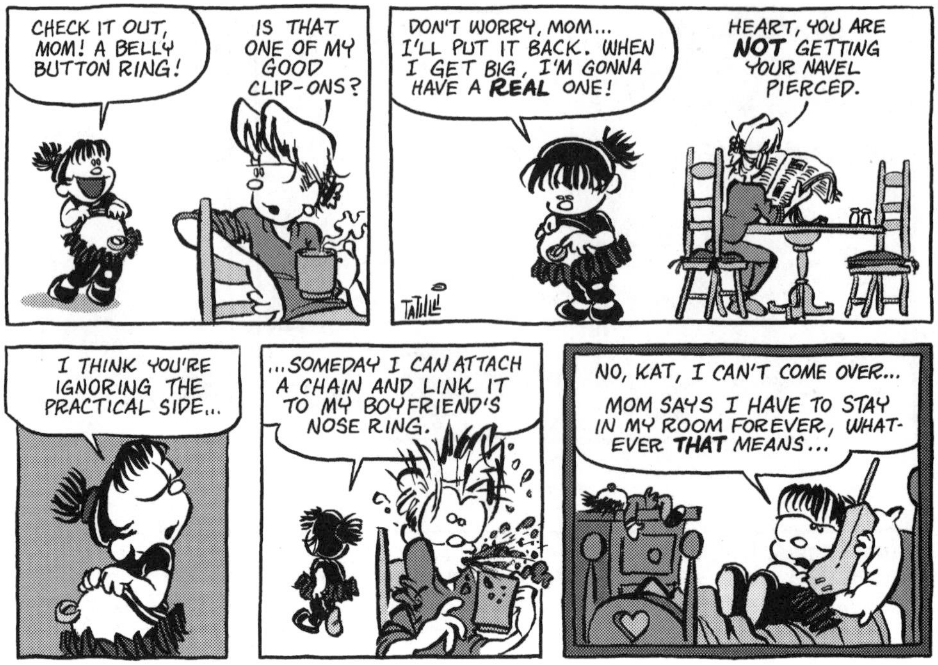

CHECK IT OUT, MOM! A BELLY BUTTON RING!
IS THAT ONE OF MY GOOD CLIP-ONS?
DON'T WORRY, MOM... I'LL PUT IT BACK. WHEN I GET BIG, I'M GONNA HAVE A **REAL** ONE!
HEART, YOU ARE **NOT** GETTING YOUR NAVEL PIERCED.
TATULLI
I THINK YOU'RE IGNORING THE PRACTICAL SIDE...
...SOMEDAY I CAN ATTACH A CHAIN AND LINK IT TO MY BOYFRIEND'S NOSE RING.
NO, KAT, I CAN'T COME OVER...
MOM SAYS I HAVE TO STAY IN MY ROOM FOREVER, WHATEVER **THAT** MEANS...

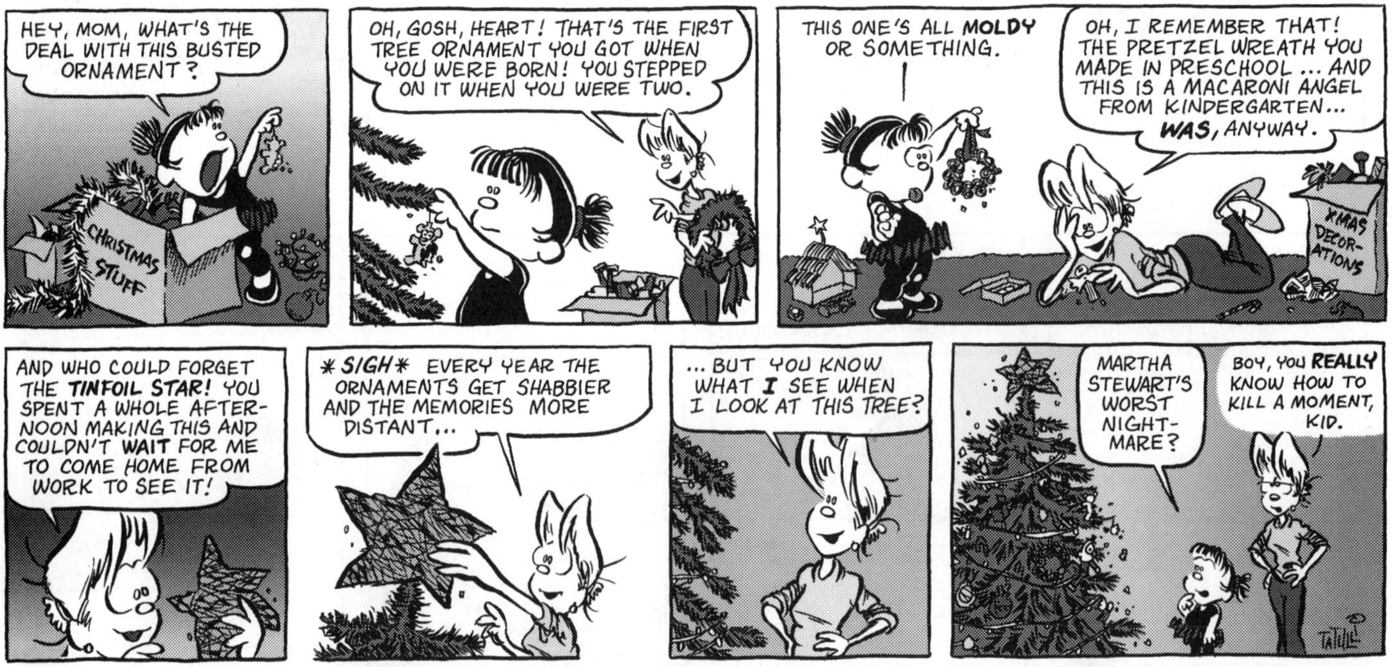

HEY, MOM, WHAT'S THE DEAL WITH THIS BUSTED ORNAMENT?
CHRISTMAS STUFF
OH, GOSH, HEART! THAT'S THE FIRST TREE ORNAMENT YOU GOT WHEN YOU WERE BORN! YOU STEPPED ON IT WHEN YOU WERE TWO.
THIS ONE'S ALL **MOLDY** OR SOMETHING.
OH, I REMEMBER THAT! THE PRETZEL WREATH YOU MADE IN PRESCHOOL ... AND THIS IS A MACARONI ANGEL FROM KINDERGARTEN... **WAS**, ANYWAY.
XMAS DECORATIONS
AND WHO COULD FORGET THE **TINFOIL STAR!** YOU SPENT A WHOLE AFTERNOON MAKING THIS AND COULDN'T **WAIT** FOR ME TO COME HOME FROM WORK TO SEE IT!
SIGH EVERY YEAR THE ORNAMENTS GET SHABBIER AND THE MEMORIES MORE DISTANT...
... BUT YOU KNOW WHAT **I** SEE WHEN I LOOK AT THIS TREE?
MARTHA STEWART'S WORST NIGHTMARE?
BOY, YOU **REALLY** KNOW HOW TO KILL A MOMENT, KID.
TATULLI

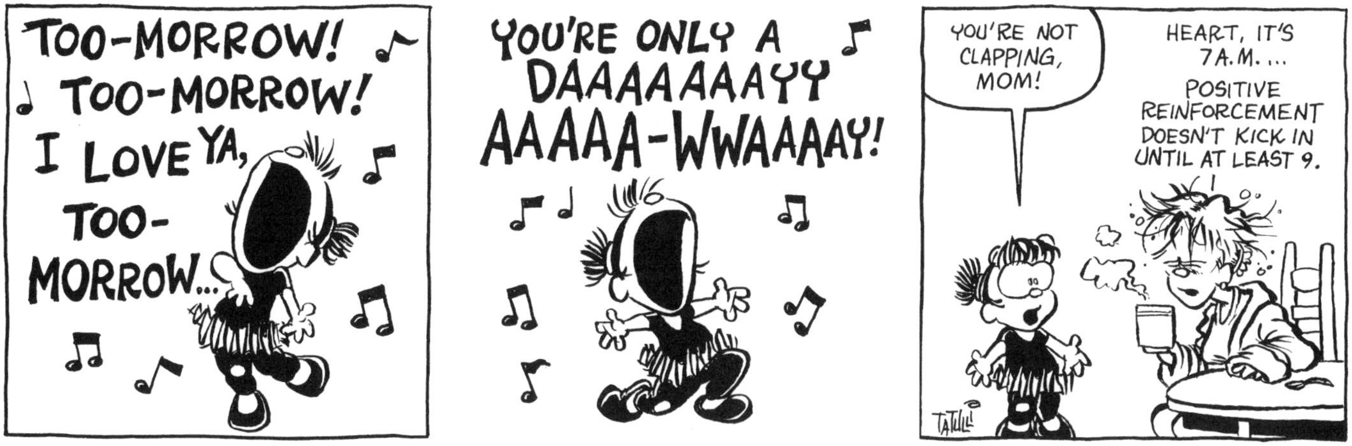
TOO-MORROW! TOO-MORROW! I LOVE YA, TOO-MORROW...
YOU'RE ONLY A DAAAAAAAYY AAAAA-WWAAAAY!
YOU'RE NOT CLAPPING, MOM!
HEART, IT'S 7 A.M. ... POSITIVE REINFORCEMENT DOESN'T KICK IN UNTIL AT LEAST 9.
TATULLI

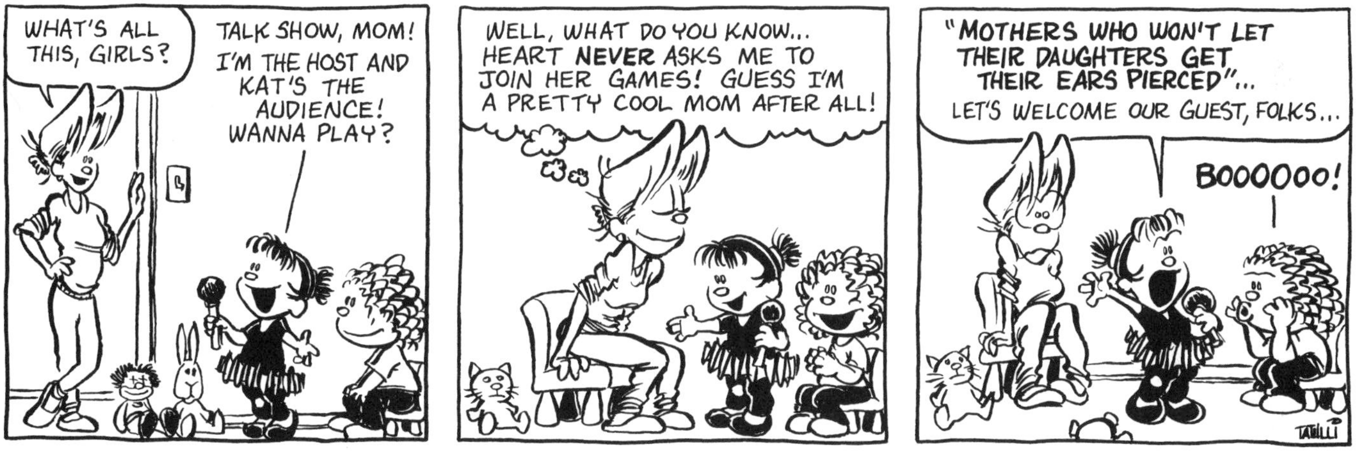
WHAT'S ALL THIS, GIRLS?
TALK SHOW, MOM! I'M THE HOST AND KAT'S THE AUDIENCE! WANNA PLAY?
WELL, WHAT DO YOU KNOW... HEART NEVER ASKS ME TO JOIN HER GAMES! GUESS I'M A PRETTY COOL MOM AFTER ALL!
"MOTHERS WHO WON'T LET THEIR DAUGHTERS GET THEIR EARS PIERCED"... LET'S WELCOME OUR GUEST, FOLKS...
BOOOOOO!
TATULLI

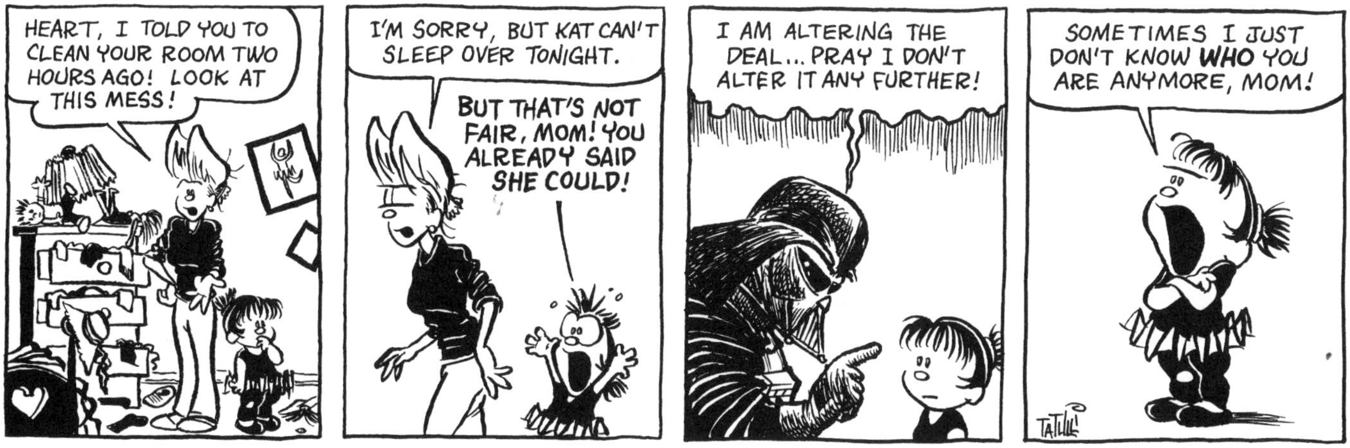
HEART, I TOLD YOU TO CLEAN YOUR ROOM TWO HOURS AGO! LOOK AT THIS MESS!
I'M SORRY, BUT KAT CAN'T SLEEP OVER TONIGHT.
BUT THAT'S NOT FAIR, MOM! YOU ALREADY SAID SHE COULD!
I AM ALTERING THE DEAL... PRAY I DON'T ALTER IT ANY FURTHER!
SOMETIMES I JUST DON'T KNOW WHO YOU ARE ANYMORE, MOM!
TATULLI

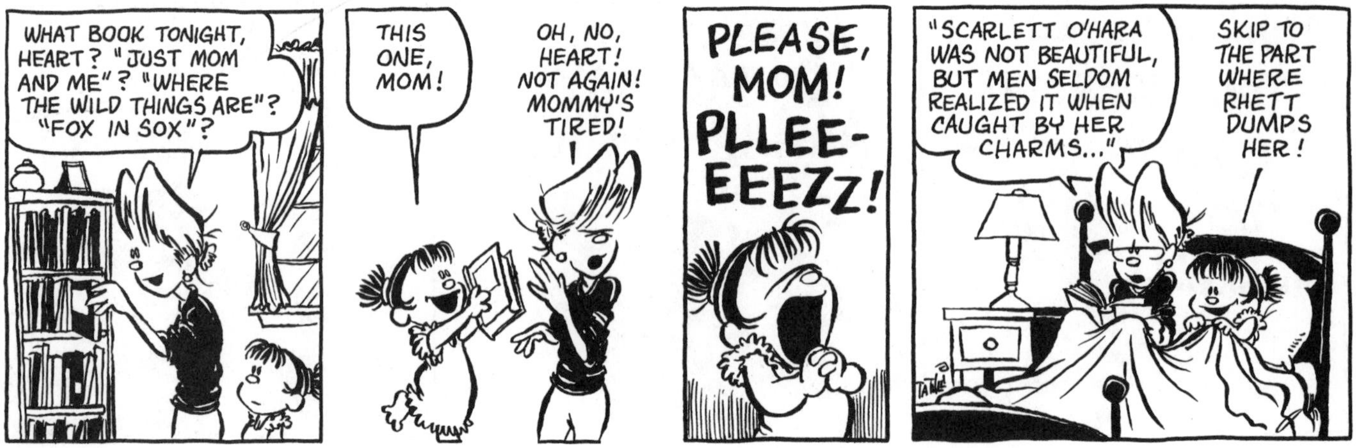
WHAT BOOK TONIGHT, HEART? "JUST MOM AND ME"? "WHERE THE WILD THINGS ARE"? "FOX IN SOX"?
THIS ONE, MOM!
OH, NO, HEART! NOT AGAIN! MOMMY'S TIRED!
PLEASE, MOM! PLLEE-EEEZZ!
"SCARLETT O'HARA WAS NOT BEAUTIFUL, BUT MEN SELDOM REALIZED IT WHEN CAUGHT BY HER CHARMS..."
SKIP TO THE PART WHERE RHETT DUMPS HER!
TATULLI

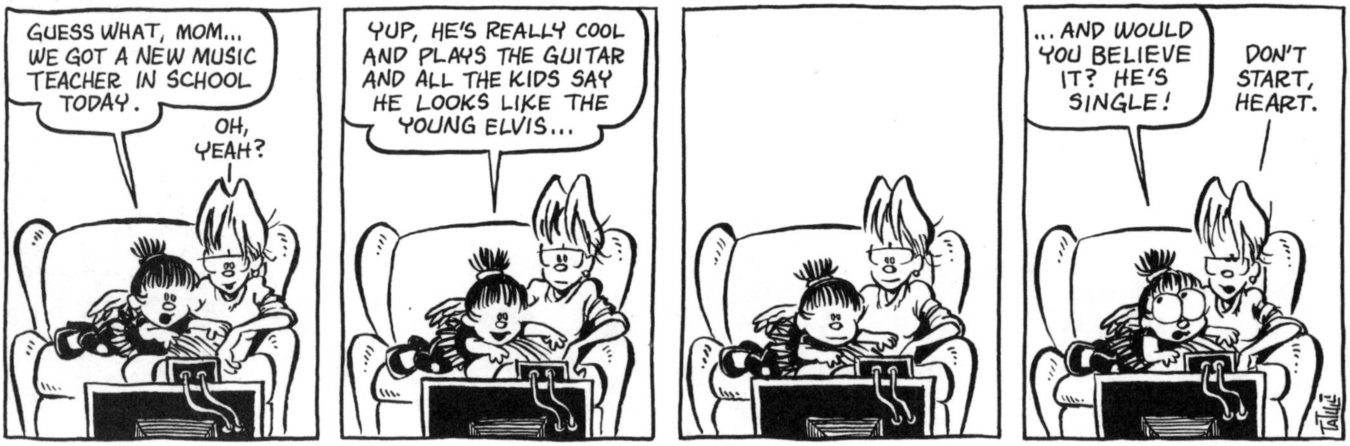
GUESS WHAT, MOM... WE GOT A NEW MUSIC TEACHER IN SCHOOL TODAY.
OH, YEAH?
YUP, HE'S REALLY COOL AND PLAYS THE GUITAR AND ALL THE KIDS SAY HE LOOKS LIKE THE YOUNG ELVIS...
... AND WOULD YOU BELIEVE IT? HE'S SINGLE!
DON'T START, HEART.
TATULLI

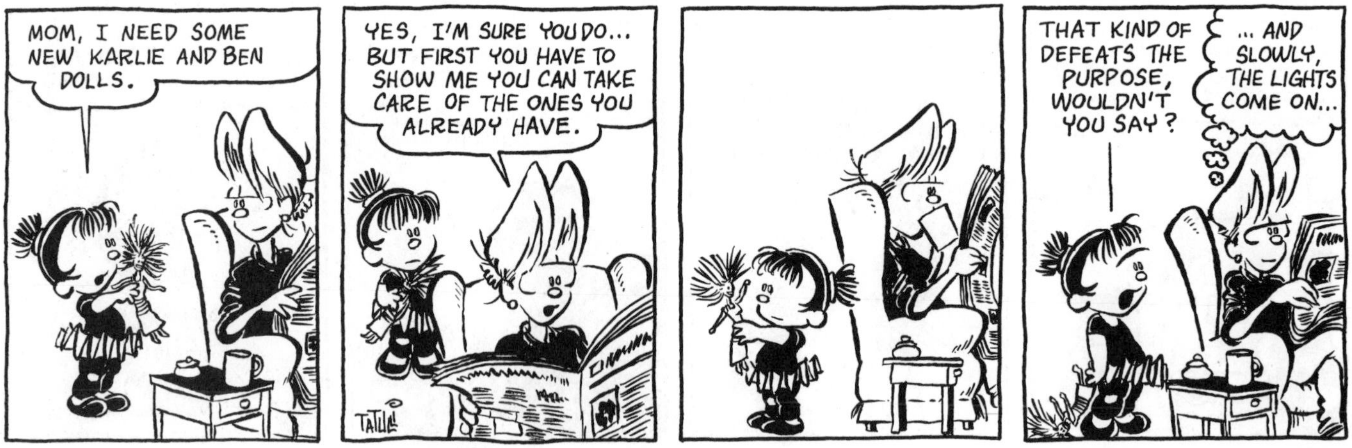
MOM, I NEED SOME NEW KARLIE AND BEN DOLLS.
YES, I'M SURE YOU DO... BUT FIRST YOU HAVE TO SHOW ME YOU CAN TAKE CARE OF THE ONES YOU ALREADY HAVE.
TATULLI
THAT KIND OF DEFEATS THE PURPOSE, WOULDN'T YOU SAY?
... AND SLOWLY, THE LIGHTS COME ON...

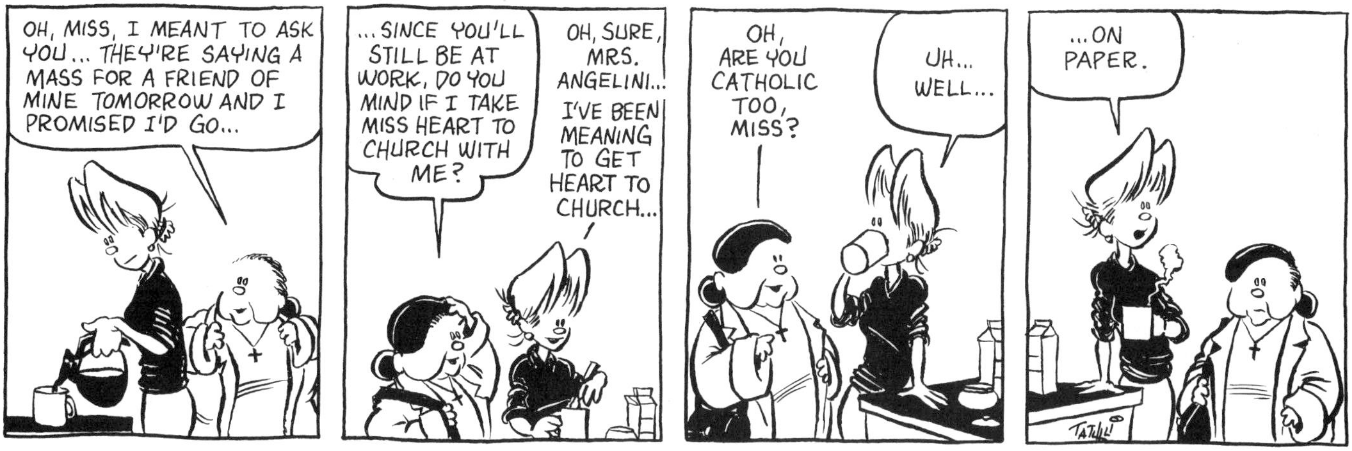
OH, MISS, I MEANT TO ASK YOU... THEY'RE SAYING A MASS FOR A FRIEND OF MINE TOMORROW AND I PROMISED I'D GO...
...SINCE YOU'LL STILL BE AT WORK, DO YOU MIND IF I TAKE MISS HEART TO CHURCH WITH ME?
OH, SURE, MRS. ANGELINI... I'VE BEEN MEANING TO GET HEART TO CHURCH...
OH, ARE YOU CATHOLIC TOO, MISS?
UH... WELL...
...ON PAPER.

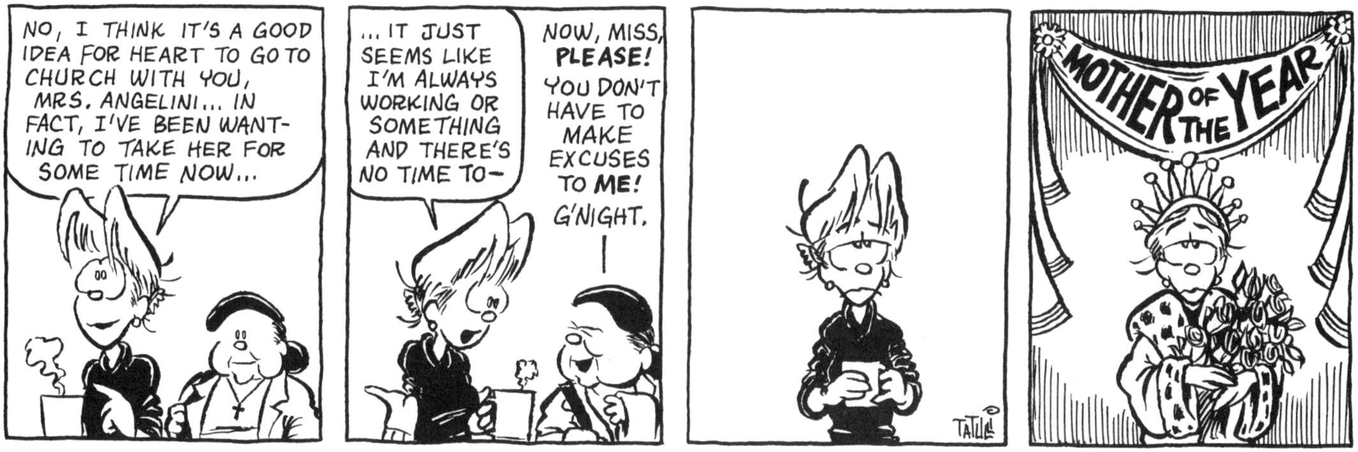
NO, I THINK IT'S A GOOD IDEA FOR HEART TO GO TO CHURCH WITH YOU, MRS. ANGELINI... IN FACT, I'VE BEEN WANTING TO TAKE HER FOR SOME TIME NOW...
...IT JUST SEEMS LIKE I'M ALWAYS WORKING OR SOMETHING AND THERE'S NO TIME TO—
NOW, MISS, PLEASE! YOU DON'T HAVE TO MAKE EXCUSES TO ME! G'NIGHT.
MOTHER OF THE YEAR

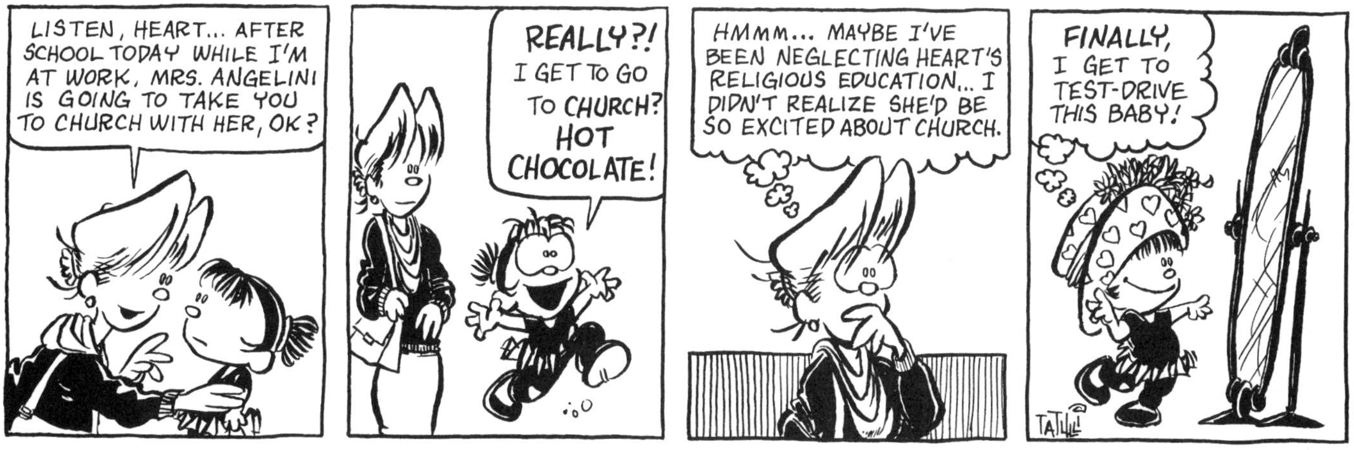
LISTEN, HEART... AFTER SCHOOL TODAY WHILE I'M AT WORK, MRS. ANGELINI IS GOING TO TAKE YOU TO CHURCH WITH HER, OK?
REALLY?! I GET TO GO TO CHURCH? HOT CHOCOLATE!
HMMM... MAYBE I'VE BEEN NEGLECTING HEART'S RELIGIOUS EDUCATION... I DIDN'T REALIZE SHE'D BE SO EXCITED ABOUT CHURCH.
FINALLY, I GET TO TEST-DRIVE THIS BABY!

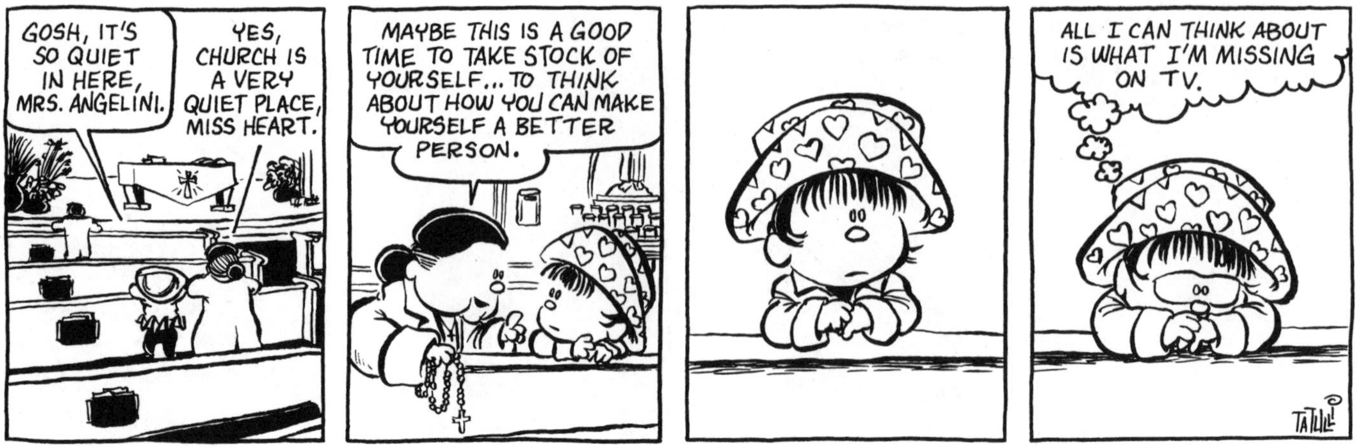
GOSH, IT'S SO QUIET IN HERE, MRS. ANGELINI.
YES, CHURCH IS A VERY QUIET PLACE, MISS HEART.
MAYBE THIS IS A GOOD TIME TO TAKE STOCK OF YOURSELF... TO THINK ABOUT HOW YOU CAN MAKE YOURSELF A BETTER PERSON.
ALL I CAN THINK ABOUT IS WHAT I'M MISSING ON TV.
TATULLI

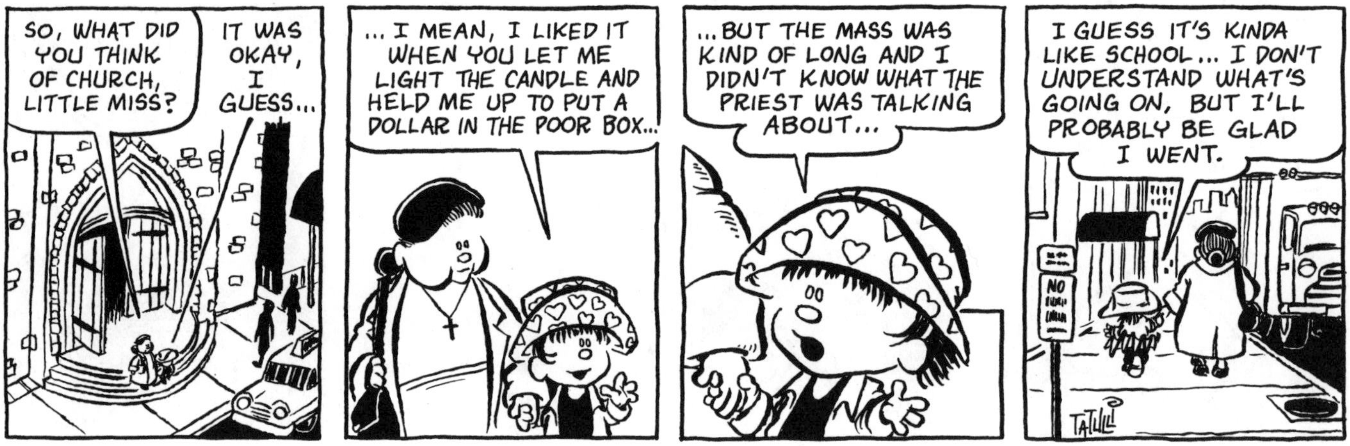
SO, WHAT DID YOU THINK OF CHURCH, LITTLE MISS?
IT WAS OKAY, I GUESS...
... I MEAN, I LIKED IT WHEN YOU LET ME LIGHT THE CANDLE AND HELD ME UP TO PUT A DOLLAR IN THE POOR BOX...
... BUT THE MASS WAS KIND OF LONG AND I DIDN'T KNOW WHAT THE PRIEST WAS TALKING ABOUT...
I GUESS IT'S KINDA LIKE SCHOOL... I DON'T UNDERSTAND WHAT'S GOING ON, BUT I'LL PROBABLY BE GLAD I WENT.
NO
TATULLI

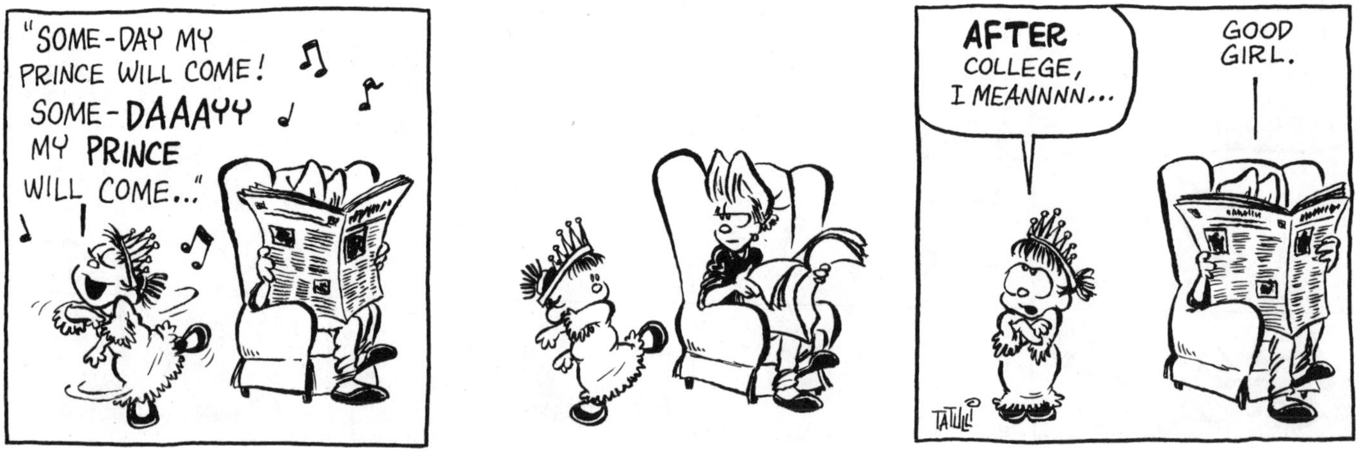
"SOME-DAY MY PRINCE WILL COME! SOME-DAAAYY MY PRINCE WILL COME..."
AFTER COLLEGE, I MEANNNN...
GOOD GIRL.
TATULLI

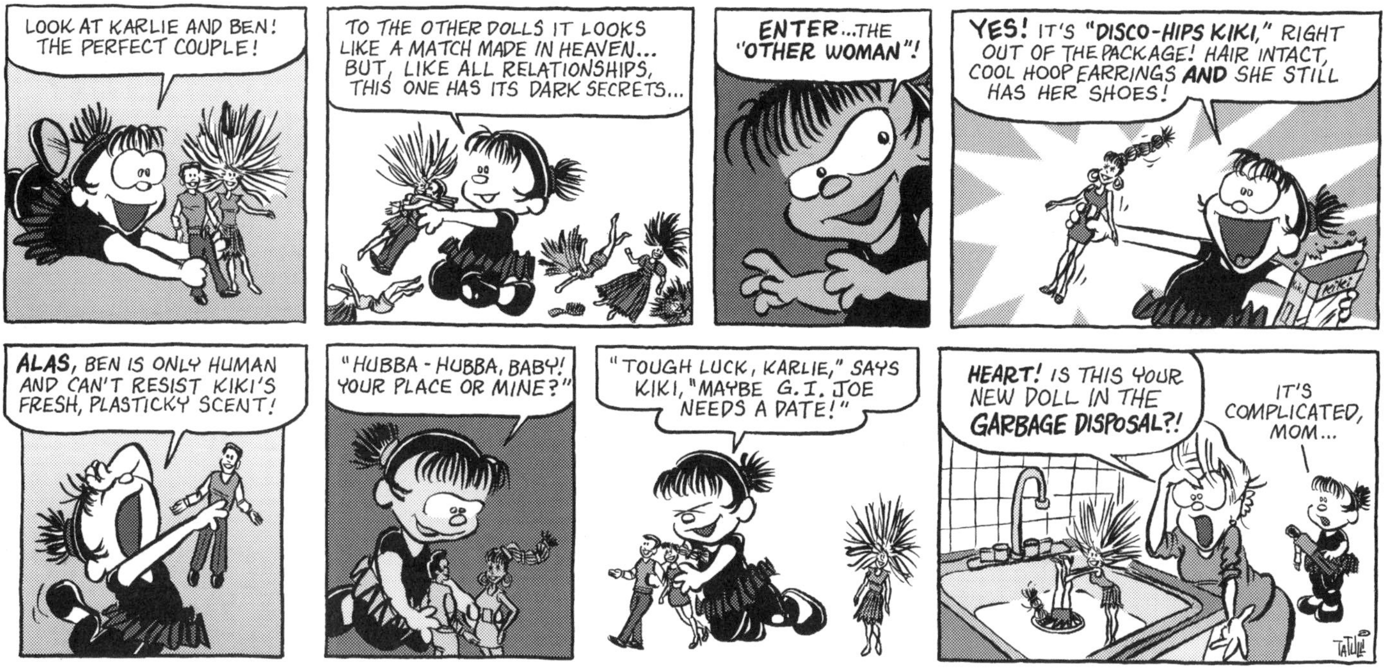
LOOK AT KARLIE AND BEN! THE PERFECT COUPLE!
TO THE OTHER DOLLS IT LOOKS LIKE A MATCH MADE IN HEAVEN... BUT, LIKE ALL RELATIONSHIPS, THIS ONE HAS ITS DARK SECRETS...
ENTER...THE "OTHER WOMAN"!
YES! IT'S "DISCO-HIPS KIKI," RIGHT OUT OF THE PACKAGE! HAIR INTACT, COOL HOOP EARRINGS AND SHE STILL HAS HER SHOES!
KIKI
ALAS, BEN IS ONLY HUMAN AND CAN'T RESIST KIKI'S FRESH, PLASTICKY SCENT!
"HUBBA-HUBBA, BABY! YOUR PLACE OR MINE?"
"TOUGH LUCK, KARLIE," SAYS KIKI, "MAYBE G.I. JOE NEEDS A DATE!"
HEART! IS THIS YOUR NEW DOLL IN THE GARBAGE DISPOSAL?!
IT'S COMPLICATED, MOM...
TATULLI

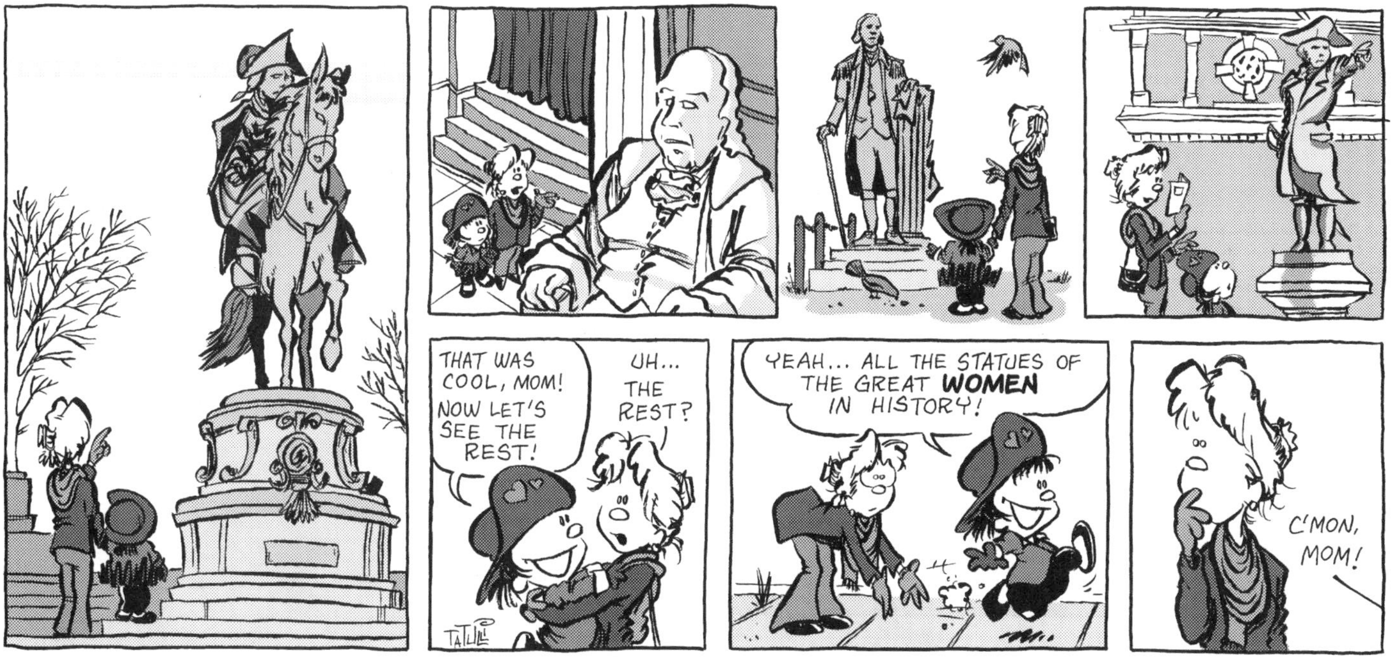
THAT WAS COOL, MOM! NOW LET'S SEE THE REST!
UH... THE REST?
TATULLI
YEAH... ALL THE STATUES OF THE GREAT WOMEN IN HISTORY!
C'MON, MOM!

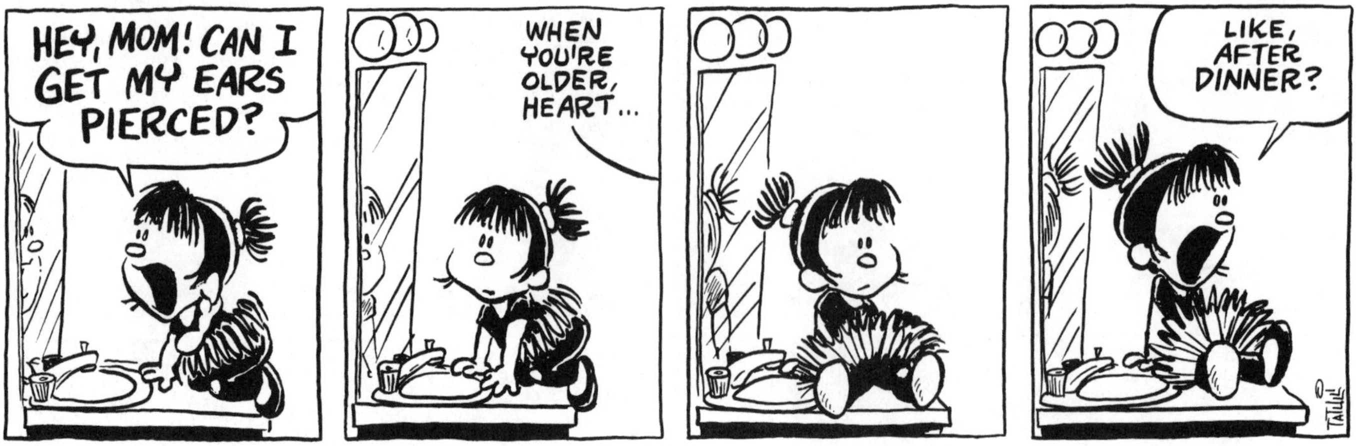
HEY, MOM! CAN I GET MY EARS PIERCED?
WHEN YOU'RE OLDER, HEART...
LIKE, AFTER DINNER?
TATULLI

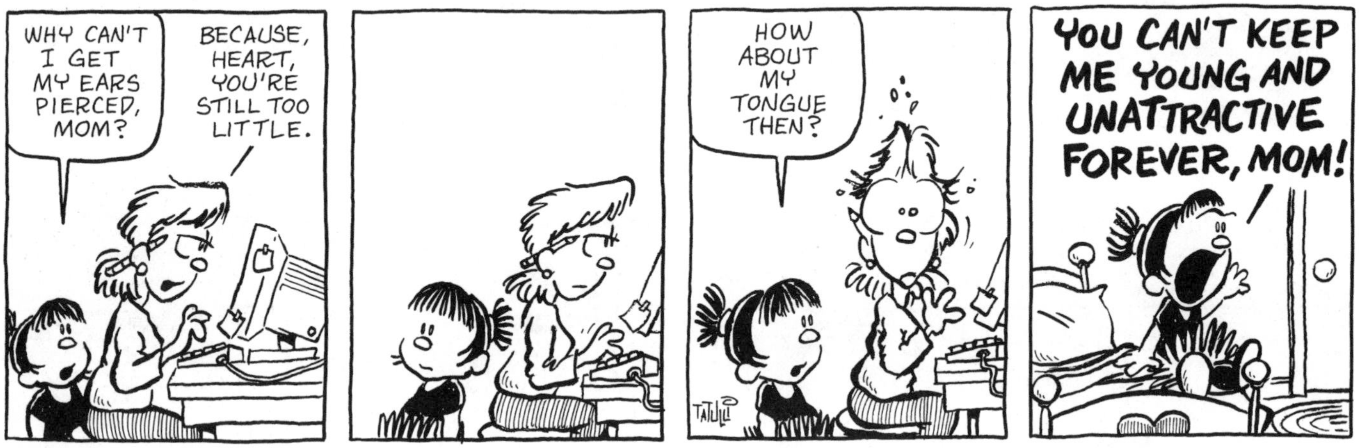
WHY CAN'T I GET MY EARS PIERCED, MOM?
BECAUSE, HEART, YOU'RE STILL TOO LITTLE.
HOW ABOUT MY TONGUE THEN?
TATULLI
YOU CAN'T KEEP ME YOUNG AND UNATTRACTIVE FOREVER, MOM!

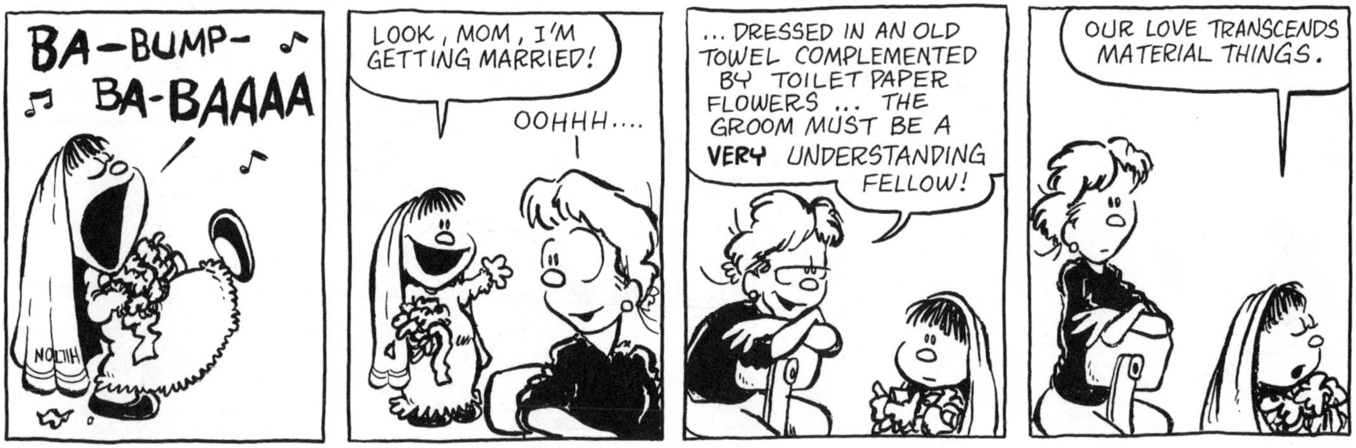
BA-BUMP-
BA-BAAAA
LOOK, MOM, I'M GETTING MARRIED!
OOHHH....
...DRESSED IN AN OLD TOWEL COMPLEMENTED BY TOILET PAPER FLOWERS ... THE GROOM MUST BE A VERY UNDERSTANDING FELLOW!
OUR LOVE TRANSCENDS MATERIAL THINGS.

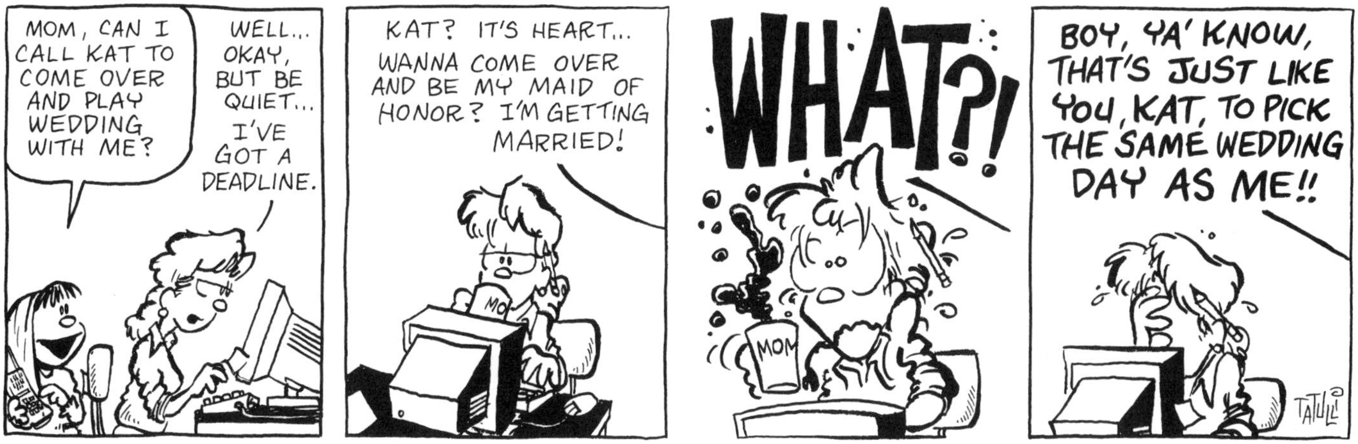
MOM, CAN I CALL KAT TO COME OVER AND PLAY WEDDING WITH ME?
WELL... OKAY, BUT BE QUIET... I'VE GOT A DEADLINE.
KAT? IT'S HEART... WANNA COME OVER AND BE MY MAID OF HONOR? I'M GETTING MARRIED!
WHAT?!
BOY, YA' KNOW, THAT'S JUST LIKE YOU, KAT, TO PICK THE SAME WEDDING DAY AS ME!!

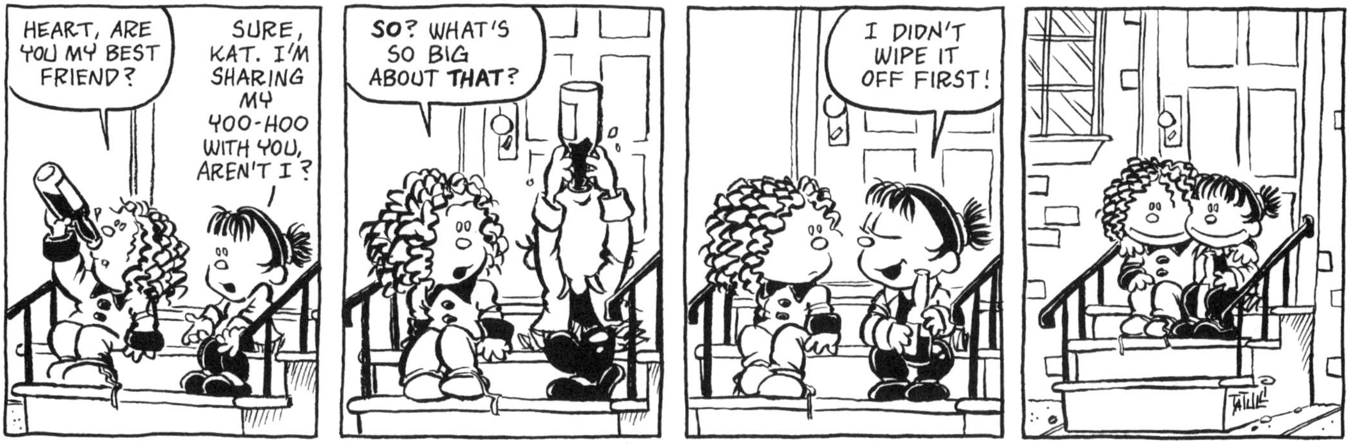
HEART, ARE YOU MY BEST FRIEND?
SURE, KAT. I'M SHARING MY YOO-HOO WITH YOU, AREN'T I?
SO? WHAT'S SO BIG ABOUT THAT?
I DIDN'T WIPE IT OFF FIRST!

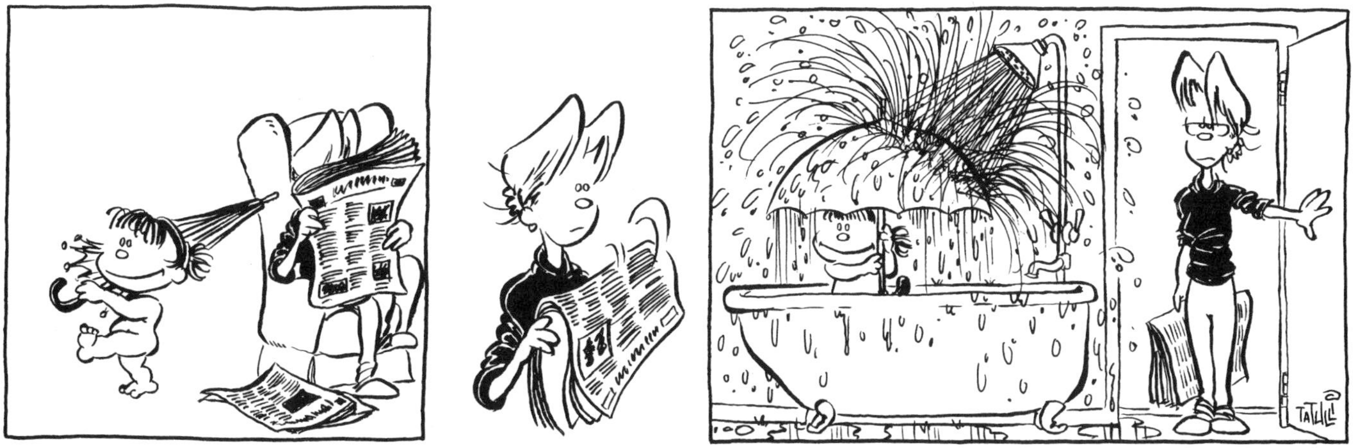

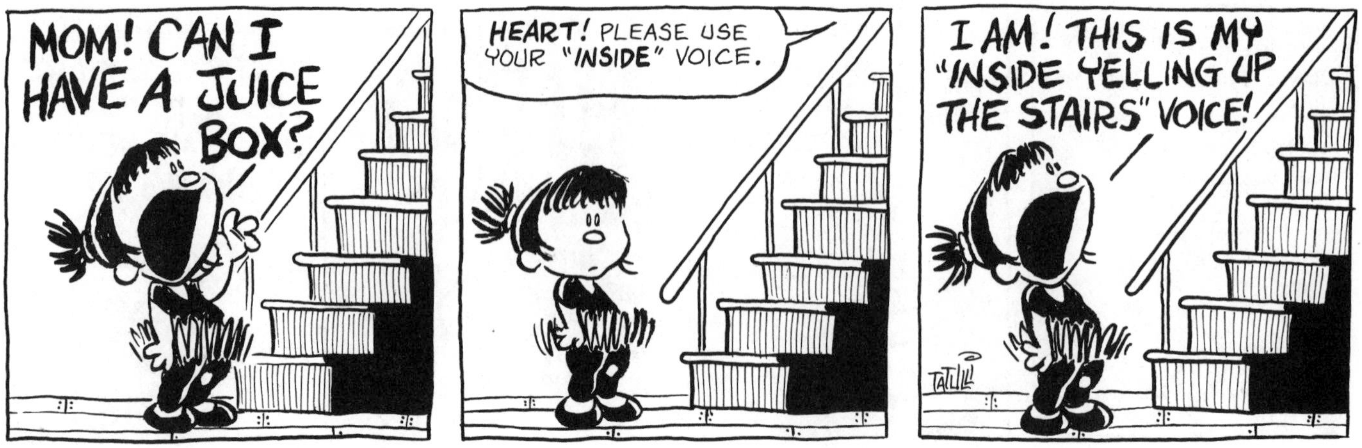
MOM! CAN I HAVE A JUICE BOX?
HEART! PLEASE USE YOUR "INSIDE" VOICE.
I AM! THIS IS MY "INSIDE YELLING UP THE STAIRS" VOICE!
TATULLI

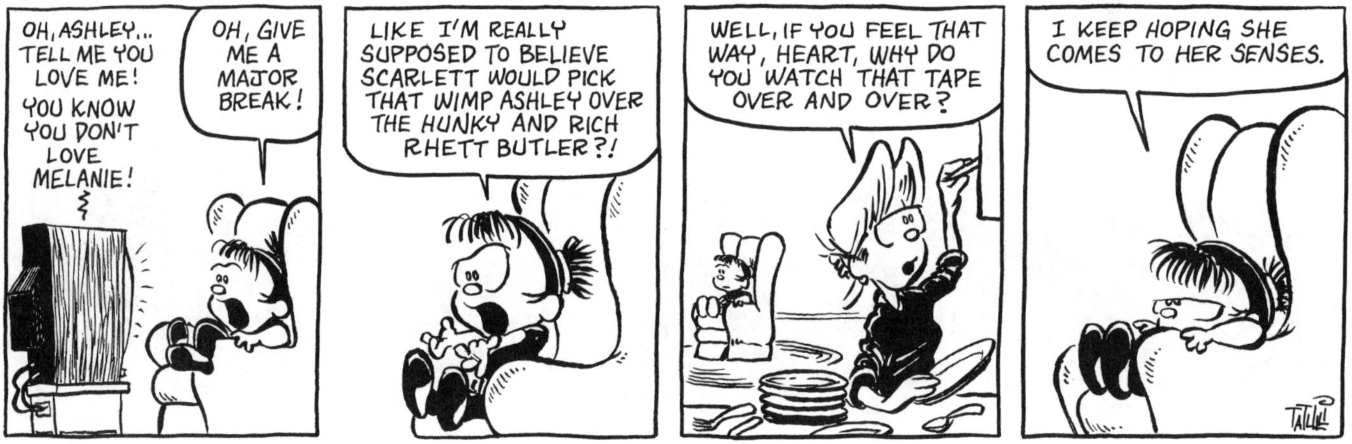
OH, ASHLEY... TELL ME YOU LOVE ME! YOU KNOW YOU DON'T LOVE MELANIE!
OH, GIVE ME A MAJOR BREAK!
LIKE I'M REALLY SUPPOSED TO BELIEVE SCARLETT WOULD PICK THAT WIMP ASHLEY OVER THE HUNKY AND RICH RHETT BUTLER?!
WELL, IF YOU FEEL THAT WAY, HEART, WHY DO YOU WATCH THAT TAPE OVER AND OVER?
I KEEP HOPING SHE COMES TO HER SENSES.
TATULLI

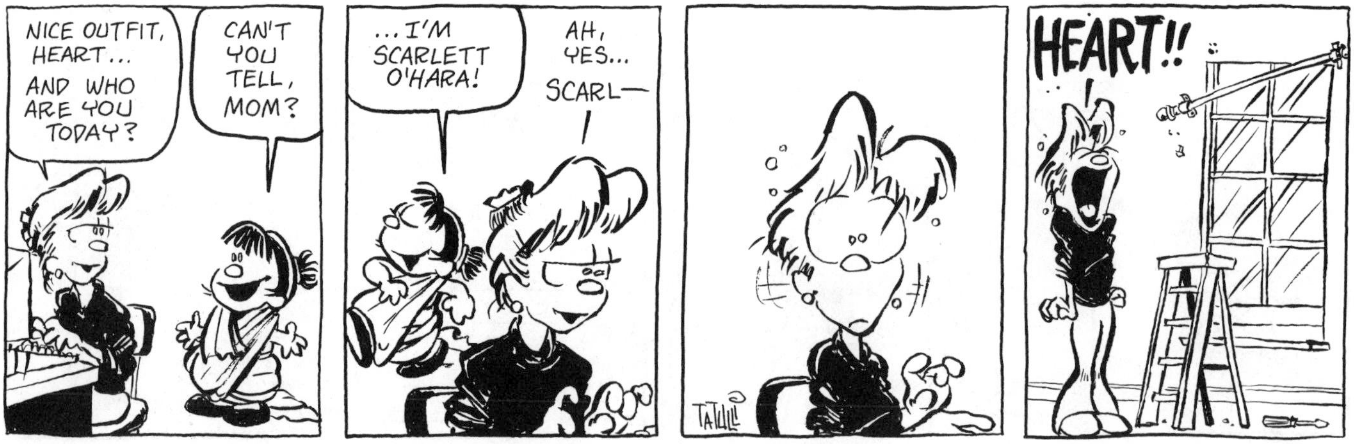
NICE OUTFIT, HEART... AND WHO ARE YOU TODAY?
CAN'T YOU TELL, MOM?
...I'M SCARLETT O'HARA!
AH, YES... SCARL—
TATULLI
HEART!!

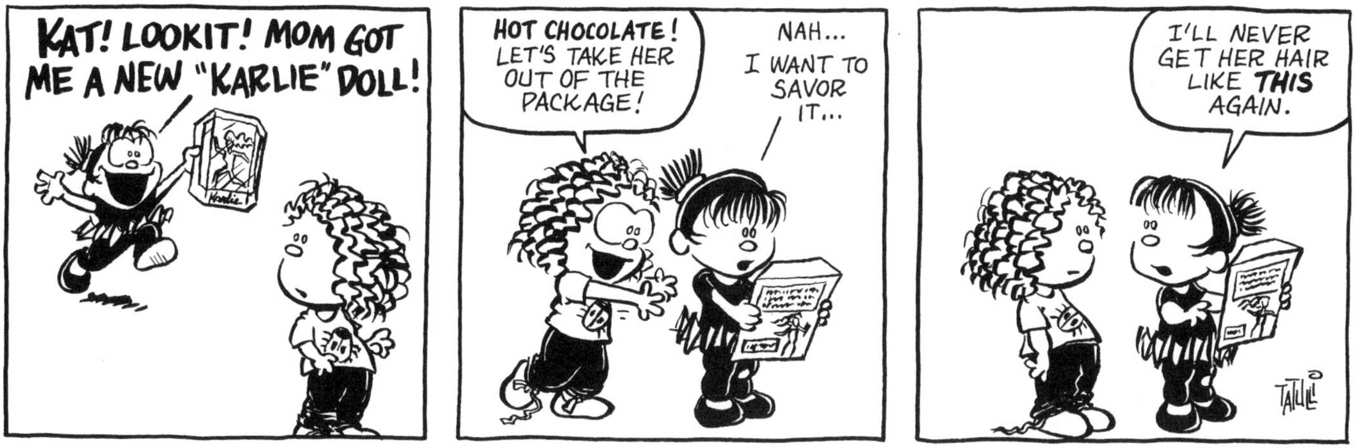
KAT! LOOKIT! MOM GOT ME A NEW "KARLIE" DOLL!
HOT CHOCOLATE! LET'S TAKE HER OUT OF THE PACKAGE!
NAH... I WANT TO SAVOR IT...
I'LL NEVER GET HER HAIR LIKE THIS AGAIN.

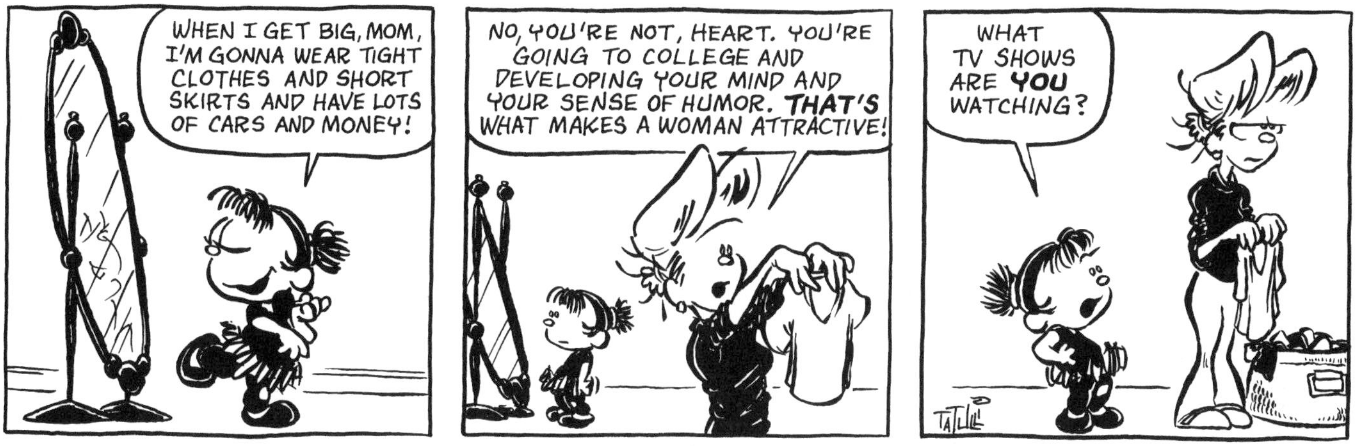
WHEN I GET BIG, MOM, I'M GONNA WEAR TIGHT CLOTHES AND SHORT SKIRTS AND HAVE LOTS OF CARS AND MONEY!
NO, YOU'RE NOT, HEART. YOU'RE GOING TO COLLEGE AND DEVELOPING YOUR MIND AND YOUR SENSE OF HUMOR. THAT'S WHAT MAKES A WOMAN ATTRACTIVE!
WHAT TV SHOWS ARE YOU WATCHING?

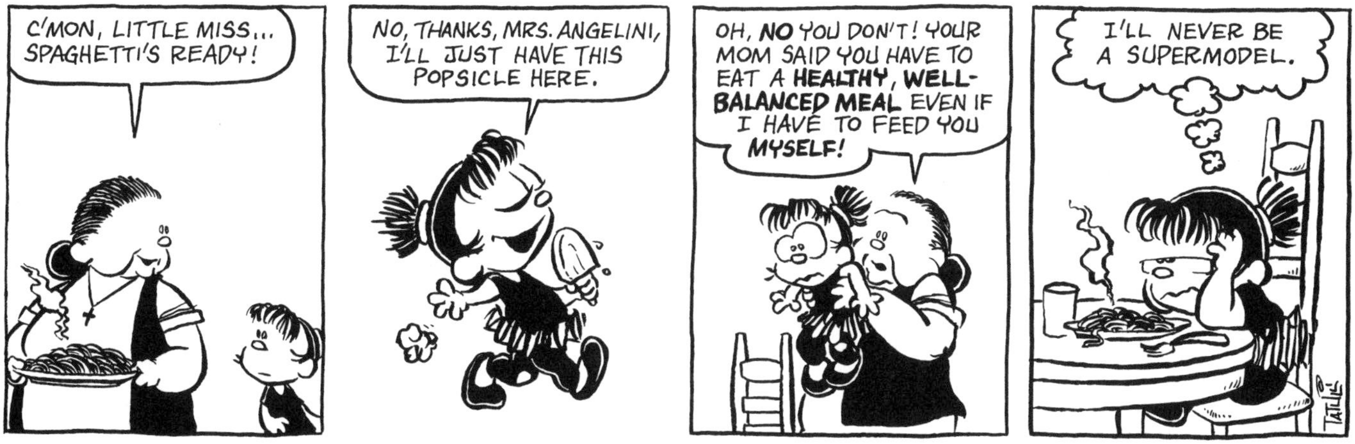
C'MON, LITTLE MISS... SPAGHETTI'S READY!
NO, THANKS, MRS. ANGELINI, I'LL JUST HAVE THIS POPSICLE HERE.
OH, NO YOU DON'T! YOUR MOM SAID YOU HAVE TO EAT A HEALTHY, WELL-BALANCED MEAL EVEN IF I HAVE TO FEED YOU MYSELF!
I'LL NEVER BE A SUPERMODEL.

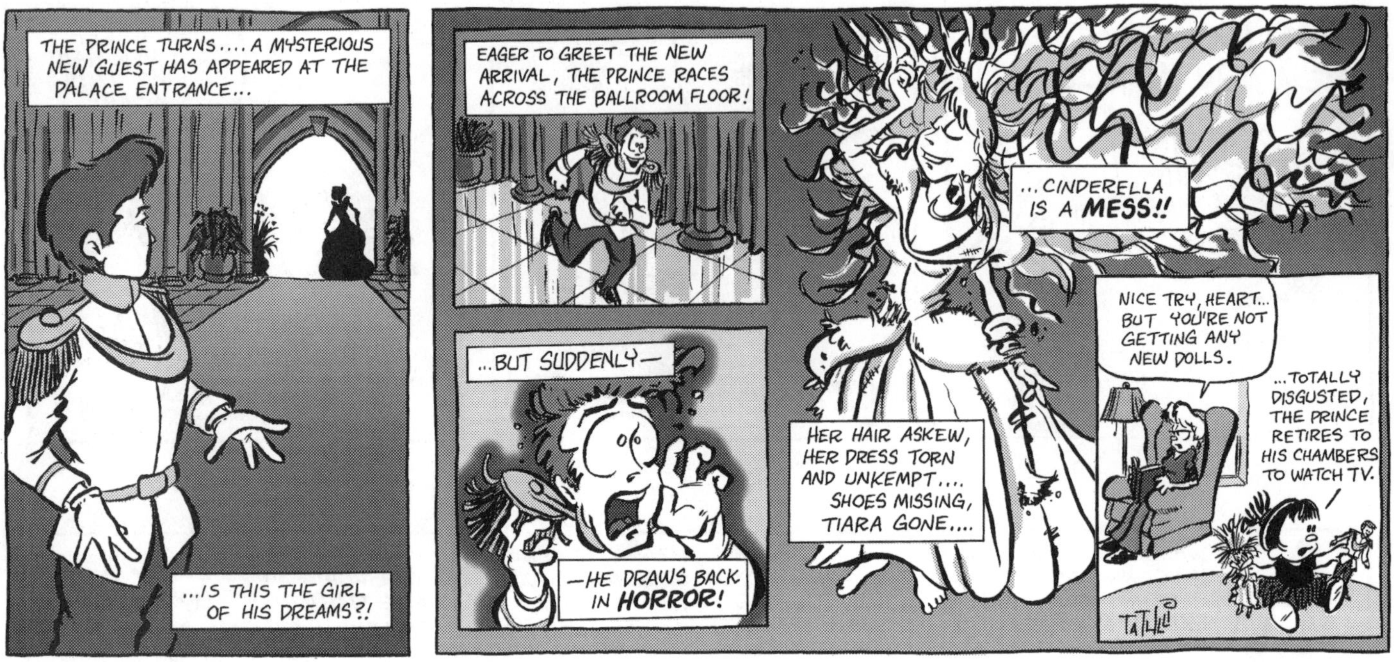
THE PRINCE TURNS.... A MYSTERIOUS NEW GUEST HAS APPEARED AT THE PALACE ENTRANCE...
...IS THIS THE GIRL OF HIS DREAMS?!
EAGER TO GREET THE NEW ARRIVAL, THE PRINCE RACES ACROSS THE BALLROOM FLOOR!
...BUT SUDDENLY—
—HE DRAWS BACK IN **HORROR!**
...CINDERELLA IS A **MESS!!**
HER HAIR ASKEW, HER DRESS TORN AND UNKEMPT.... SHOES MISSING, TIARA GONE....
NICE TRY, HEART... BUT YOU'RE NOT GETTING ANY NEW DOLLS.
...TOTALLY DISGUSTED, THE PRINCE RETIRES TO HIS CHAMBERS TO WATCH TV.

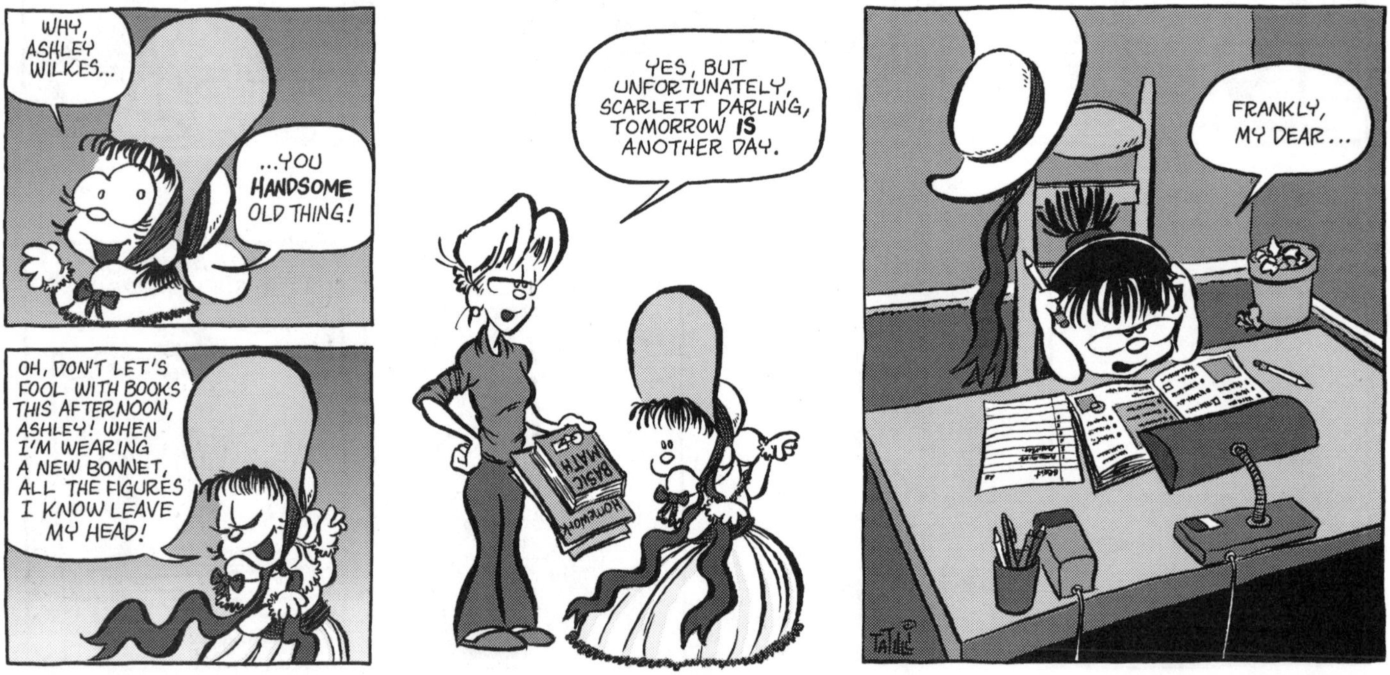
WHY, ASHLEY WILKES...
...YOU **HANDSOME** OLD THING!
OH, DON'T LET'S FOOL WITH BOOKS THIS AFTERNOON, ASHLEY! WHEN I'M WEARING A NEW BONNET, ALL THE FIGURES I KNOW LEAVE MY HEAD!
YES, BUT UNFORTUNATELY, SCARLETT DARLING, TOMORROW **IS** ANOTHER DAY.
BASIC MATH
FRANKLY, MY DEAR...

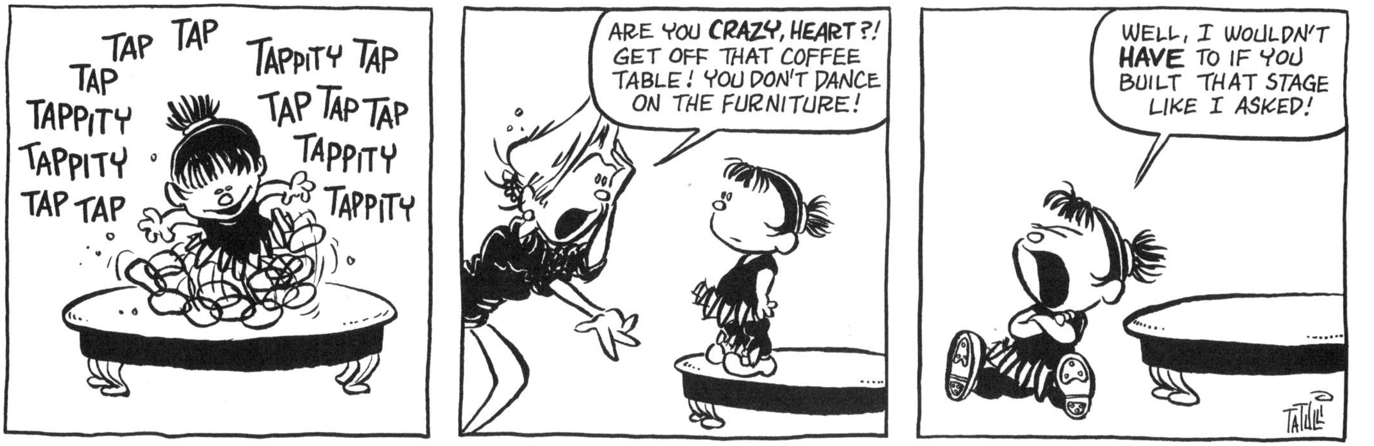
TAP TAP
TAP
TAPPITY
TAPPITY
TAP TAP
TAPPITY TAP
TAP TAP TAP
TAPPITY
TAPPITY
ARE YOU CRAZY, HEART?! GET OFF THAT COFFEE TABLE! YOU DON'T DANCE ON THE FURNITURE!
WELL, I WOULDN'T HAVE TO IF YOU BUILT THAT STAGE LIKE I ASKED!
TATULLI

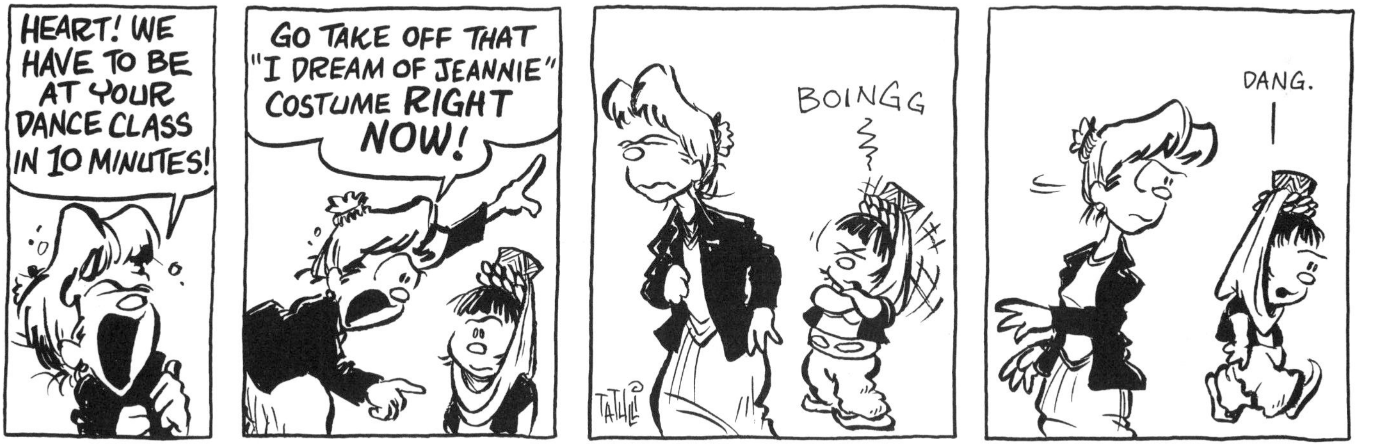
HEART! WE HAVE TO BE AT YOUR DANCE CLASS IN 10 MINUTES!
GO TAKE OFF THAT "I DREAM OF JEANNIE" COSTUME RIGHT NOW!
BOINGG
TATULLI
DANG.

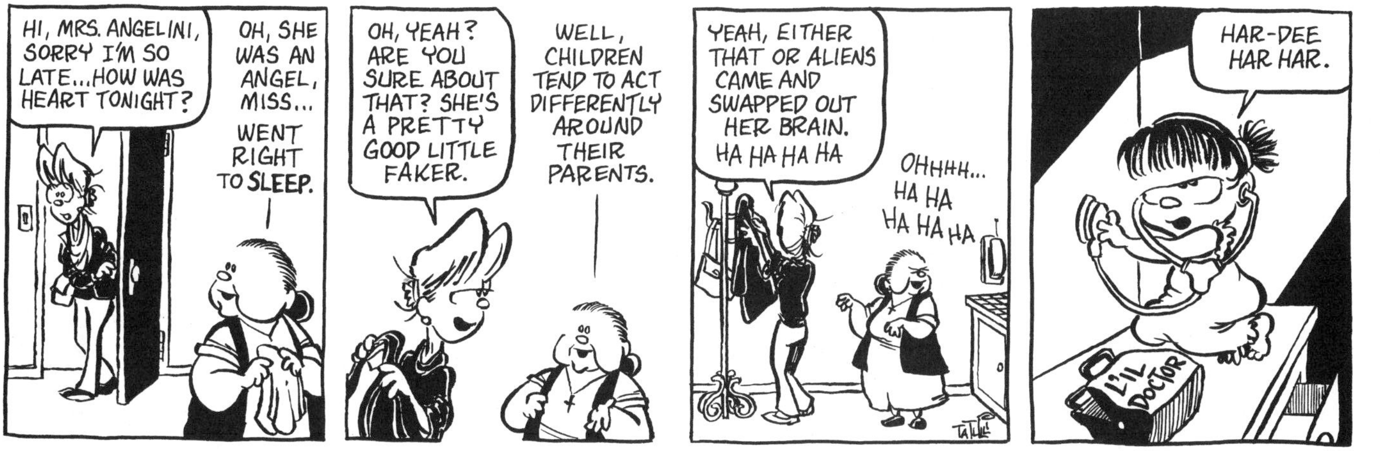
HI, MRS. ANGELINI, SORRY I'M SO LATE...HOW WAS HEART TONIGHT?
OH, SHE WAS AN ANGEL, MISS...
WENT RIGHT TO SLEEP.
OH, YEAH? ARE YOU SURE ABOUT THAT? SHE'S A PRETTY GOOD LITTLE FAKER.
WELL, CHILDREN TEND TO ACT DIFFERENTLY AROUND THEIR PARENTS.
YEAH, EITHER THAT OR ALIENS CAME AND SWAPPED OUT HER BRAIN. HA HA HA HA
OHHHH... HA HA HA HA HA
TATULLI
HAR-DEE HAR HAR.
L'IL DOCTOR

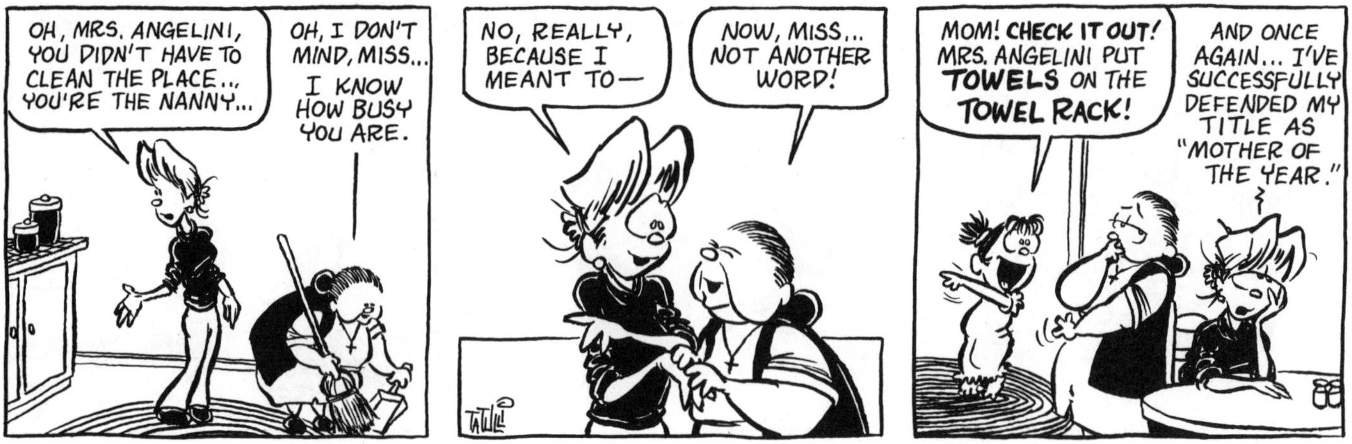
OH, MRS. ANGELINI, YOU DIDN'T HAVE TO CLEAN THE PLACE... YOU'RE THE NANNY...
OH, I DON'T MIND, MISS...
I KNOW HOW BUSY YOU ARE.
NO, REALLY, BECAUSE I MEANT TO—
NOW, MISS... NOT ANOTHER WORD!
MOM! **CHECK IT OUT!** MRS. ANGELINI PUT **TOWELS** ON THE **TOWEL RACK!**
AND ONCE AGAIN... I'VE SUCCESSFULLY DEFENDED MY TITLE AS "MOTHER OF THE YEAR."

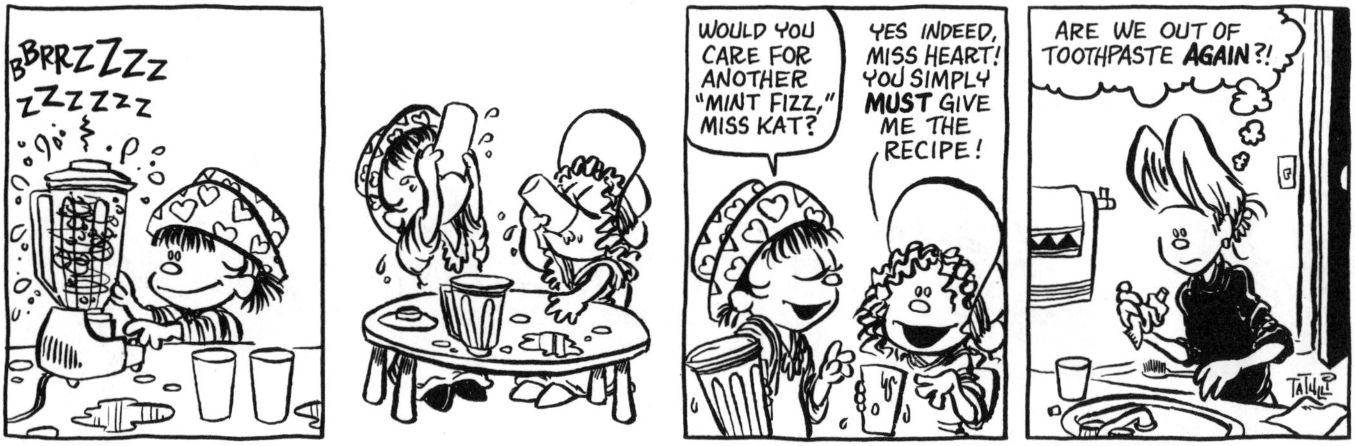
BBRRZZZZZ
ZZZZZZ
WOULD YOU CARE FOR ANOTHER "MINT FIZZ," MISS KAT?
YES INDEED, MISS HEART! YOU SIMPLY **MUST** GIVE ME THE RECIPE!
ARE WE OUT OF TOOTHPASTE **AGAIN**?!

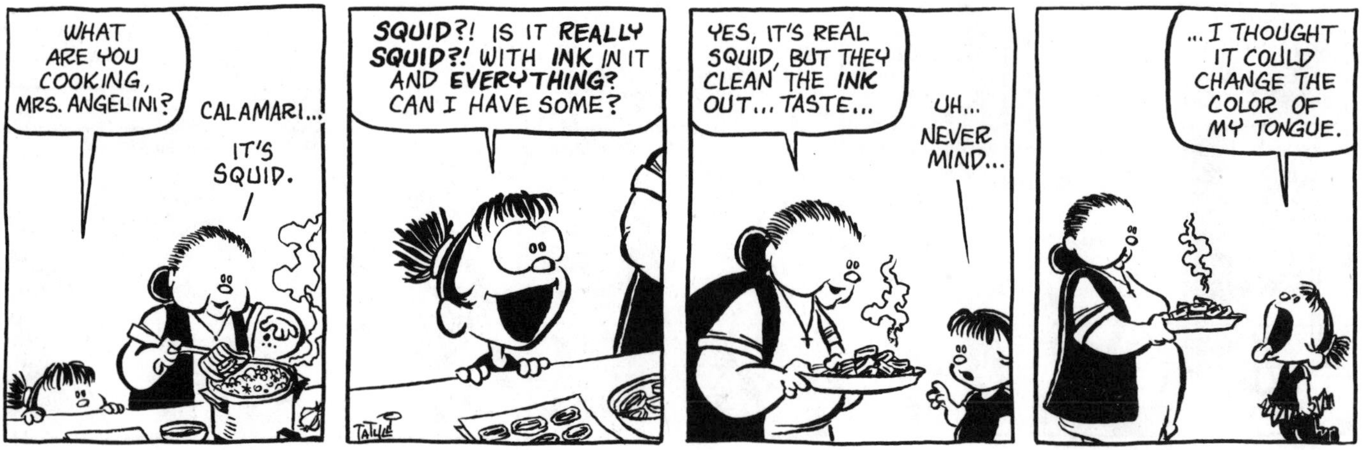
WHAT ARE YOU COOKING, MRS. ANGELINI?
CALAMARI...
IT'S SQUID.
SQUID?! IS IT **REALLY SQUID?!** WITH **INK** IN IT AND **EVERYTHING?** CAN I HAVE SOME?
YES, IT'S REAL SQUID, BUT THEY CLEAN THE **INK** OUT... TASTE...
UH... NEVER MIND...
...I THOUGHT IT COULD CHANGE THE COLOR OF MY TONGUE.

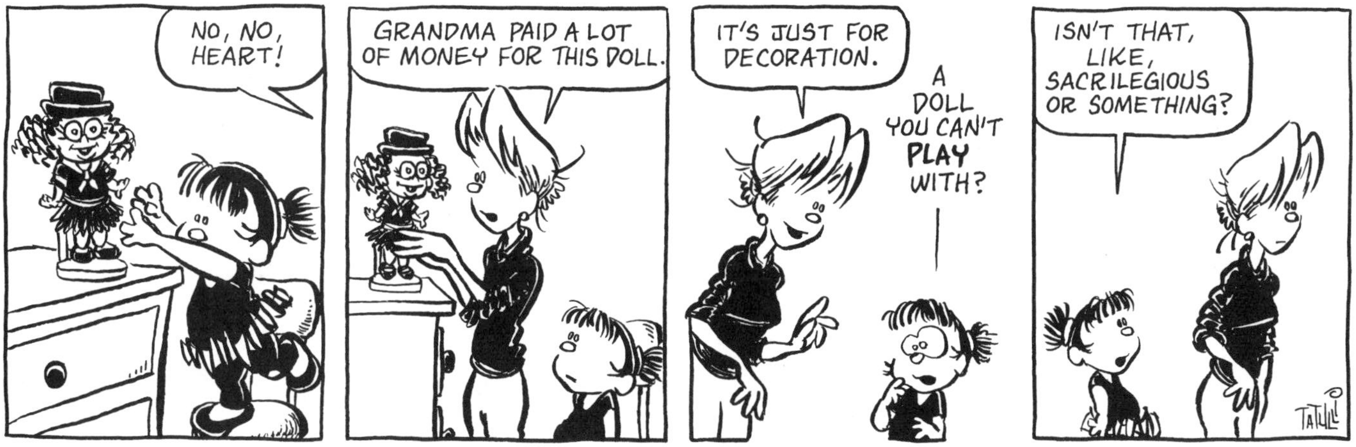
NO, NO, HEART!
GRANDMA PAID A LOT OF MONEY FOR THIS DOLL.
IT'S JUST FOR DECORATION.
A DOLL YOU CAN'T **PLAY** WITH?
ISN'T THAT, LIKE, SACRILEGIOUS OR SOMETHING?

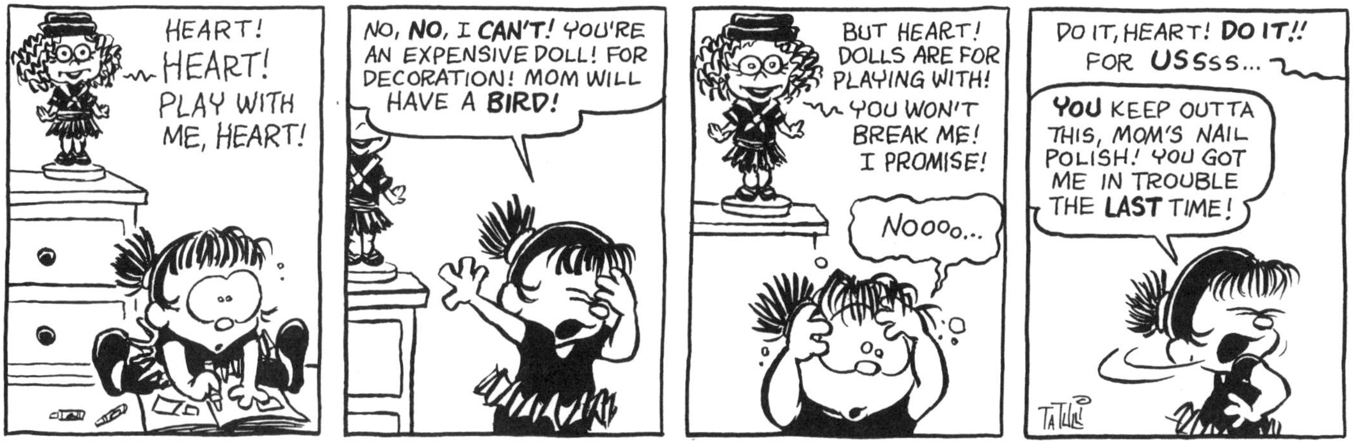
HEART! HEART! PLAY WITH ME, HEART!
NO, **NO**, I **CAN'T**! YOU'RE AN EXPENSIVE DOLL! FOR DECORATION! MOM WILL HAVE A **BIRD**!
BUT HEART! DOLLS ARE FOR PLAYING WITH! YOU WON'T BREAK ME! I PROMISE!
NOooo...
DO IT, HEART! **DO IT**!! FOR **US**sss...
YOU KEEP OUTTA THIS, MOM'S NAIL POLISH! YOU GOT ME IN TROUBLE THE **LAST** TIME!

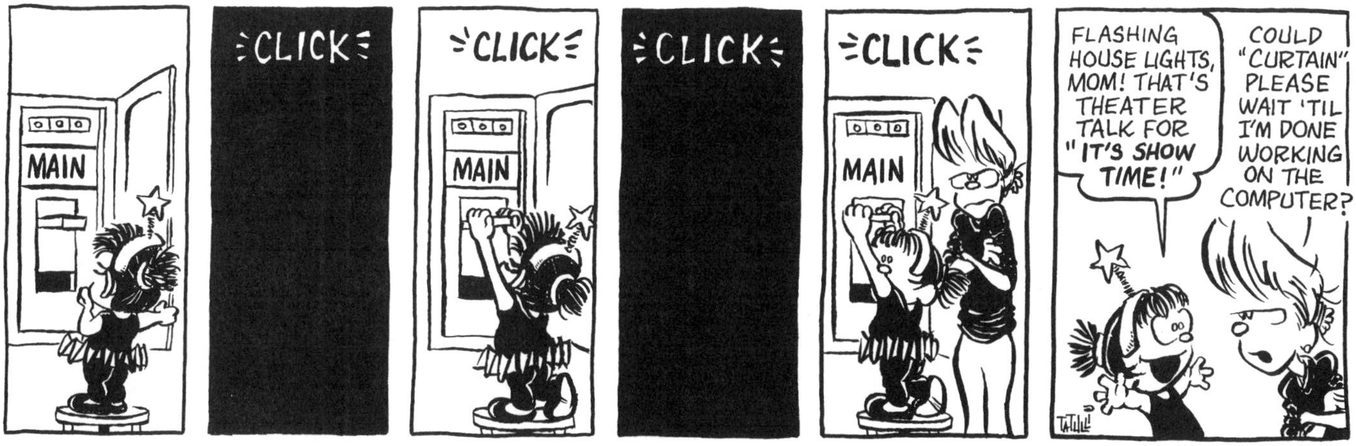
MAIN
CLICK
CLICK
MAIN
CLICK
CLICK
MAIN
FLASHING HOUSE LIGHTS, MOM! THAT'S THEATER TALK FOR "**IT'S SHOW TIME!**"
COULD "CURTAIN" PLEASE WAIT 'TIL I'M DONE WORKING ON THE COMPUTER?

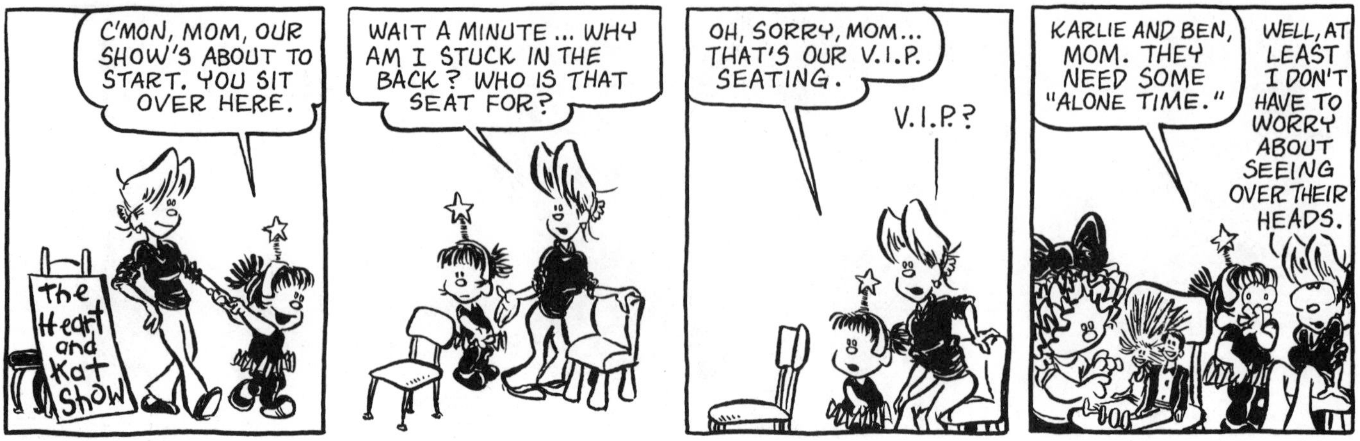

C'MON, MOM, OUR SHOW'S ABOUT TO START. YOU SIT OVER HERE.
The Heart and Kat Show
WAIT A MINUTE ... WHY AM I STUCK IN THE BACK? WHO IS THAT SEAT FOR?
OH, SORRY, MOM... THAT'S OUR V.I.P. SEATING.
V.I.P.?
KARLIE AND BEN, MOM. THEY NEED SOME "ALONE TIME."
WELL, AT LEAST I DON'T HAVE TO WORRY ABOUT SEEING OVER THEIR HEADS.

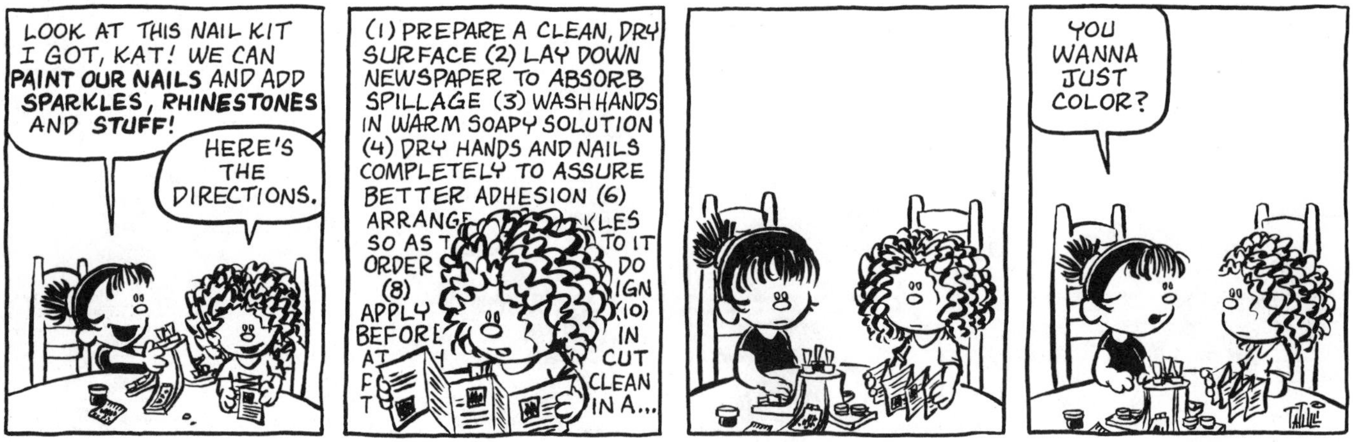

LOOK AT THIS NAIL KIT I GOT, KAT! WE CAN **PAINT OUR NAILS** AND ADD **SPARKLES, RHINESTONES** AND **STUFF**!
HERE'S THE DIRECTIONS.
(1) PREPARE A CLEAN, DRY SURFACE (2) LAY DOWN NEWSPAPER TO ABSORB SPILLAGE (3) WASH HANDS IN WARM SOAPY SOLUTION (4) DRY HANDS AND NAILS COMPLETELY TO ASSURE BETTER ADHESION (6)
YOU WANNA JUST COLOR?
TATULLI

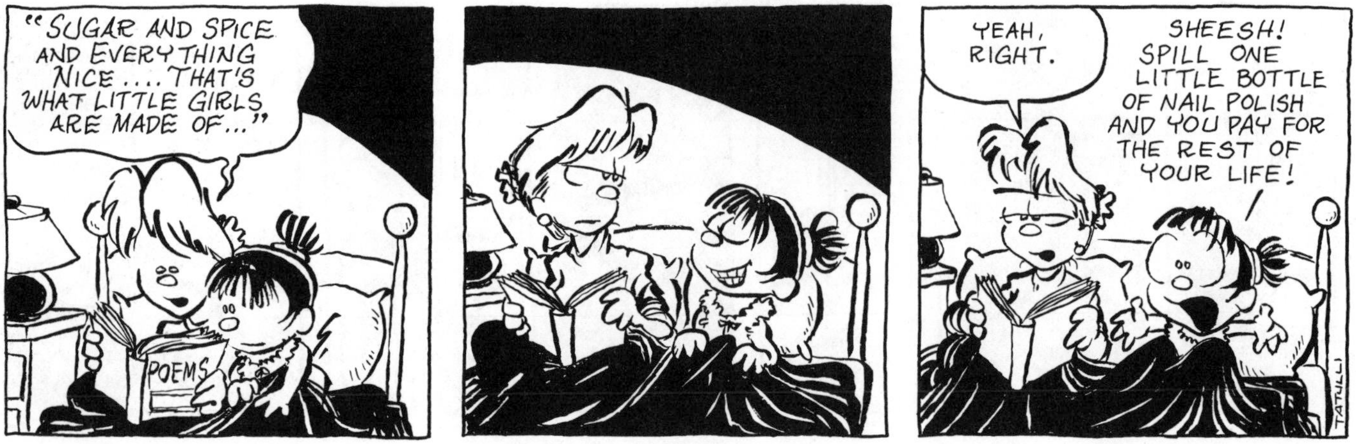

"SUGAR AND SPICE AND EVERYTHING NICE .... THAT'S WHAT LITTLE GIRLS ARE MADE OF..."
POEMS
YEAH, RIGHT.
SHEESH! SPILL ONE LITTLE BOTTLE OF NAIL POLISH AND YOU PAY FOR THE REST OF YOUR LIFE!
TATULLI

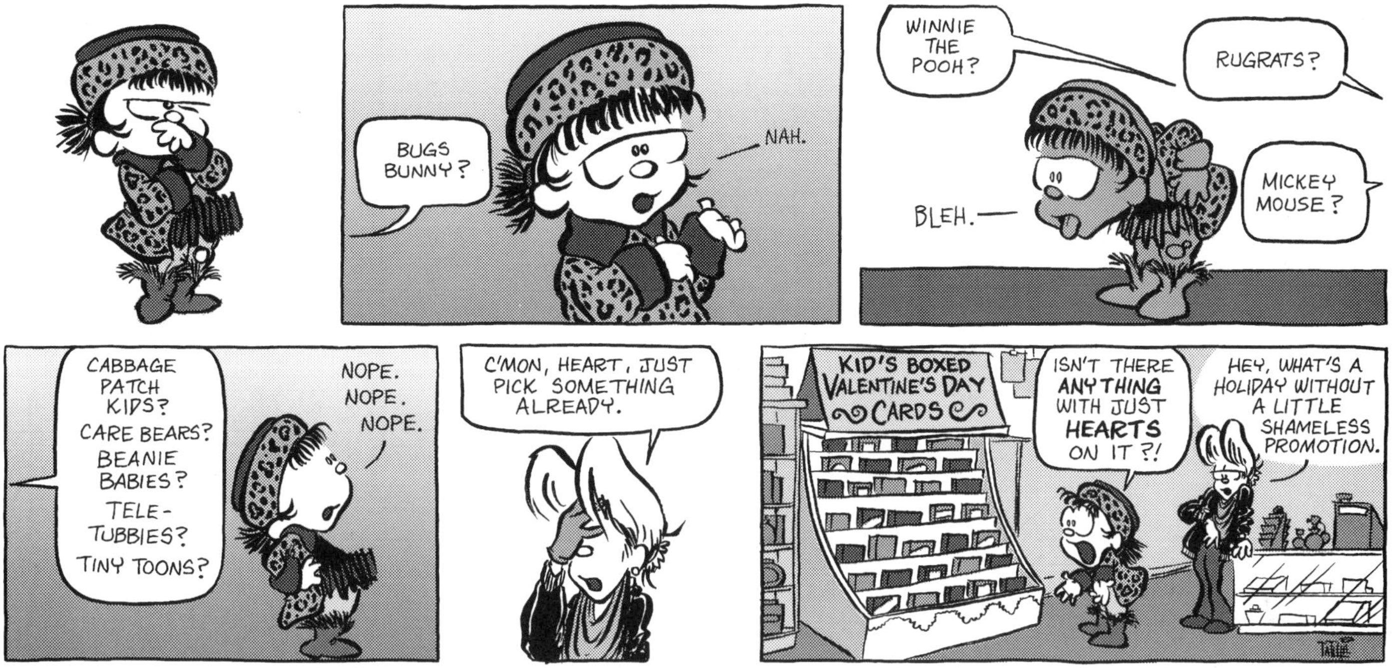
BUGS BUNNY?
NAH.
WINNIE THE POOH?
RUGRATS?
MICKEY MOUSE?
BLEH.
CABBAGE PATCH KIDS? CARE BEARS? BEANIE BABIES? TELE-TUBBIES? TINY TOONS?
NOPE. NOPE. NOPE.
C'MON, HEART, JUST PICK SOMETHING ALREADY.
KID'S BOXED VALENTINE'S DAY CARDS
ISN'T THERE **ANYTHING** WITH JUST **HEARTS** ON IT?!
HEY, WHAT'S A HOLIDAY WITHOUT A LITTLE SHAMELESS PROMOTION.

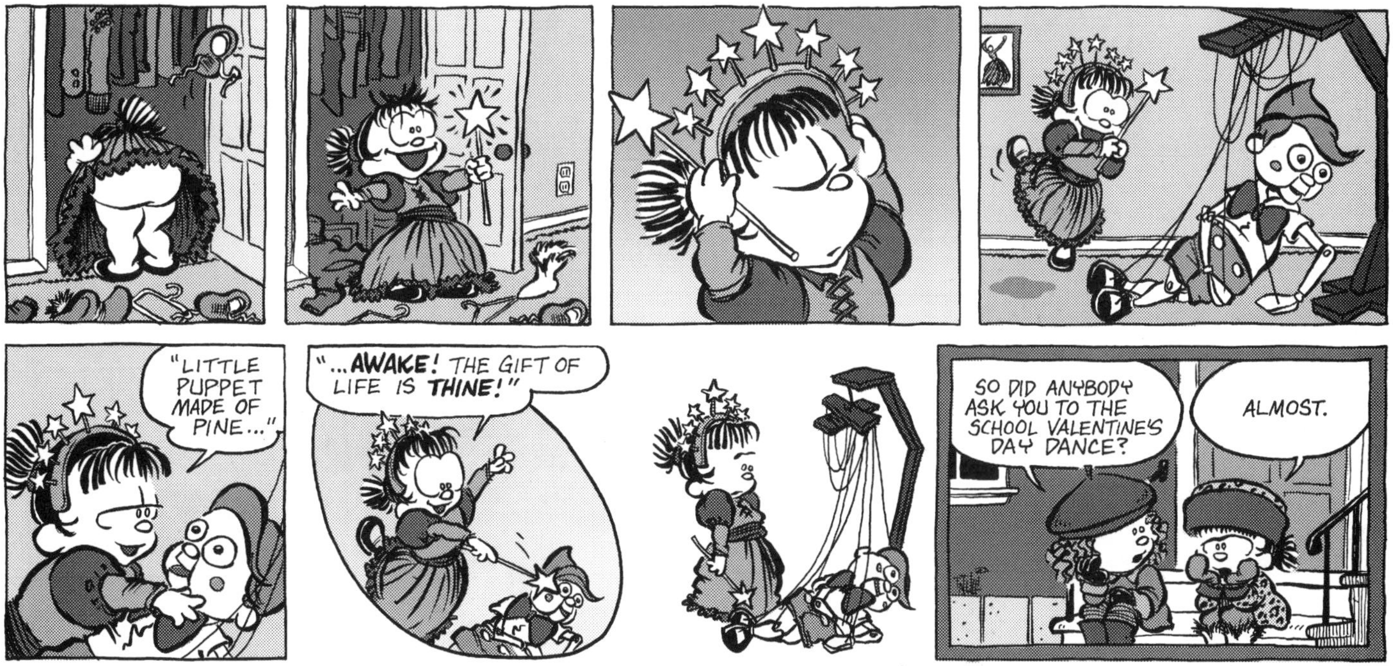
"LITTLE PUPPET MADE OF PINE..."
"...**AWAKE!** THE GIFT OF LIFE IS **THINE!**"
SO DID ANYBODY ASK YOU TO THE SCHOOL VALENTINE'S DAY DANCE?
ALMOST.

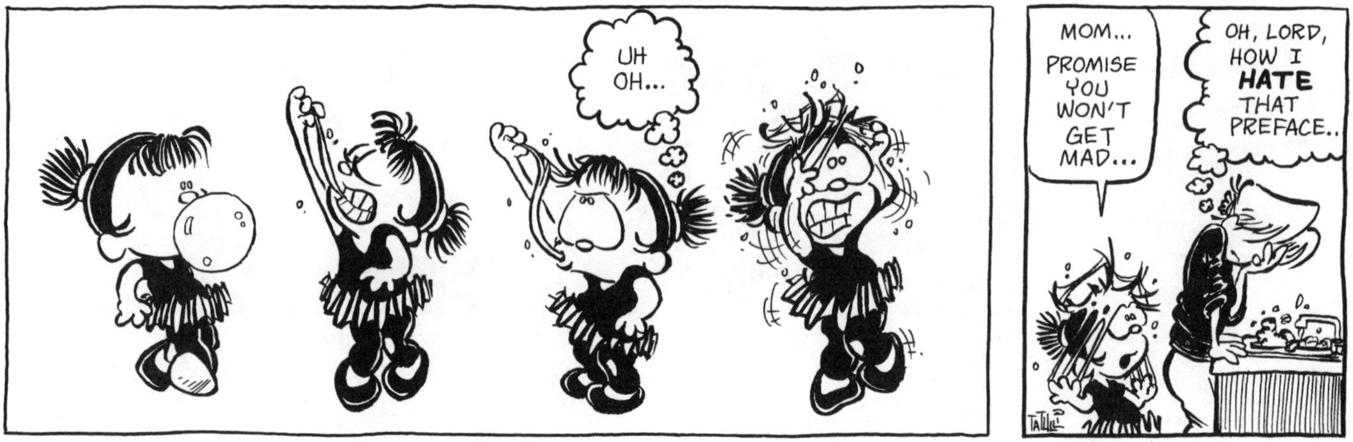
UH OH...
MOM... PROMISE YOU WON'T GET MAD...
OH, LORD, HOW I **HATE** THAT PREFACE..

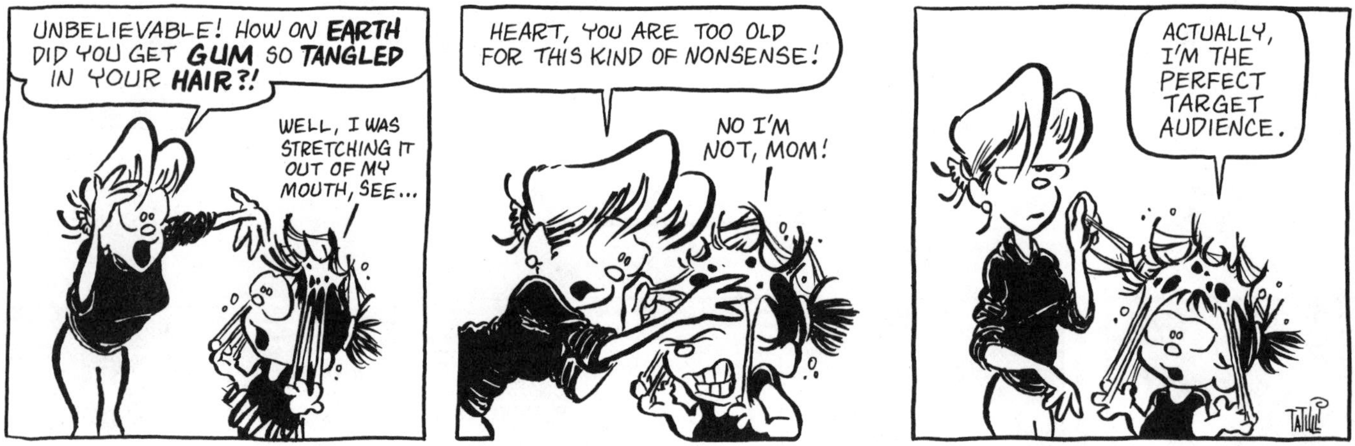
UNBELIEVABLE! HOW ON **EARTH** DID YOU GET **GUM** SO **TANGLED** IN YOUR **HAIR**?!
WELL, I WAS STRETCHING IT OUT OF MY MOUTH, SEE...
HEART, YOU ARE TOO OLD FOR THIS KIND OF NONSENSE!
NO I'M NOT, MOM!
ACTUALLY, I'M THE PERFECT TARGET AUDIENCE.

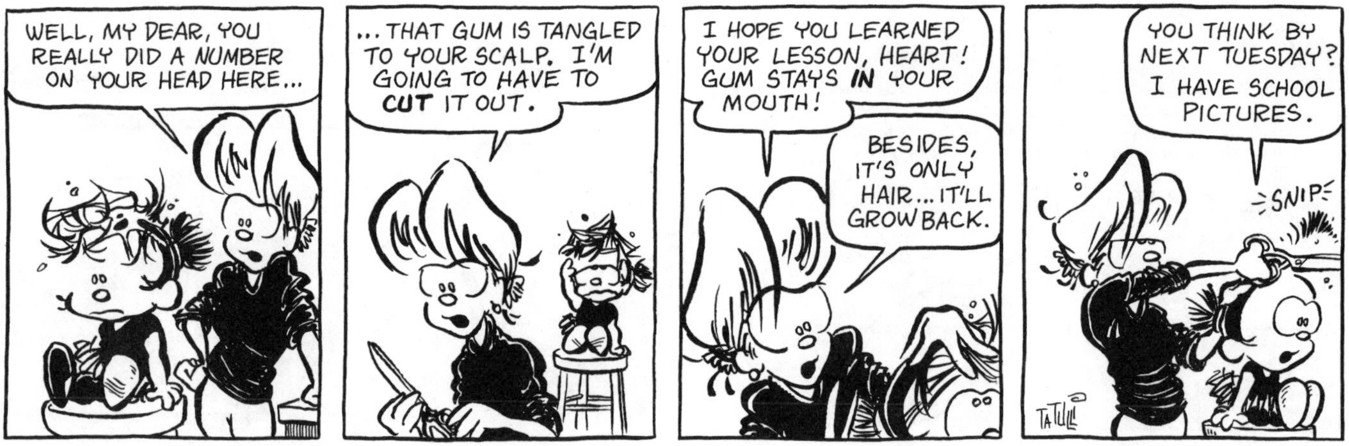
WELL, MY DEAR, YOU REALLY DID A NUMBER ON YOUR HEAD HERE...
...THAT GUM IS TANGLED TO YOUR SCALP. I'M GOING TO HAVE TO **CUT** IT OUT.
I HOPE YOU LEARNED YOUR LESSON, HEART! GUM STAYS **IN** YOUR MOUTH!
BESIDES, IT'S ONLY HAIR... IT'LL GROW BACK.
YOU THINK BY NEXT TUESDAY? I HAVE SCHOOL PICTURES.
SNIP

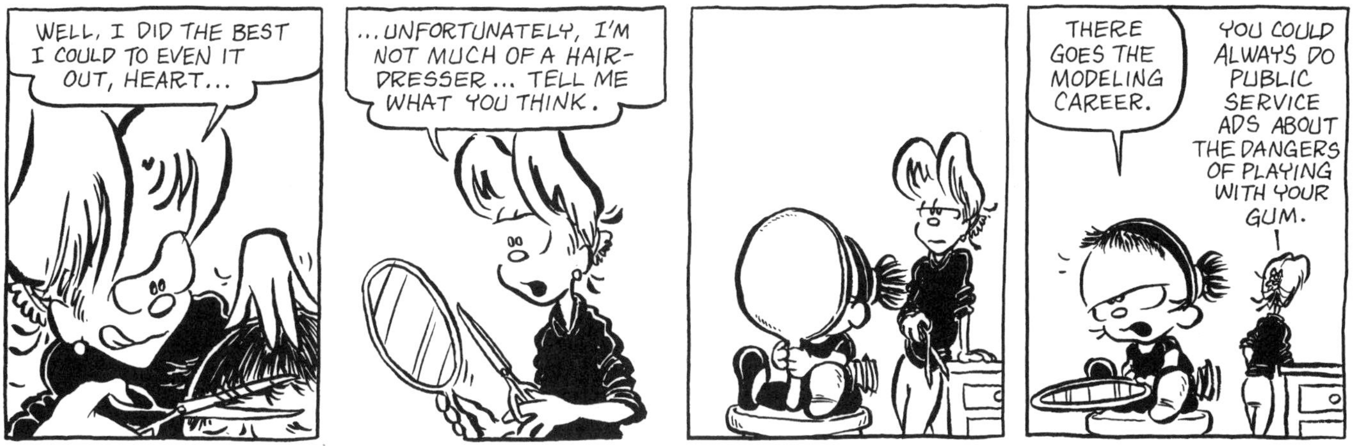
WELL, I DID THE BEST I COULD TO EVEN IT OUT, HEART...
...UNFORTUNATELY, I'M NOT MUCH OF A HAIR-DRESSER ... TELL ME WHAT YOU THINK.
THERE GOES THE MODELING CAREER.
YOU COULD ALWAYS DO PUBLIC SERVICE ADS ABOUT THE DANGERS OF PLAYING WITH YOUR GUM.

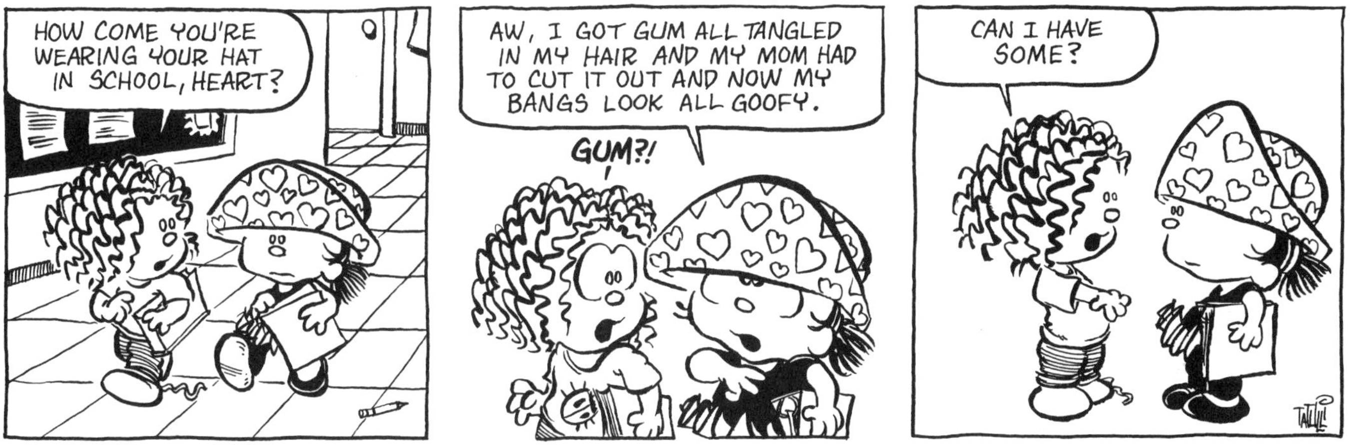
HOW COME YOU'RE WEARING YOUR HAT IN SCHOOL, HEART?
AW, I GOT GUM ALL TANGLED IN MY HAIR AND MY MOM HAD TO CUT IT OUT AND NOW MY BANGS LOOK ALL GOOFY.
GUM?!
CAN I HAVE SOME?

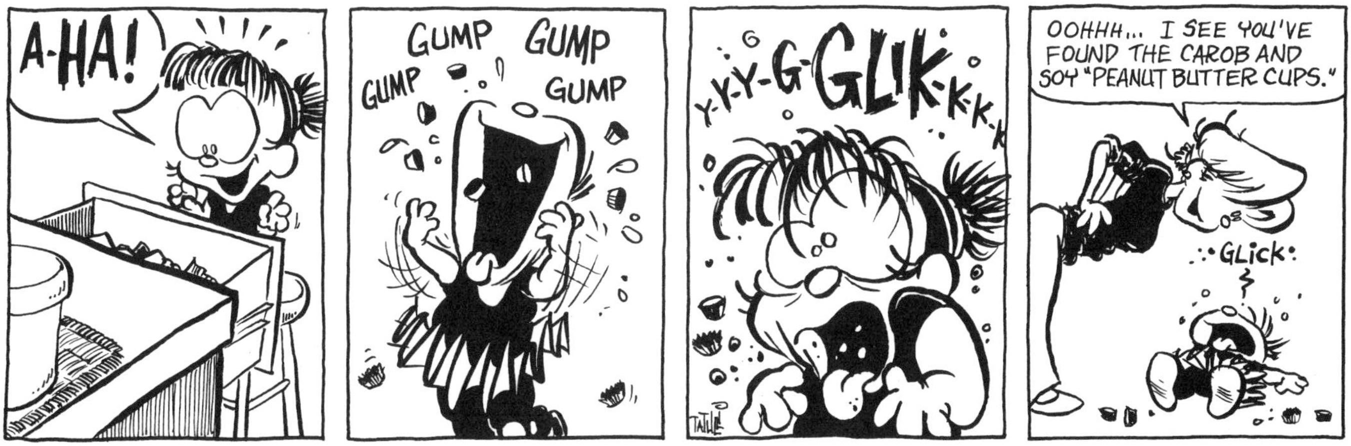
A-HA!
GUMP GUMP GUMP GUMP
Y-Y-Y-G-GLIK-K-K-K
OOHHH... I SEE YOU'VE FOUND THE CAROB AND SOY "PEANUT BUTTER CUPS."
GLICK

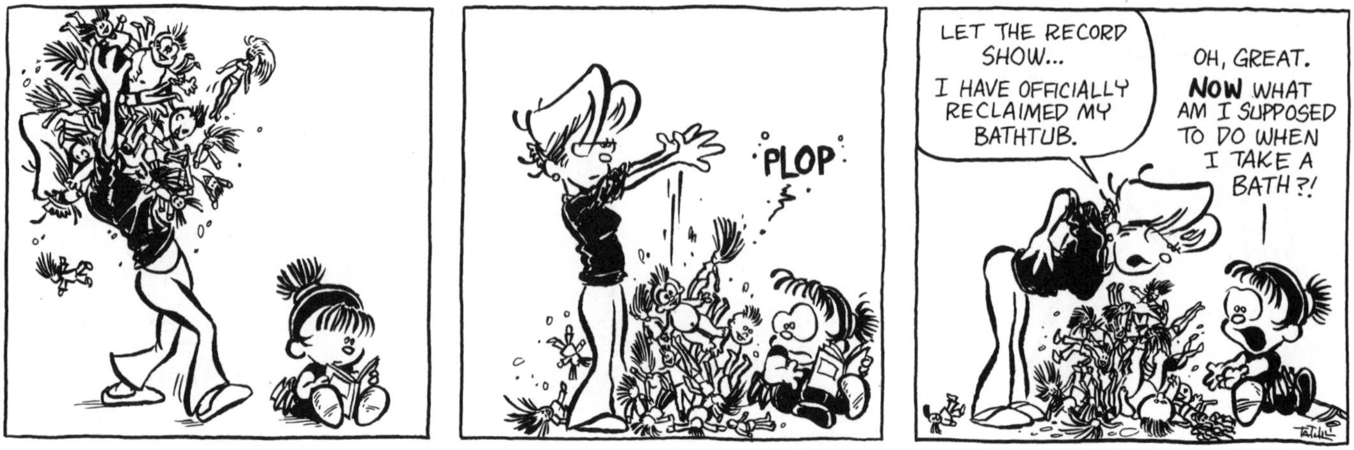
PLOP
LET THE RECORD SHOW... I HAVE OFFICIALLY RECLAIMED MY BATHTUB.
OH, GREAT. NOW WHAT AM I SUPPOSED TO DO WHEN I TAKE A BATH?!

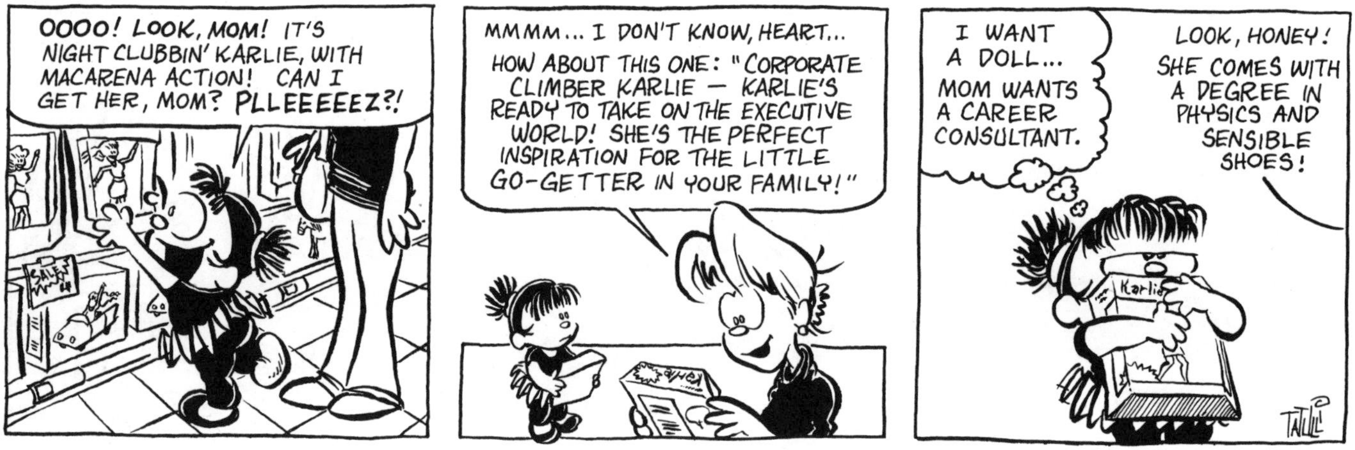
OOOO! LOOK, MOM! IT'S NIGHT CLUBBIN' KARLIE, WITH MACARENA ACTION! CAN I GET HER, MOM? PLLEEEEEZ?!
MMMM... I DON'T KNOW, HEART... HOW ABOUT THIS ONE: "CORPORATE CLIMBER KARLIE — KARLIE'S READY TO TAKE ON THE EXECUTIVE WORLD! SHE'S THE PERFECT INSPIRATION FOR THE LITTLE GO-GETTER IN YOUR FAMILY!"
I WANT A DOLL... MOM WANTS A CAREER CONSULTANT.
LOOK, HONEY! SHE COMES WITH A DEGREE IN PHYSICS AND SENSIBLE SHOES!

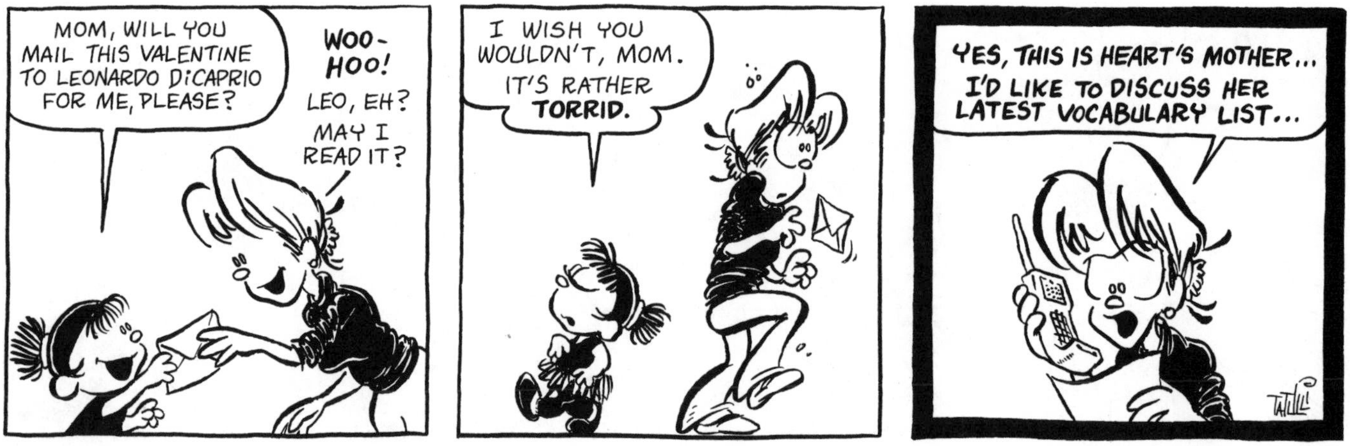
MOM, WILL YOU MAIL THIS VALENTINE TO LEONARDO DiCAPRIO FOR ME, PLEASE?
WOO-HOO! LEO, EH? MAY I READ IT?
I WISH YOU WOULDN'T, MOM. IT'S RATHER TORRID.
YES, THIS IS HEART'S MOTHER... I'D LIKE TO DISCUSS HER LATEST VOCABULARY LIST...

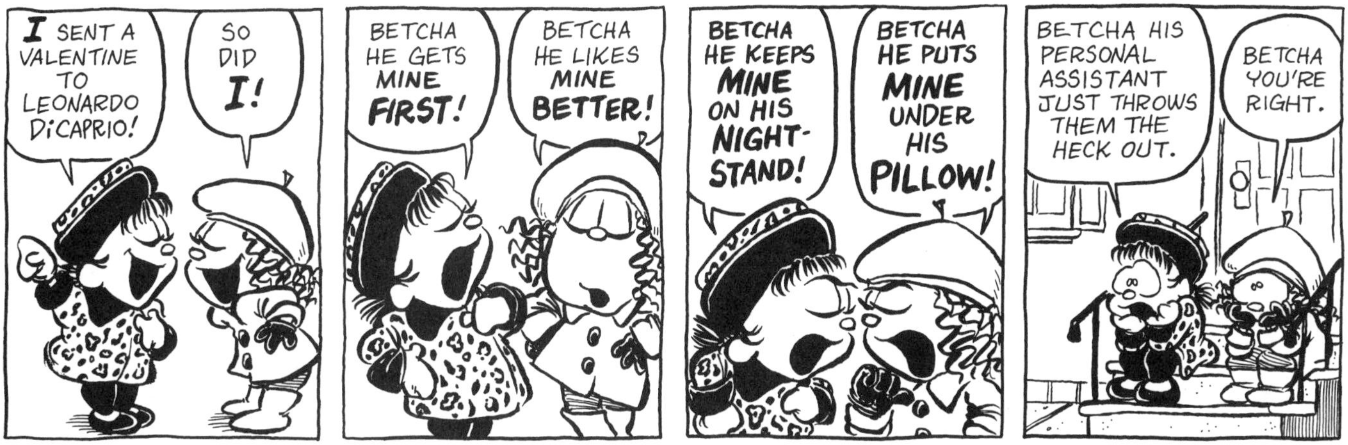
I SENT A VALENTINE TO LEONARDO DiCAPRIO!
SO DID I!
BETCHA HE GETS MINE FIRST!
BETCHA HE LIKES MINE BETTER!
BETCHA HE KEEPS MINE ON HIS NIGHT-STAND!
BETCHA HE PUTS MINE UNDER HIS PILLOW!
BETCHA HIS PERSONAL ASSISTANT JUST THROWS THEM THE HECK OUT.
BETCHA YOU'RE RIGHT.

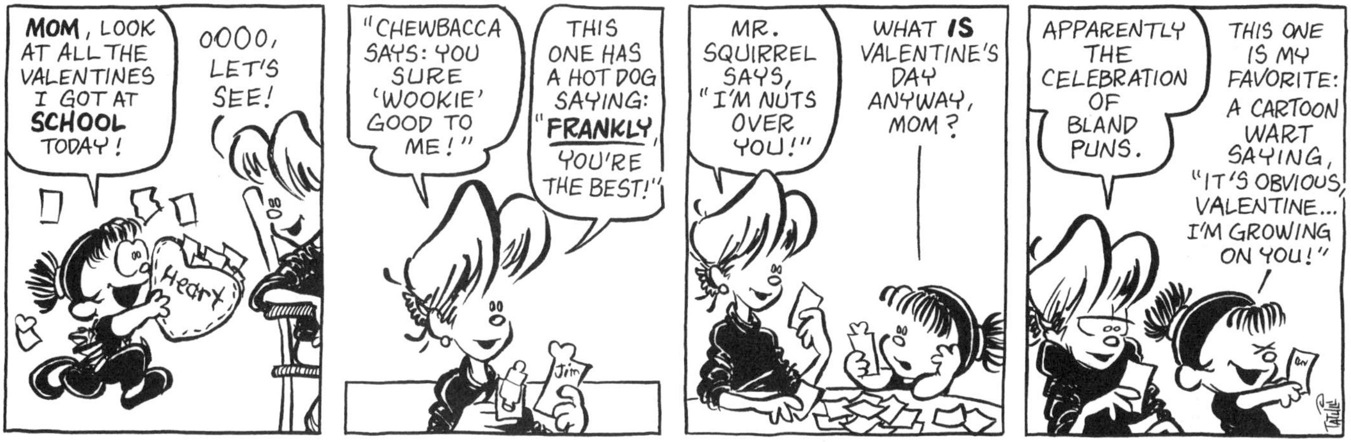
MOM, LOOK AT ALL THE VALENTINES I GOT AT SCHOOL TODAY!
OOOO, LET'S SEE!
Heart
"CHEWBACCA SAYS: YOU SURE 'WOOKIE' GOOD TO ME!"
THIS ONE HAS A HOT DOG SAYING: "FRANKLY, YOU'RE THE BEST!"
MR. SQUIRREL SAYS, "I'M NUTS OVER YOU!"
WHAT IS VALENTINE'S DAY ANYWAY, MOM?
APPARENTLY THE CELEBRATION OF BLAND PUNS.
THIS ONE IS MY FAVORITE: A CARTOON WART SAYING, "IT'S OBVIOUS, VALENTINE... I'M GROWING ON YOU!"

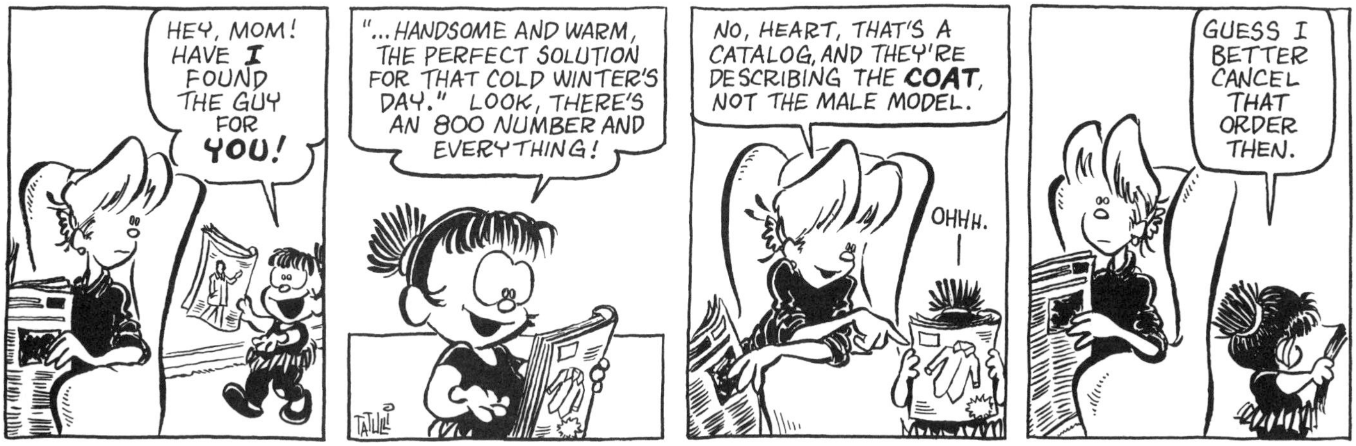
HEY, MOM! HAVE I FOUND THE GUY FOR YOU!
"...HANDSOME AND WARM, THE PERFECT SOLUTION FOR THAT COLD WINTER'S DAY." LOOK, THERE'S AN 800 NUMBER AND EVERYTHING!
NO, HEART, THAT'S A CATALOG, AND THEY'RE DESCRIBING THE COAT, NOT THE MALE MODEL.
OHHH.
GUESS I BETTER CANCEL THAT ORDER THEN.

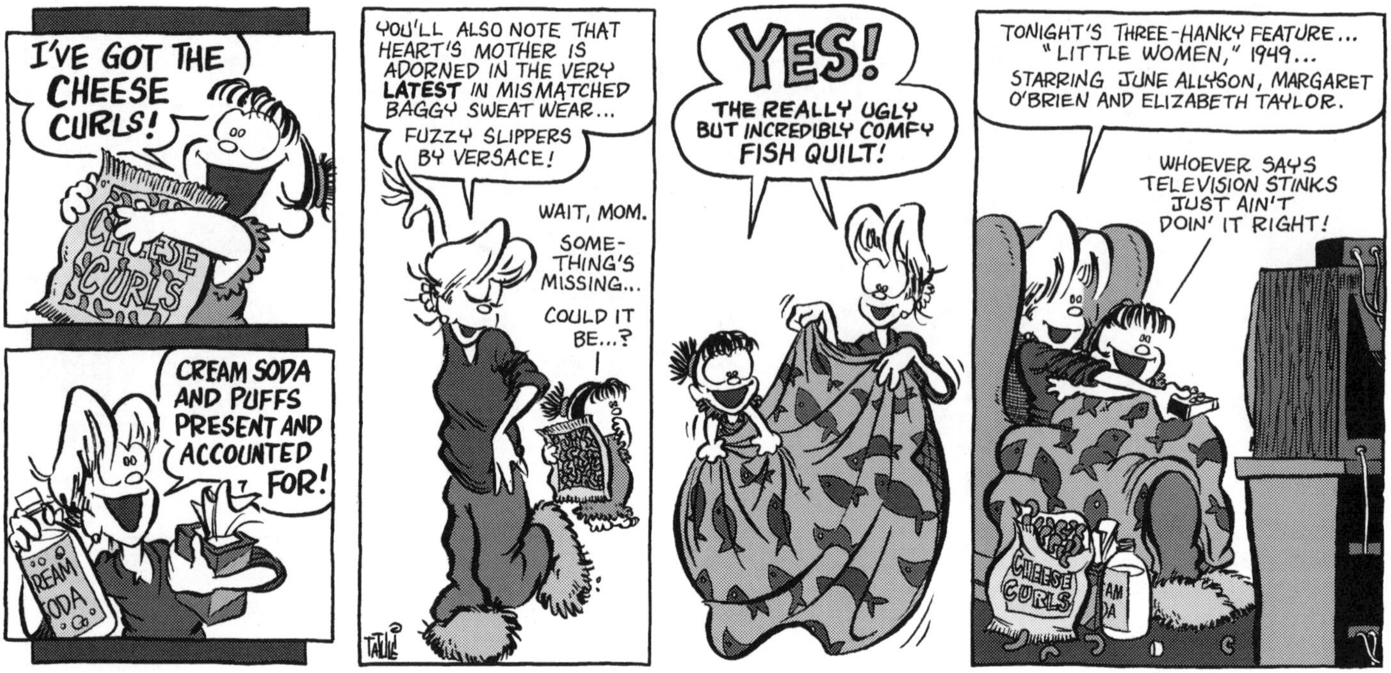
I'VE GOT THE CHEESE CURLS!
CHEESE CURLS
CREAM SODA AND PUFFS PRESENT AND ACCOUNTED FOR!
YOU'LL ALSO NOTE THAT HEART'S MOTHER IS ADORNED IN THE VERY **LATEST** IN MISMATCHED BAGGY SWEAT WEAR...
FUZZY SLIPPERS BY VERSACE!
WAIT, MOM.
SOME-THING'S MISSING...
COULD IT BE...?
YES!
THE REALLY UGLY BUT INCREDIBLY COMFY FISH QUILT!
TONIGHT'S THREE-HANKY FEATURE... "LITTLE WOMEN," 1949... STARRING JUNE ALLYSON, MARGARET O'BRIEN AND ELIZABETH TAYLOR.
WHOEVER SAYS TELEVISION STINKS JUST AIN'T DOIN' IT RIGHT!
CHEESE CURLS

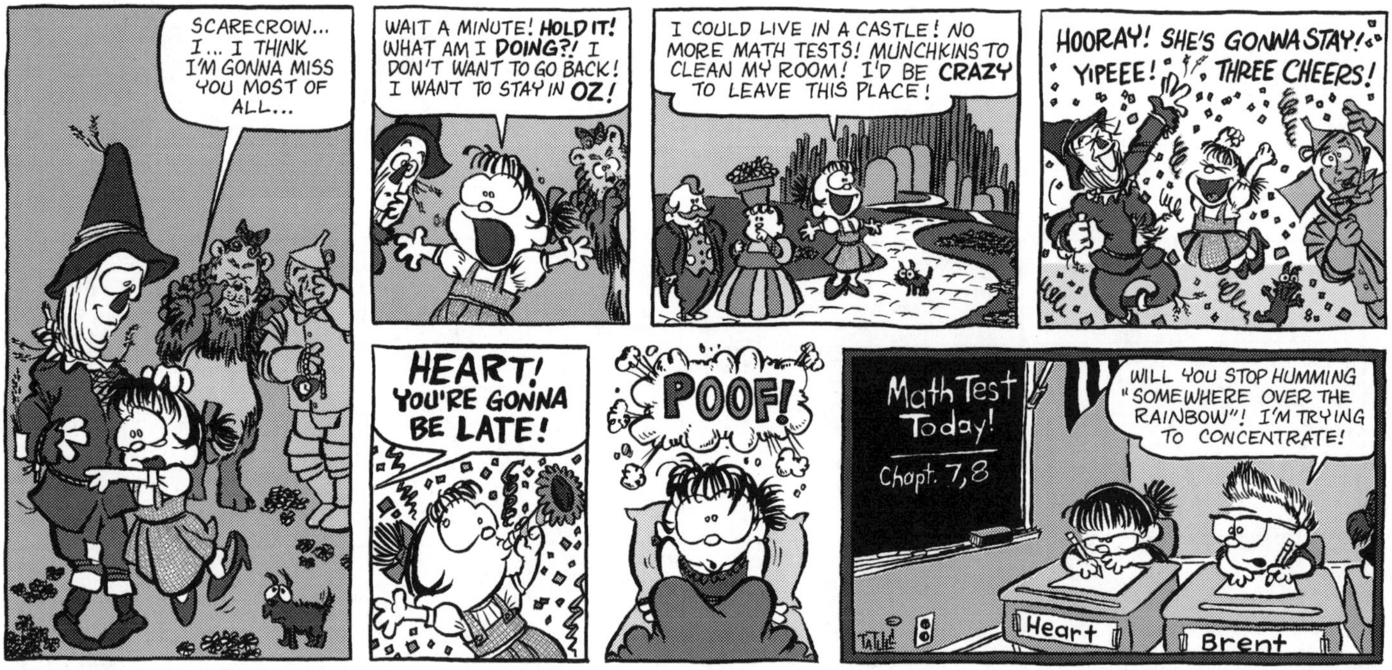
SCARECROW... I... I THINK I'M GONNA MISS YOU MOST OF ALL...
WAIT A MINUTE! **HOLD IT!** WHAT AM I **DOING?!** I DON'T WANT TO GO BACK! I WANT TO STAY IN **OZ!**
I COULD LIVE IN A CASTLE! NO MORE MATH TESTS! MUNCHKINS TO CLEAN MY ROOM! I'D BE **CRAZY** TO LEAVE THIS PLACE!
HOORAY! SHE'S GONNA STAY!
YIPEEE!
THREE CHEERS!
HEART! YOU'RE GONNA BE LATE!
POOF!
Math Test Today!
Chapt. 7,8
WILL YOU STOP HUMMING "SOMEWHERE OVER THE RAINBOW"! I'M TRYING TO CONCENTRATE!
Heart
Brent

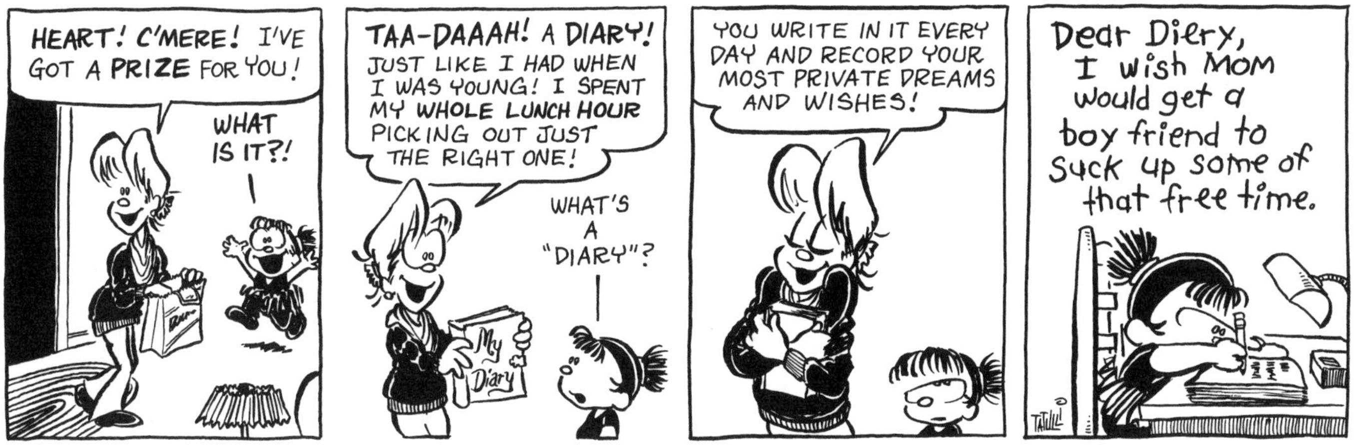
HEART! C'MERE! I'VE GOT A PRIZE FOR YOU!
WHAT IS IT?!
TAA-DAAAH! A DIARY! JUST LIKE I HAD WHEN I WAS YOUNG! I SPENT MY WHOLE LUNCH HOUR PICKING OUT JUST THE RIGHT ONE!
WHAT'S A "DIARY"?
My Diary
YOU WRITE IN IT EVERY DAY AND RECORD YOUR MOST PRIVATE DREAMS AND WISHES!
Dear Diery,
I wish MOM would get a boy friend to suck up some of that free time.

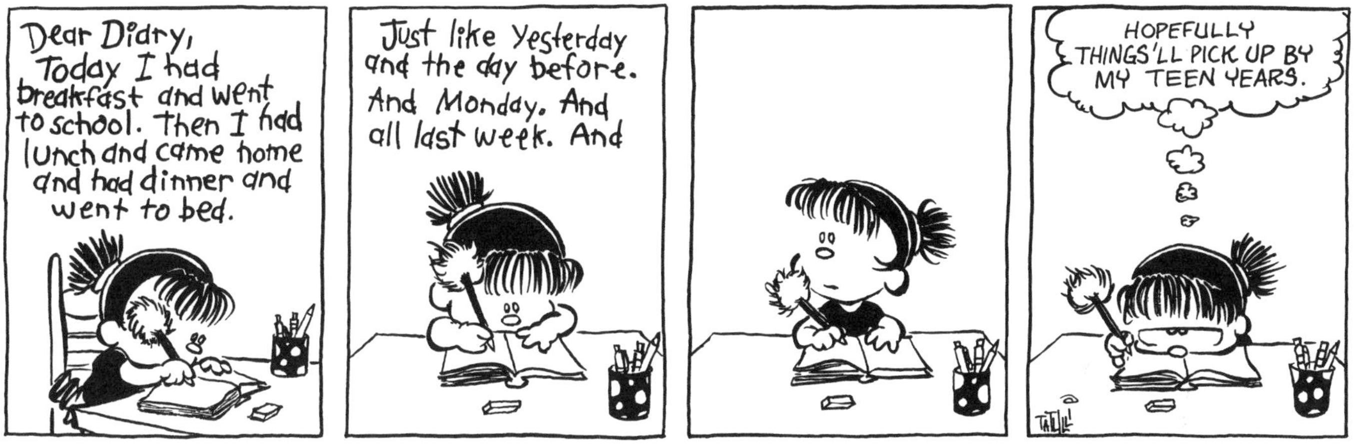
Dear Didry,
Today I had breakfast and went to school. Then I had lunch and came home and had dinner and went to bed.
Just like yesterday and the day before. And Monday. And all last week. And
HOPEFULLY THINGS'LL PICK UP BY MY TEEN YEARS.

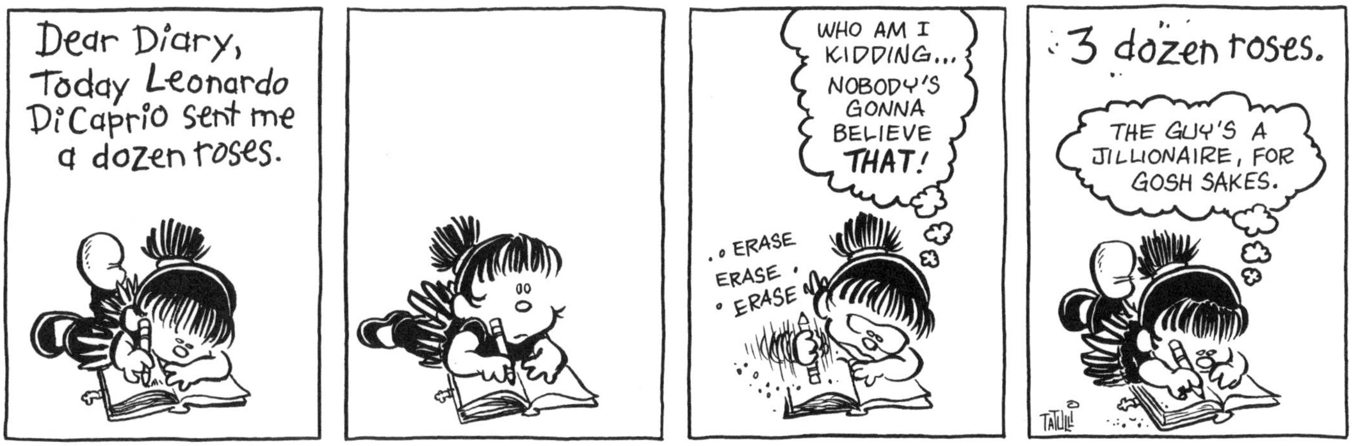
Dear Diary,
Today Leonardo DiCaprio sent me a dozen roses.
WHO AM I KIDDING... NOBODY'S GONNA BELIEVE THAT!
ERASE
ERASE
ERASE
3 dozen roses.
THE GUY'S A JILLIONAIRE, FOR GOSH SAKES.

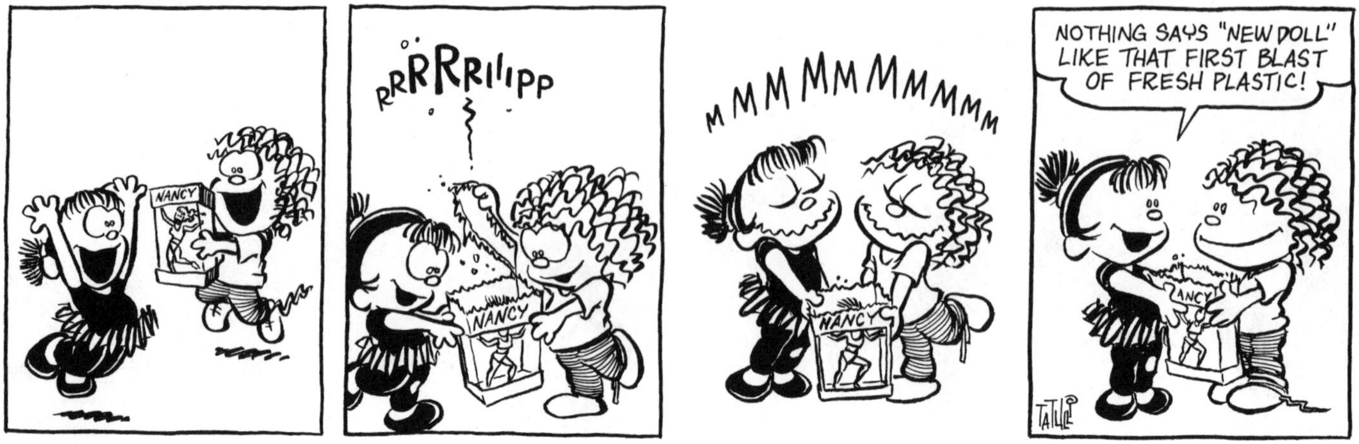
RRRRRIIIPP
MMMMMMMMMMMM
NOTHING SAYS "NEW DOLL" LIKE THAT FIRST BLAST OF FRESH PLASTIC!

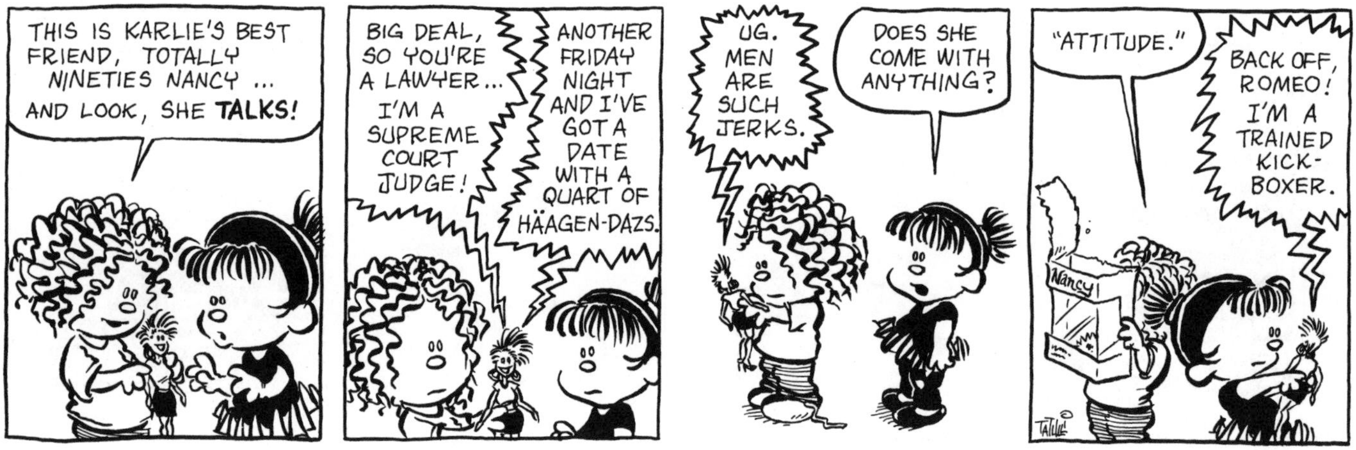
THIS IS KARLIE'S BEST FRIEND, TOTALLY NINETIES NANCY ... AND LOOK, SHE **TALKS**!
BIG DEAL, SO YOU'RE A LAWYER... I'M A SUPREME COURT JUDGE!
ANOTHER FRIDAY NIGHT AND I'VE GOT A DATE WITH A QUART OF HÄAGEN-DAZS.
UG. MEN ARE SUCH JERKS.
DOES SHE COME WITH ANYTHING?
"ATTITUDE."
BACK OFF, ROMEO! I'M A TRAINED KICK-BOXER.

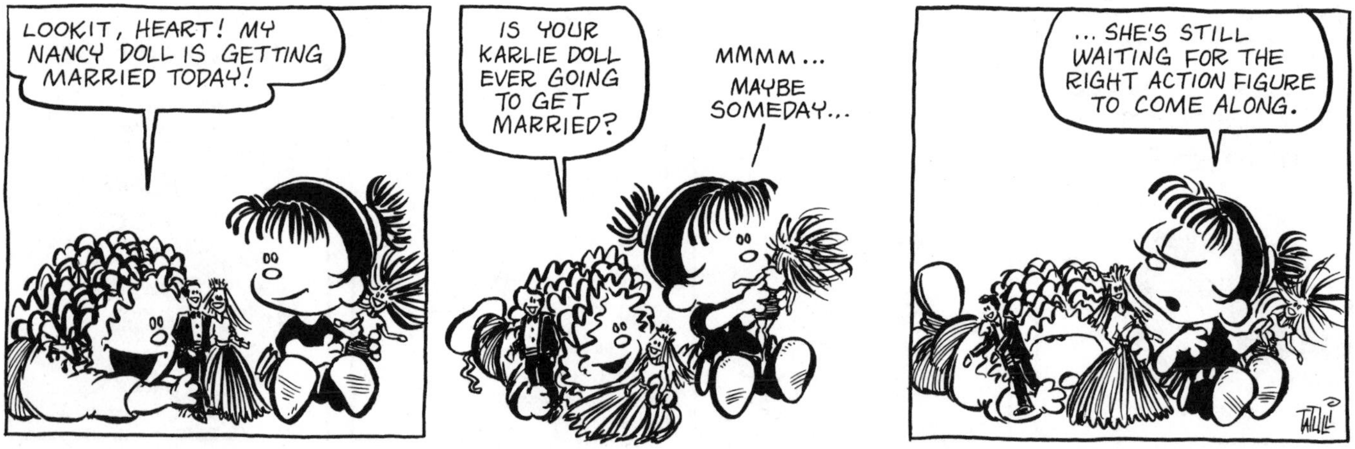
LOOKIT, HEART! MY NANCY DOLL IS GETTING MARRIED TODAY!
IS YOUR KARLIE DOLL EVER GOING TO GET MARRIED?
MMMM... MAYBE SOMEDAY...
... SHE'S STILL WAITING FOR THE RIGHT ACTION FIGURE TO COME ALONG.

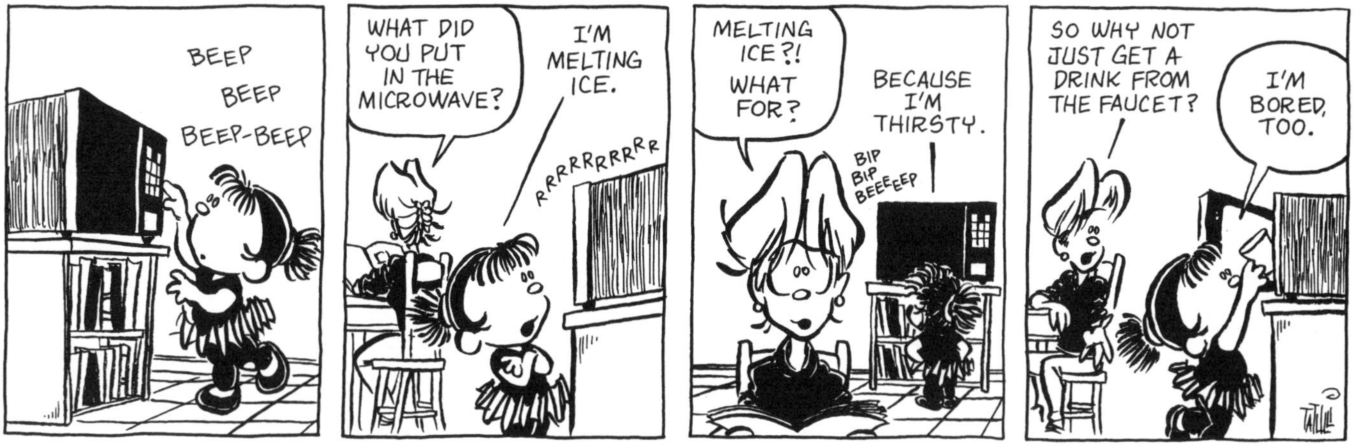
BEEP
BEEP
BEEP-BEEP
WHAT DID YOU PUT IN THE MICROWAVE?
I'M MELTING ICE.
RRRRRRRRRRR
MELTING ICE?! WHAT FOR?
BECAUSE I'M THIRSTY.
BIP BIP BEEEEEEP
SO WHY NOT JUST GET A DRINK FROM THE FAUCET?
I'M BORED, TOO.

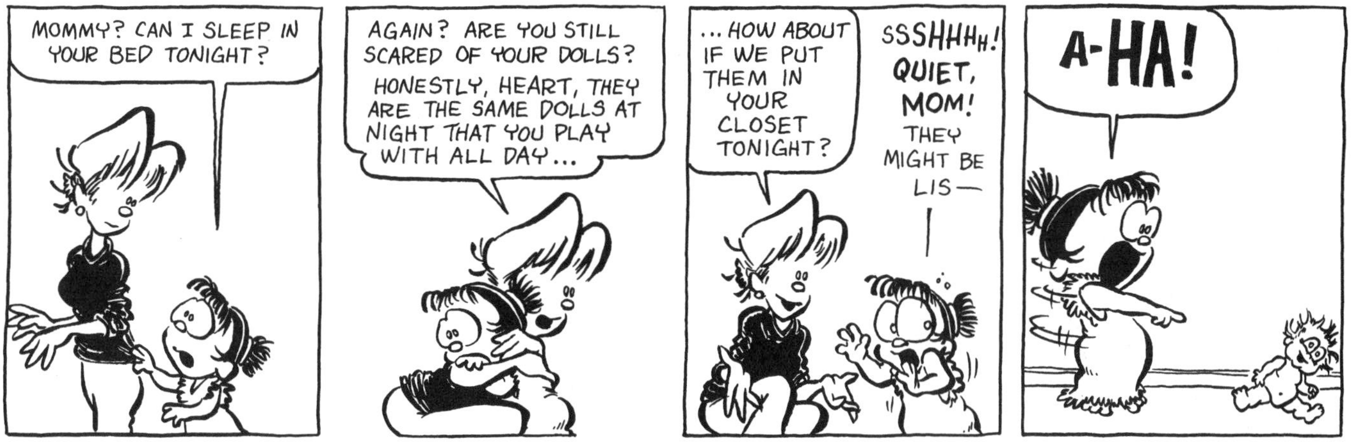
MOMMY? CAN I SLEEP IN YOUR BED TONIGHT?
AGAIN? ARE YOU STILL SCARED OF YOUR DOLLS?
HONESTLY, HEART, THEY ARE THE SAME DOLLS AT NIGHT THAT YOU PLAY WITH ALL DAY...
...HOW ABOUT IF WE PUT THEM IN YOUR CLOSET TONIGHT?
SSSHHHH! QUIET, MOM! THEY MIGHT BE LIS—
A-HA!

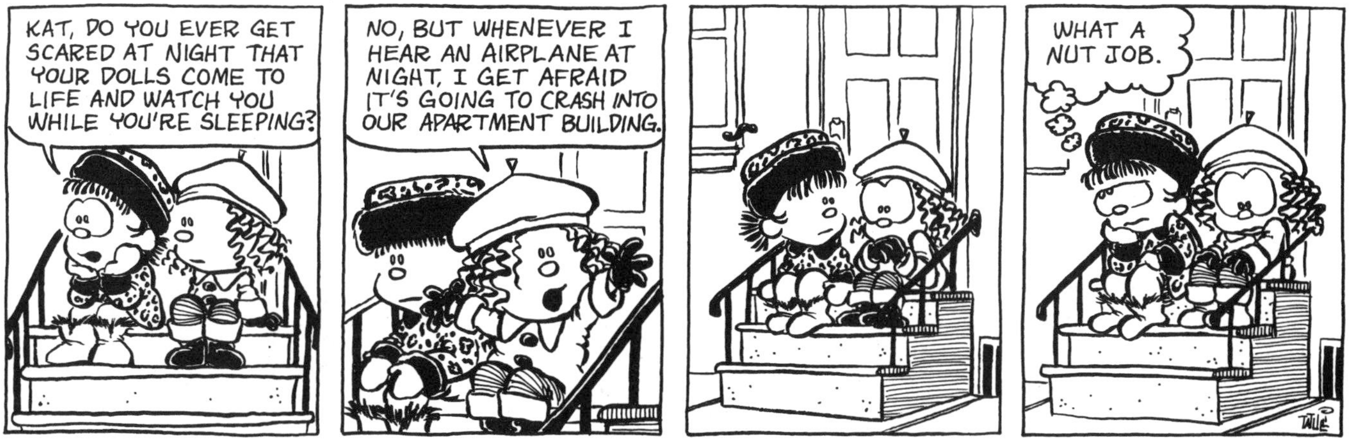
KAT, DO YOU EVER GET SCARED AT NIGHT THAT YOUR DOLLS COME TO LIFE AND WATCH YOU WHILE YOU'RE SLEEPING?
NO, BUT WHENEVER I HEAR AN AIRPLANE AT NIGHT, I GET AFRAID IT'S GOING TO CRASH INTO OUR APARTMENT BUILDING.
WHAT A NUT JOB.

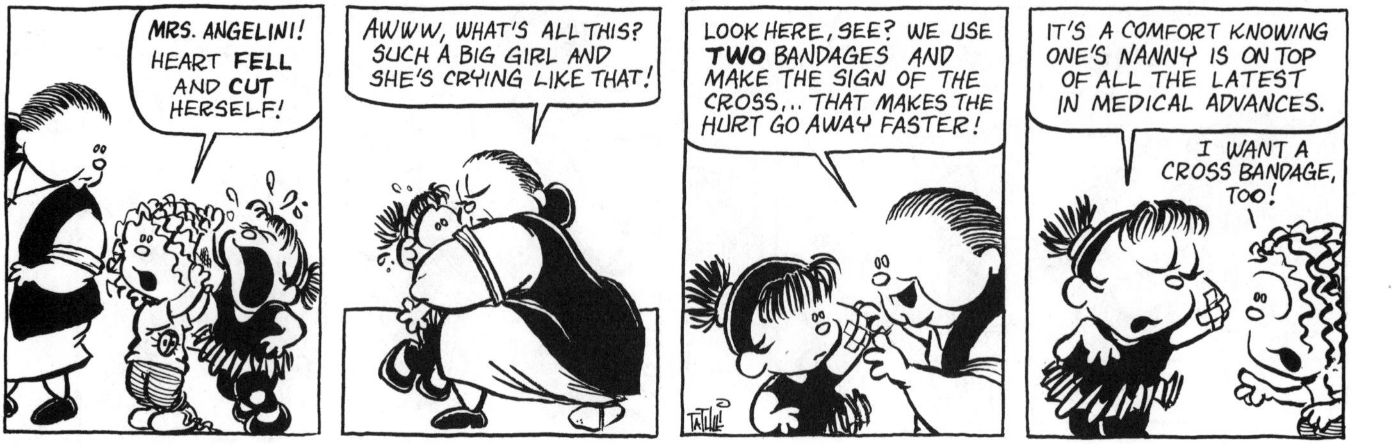
MRS. ANGELINI! HEART FELL AND CUT HERSELF!
AWWW, WHAT'S ALL THIS? SUCH A BIG GIRL AND SHE'S CRYING LIKE THAT!
LOOK HERE, SEE? WE USE TWO BANDAGES AND MAKE THE SIGN OF THE CROSS,.. THAT MAKES THE HURT GO AWAY FASTER!
IT'S A COMFORT KNOWING ONE'S NANNY IS ON TOP OF ALL THE LATEST IN MEDICAL ADVANCES.
I WANT A CROSS BANDAGE, TOO!

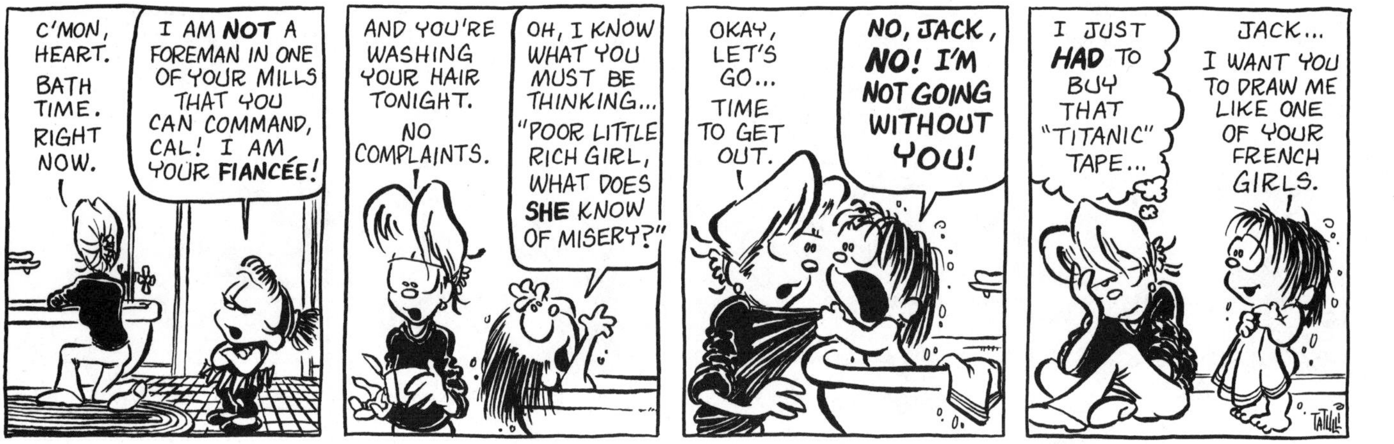
C'MON, HEART. BATH TIME. RIGHT NOW.
I AM NOT A FOREMAN IN ONE OF YOUR MILLS THAT YOU CAN COMMAND, CAL! I AM YOUR FIANCÉE!
AND YOU'RE WASHING YOUR HAIR TONIGHT.
NO COMPLAINTS.
OH, I KNOW WHAT YOU MUST BE THINKING... "POOR LITTLE RICH GIRL, WHAT DOES SHE KNOW OF MISERY?"
OKAY, LET'S GO...
TIME TO GET OUT.
NO, JACK, NO! I'M NOT GOING WITHOUT YOU!
I JUST HAD TO BUY THAT "TITANIC" TAPE...
JACK... I WANT YOU TO DRAW ME LIKE ONE OF YOUR FRENCH GIRLS.

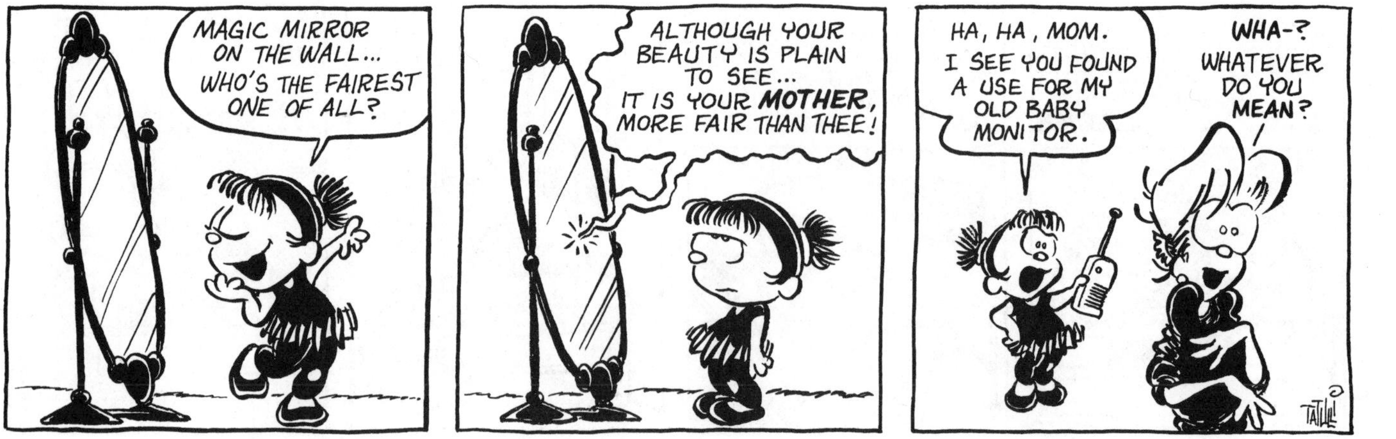
MAGIC MIRROR ON THE WALL... WHO'S THE FAIREST ONE OF ALL?
ALTHOUGH YOUR BEAUTY IS PLAIN TO SEE... IT IS YOUR MOTHER, MORE FAIR THAN THEE!
HA, HA, MOM. I SEE YOU FOUND A USE FOR MY OLD BABY MONITOR.
WHA-? WHATEVER DO YOU MEAN?

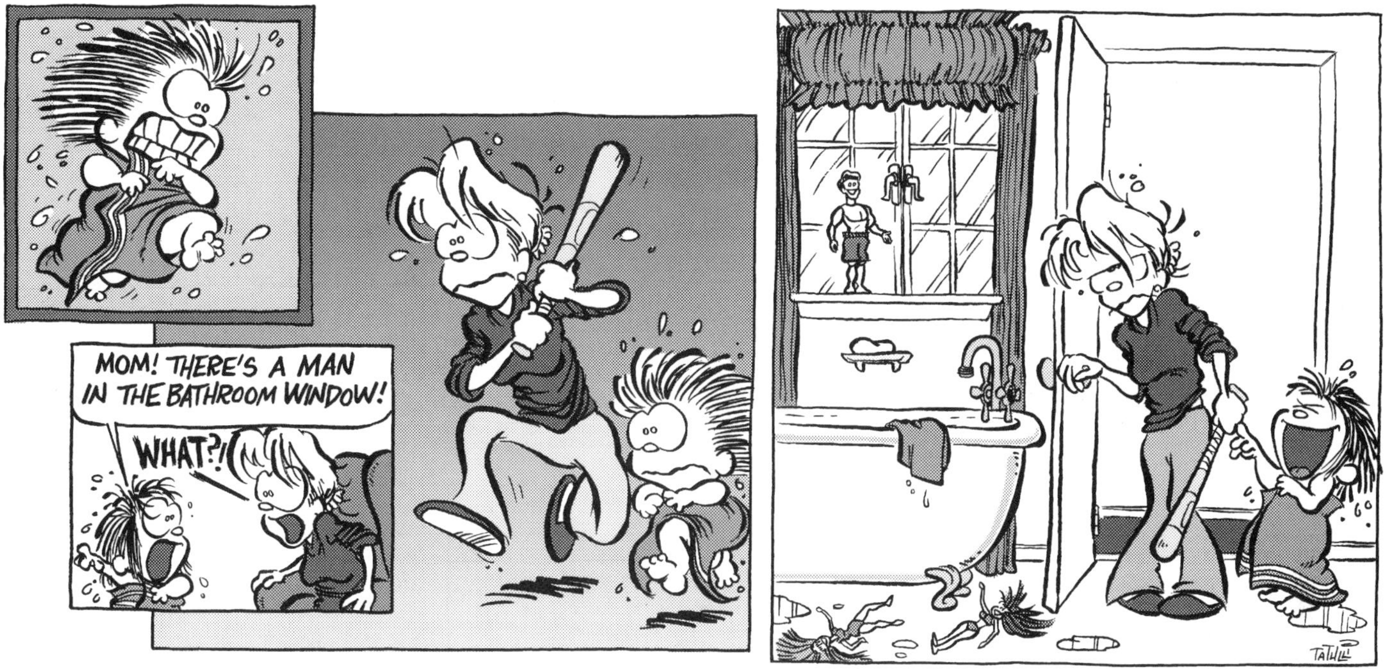
MOM! THERE'S A MAN IN THE BATHROOM WINDOW!
WHAT?!

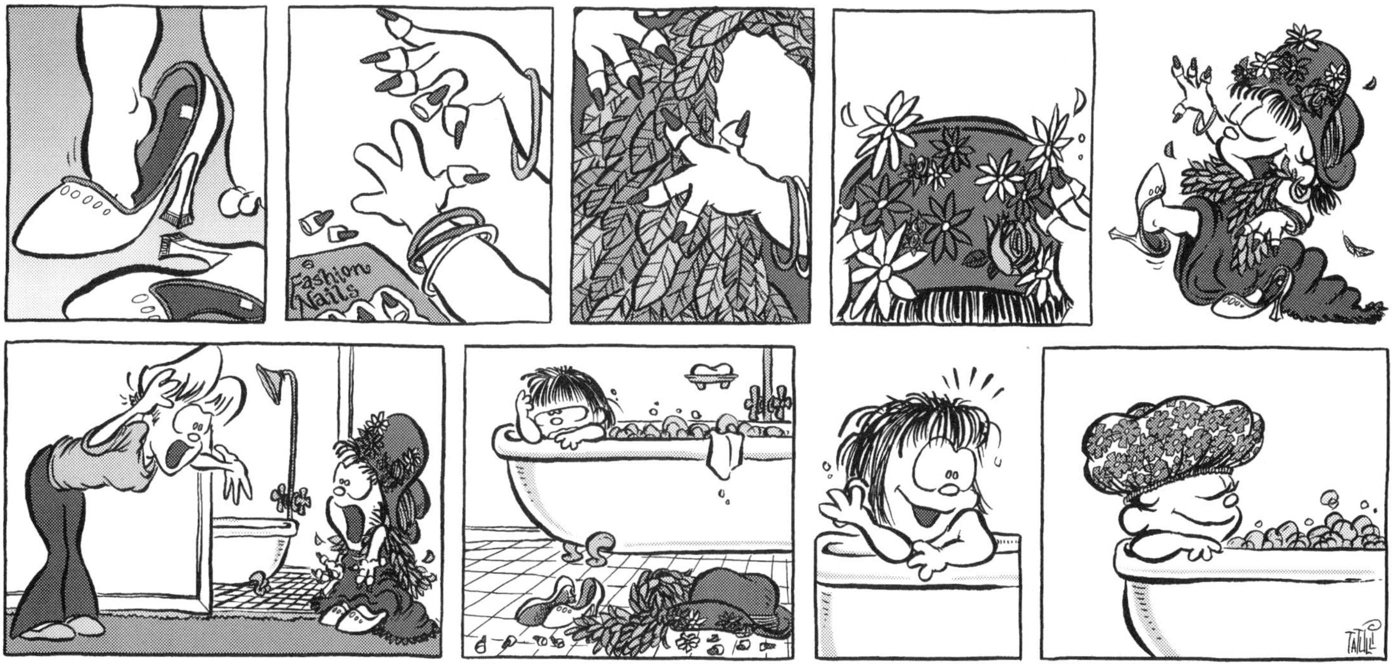
Fashion Nails

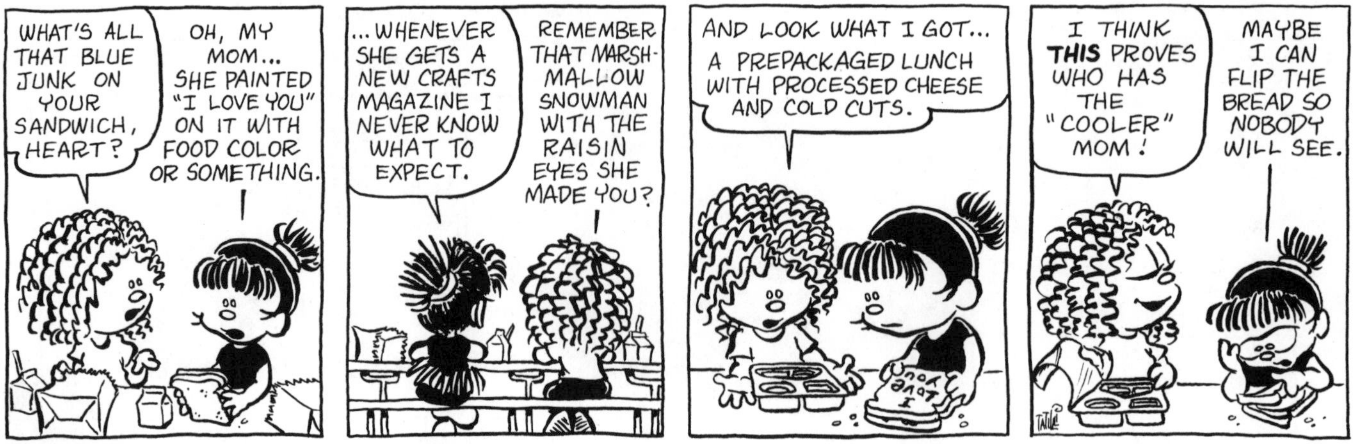
WHAT'S ALL THAT BLUE JUNK ON YOUR SANDWICH, HEART?
OH, MY MOM... SHE PAINTED "I LOVE YOU" ON IT WITH FOOD COLOR OR SOMETHING.
...WHENEVER SHE GETS A NEW CRAFTS MAGAZINE I NEVER KNOW WHAT TO EXPECT.
REMEMBER THAT MARSHMALLOW SNOWMAN WITH THE RAISIN EYES SHE MADE YOU?
AND LOOK WHAT I GOT... A PREPACKAGED LUNCH WITH PROCESSED CHEESE AND COLD CUTS.
I THINK THIS PROVES WHO HAS THE "COOLER" MOM!
MAYBE I CAN FLIP THE BREAD SO NOBODY WILL SEE.

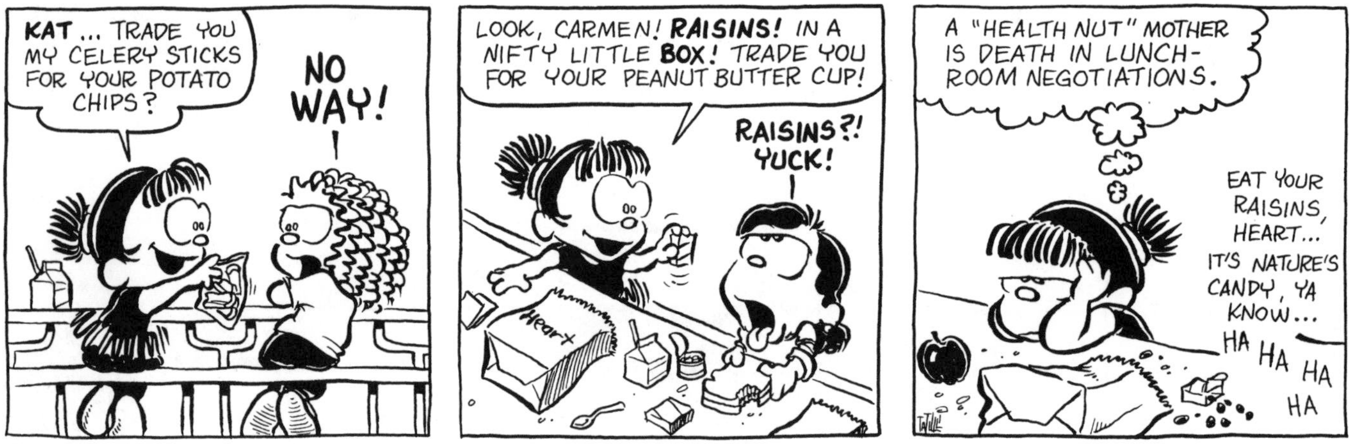
KAT... TRADE YOU MY CELERY STICKS FOR YOUR POTATO CHIPS?
NO WAY!
LOOK, CARMEN! RAISINS! IN A NIFTY LITTLE BOX! TRADE YOU FOR YOUR PEANUT BUTTER CUP!
RAISINS?! YUCK!
A "HEALTH NUT" MOTHER IS DEATH IN LUNCHROOM NEGOTIATIONS.
EAT YOUR RAISINS, HEART... IT'S NATURE'S CANDY, YA KNOW...
HA HA HA HA

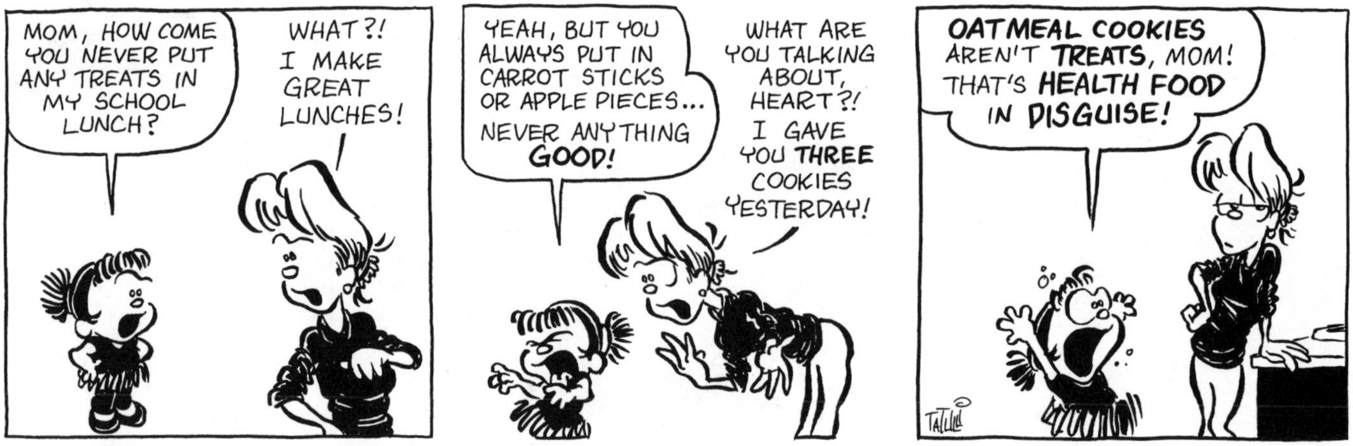
MOM, HOW COME YOU NEVER PUT ANY TREATS IN MY SCHOOL LUNCH?
WHAT?! I MAKE GREAT LUNCHES!
YEAH, BUT YOU ALWAYS PUT IN CARROT STICKS OR APPLE PIECES... NEVER ANYTHING GOOD!
WHAT ARE YOU TALKING ABOUT, HEART?! I GAVE YOU THREE COOKIES YESTERDAY!
OATMEAL COOKIES AREN'T TREATS, MOM! THAT'S HEALTH FOOD IN DISGUISE!

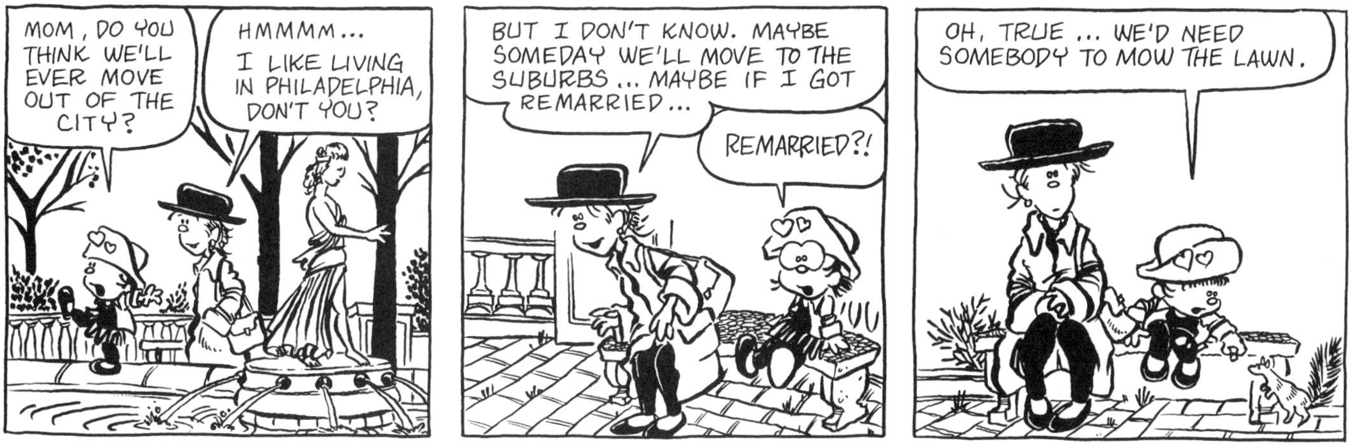
MOM, DO YOU THINK WE'LL EVER MOVE OUT OF THE CITY?
HMMMM... I LIKE LIVING IN PHILADELPHIA, DON'T YOU?
BUT I DON'T KNOW. MAYBE SOMEDAY WE'LL MOVE TO THE SUBURBS ... MAYBE IF I GOT REMARRIED...
REMARRIED?!
OH, TRUE ... WE'D NEED SOMEBODY TO MOW THE LAWN.

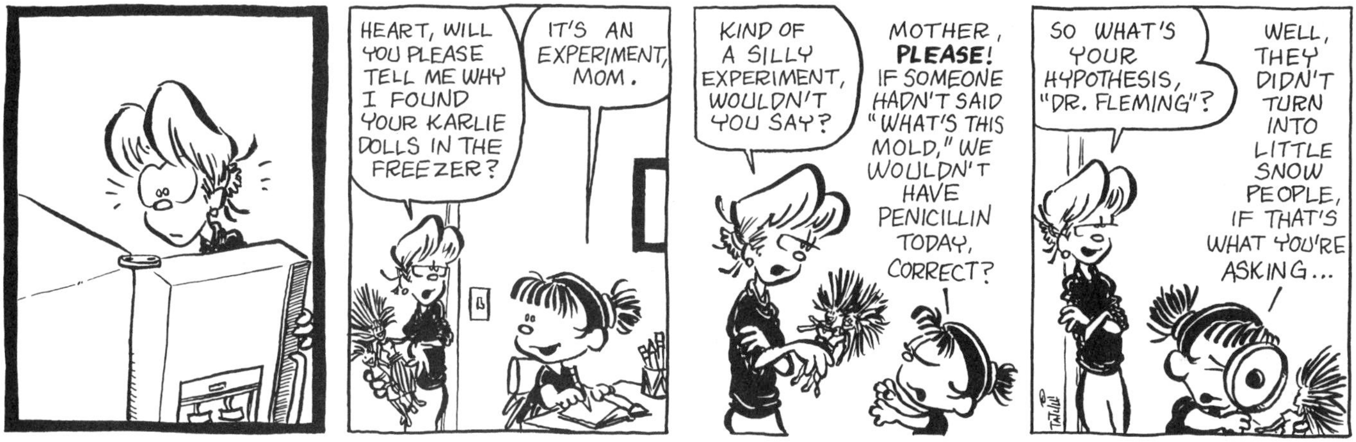
HEART, WILL YOU PLEASE TELL ME WHY I FOUND YOUR KARLIE DOLLS IN THE FREEZER?
IT'S AN EXPERIMENT, MOM.
KIND OF A SILLY EXPERIMENT, WOULDN'T YOU SAY?
MOTHER, **PLEASE!** IF SOMEONE HADN'T SAID "WHAT'S THIS MOLD," WE WOULDN'T HAVE PENICILLIN TODAY, CORRECT?
SO WHAT'S YOUR HYPOTHESIS, "DR. FLEMING"?
WELL, THEY DIDN'T TURN INTO LITTLE SNOW PEOPLE, IF THAT'S WHAT YOU'RE ASKING...

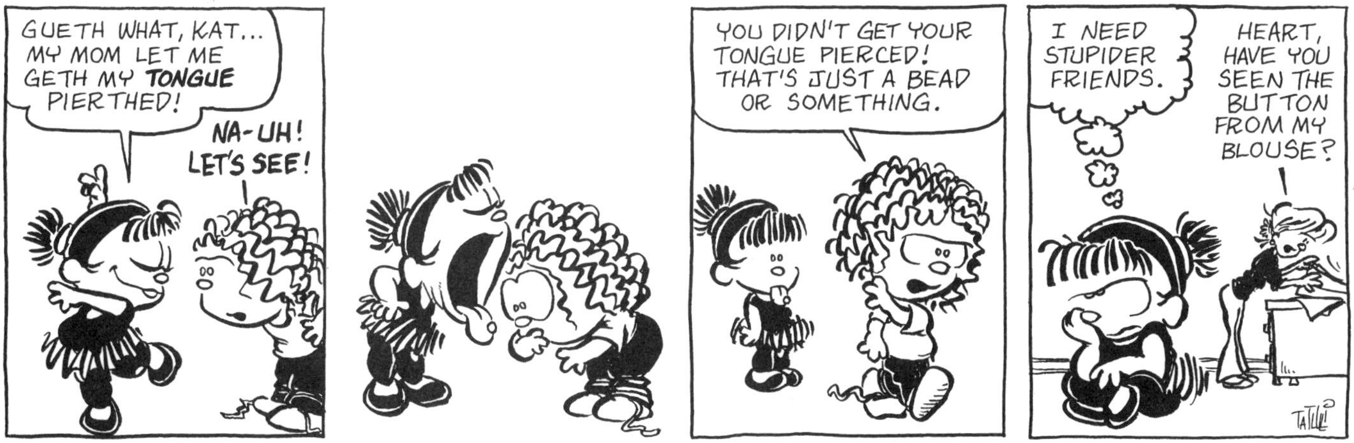
GUETH WHAT, KAT... MY MOM LET ME GETH MY **TONGUE** PIERTHED!
NA-UH! LET'S SEE!
YOU DIDN'T GET YOUR TONGUE PIERCED! THAT'S JUST A BEAD OR SOMETHING.
I NEED STUPIDER FRIENDS.
HEART, HAVE YOU SEEN THE BUTTON FROM MY BLOUSE?

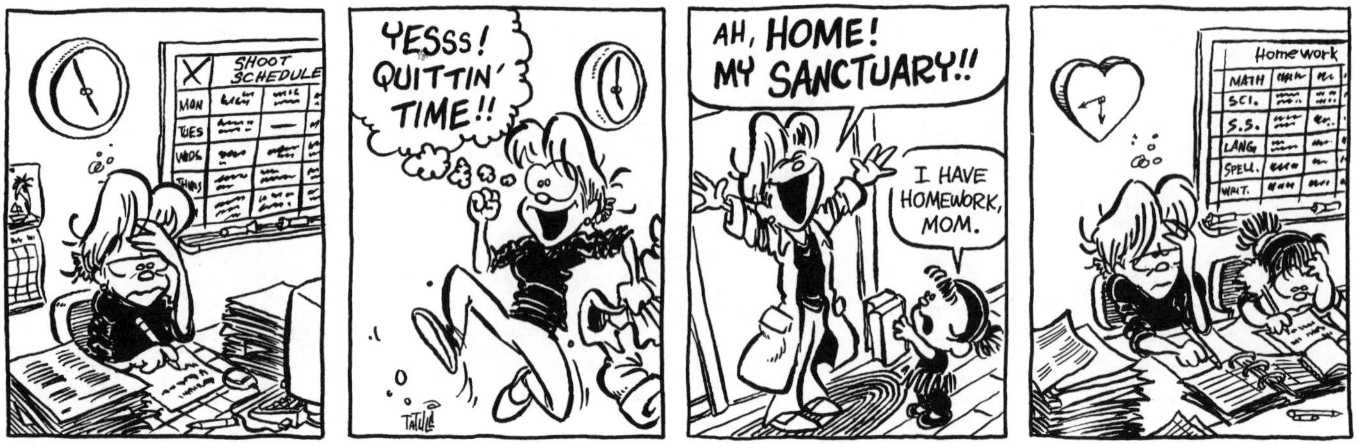
SHOOT SCHEDULE
MON
TUES
WEDS
THURS
YESSS! QUITTIN' TIME!!
TATULLI
AH, **HOME**! MY **SANCTUARY**!!
I HAVE HOMEWORK, MOM.
Homework
MATH
SCI.
S.S.
LANG.
SPELL.
WRIT.

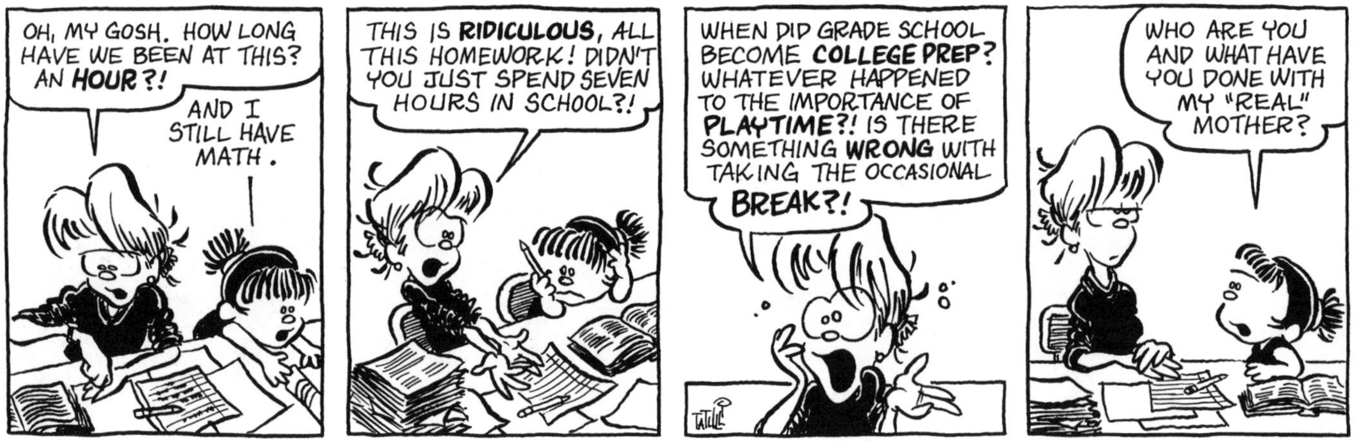
OH, MY GOSH. HOW LONG HAVE WE BEEN AT THIS? AN **HOUR**?!
AND I STILL HAVE MATH.
THIS IS **RIDICULOUS**, ALL THIS HOMEWORK! DIDN'T YOU JUST SPEND SEVEN HOURS IN SCHOOL?!
WHEN DID GRADE SCHOOL BECOME **COLLEGE PREP**? WHATEVER HAPPENED TO THE IMPORTANCE OF **PLAYTIME**?! IS THERE SOMETHING **WRONG** WITH TAKING THE OCCASIONAL **BREAK**?!
TATULLI
WHO ARE YOU AND WHAT HAVE YOU DONE WITH MY "REAL" MOTHER?

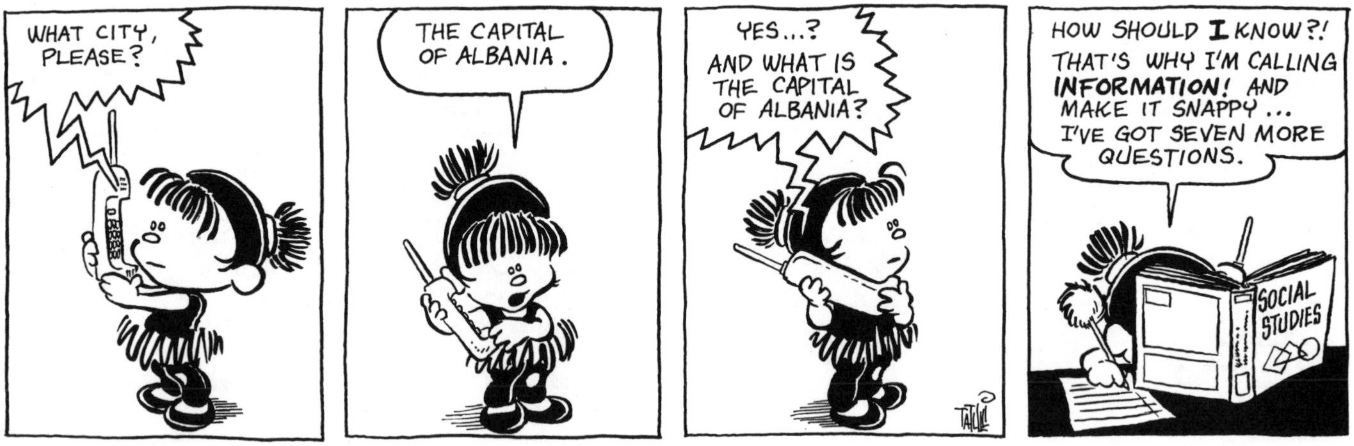
WHAT CITY, PLEASE?
THE CAPITAL OF ALBANIA.
YES...? AND WHAT IS THE CAPITAL OF ALBANIA?
TATULLI
HOW SHOULD **I** KNOW?! THAT'S WHY I'M CALLING **INFORMATION**! AND MAKE IT SNAPPY... I'VE GOT SEVEN MORE QUESTIONS.
SOCIAL STUDIES

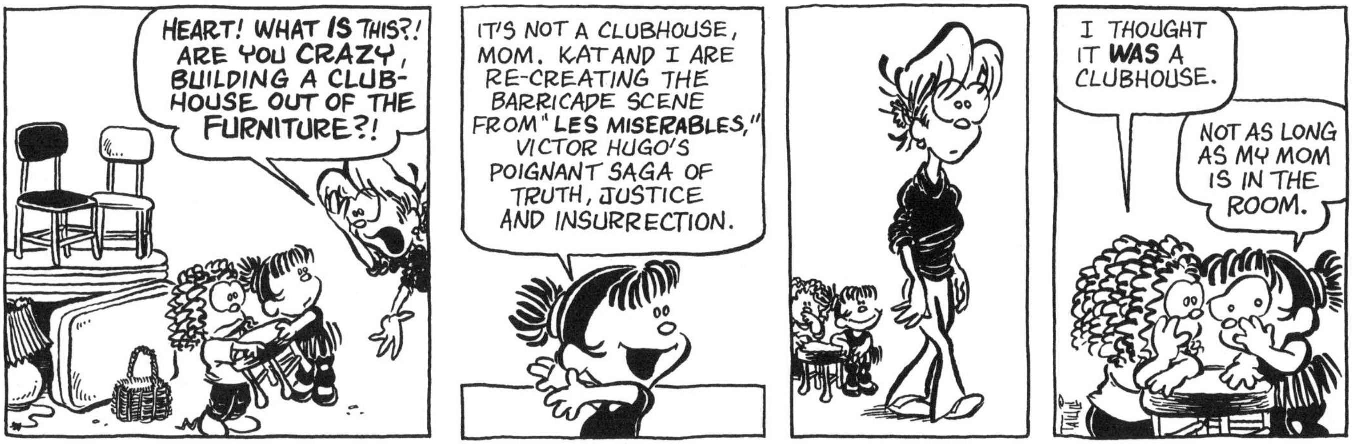
HEART! WHAT IS THIS?! ARE YOU CRAZY, BUILDING A CLUB-HOUSE OUT OF THE FURNITURE?!
IT'S NOT A CLUBHOUSE, MOM. KAT AND I ARE RE-CREATING THE BARRICADE SCENE FROM "LES MISERABLES," VICTOR HUGO'S POIGNANT SAGA OF TRUTH, JUSTICE AND INSURRECTION.
I THOUGHT IT WAS A CLUBHOUSE.
NOT AS LONG AS MY MOM IS IN THE ROOM.

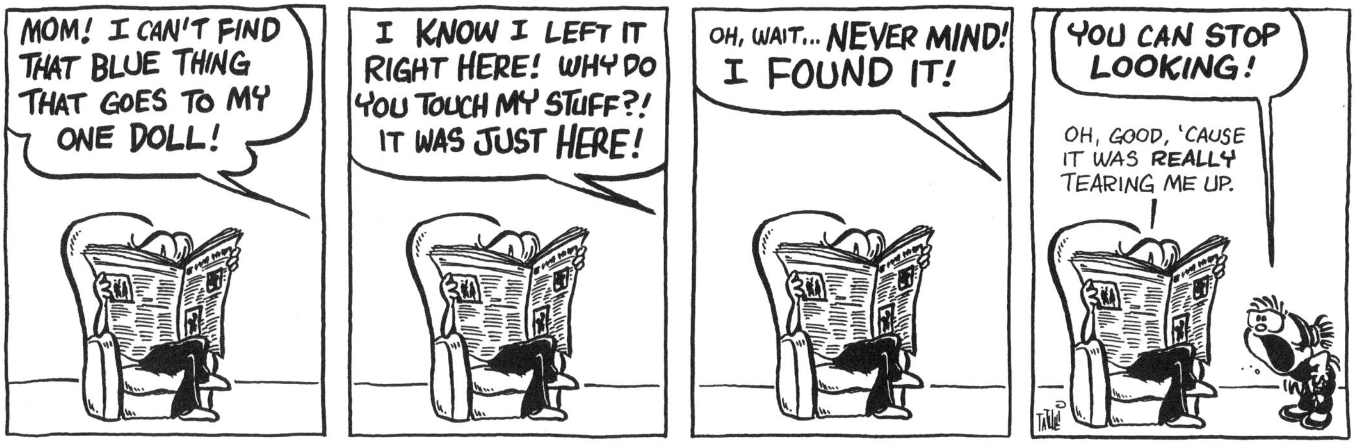
MOM! I CAN'T FIND THAT BLUE THING THAT GOES TO MY ONE DOLL!
I KNOW I LEFT IT RIGHT HERE! WHY DO YOU TOUCH MY STUFF?! IT WAS JUST HERE!
OH, WAIT... NEVER MIND! I FOUND IT!
YOU CAN STOP LOOKING!
OH, GOOD, 'CAUSE IT WAS REALLY TEARING ME UP.

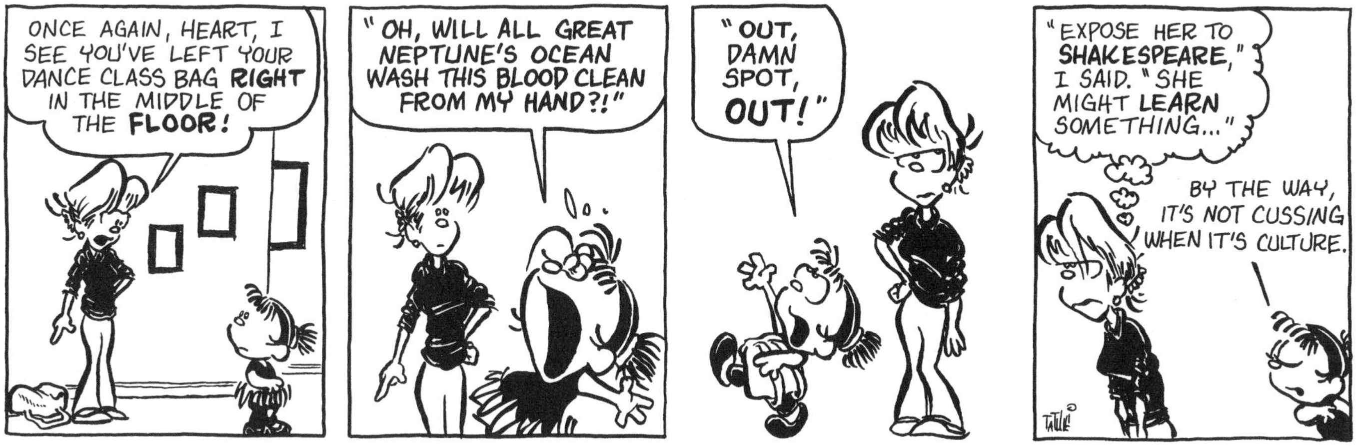
ONCE AGAIN, HEART, I SEE YOU'VE LEFT YOUR DANCE CLASS BAG RIGHT IN THE MIDDLE OF THE FLOOR!
"OH, WILL ALL GREAT NEPTUNE'S OCEAN WASH THIS BLOOD CLEAN FROM MY HAND?!"
"OUT, DAMN SPOT, OUT!"
"EXPOSE HER TO SHAKESPEARE," I SAID. "SHE MIGHT LEARN SOMETHING..."
BY THE WAY, IT'S NOT CUSSING WHEN IT'S CULTURE.

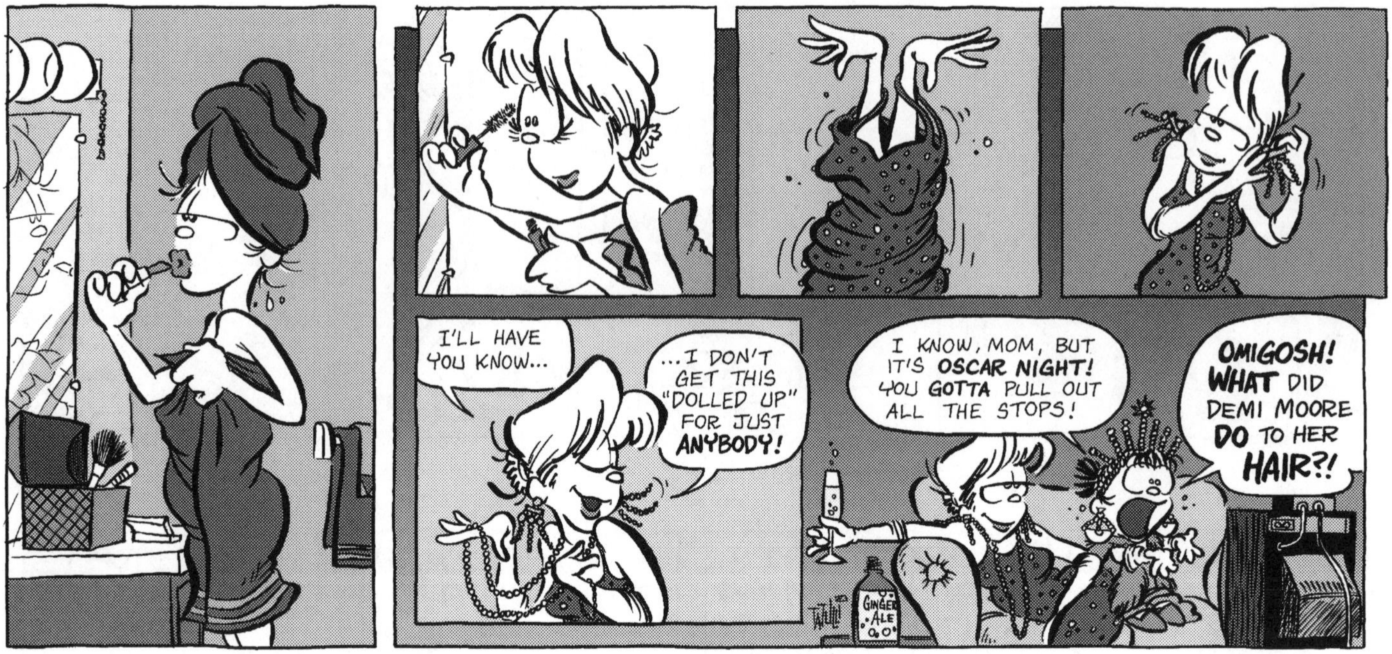
I'LL HAVE YOU KNOW...
...I DON'T GET THIS "DOLLED UP" FOR JUST ANYBODY!
I KNOW, MOM, BUT IT'S OSCAR NIGHT! YOU GOTTA PULL OUT ALL THE STOPS!
OMIGOSH! WHAT DID DEMI MOORE DO TO HER HAIR?!
GINGER ALE

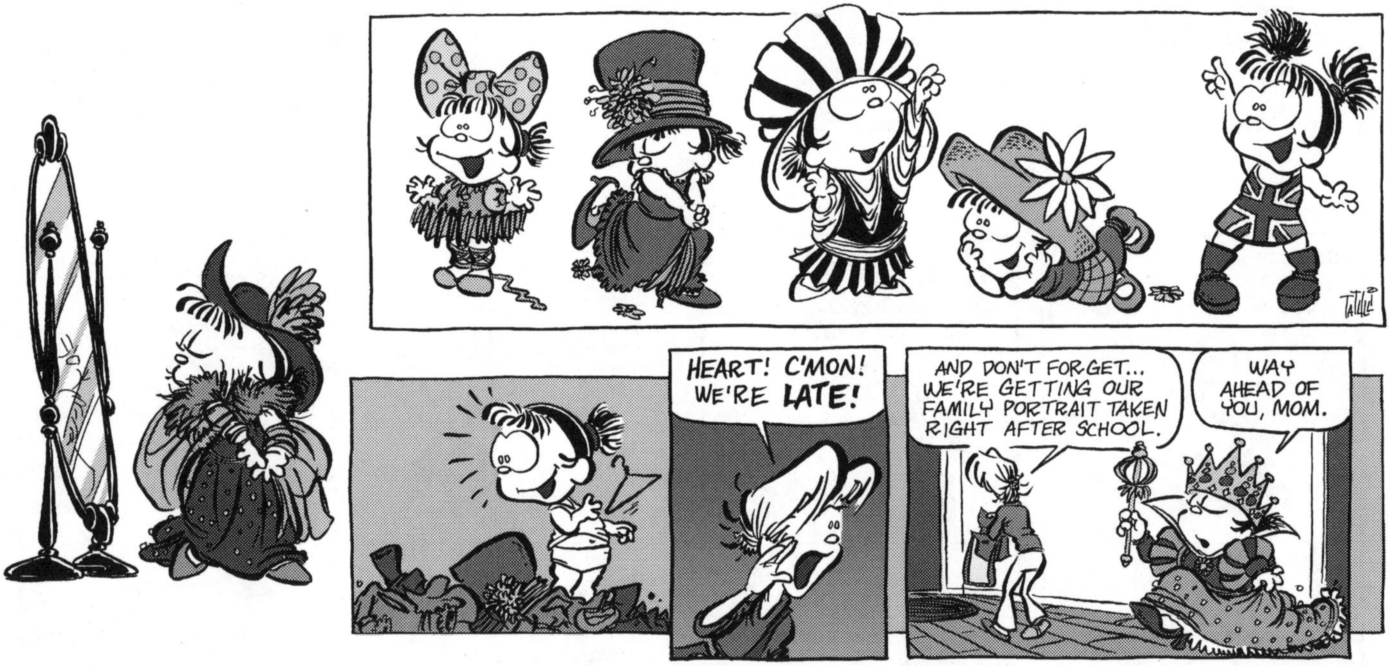
HEART! C'MON! WE'RE LATE!
AND DON'T FORGET... WE'RE GETTING OUR FAMILY PORTRAIT TAKEN RIGHT AFTER SCHOOL.
WAY AHEAD OF YOU, MOM.

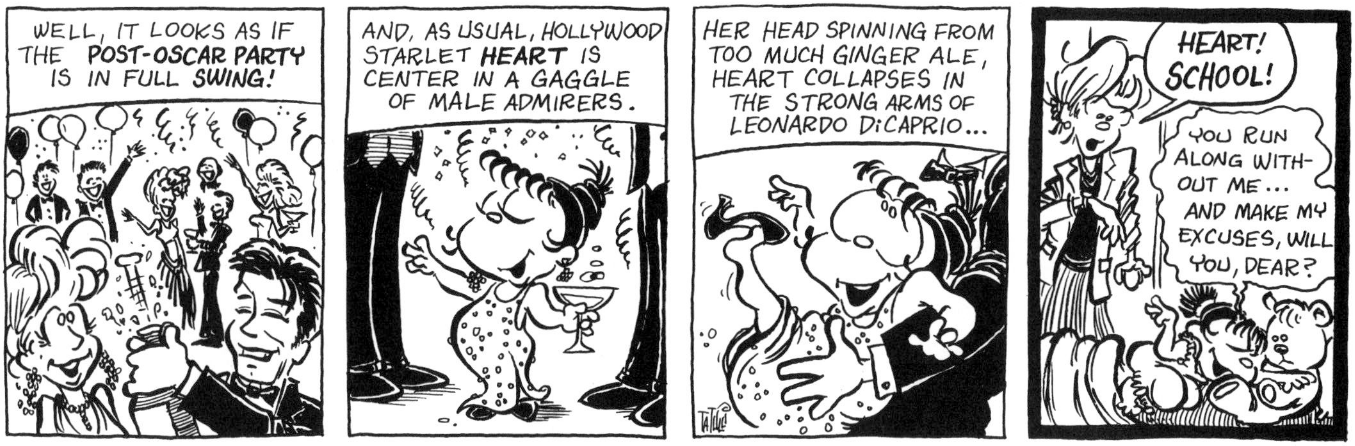
WELL, IT LOOKS AS IF THE POST-OSCAR PARTY IS IN FULL SWING!
AND, AS USUAL, HOLLYWOOD STARLET HEART IS CENTER IN A GAGGLE OF MALE ADMIRERS.
HER HEAD SPINNING FROM TOO MUCH GINGER ALE, HEART COLLAPSES IN THE STRONG ARMS OF LEONARDO DiCAPRIO...
HEART! SCHOOL!
YOU RUN ALONG WITHOUT ME... AND MAKE MY EXCUSES, WILL YOU, DEAR?

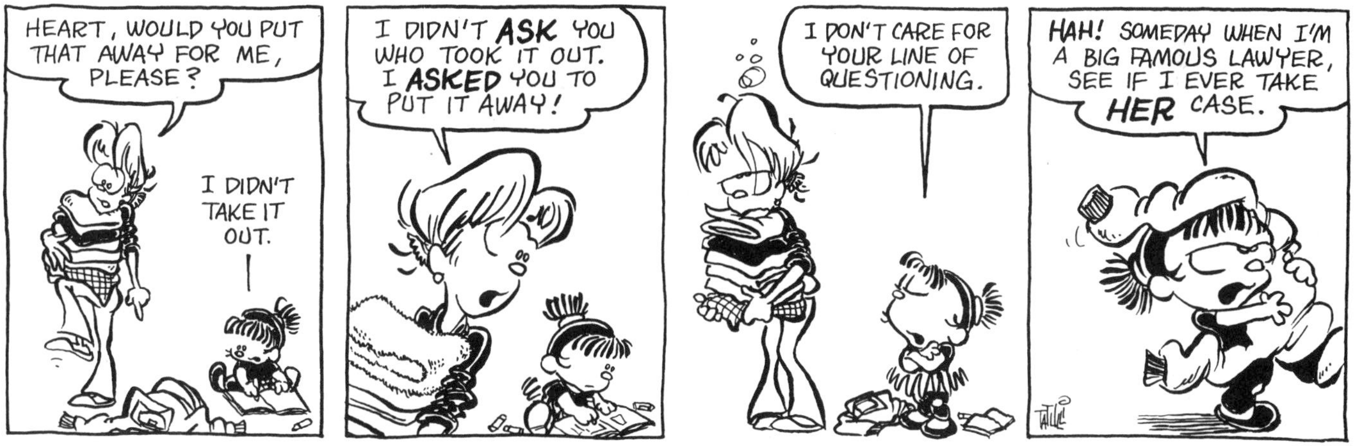
HEART, WOULD YOU PUT THAT AWAY FOR ME, PLEASE?
I DIDN'T TAKE IT OUT.
I DIDN'T ASK YOU WHO TOOK IT OUT. I ASKED YOU TO PUT IT AWAY!
I DON'T CARE FOR YOUR LINE OF QUESTIONING.
HAH! SOMEDAY WHEN I'M A BIG FAMOUS LAWYER, SEE IF I EVER TAKE HER CASE.

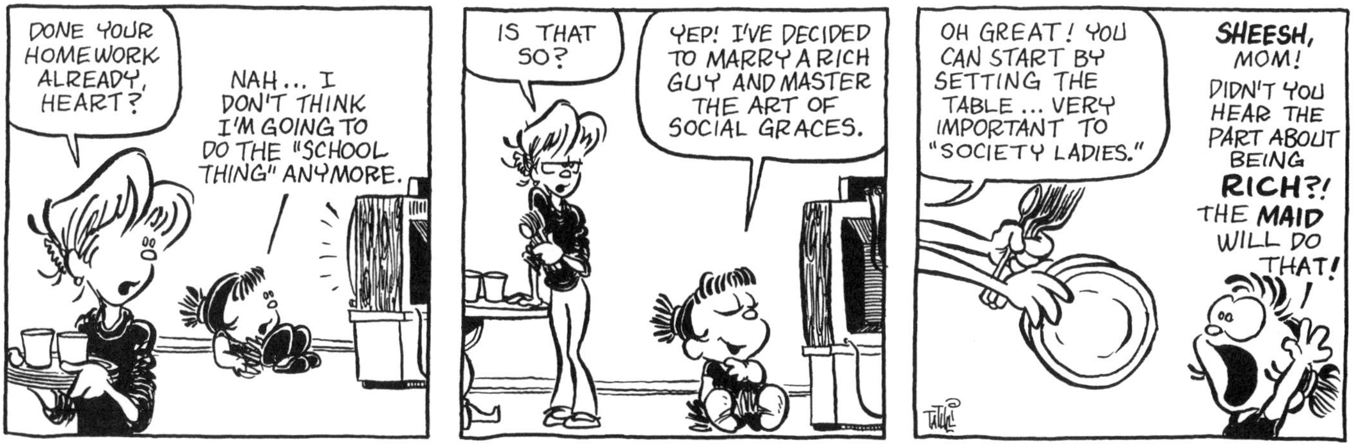
DONE YOUR HOMEWORK ALREADY, HEART?
NAH... I DON'T THINK I'M GOING TO DO THE "SCHOOL THING" ANYMORE.
IS THAT SO?
YEP! I'VE DECIDED TO MARRY A RICH GUY AND MASTER THE ART OF SOCIAL GRACES.
OH GREAT! YOU CAN START BY SETTING THE TABLE... VERY IMPORTANT TO "SOCIETY LADIES."
SHEESH, MOM! DIDN'T YOU HEAR THE PART ABOUT BEING RICH?! THE MAID WILL DO THAT!

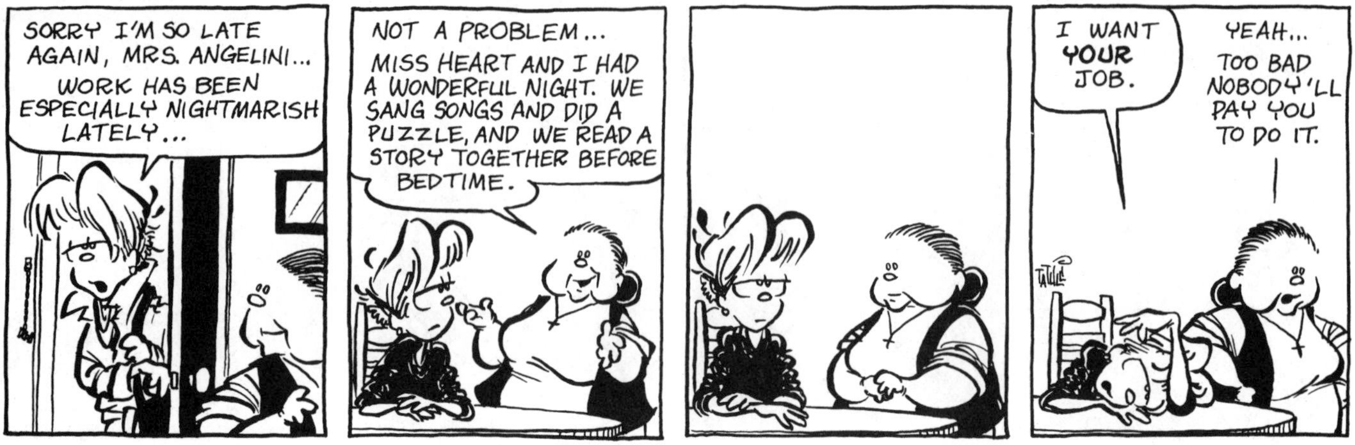
SORRY I'M SO LATE AGAIN, MRS. ANGELINI... WORK HAS BEEN ESPECIALLY NIGHTMARISH LATELY...
NOT A PROBLEM... MISS HEART AND I HAD A WONDERFUL NIGHT. WE SANG SONGS AND DID A PUZZLE, AND WE READ A STORY TOGETHER BEFORE BEDTIME.
I WANT **YOUR** JOB.
YEAH... TOO BAD NOBODY'LL PAY YOU TO DO IT.

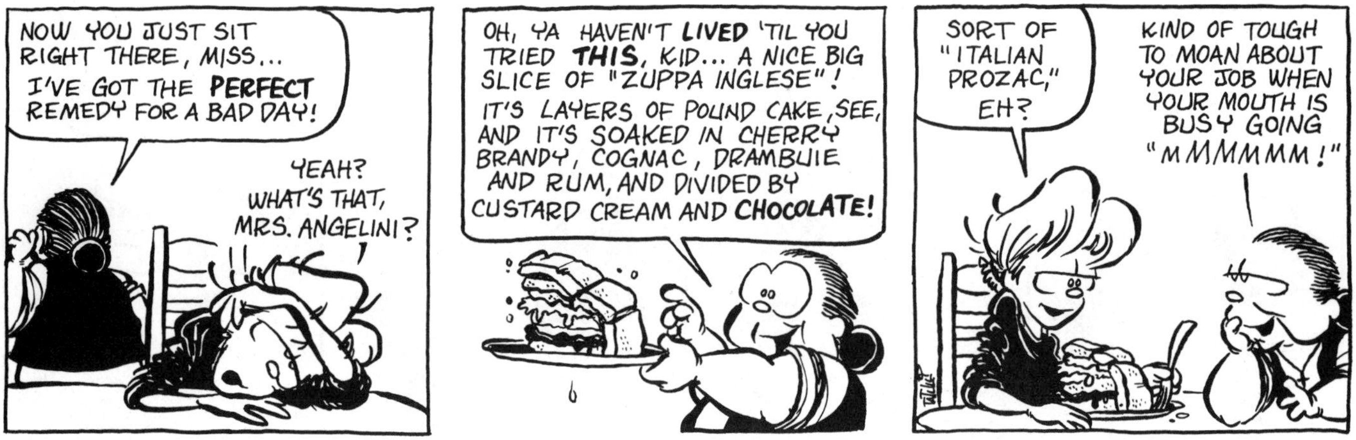
NOW YOU JUST SIT RIGHT THERE, MISS... I'VE GOT THE **PERFECT** REMEDY FOR A BAD DAY!
YEAH? WHAT'S THAT, MRS. ANGELINI?
OH, YA HAVEN'T **LIVED** 'TIL YOU TRIED **THIS**, KID... A NICE BIG SLICE OF "ZUPPA INGLESE"! IT'S LAYERS OF POUND CAKE, SEE, AND IT'S SOAKED IN CHERRY BRANDY, COGNAC, DRAMBUIE AND RUM, AND DIVIDED BY CUSTARD CREAM AND **CHOCOLATE**!
SORT OF "ITALIAN PROZAC," EH?
KIND OF TOUGH TO MOAN ABOUT YOUR JOB WHEN YOUR MOUTH IS BUSY GOING "MMMMMM!"

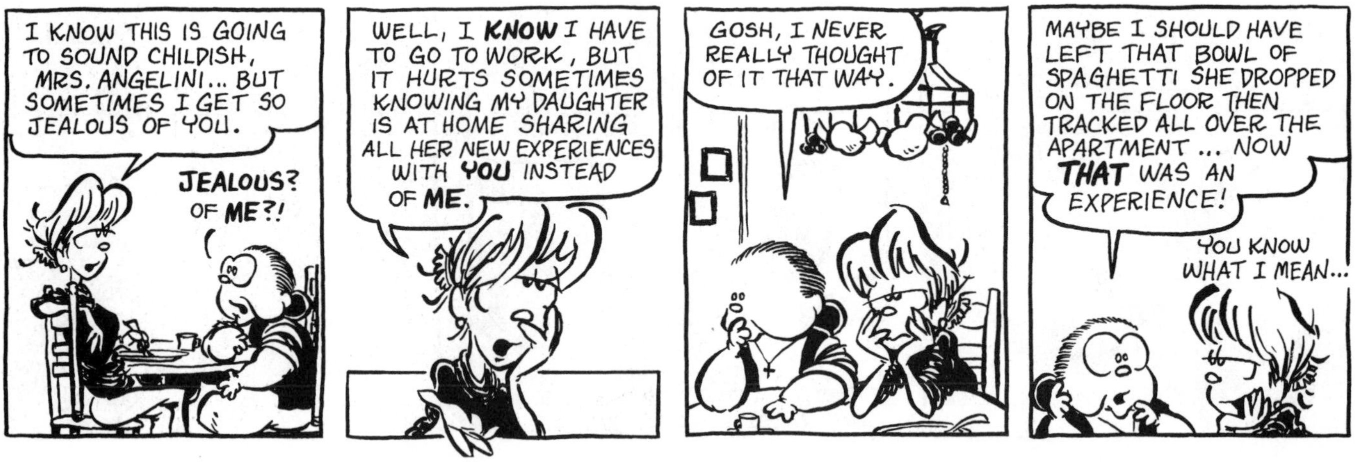
I KNOW THIS IS GOING TO SOUND CHILDISH, MRS. ANGELINI... BUT SOMETIMES I GET SO JEALOUS OF YOU.
JEALOUS? OF ME?!
WELL, I **KNOW** I HAVE TO GO TO WORK, BUT IT HURTS SOMETIMES KNOWING MY DAUGHTER IS AT HOME SHARING ALL HER NEW EXPERIENCES WITH **YOU** INSTEAD OF **ME**.
GOSH, I NEVER REALLY THOUGHT OF IT THAT WAY.
MAYBE I SHOULD HAVE LEFT THAT BOWL OF SPAGHETTI SHE DROPPED ON THE FLOOR THEN TRACKED ALL OVER THE APARTMENT ... NOW **THAT** WAS AN EXPERIENCE!
YOU KNOW WHAT I MEAN...

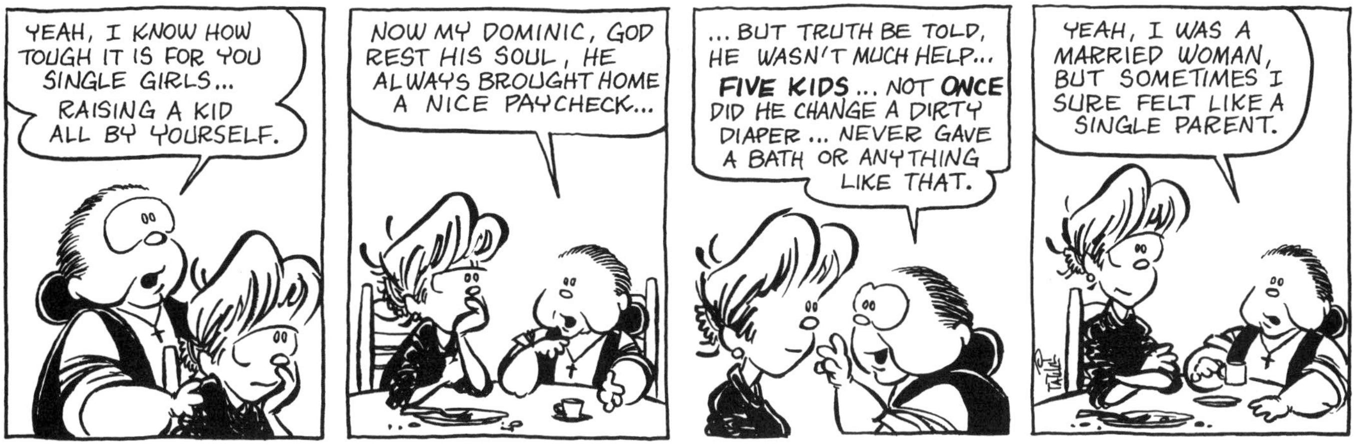
YEAH, I KNOW HOW TOUGH IT IS FOR YOU SINGLE GIRLS... RAISING A KID ALL BY YOURSELF.
NOW MY DOMINIC, GOD REST HIS SOUL, HE ALWAYS BROUGHT HOME A NICE PAYCHECK...
... BUT TRUTH BE TOLD, HE WASN'T MUCH HELP... **FIVE KIDS**... NOT **ONCE** DID HE CHANGE A DIRTY DIAPER... NEVER GAVE A BATH OR ANYTHING LIKE THAT.
YEAH, I WAS A MARRIED WOMAN, BUT SOMETIMES I SURE FELT LIKE A SINGLE PARENT.

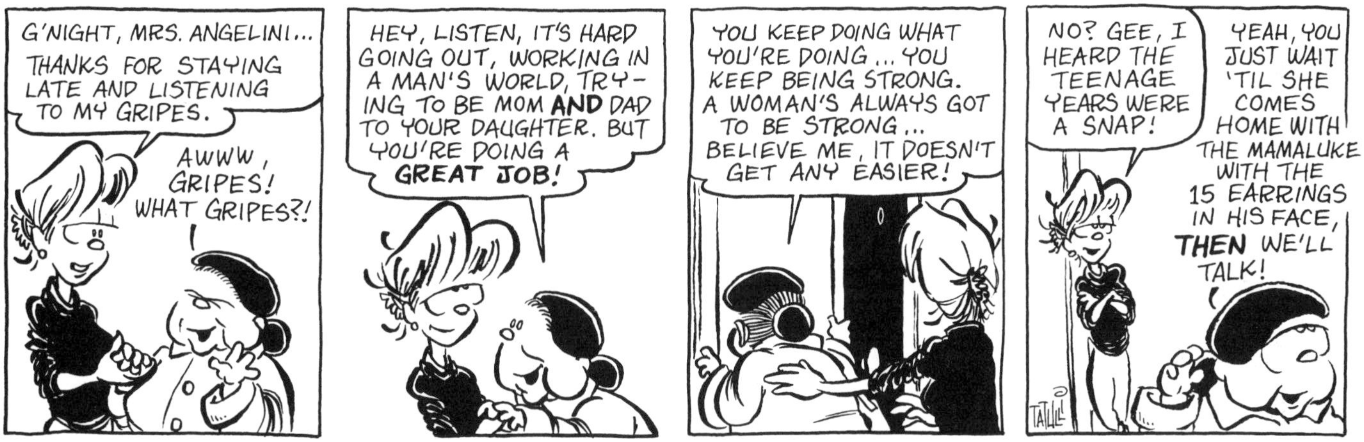
G'NIGHT, MRS. ANGELINI... THANKS FOR STAYING LATE AND LISTENING TO MY GRIPES.
AWWW, GRIPES! WHAT GRIPES?!
HEY, LISTEN, IT'S HARD GOING OUT, WORKING IN A MAN'S WORLD, TRYING TO BE MOM **AND** DAD TO YOUR DAUGHTER. BUT YOU'RE DOING A **GREAT JOB**!
YOU KEEP DOING WHAT YOU'RE DOING... YOU KEEP BEING STRONG. A WOMAN'S ALWAYS GOT TO BE STRONG... BELIEVE ME, IT DOESN'T GET ANY EASIER!
NO? GEE, I HEARD THE TEENAGE YEARS WERE A SNAP!
YEAH, YOU JUST WAIT 'TIL SHE COMES HOME WITH THE MAMALUKE WITH THE 15 EARRINGS IN HIS FACE, **THEN** WE'LL TALK!

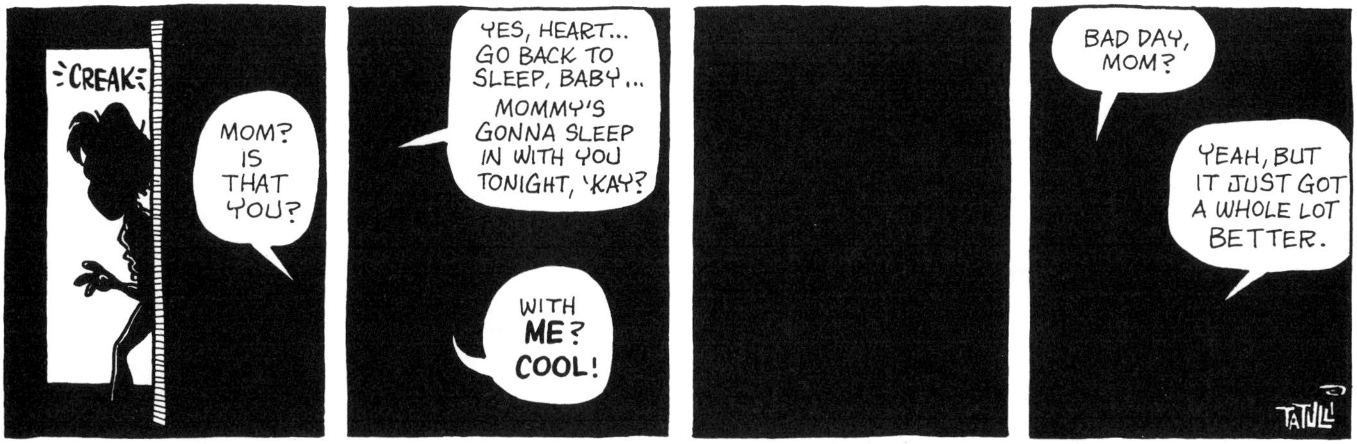
CREAK
MOM? IS THAT YOU?
YES, HEART... GO BACK TO SLEEP, BABY... MOMMY'S GONNA SLEEP IN WITH YOU TONIGHT, 'KAY?
WITH **ME**? **COOL**!
BAD DAY, MOM?
YEAH, BUT IT JUST GOT A WHOLE LOT BETTER.

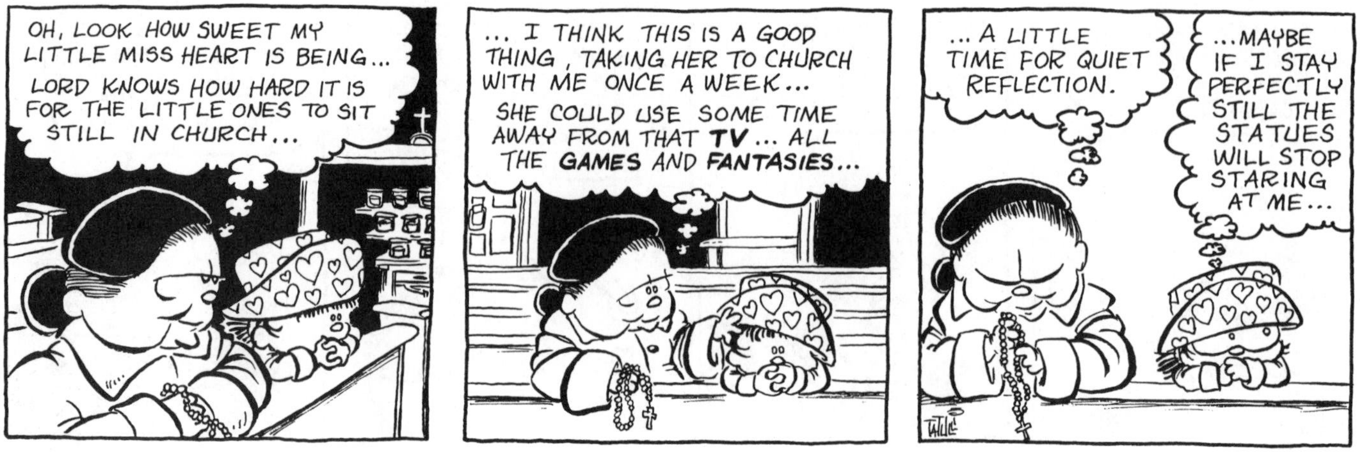
OH, LOOK HOW SWEET MY LITTLE MISS HEART IS BEING...
LORD KNOWS HOW HARD IT IS FOR THE LITTLE ONES TO SIT STILL IN CHURCH...
... I THINK THIS IS A GOOD THING, TAKING HER TO CHURCH WITH ME ONCE A WEEK...
SHE COULD USE SOME TIME AWAY FROM THAT TV ... ALL THE GAMES AND FANTASIES...
... A LITTLE TIME FOR QUIET REFLECTION.
...MAYBE IF I STAY PERFECTLY STILL THE STATUES WILL STOP STARING AT ME...

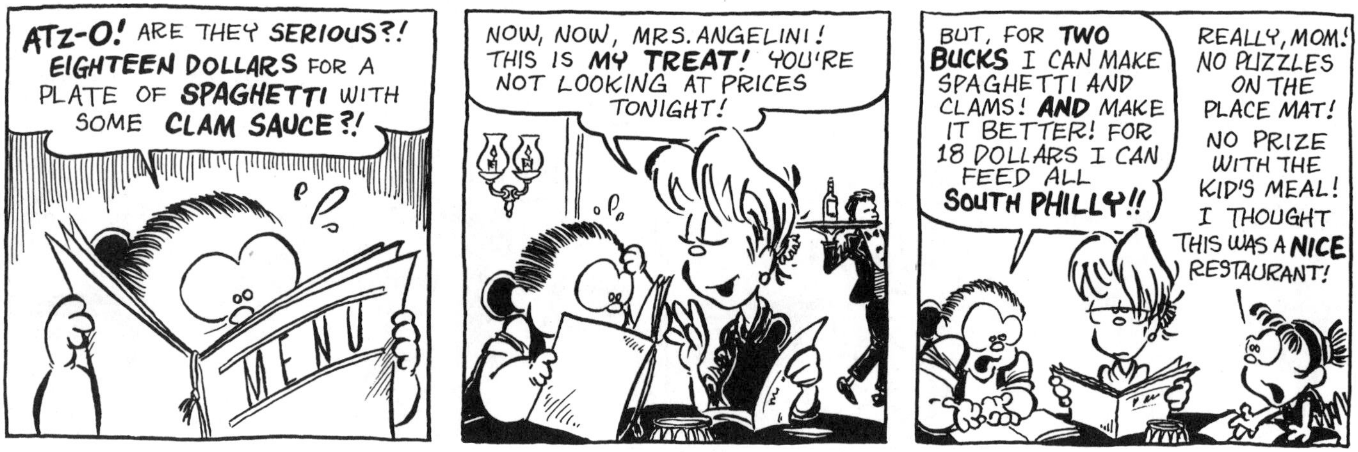
ATZ-O! ARE THEY SERIOUS?! EIGHTEEN DOLLARS FOR A PLATE OF SPAGHETTI WITH SOME CLAM SAUCE?!
MENU
NOW, NOW, MRS. ANGELINI! THIS IS MY TREAT! YOU'RE NOT LOOKING AT PRICES TONIGHT!
BUT, FOR TWO BUCKS I CAN MAKE SPAGHETTI AND CLAMS! AND MAKE IT BETTER! FOR 18 DOLLARS I CAN FEED ALL SOUTH PHILLY!!
REALLY, MOM! NO PUZZLES ON THE PLACE MAT! NO PRIZE WITH THE KID'S MEAL! I THOUGHT THIS WAS A NICE RESTAURANT!

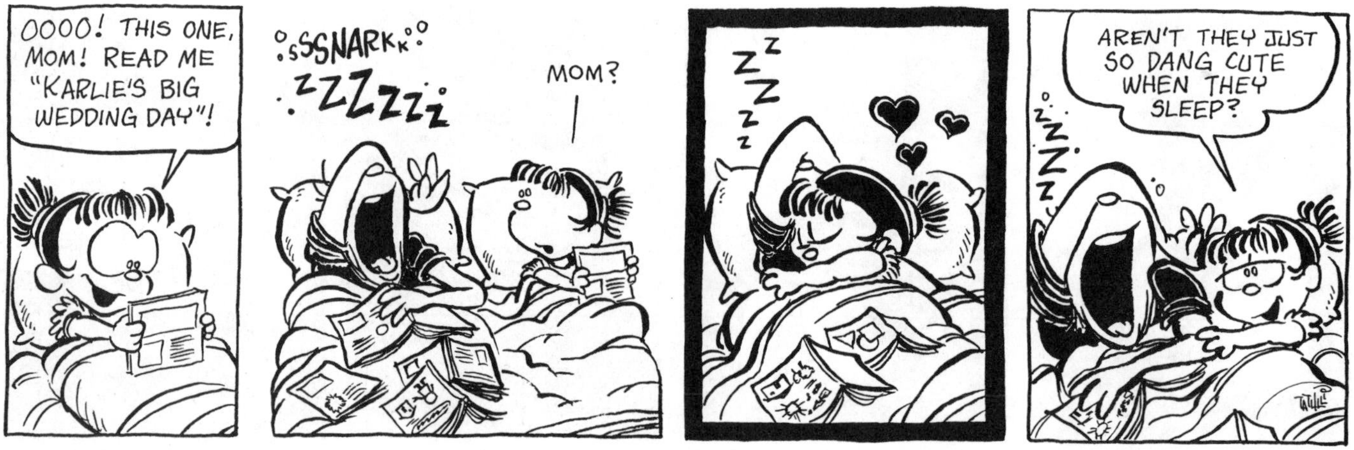
OOOO! THIS ONE, MOM! READ ME "KARLIE'S BIG WEDDING DAY"!
SSNARKK
ZZZzzz
MOM?
ZZZZZ
AREN'T THEY JUST SO DANG CUTE WHEN THEY SLEEP?

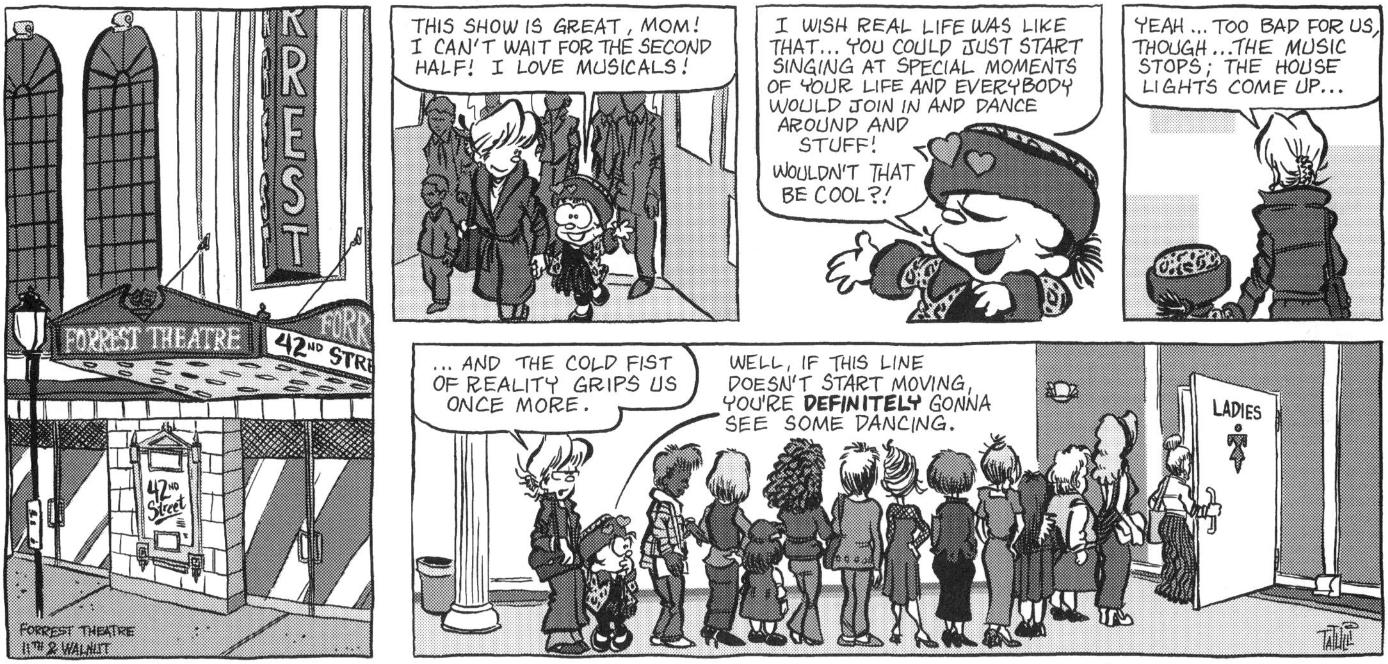
RREST
FORREST THEATRE
42ND STRE
42ND Street
FORREST THEATRE
11TH & WALNUT
THIS SHOW IS GREAT, MOM! I CAN'T WAIT FOR THE SECOND HALF! I LOVE MUSICALS!
I WISH REAL LIFE WAS LIKE THAT... YOU COULD JUST START SINGING AT SPECIAL MOMENTS OF YOUR LIFE AND EVERYBODY WOULD JOIN IN AND DANCE AROUND AND STUFF!
WOULDN'T THAT BE COOL?!
YEAH ... TOO BAD FOR US, THOUGH ... THE MUSIC STOPS; THE HOUSE LIGHTS COME UP...
... AND THE COLD FIST OF REALITY GRIPS US ONCE MORE.
WELL, IF THIS LINE DOESN'T START MOVING, YOU'RE **DEFINITELY** GONNA SEE SOME DANCING.
LADIES
TATULLI

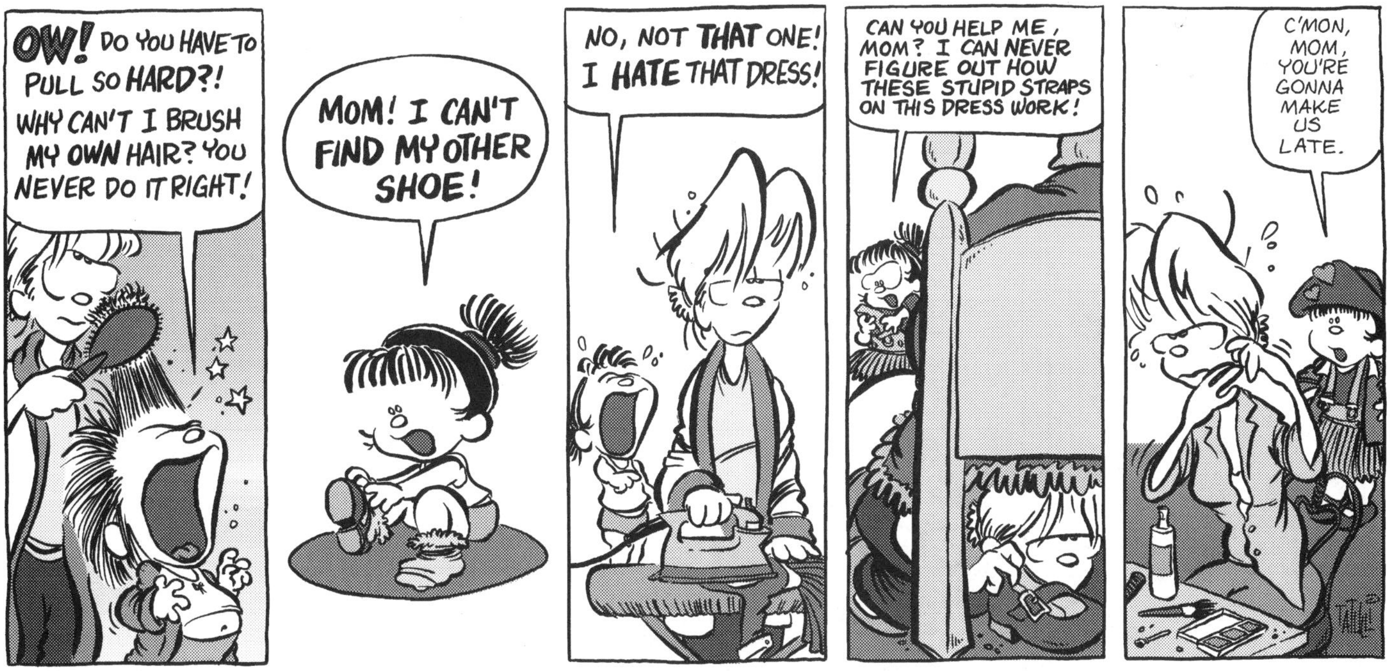
OW! DO YOU HAVE TO PULL SO **HARD?!**
WHY CAN'T I BRUSH MY **OWN** HAIR? YOU NEVER DO IT RIGHT!
MOM! I CAN'T FIND MY OTHER SHOE!
NO, NOT **THAT** ONE! I **HATE** THAT DRESS!
CAN YOU HELP ME, MOM? I CAN NEVER FIGURE OUT HOW THESE STUPID STRAPS ON THIS DRESS WORK!
C'MON, MOM, YOU'RE GONNA MAKE US LATE.
TATULLI

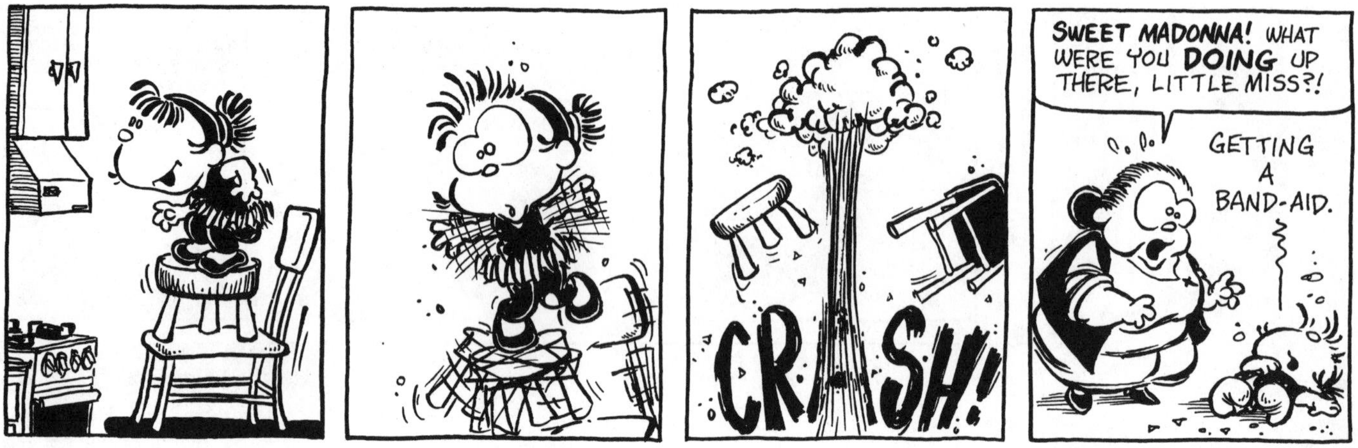
CRASH!
SWEET MADONNA! WHAT WERE YOU DOING UP THERE, LITTLE MISS?!
GETTING A BAND-AID.

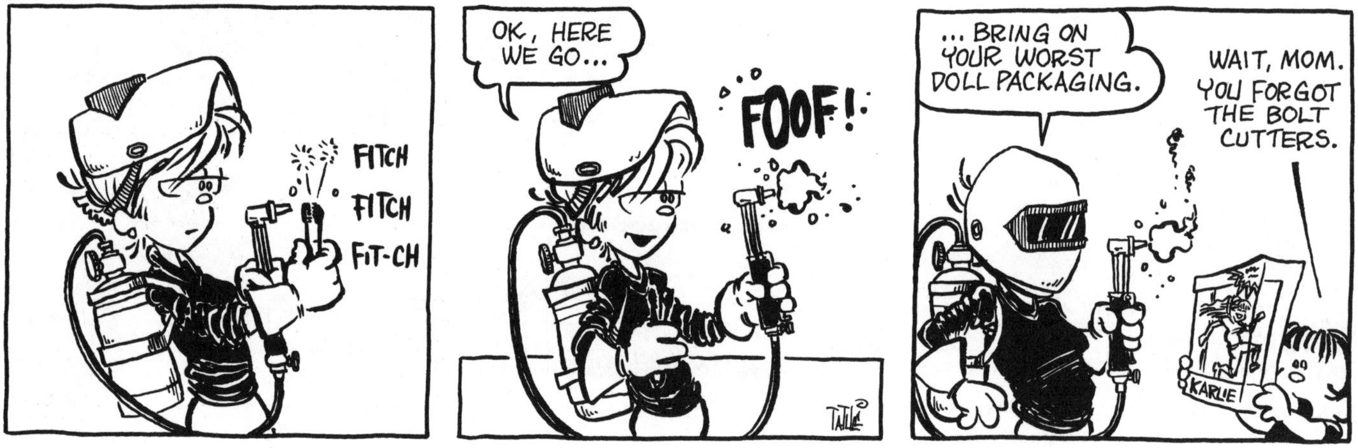
FITCH
FITCH
FIT-CH
OK, HERE WE GO...
FOOF!
... BRING ON YOUR WORST DOLL PACKAGING.
WAIT, MOM. YOU FORGOT THE BOLT CUTTERS.
KARLIE

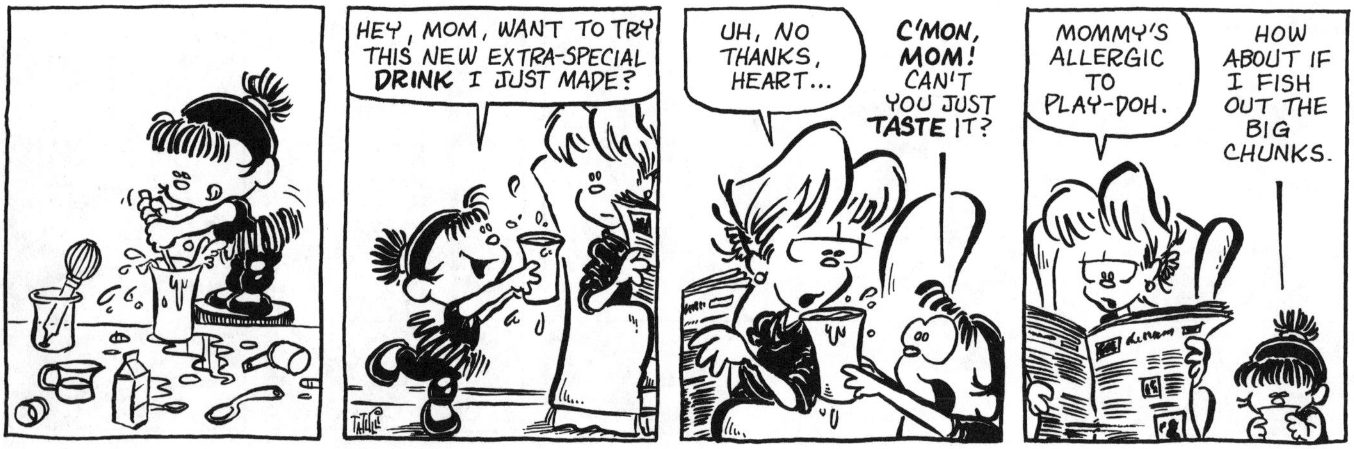
HEY, MOM, WANT TO TRY THIS NEW EXTRA-SPECIAL DRINK I JUST MADE?
UH, NO THANKS, HEART...
C'MON, MOM! CAN'T YOU JUST TASTE IT?
MOMMY'S ALLERGIC TO PLAY-DOH.
HOW ABOUT IF I FISH OUT THE BIG CHUNKS.

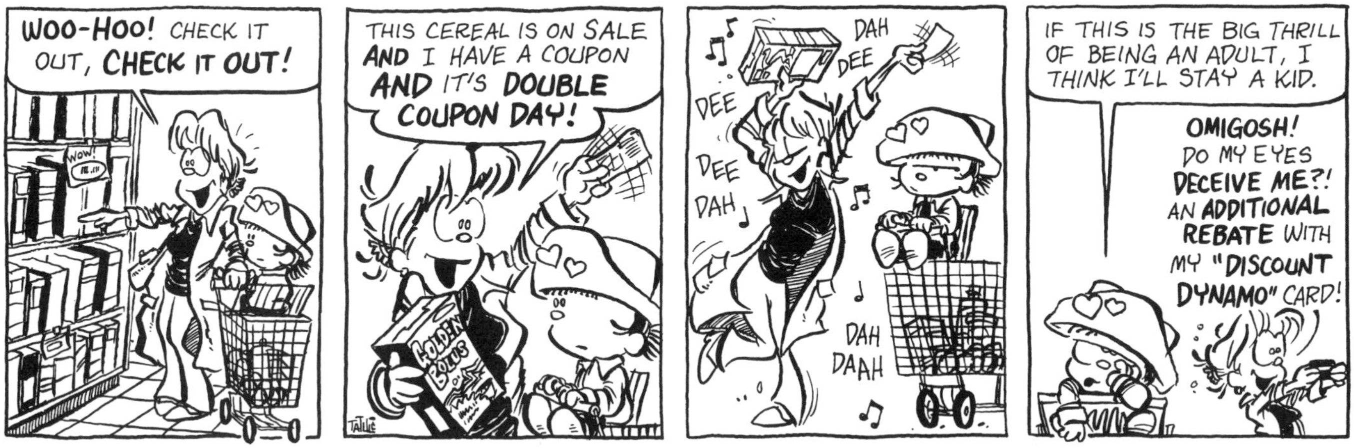
WOO-HOO! CHECK IT OUT, CHECK IT OUT!
THIS CEREAL IS ON SALE AND I HAVE A COUPON AND IT'S DOUBLE COUPON DAY!
DAH DEE
DEE DEE DAH
DAH DAAH
IF THIS IS THE BIG THRILL OF BEING AN ADULT, I THINK I'LL STAY A KID.
OMIGOSH! DO MY EYES DECEIVE ME?! AN ADDITIONAL REBATE WITH MY "DISCOUNT DYNAMO" CARD!

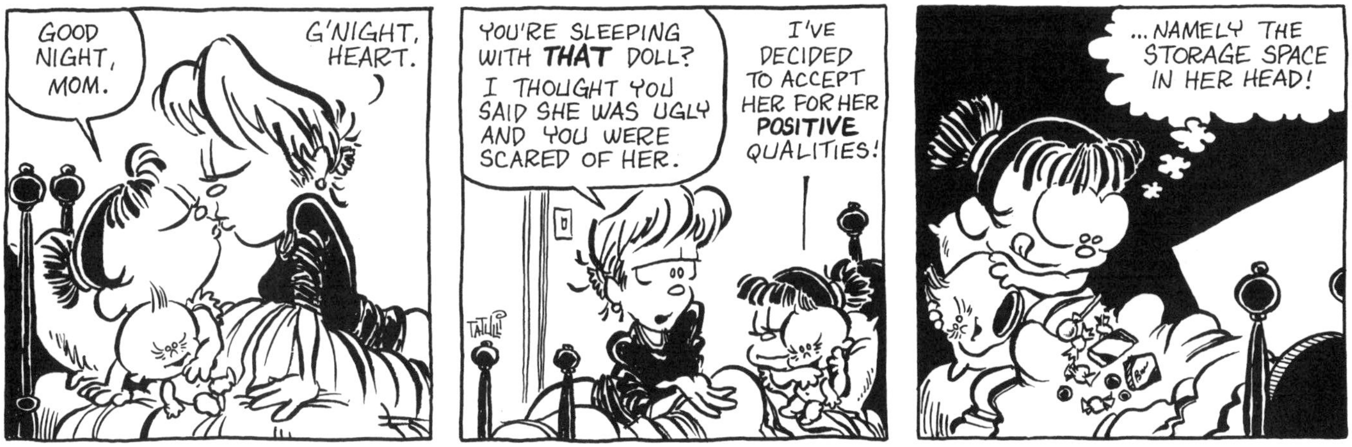
GOOD NIGHT, MOM.
G'NIGHT, HEART.
YOU'RE SLEEPING WITH THAT DOLL? I THOUGHT YOU SAID SHE WAS UGLY AND YOU WERE SCARED OF HER.
I'VE DECIDED TO ACCEPT HER FOR HER POSITIVE QUALITIES!
...NAMELY THE STORAGE SPACE IN HER HEAD!

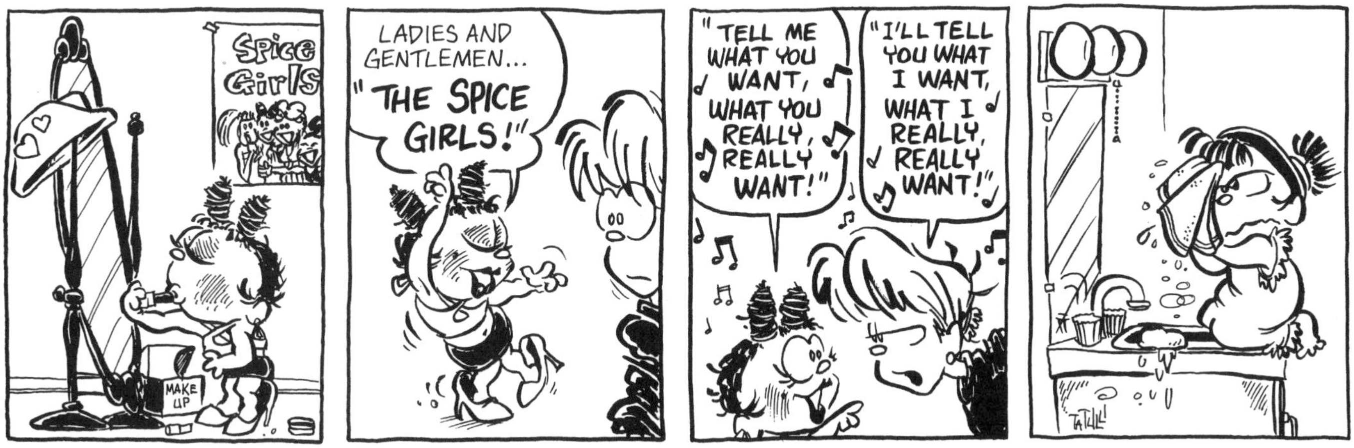
Spice Girls
MAKE UP
LADIES AND GENTLEMEN... "THE SPICE GIRLS!"
"TELL ME WHAT YOU WANT, WHAT YOU REALLY, REALLY WANT!"
"I'LL TELL YOU WHAT I WANT, WHAT I REALLY, REALLY WANT!"

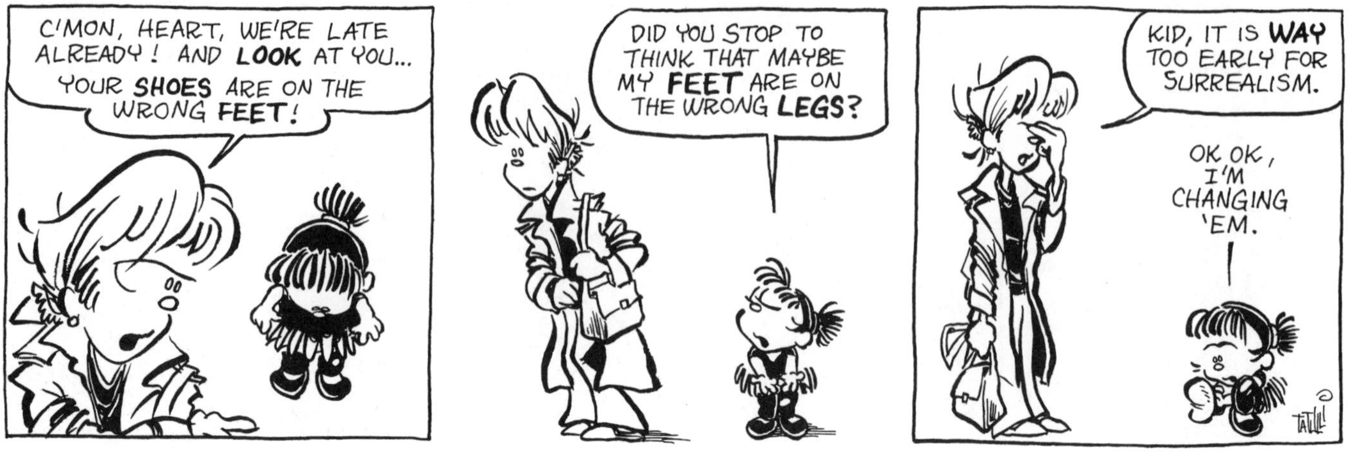
C'MON, HEART, WE'RE LATE ALREADY! AND **LOOK** AT YOU... YOUR **SHOES** ARE ON THE WRONG **FEET**!
DID YOU STOP TO THINK THAT MAYBE MY **FEET** ARE ON THE WRONG **LEGS**?
KID, IT IS **WAY** TOO EARLY FOR SURREALISM.
OK OK, I'M CHANGING 'EM.

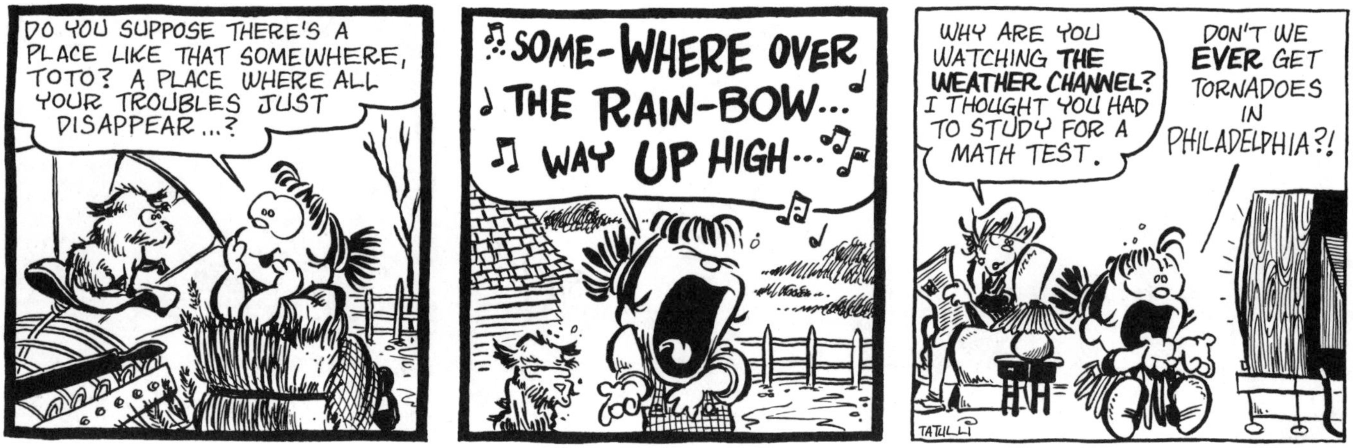
DO YOU SUPPOSE THERE'S A PLACE LIKE THAT SOMEWHERE, TOTO? A PLACE WHERE ALL YOUR TROUBLES JUST DISAPPEAR...?
SOME-WHERE OVER THE RAIN-BOW... WAY UP HIGH...
WHY ARE YOU WATCHING **THE WEATHER CHANNEL**? I THOUGHT YOU HAD TO STUDY FOR A MATH TEST.
DON'T WE **EVER** GET TORNADOES IN PHILADELPHIA?!

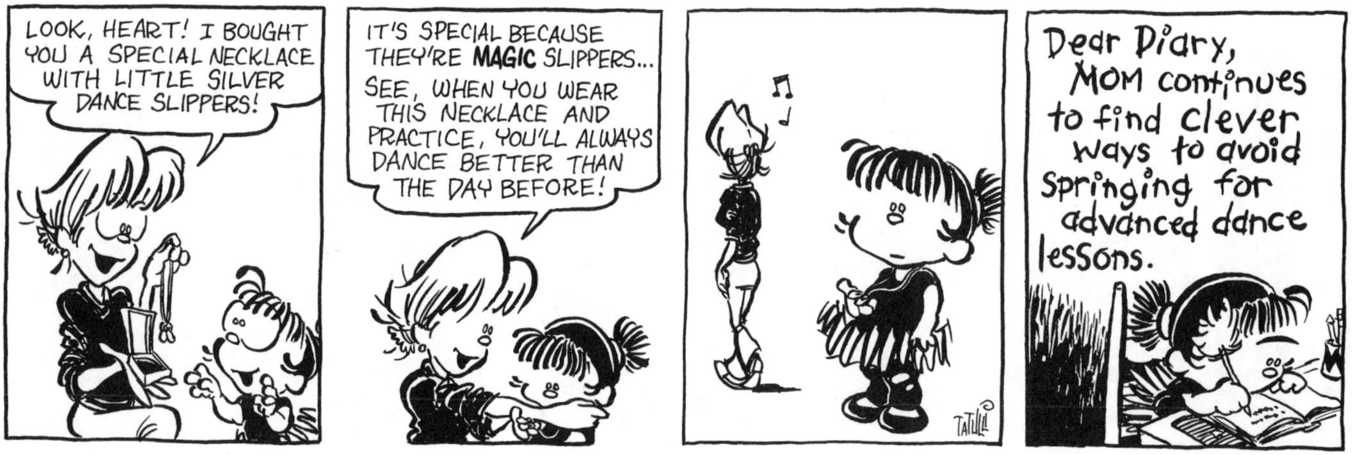
LOOK, HEART! I BOUGHT YOU A SPECIAL NECKLACE WITH LITTLE SILVER DANCE SLIPPERS!
IT'S SPECIAL BECAUSE THEY'RE **MAGIC** SLIPPERS... SEE, WHEN YOU WEAR THIS NECKLACE AND PRACTICE, YOU'LL ALWAYS DANCE BETTER THAN THE DAY BEFORE!
Dear Diary, MOM continues to find clever ways to avoid springing for advanced dance lessons.

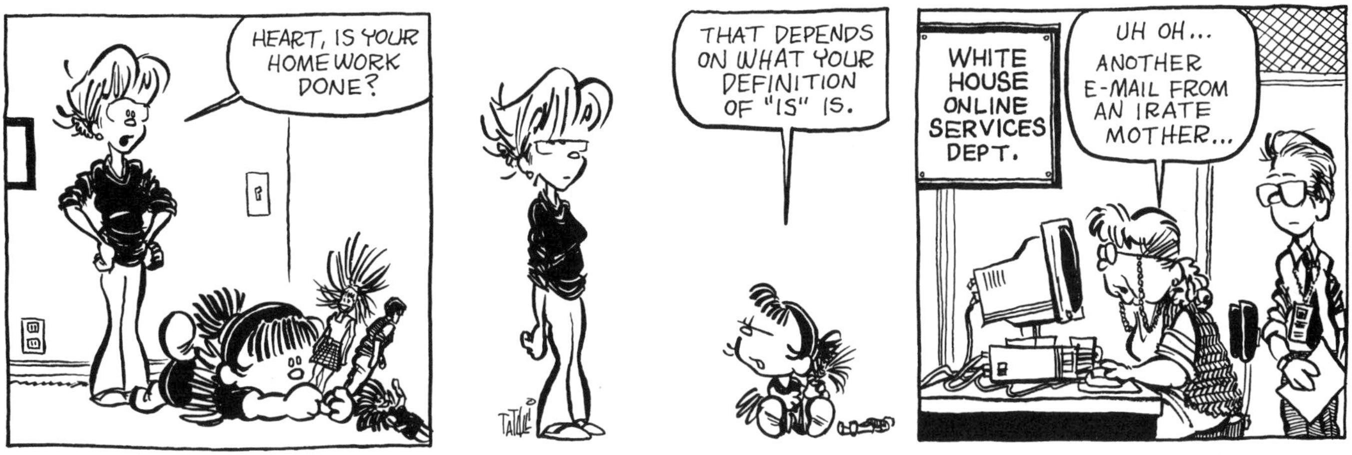
HEART, IS YOUR HOMEWORK DONE?
THAT DEPENDS ON WHAT YOUR DEFINITION OF "IS" IS.
WHITE HOUSE ONLINE SERVICES DEPT.
UH OH... ANOTHER E-MAIL FROM AN IRATE MOTHER...

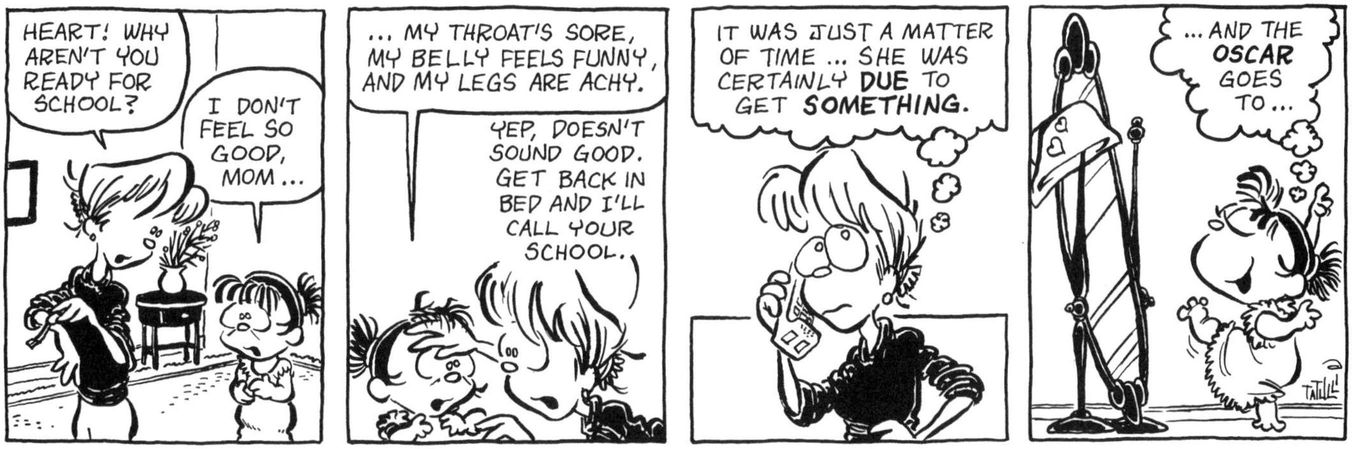
HEART! WHY AREN'T YOU READY FOR SCHOOL?
I DON'T FEEL SO GOOD, MOM...
... MY THROAT'S SORE, MY BELLY FEELS FUNNY, AND MY LEGS ARE ACHY.
YEP, DOESN'T SOUND GOOD. GET BACK IN BED AND I'LL CALL YOUR SCHOOL.
IT WAS JUST A MATTER OF TIME ... SHE WAS CERTAINLY **DUE** TO GET **SOMETHING**.
... AND THE **OSCAR** GOES TO ...

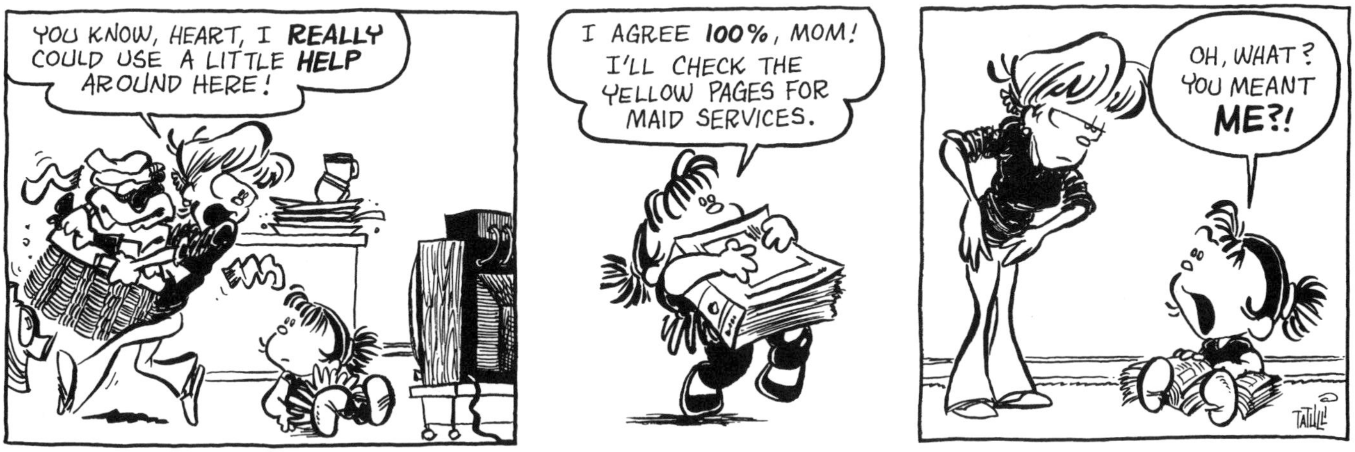
YOU KNOW, HEART, I **REALLY** COULD USE A LITTLE **HELP** AROUND HERE!
I AGREE **100%**, MOM! I'LL CHECK THE YELLOW PAGES FOR MAID SERVICES.
OH, WHAT? YOU MEANT **ME?!**

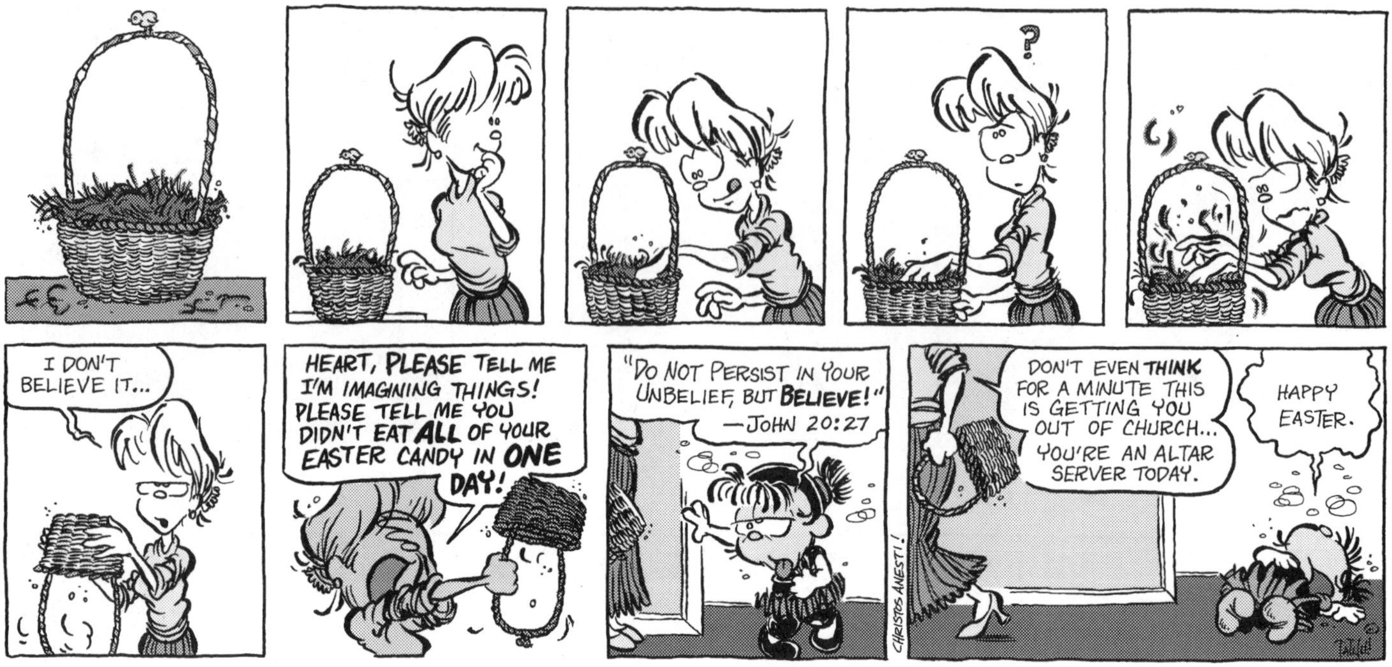
I DON'T BELIEVE IT...
HEART, PLEASE TELL ME I'M IMAGINING THINGS! PLEASE TELL ME YOU DIDN'T EAT ALL OF YOUR EASTER CANDY IN ONE DAY!
"DO NOT PERSIST IN YOUR UNBELIEF, BUT BELIEVE!" —JOHN 20:27
CHRISTOS ANESTI!
DON'T EVEN THINK FOR A MINUTE THIS IS GETTING YOU OUT OF CHURCH... YOU'RE AN ALTAR SERVER TODAY.
HAPPY EASTER.

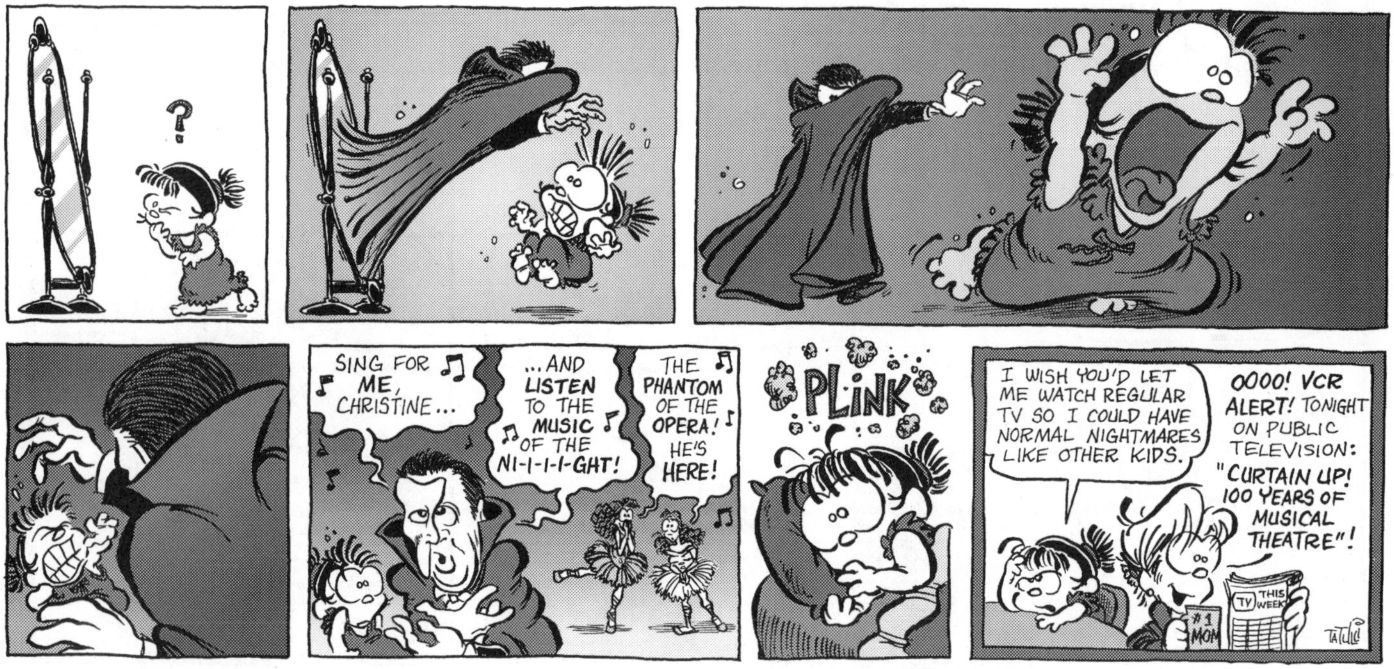
SING FOR ME, CHRISTINE...
...AND LISTEN TO THE MUSIC OF THE NI-I-I-I-GHT!
THE PHANTOM OF THE OPERA! HE'S HERE!
PLINK
I WISH YOU'D LET ME WATCH REGULAR TV SO I COULD HAVE NORMAL NIGHTMARES LIKE OTHER KIDS.
OOOO! VCR ALERT! TONIGHT ON PUBLIC TELEVISION: "CURTAIN UP! 100 YEARS OF MUSICAL THEATRE"!
TV THIS WEEK
#1 MOM

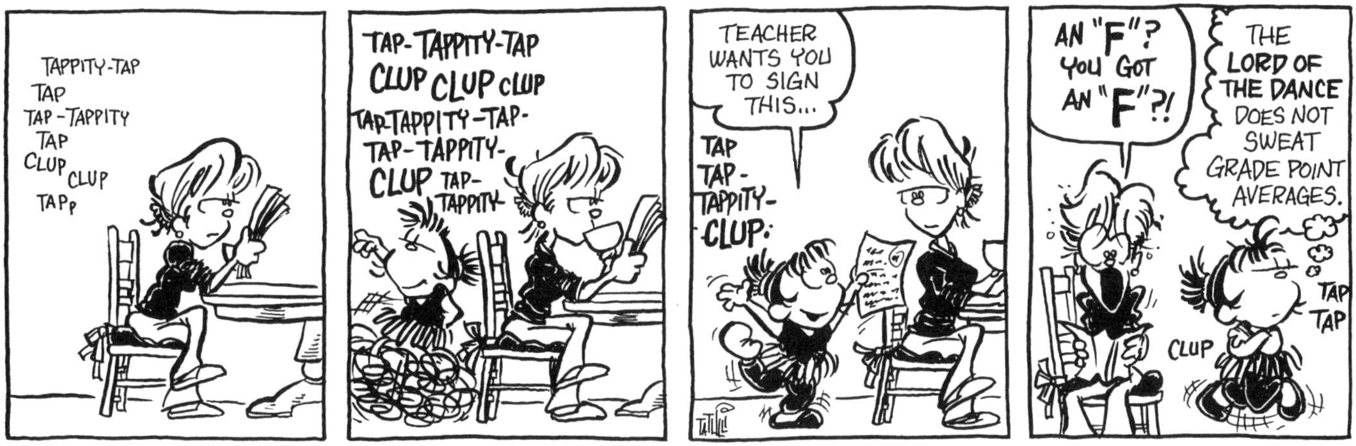
TAPPITY-TAP
TAP
TAP-TAPPITY
TAP
CLUP CLUP
TAPP
TAP-TAPPITY-TAP
CLUP CLUP CLUP
TAP-TAPPITY-TAP-
TAP-TAPPITY-
CLUP TAP-
TAPPITY-
TEACHER WANTS YOU TO SIGN THIS...
TAP
TAP-
TAPPITY-
CLUP.
AN "F"? YOU GOT AN "F"?!
THE LORD OF THE DANCE DOES NOT SWEAT GRADE POINT AVERAGES.
TAP
TAP
CLUP

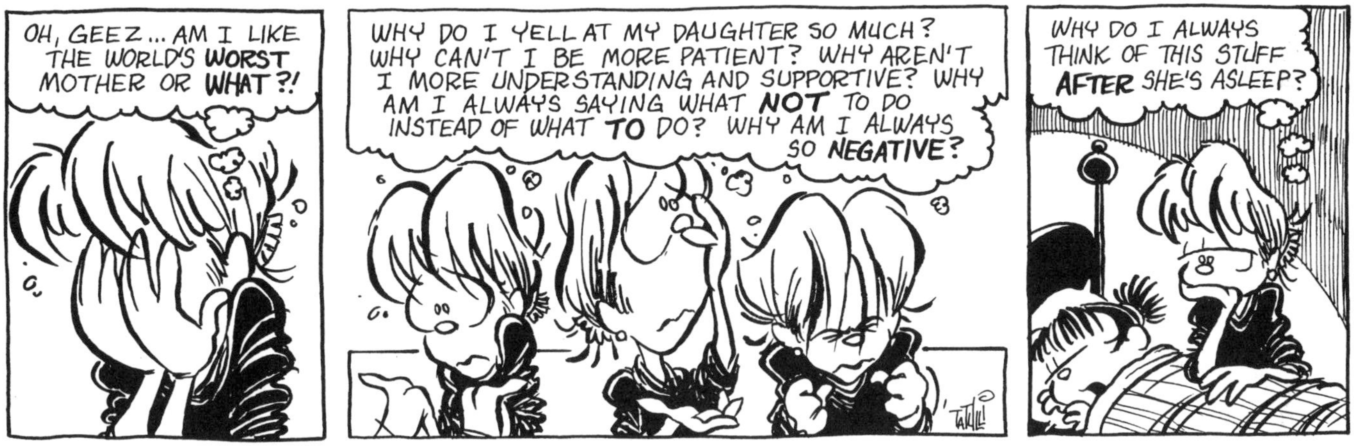
OH, GEEZ... AM I LIKE THE WORLD'S WORST MOTHER OR WHAT?!
WHY DO I YELL AT MY DAUGHTER SO MUCH? WHY CAN'T I BE MORE PATIENT? WHY AREN'T I MORE UNDERSTANDING AND SUPPORTIVE? WHY AM I ALWAYS SAYING WHAT NOT TO DO INSTEAD OF WHAT TO DO? WHY AM I ALWAYS SO NEGATIVE?
WHY DO I ALWAYS THINK OF THIS STUFF AFTER SHE'S ASLEEP?

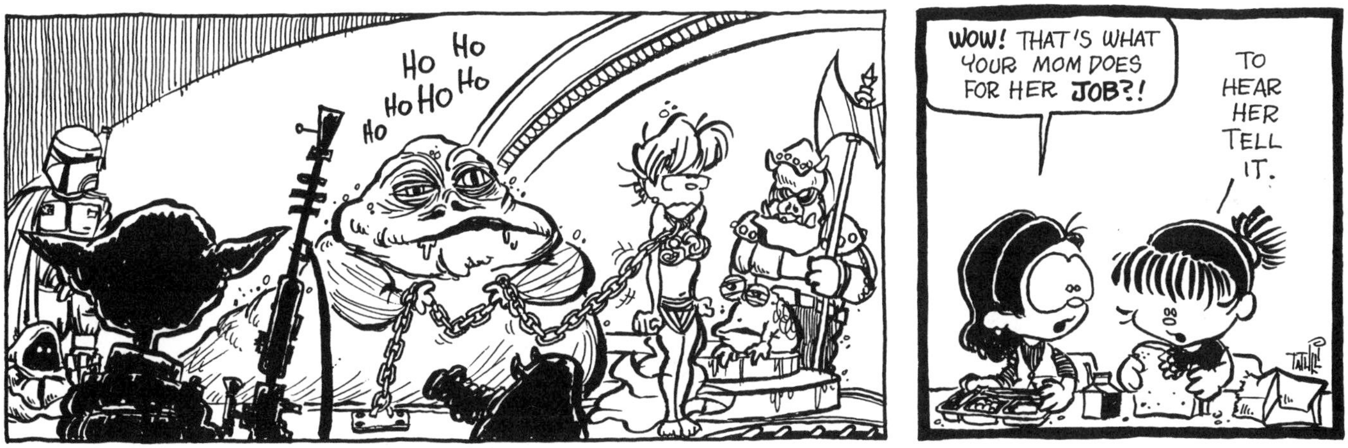
HO HO
HO HO HO HO HO
WOW! THAT'S WHAT YOUR MOM DOES FOR HER JOB?!
TO HEAR HER TELL IT.

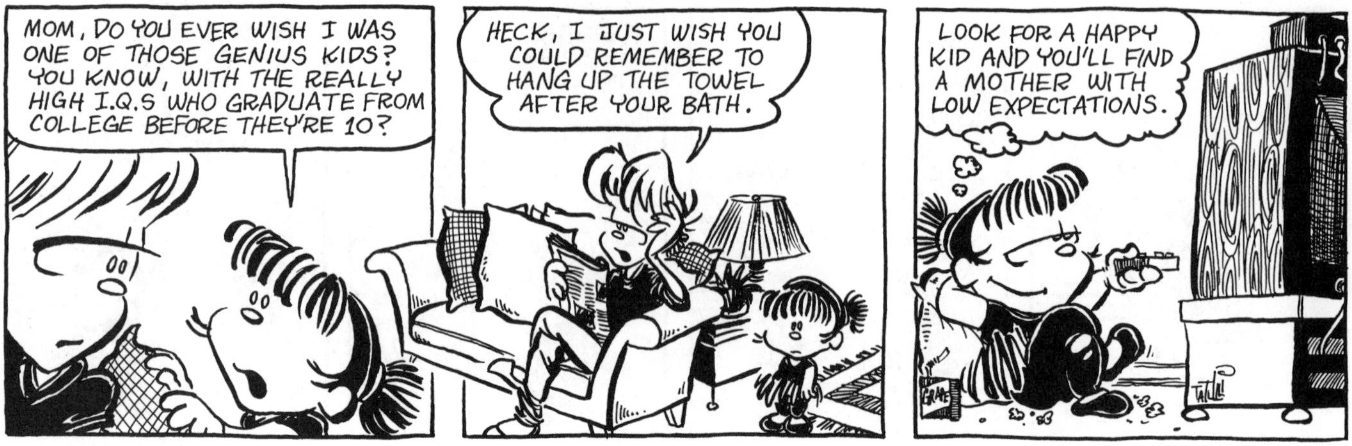
MOM, DO YOU EVER WISH I WAS ONE OF THOSE GENIUS KIDS? YOU KNOW, WITH THE REALLY HIGH I.Q.S WHO GRADUATE FROM COLLEGE BEFORE THEY'RE 10?
HECK, I JUST WISH YOU COULD REMEMBER TO HANG UP THE TOWEL AFTER YOUR BATH.
LOOK FOR A HAPPY KID AND YOU'LL FIND A MOTHER WITH LOW EXPECTATIONS.

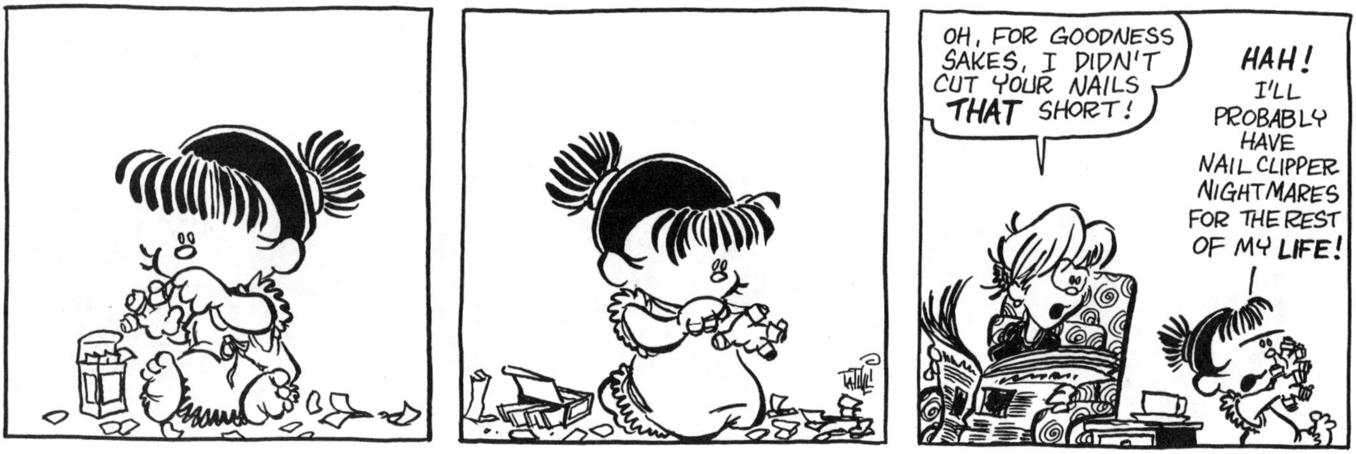
OH, FOR GOODNESS SAKES, I DIDN'T CUT YOUR NAILS THAT SHORT!
HAH! I'LL PROBABLY HAVE NAIL CLIPPER NIGHTMARES FOR THE REST OF MY LIFE!

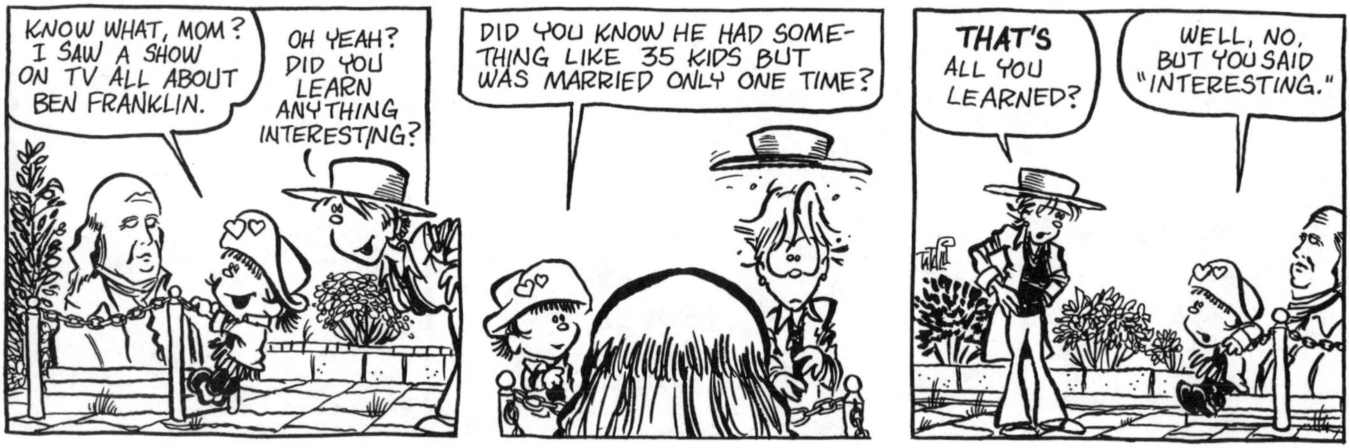
KNOW WHAT, MOM? I SAW A SHOW ON TV ALL ABOUT BEN FRANKLIN.
OH YEAH? DID YOU LEARN ANYTHING INTERESTING?
DID YOU KNOW HE HAD SOMETHING LIKE 35 KIDS BUT WAS MARRIED ONLY ONE TIME?
THAT'S ALL YOU LEARNED?
WELL, NO, BUT YOU SAID "INTERESTING."

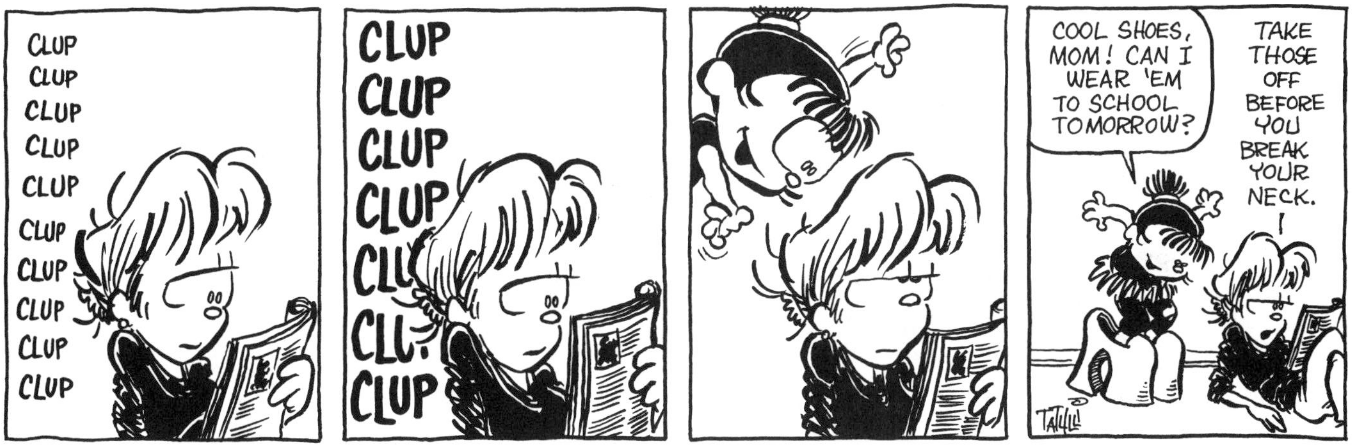
CLUP
CLUP
CLUP
CLUP
CLUP
CLUP
CLUP
CLUP
CLUP
CLUP
CLUP
CLUP
CLUP
CLUP
CLUP
CLUP
CLUP
COOL SHOES, MOM! CAN I WEAR 'EM TO SCHOOL TOMORROW?
TAKE THOSE OFF BEFORE YOU BREAK YOUR NECK.
TATULLI

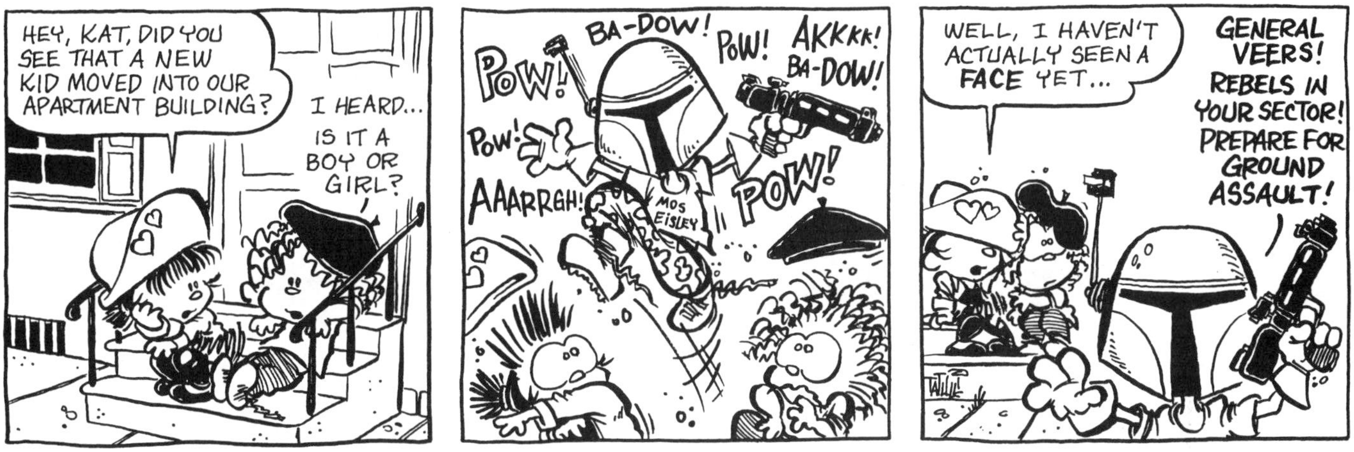
HEY, KAT, DID YOU SEE THAT A NEW KID MOVED INTO OUR APARTMENT BUILDING?
I HEARD... IS IT A BOY OR GIRL?
POW!
BA-DOW!
POW!
AKKKK!
BA-DOW!
POW!
AAARRGH!
MOS EISLEY
POW!
WELL, I HAVEN'T ACTUALLY SEEN A FACE YET...
GENERAL VEERS! REBELS IN YOUR SECTOR! PREPARE FOR GROUND ASSAULT!
TATULLI

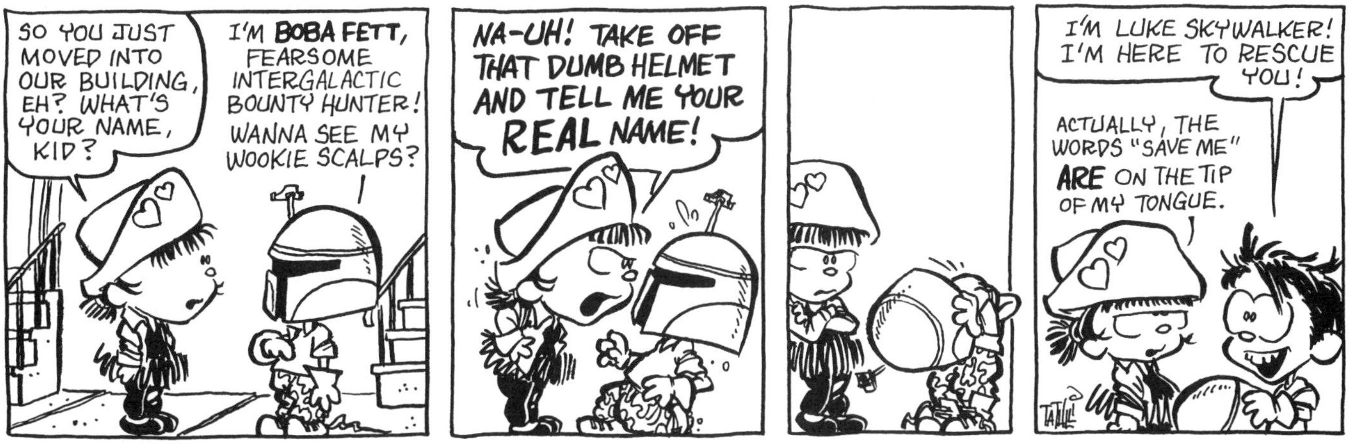
SO YOU JUST MOVED INTO OUR BUILDING, EH? WHAT'S YOUR NAME, KID?
I'M BOBA FETT, FEARSOME INTERGALACTIC BOUNTY HUNTER!
WANNA SEE MY WOOKIE SCALPS?
NA-UH! TAKE OFF THAT DUMB HELMET AND TELL ME YOUR REAL NAME!
I'M LUKE SKYWALKER! I'M HERE TO RESCUE YOU!
ACTUALLY, THE WORDS "SAVE ME" ARE ON THE TIP OF MY TONGUE.
TATULLI

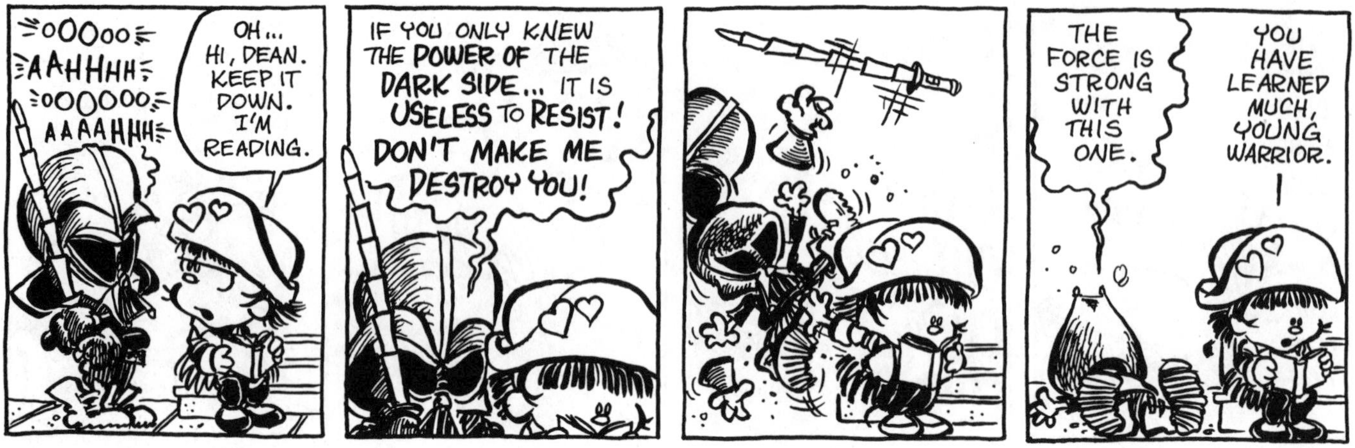
OOOoo
AAHHHH
OOOOOO
AAAAHHH
OH... HI, DEAN. KEEP IT DOWN. I'M READING.
IF YOU ONLY KNEW THE POWER OF THE DARK SIDE... IT IS USELESS TO RESIST! DON'T MAKE ME DESTROY YOU!
THE FORCE IS STRONG WITH THIS ONE.
YOU HAVE LEARNED MUCH, YOUNG WARRIOR.

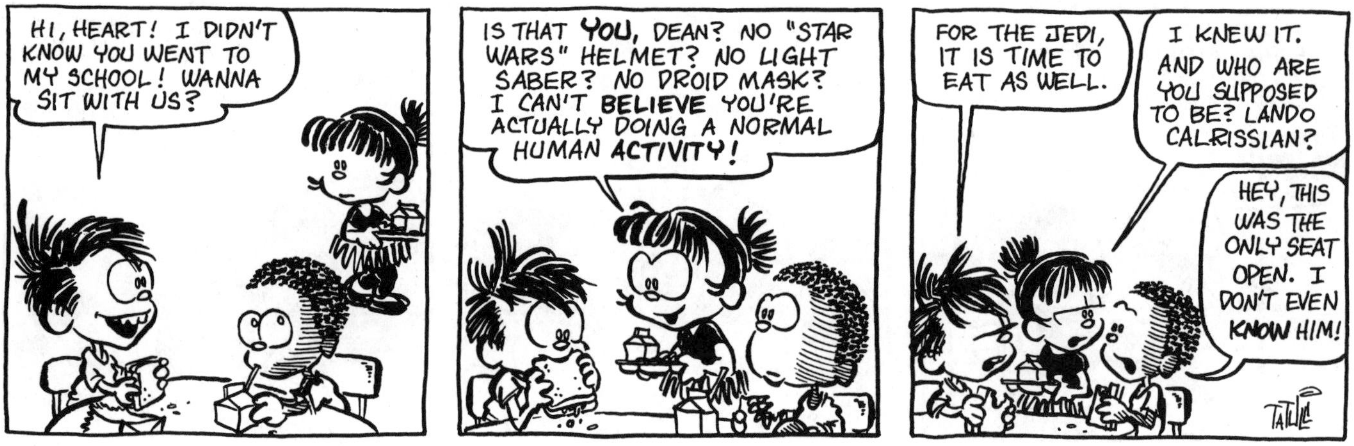
HI, HEART! I DIDN'T KNOW YOU WENT TO MY SCHOOL! WANNA SIT WITH US?
IS THAT YOU, DEAN? NO "STAR WARS" HELMET? NO LIGHT SABER? NO DROID MASK? I CAN'T BELIEVE YOU'RE ACTUALLY DOING A NORMAL HUMAN ACTIVITY!
FOR THE JEDI, IT IS TIME TO EAT AS WELL.
I KNEW IT. AND WHO ARE YOU SUPPOSED TO BE? LANDO CALRISSIAN?
HEY, THIS WAS THE ONLY SEAT OPEN. I DON'T EVEN KNOW HIM!

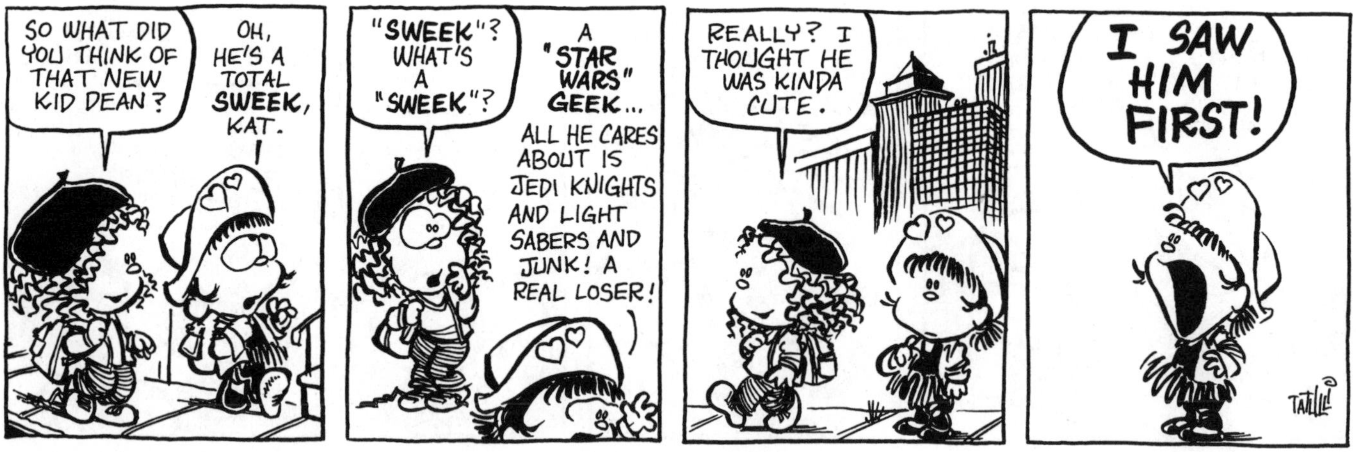
SO WHAT DID YOU THINK OF THAT NEW KID DEAN?
OH, HE'S A TOTAL SWEEK, KAT.
"SWEEK"? WHAT'S A "SWEEK"?
A "STAR WARS" GEEK... ALL HE CARES ABOUT IS JEDI KNIGHTS AND LIGHT SABERS AND JUNK! A REAL LOSER!
REALLY? I THOUGHT HE WAS KINDA CUTE.
I SAW HIM FIRST!

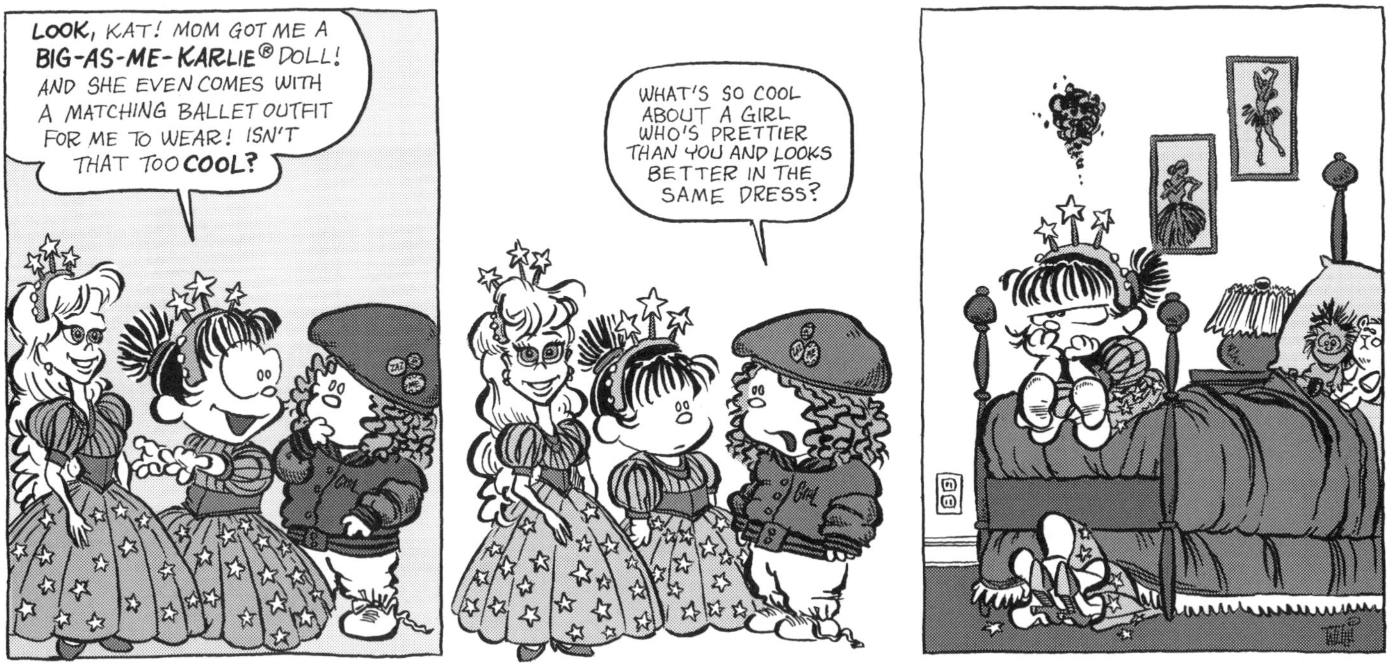
LOOK, KAT! MOM GOT ME A BIG-AS-ME-KARLIE® DOLL! AND SHE EVEN COMES WITH A MATCHING BALLET OUTFIT FOR ME TO WEAR! ISN'T THAT TOO COOL?
WHAT'S SO COOL ABOUT A GIRL WHO'S PRETTIER THAN YOU AND LOOKS BETTER IN THE SAME DRESS?

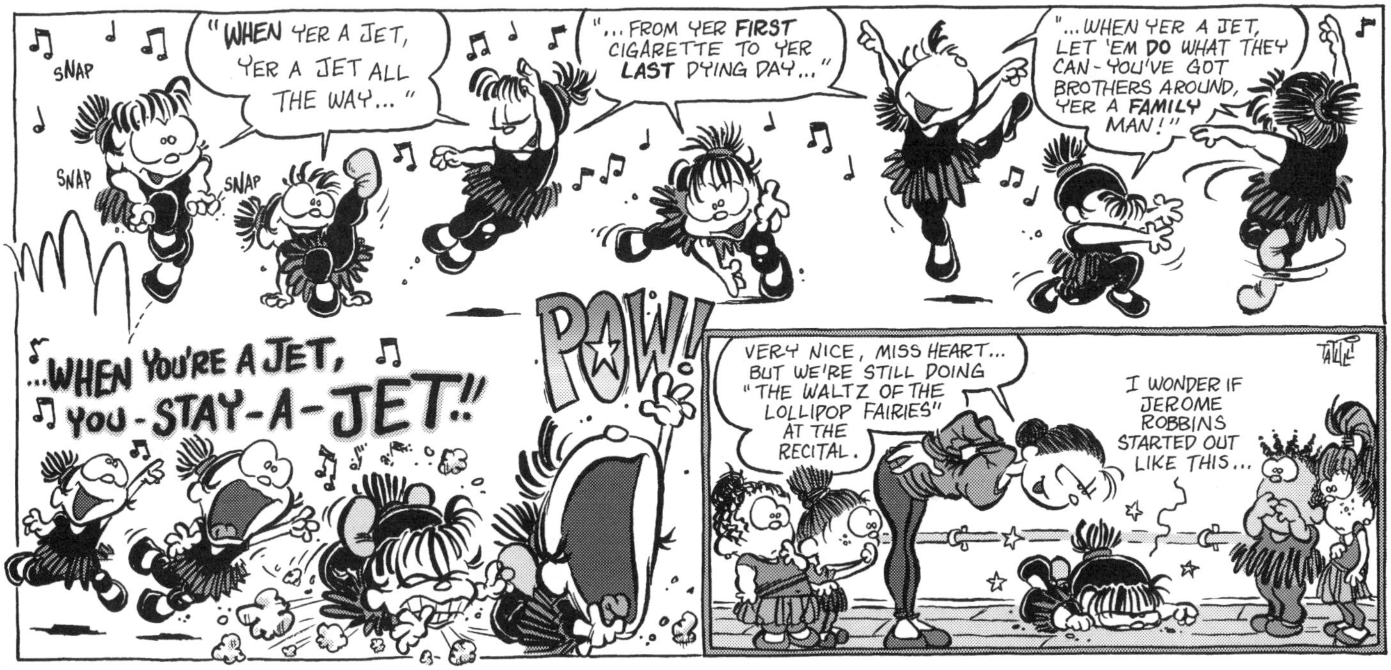
SNAP
SNAP
SNAP
"WHEN YER A JET, YER A JET ALL THE WAY..."
"...FROM YER FIRST CIGARETTE TO YER LAST DYING DAY..."
"...WHEN YER A JET, LET 'EM DO WHAT THEY CAN - YOU'VE GOT BROTHERS AROUND, YER A FAMILY MAN!"
"...WHEN YOU'RE A JET, YOU - STAY - A - JET!!"
POW!
VERY NICE, MISS HEART... BUT WE'RE STILL DOING "THE WALTZ OF THE LOLLIPOP FAIRIES" AT THE RECITAL.
I WONDER IF JEROME ROBBINS STARTED OUT LIKE THIS...

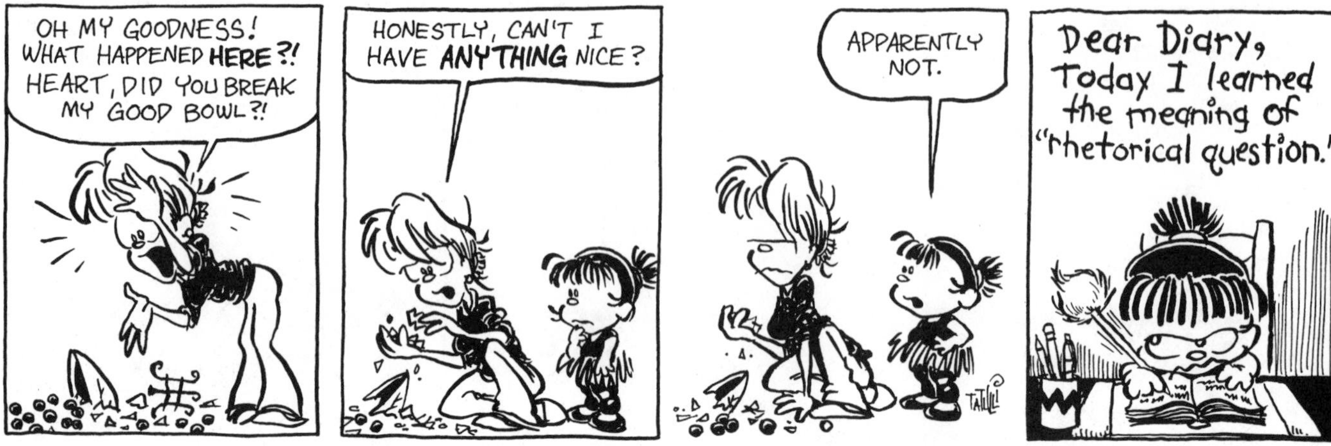
OH MY GOODNESS! WHAT HAPPENED HERE?! HEART, DID YOU BREAK MY GOOD BOWL?!
HONESTLY, CAN'T I HAVE ANYTHING NICE?
APPARENTLY NOT.
Dear Diary, Today I learned the meaning of "rhetorical question."
TATULLI

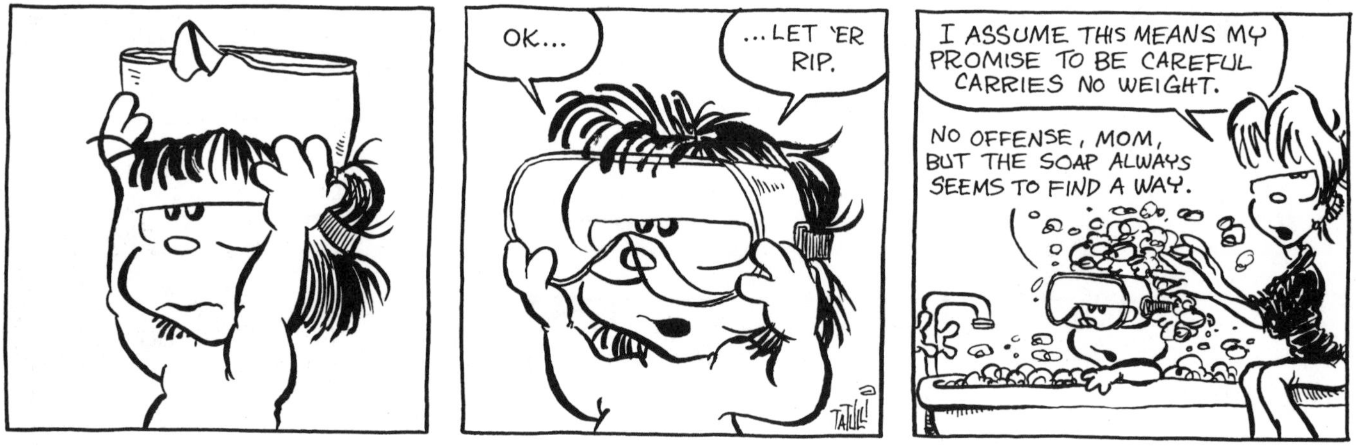
OK...
...LET 'ER RIP.
TATULLI
I ASSUME THIS MEANS MY PROMISE TO BE CAREFUL CARRIES NO WEIGHT.
NO OFFENSE, MOM, BUT THE SOAP ALWAYS SEEMS TO FIND A WAY.

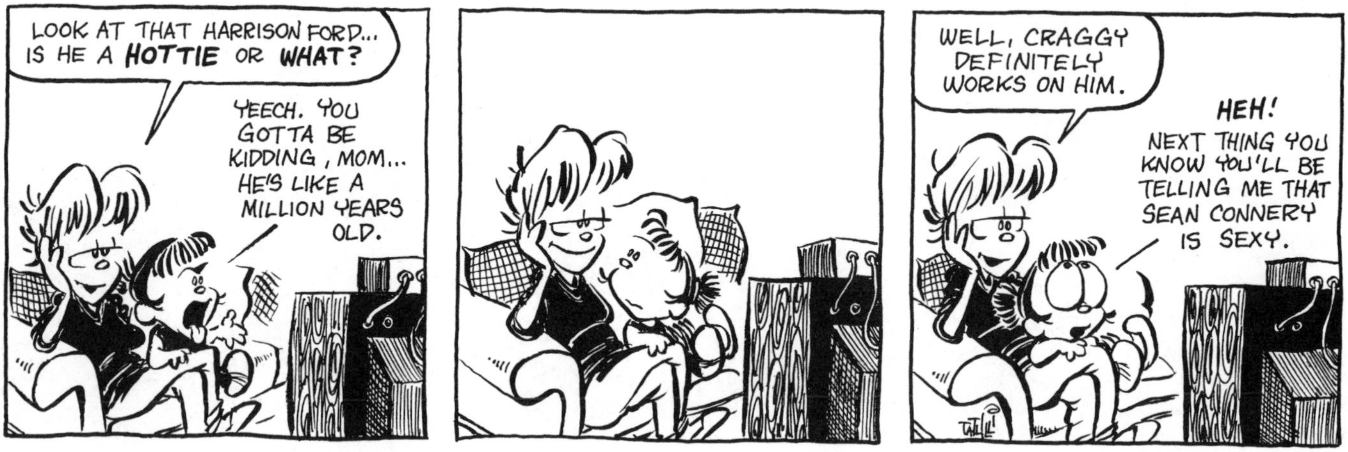
LOOK AT THAT HARRISON FORD... IS HE A HOTTIE OR WHAT?
YEECH. YOU GOTTA BE KIDDING, MOM... HE'S LIKE A MILLION YEARS OLD.
WELL, CRAGGY DEFINITELY WORKS ON HIM.
HEH! NEXT THING YOU KNOW YOU'LL BE TELLING ME THAT SEAN CONNERY IS SEXY.
TATULLI

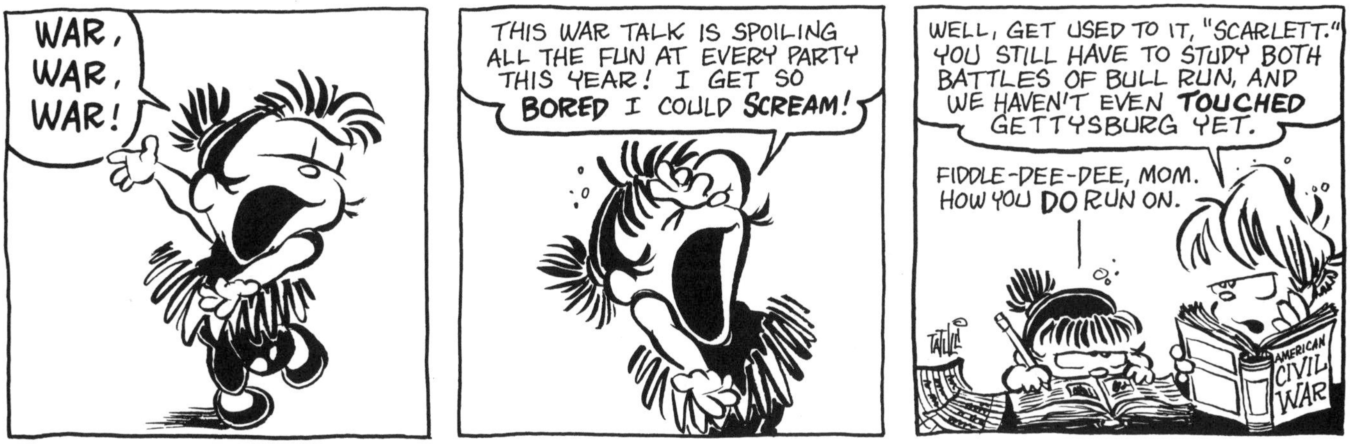
WAR, WAR, WAR!
THIS WAR TALK IS SPOILING ALL THE FUN AT EVERY PARTY THIS YEAR! I GET SO **BORED** I COULD **SCREAM**!
WELL, GET USED TO IT, "SCARLETT." YOU STILL HAVE TO STUDY BOTH BATTLES OF BULL RUN, AND WE HAVEN'T EVEN **TOUCHED** GETTYSBURG YET.
FIDDLE-DEE-DEE, MOM. HOW YOU **DO** RUN ON.
AMERICAN CIVIL WAR

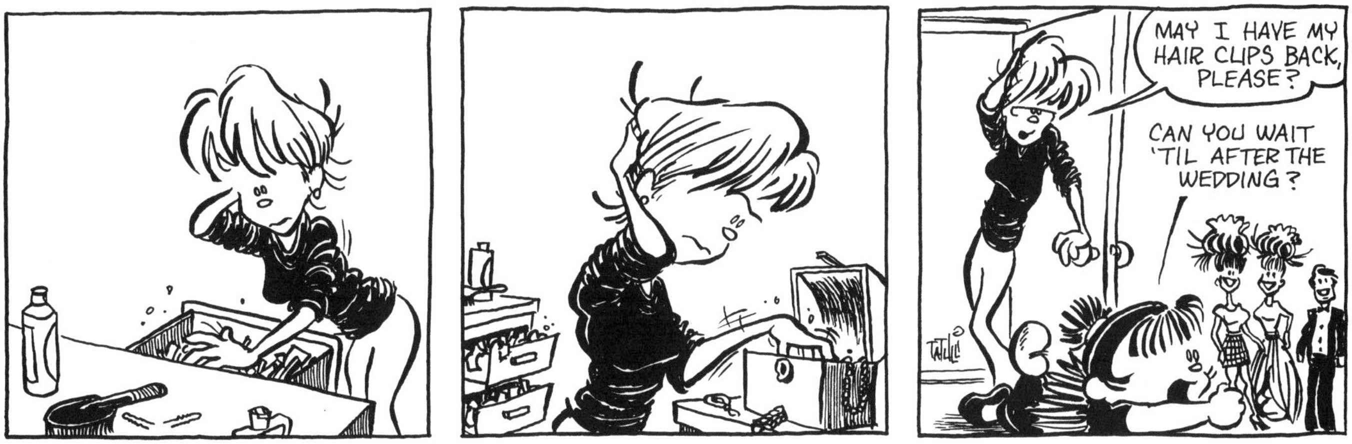
MAY I HAVE MY HAIR CLIPS BACK, PLEASE?
CAN YOU WAIT 'TIL AFTER THE WEDDING?

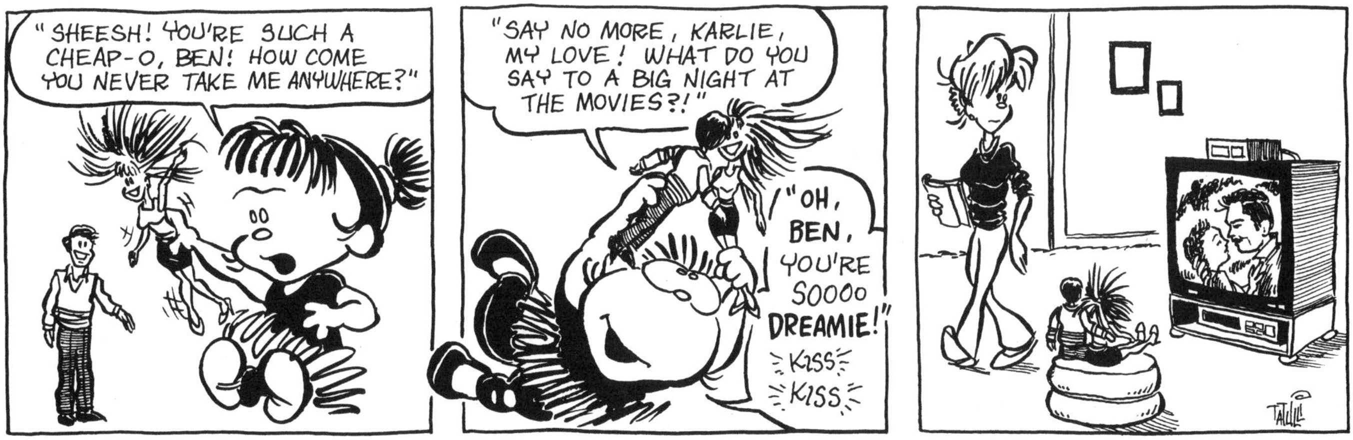
"SHEESH! YOU'RE SUCH A CHEAP-O, BEN! HOW COME YOU NEVER TAKE ME ANYWHERE?"
"SAY NO MORE, KARLIE, MY LOVE! WHAT DO YOU SAY TO A BIG NIGHT AT THE MOVIES?!"
"OH, BEN, YOU'RE SOOOO DREAMIE!"
KISS KISS

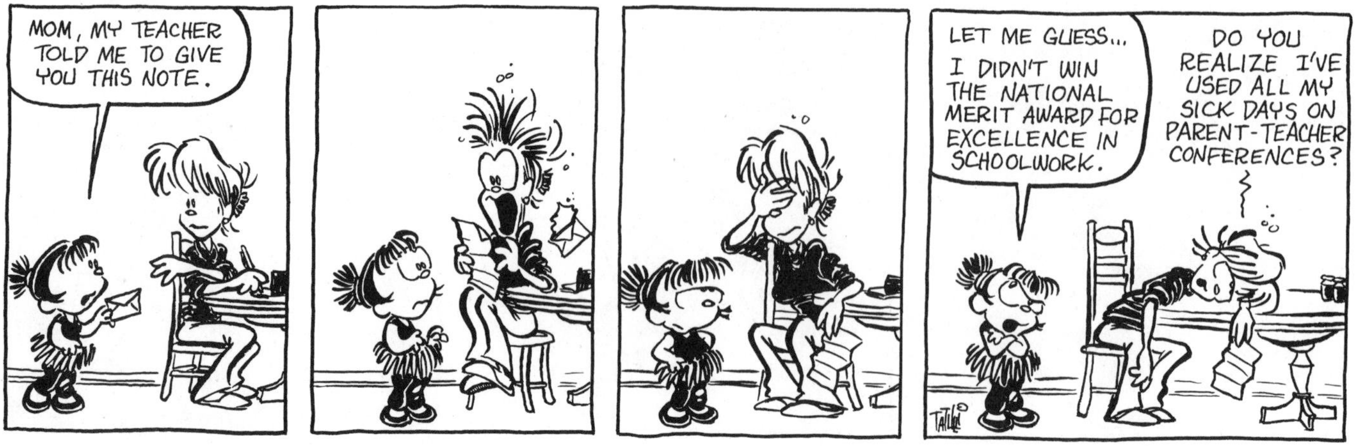
MOM, MY TEACHER TOLD ME TO GIVE YOU THIS NOTE.
LET ME GUESS... I DIDN'T WIN THE NATIONAL MERIT AWARD FOR EXCELLENCE IN SCHOOLWORK.
DO YOU REALIZE I'VE USED ALL MY SICK DAYS ON PARENT-TEACHER CONFERENCES?

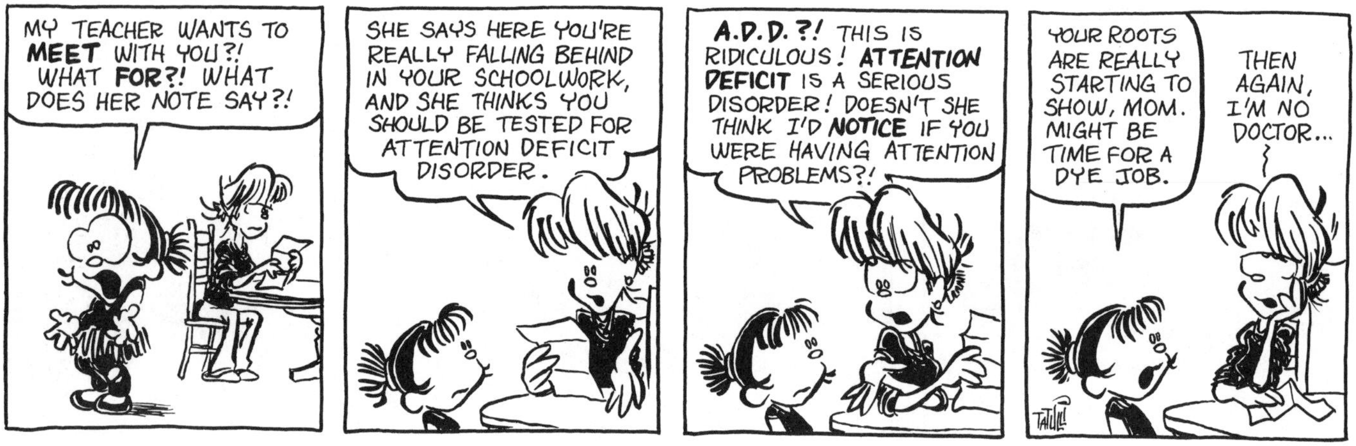
MY TEACHER WANTS TO **MEET** WITH YOU?! WHAT **FOR?!** WHAT DOES HER NOTE SAY?!
SHE SAYS HERE YOU'RE REALLY FALLING BEHIND IN YOUR SCHOOLWORK, AND SHE THINKS YOU SHOULD BE TESTED FOR ATTENTION DEFICIT DISORDER.
A.D.D.?! THIS IS RIDICULOUS! **ATTENTION DEFICIT** IS A SERIOUS DISORDER! DOESN'T SHE THINK I'D **NOTICE** IF YOU WERE HAVING ATTENTION PROBLEMS?!
YOUR ROOTS ARE REALLY STARTING TO SHOW, MOM. MIGHT BE TIME FOR A DYE JOB.
THEN AGAIN, I'M NO DOCTOR...

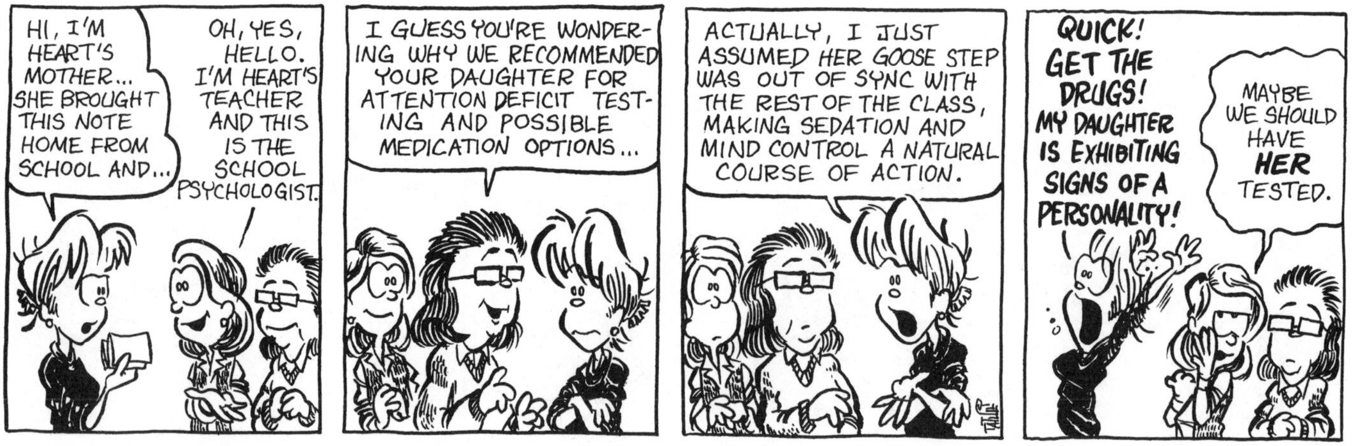
HI, I'M HEART'S MOTHER... SHE BROUGHT THIS NOTE HOME FROM SCHOOL AND...
OH, YES, HELLO. I'M HEART'S TEACHER AND THIS IS THE SCHOOL PSYCHOLOGIST.
I GUESS YOU'RE WONDERING WHY WE RECOMMENDED YOUR DAUGHTER FOR ATTENTION DEFICIT TESTING AND POSSIBLE MEDICATION OPTIONS...
ACTUALLY, I JUST ASSUMED HER GOOSE STEP WAS OUT OF SYNC WITH THE REST OF THE CLASS, MAKING SEDATION AND MIND CONTROL A NATURAL COURSE OF ACTION.
QUICK! GET THE DRUGS! MY DAUGHTER IS EXHIBITING SIGNS OF A PERSONALITY!
MAYBE WE SHOULD HAVE **HER** TESTED.

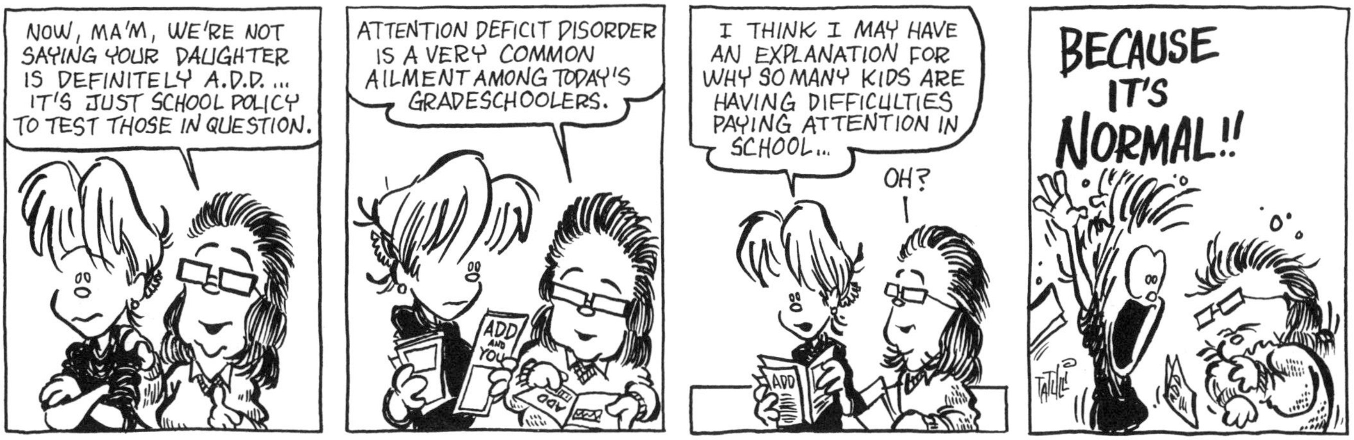
NOW, MA'M, WE'RE NOT SAYING YOUR DAUGHTER IS DEFINITELY A.D.D. ... IT'S JUST SCHOOL POLICY TO TEST THOSE IN QUESTION.
ATTENTION DEFICIT DISORDER IS A VERY COMMON AILMENT AMONG TODAY'S GRADESCHOOLERS.
ADD AND YOU
I THINK I MAY HAVE AN EXPLANATION FOR WHY SO MANY KIDS ARE HAVING DIFFICULTIES PAYING ATTENTION IN SCHOOL...
OH?
ADD
BECAUSE IT'S NORMAL!!

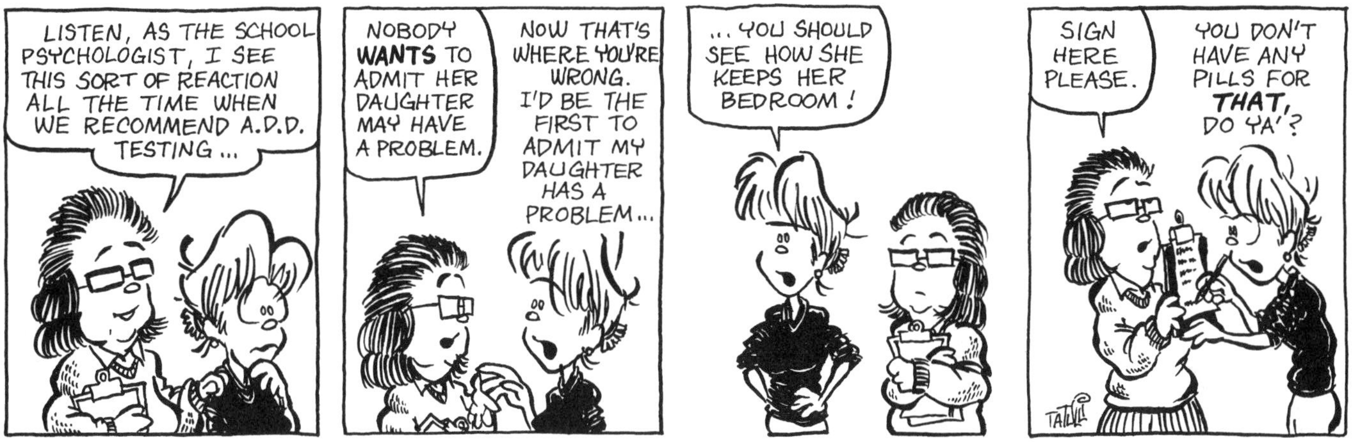
LISTEN, AS THE SCHOOL PSYCHOLOGIST, I SEE THIS SORT OF REACTION ALL THE TIME WHEN WE RECOMMEND A.D.D. TESTING...
NOBODY **WANTS** TO ADMIT HER DAUGHTER MAY HAVE A PROBLEM.
NOW THAT'S WHERE YOU'RE WRONG. I'D BE THE FIRST TO ADMIT MY DAUGHTER HAS A PROBLEM...
...YOU SHOULD SEE HOW SHE KEEPS HER BEDROOM!
SIGN HERE PLEASE.
YOU DON'T HAVE ANY PILLS FOR **THAT**, DO YA'?

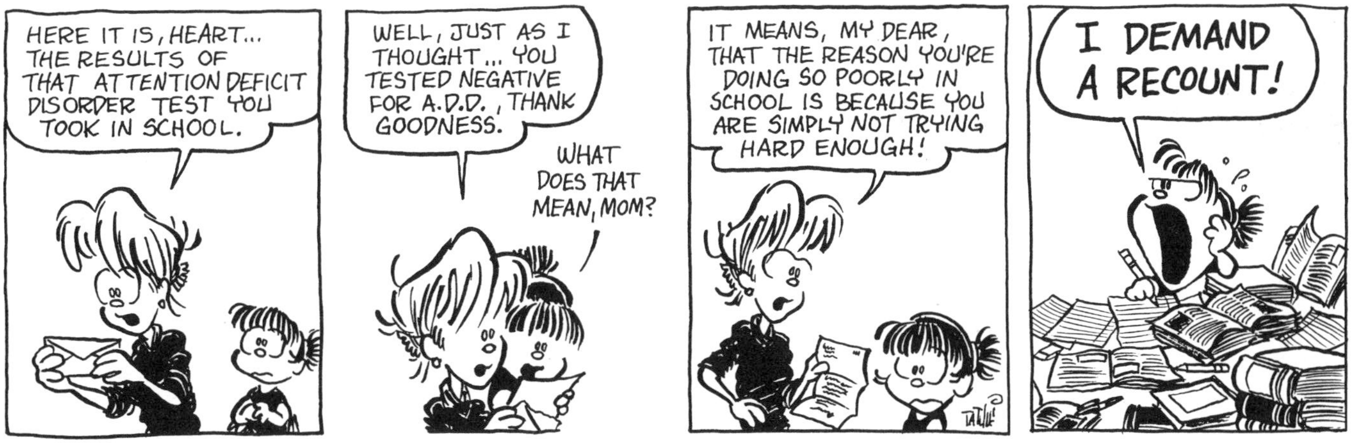
HERE IT IS, HEART... THE RESULTS OF THAT ATTENTION DEFICIT DISORDER TEST YOU TOOK IN SCHOOL.
WELL, JUST AS I THOUGHT... YOU TESTED NEGATIVE FOR A.D.D., THANK GOODNESS.
WHAT DOES THAT MEAN, MOM?
IT MEANS, MY DEAR, THAT THE REASON YOU'RE DOING SO POORLY IN SCHOOL IS BECAUSE YOU ARE SIMPLY NOT TRYING HARD ENOUGH!
I DEMAND A RECOUNT!

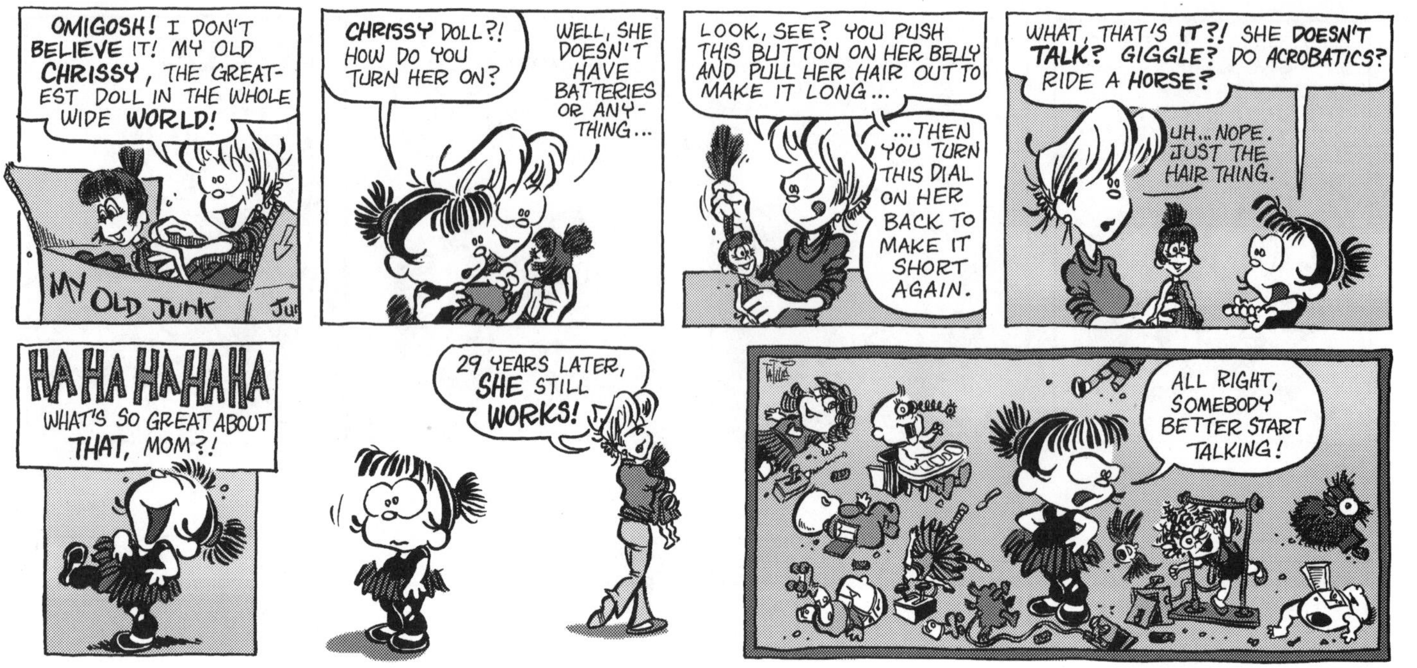
OMIGOSH! I DON'T BELIEVE IT! MY OLD CHRISSY, THE GREATEST DOLL IN THE WHOLE WIDE WORLD!
MY OLD JUNK
CHRISSY DOLL?! HOW DO YOU TURN HER ON?
WELL, SHE DOESN'T HAVE BATTERIES OR ANYTHING...
LOOK, SEE? YOU PUSH THIS BUTTON ON HER BELLY AND PULL HER HAIR OUT TO MAKE IT LONG...
...THEN YOU TURN THIS DIAL ON HER BACK TO MAKE IT SHORT AGAIN.
WHAT, THAT'S IT?! SHE DOESN'T TALK? GIGGLE? DO ACROBATICS? RIDE A HORSE?
UH... NOPE. JUST THE HAIR THING.
HA HA HAHAHA
WHAT'S SO GREAT ABOUT THAT, MOM?!
29 YEARS LATER, SHE STILL WORKS!
ALL RIGHT, SOMEBODY BETTER START TALKING!

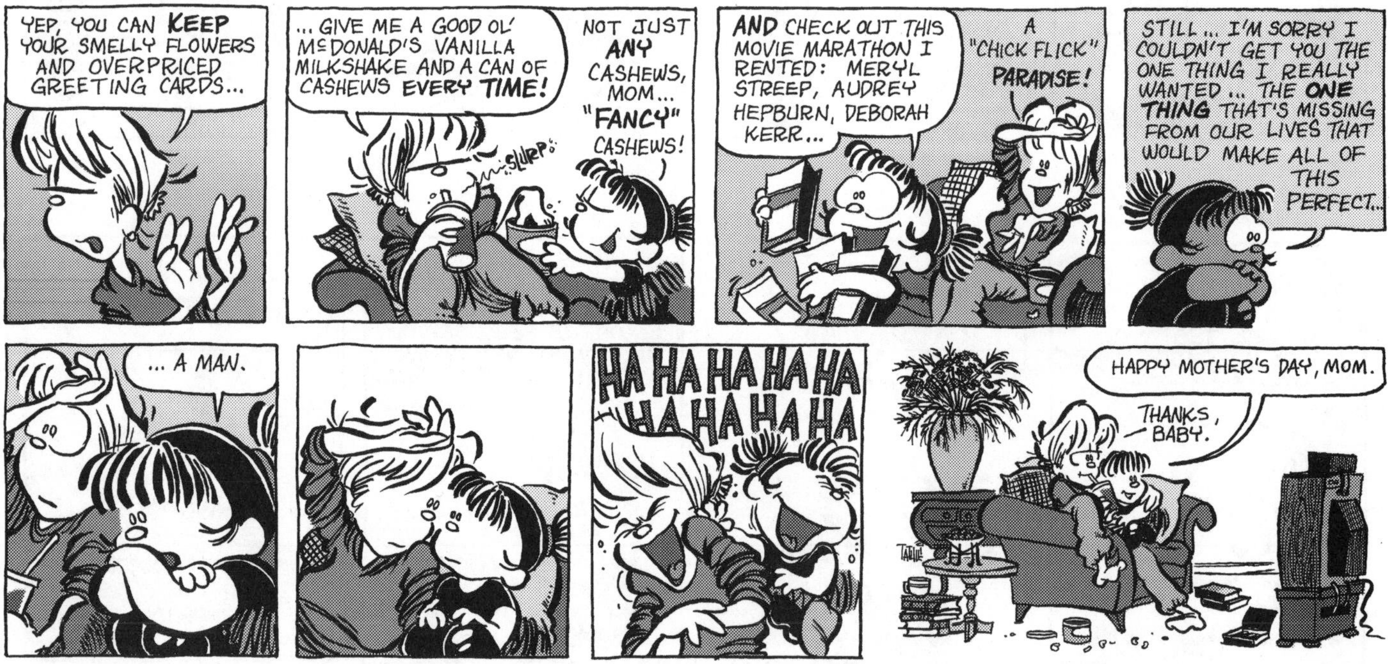
YEP, YOU CAN KEEP YOUR SMELLY FLOWERS AND OVERPRICED GREETING CARDS...
...GIVE ME A GOOD OL' McDONALD'S VANILLA MILKSHAKE AND A CAN OF CASHEWS EVERY TIME!
SLURP
NOT JUST ANY CASHEWS, MOM... "FANCY" CASHEWS!
AND CHECK OUT THIS MOVIE MARATHON I RENTED: MERYL STREEP, AUDREY HEPBURN, DEBORAH KERR...
A "CHICK FLICK" PARADISE!
STILL... I'M SORRY I COULDN'T GET YOU THE ONE THING I REALLY WANTED... THE ONE THING THAT'S MISSING FROM OUR LIVES THAT WOULD MAKE ALL OF THIS PERFECT...
... A MAN.
HA HA HA HA HA HA HA HA HA HA HA
HAPPY MOTHER'S DAY, MOM.
THANKS, BABY.

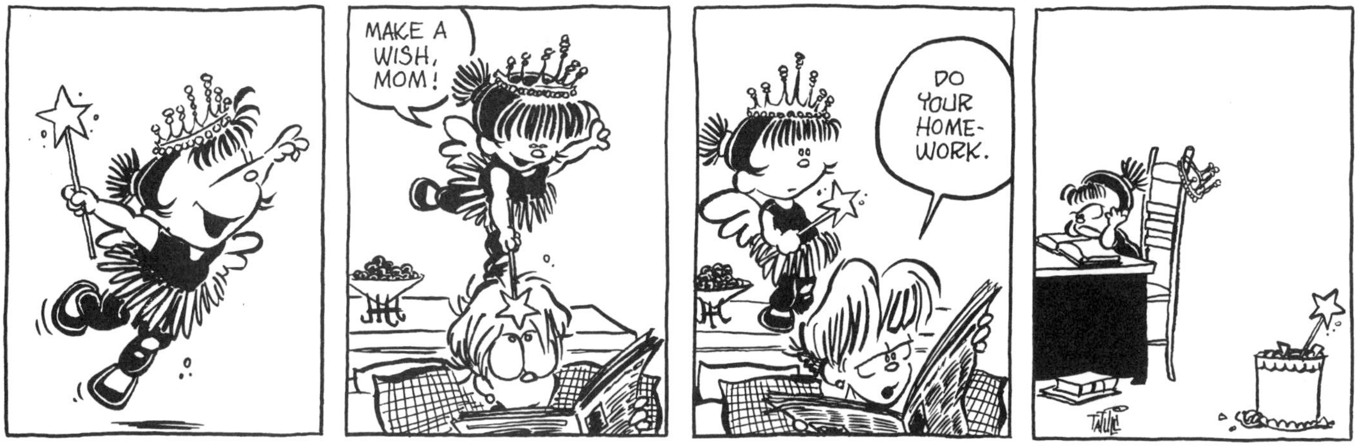
MAKE A WISH, MOM!
DO YOUR HOME-WORK.

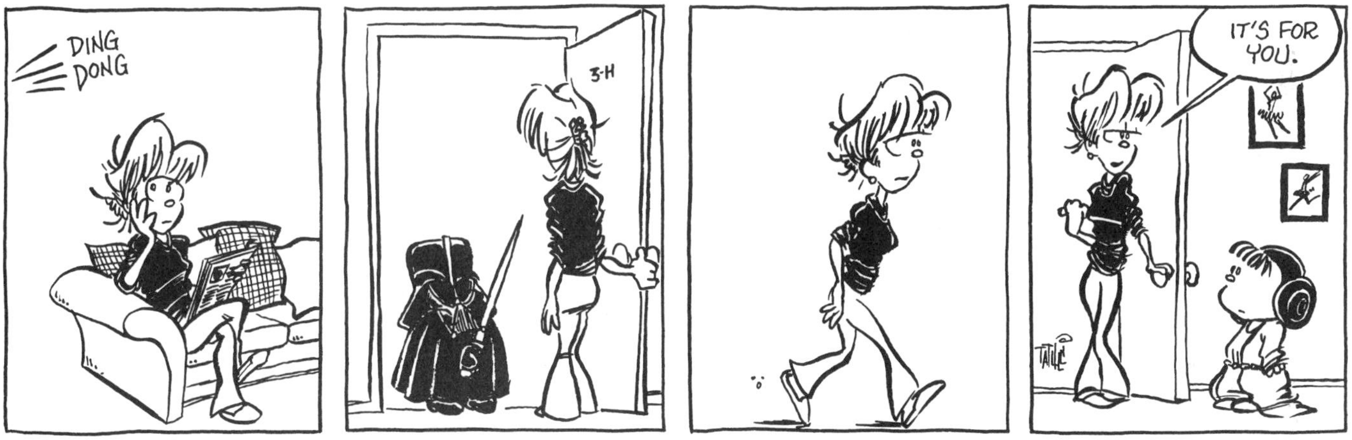
DING DONG
IT'S FOR YOU.

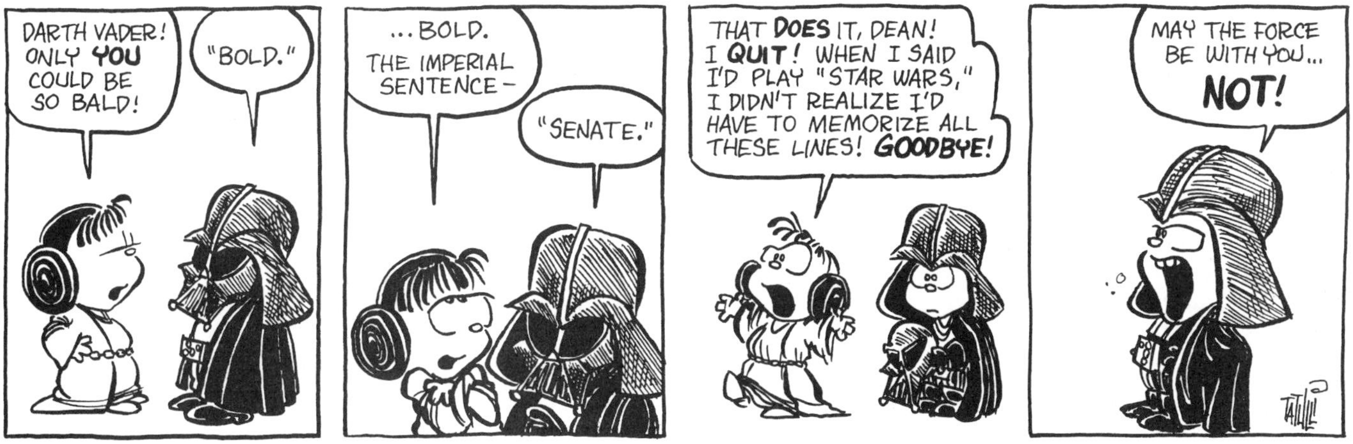
DARTH VADER! ONLY **YOU** COULD BE SO BALD!
"BOLD."
...BOLD. THE IMPERIAL SENTENCE–
"SENATE."
THAT **DOES** IT, DEAN! I **QUIT**! WHEN I SAID I'D PLAY "STAR WARS," I DIDN'T REALIZE I'D HAVE TO MEMORIZE ALL THESE LINES! **GOODBYE**!
MAY THE FORCE BE WITH YOU... **NOT!**

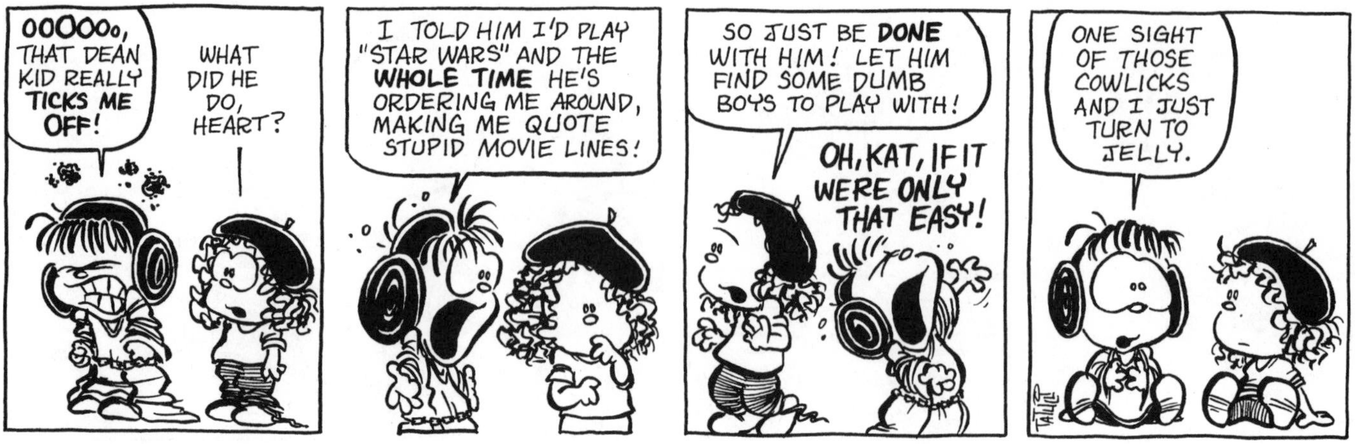
OOOOOo, THAT DEAN KID REALLY TICKS ME OFF!
WHAT DID HE DO, HEART?
I TOLD HIM I'D PLAY "STAR WARS" AND THE WHOLE TIME HE'S ORDERING ME AROUND, MAKING ME QUOTE STUPID MOVIE LINES!
SO JUST BE DONE WITH HIM! LET HIM FIND SOME DUMB BOYS TO PLAY WITH!
OH, KAT, IF IT WERE ONLY THAT EASY!
ONE SIGHT OF THOSE COWLICKS AND I JUST TURN TO JELLY.

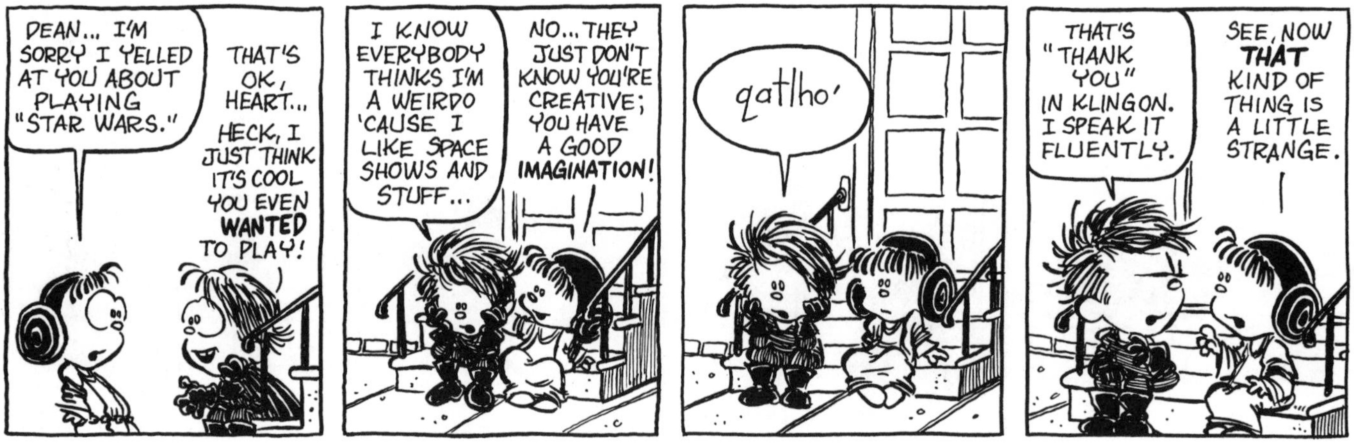
DEAN... I'M SORRY I YELLED AT YOU ABOUT PLAYING "STAR WARS."
THAT'S OK, HEART... HECK, I JUST THINK IT'S COOL YOU EVEN WANTED TO PLAY!
I KNOW EVERYBODY THINKS I'M A WEIRDO 'CAUSE I LIKE SPACE SHOWS AND STUFF...
NO... THEY JUST DON'T KNOW YOU'RE CREATIVE; YOU HAVE A GOOD IMAGINATION!
qatlho'
THAT'S "THANK YOU" IN KLINGON. I SPEAK IT FLUENTLY.
SEE, NOW THAT KIND OF THING IS A LITTLE STRANGE.

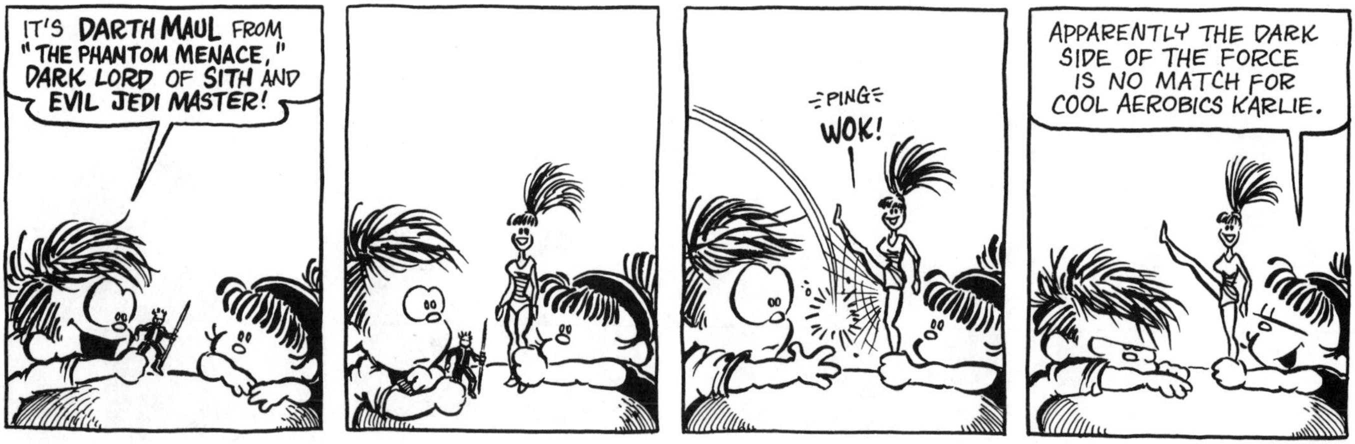
IT'S DARTH MAUL FROM "THE PHANTOM MENACE," DARK LORD OF SITH AND EVIL JEDI MASTER!
PING
WOK!
APPARENTLY THE DARK SIDE OF THE FORCE IS NO MATCH FOR COOL AEROBICS KARLIE.

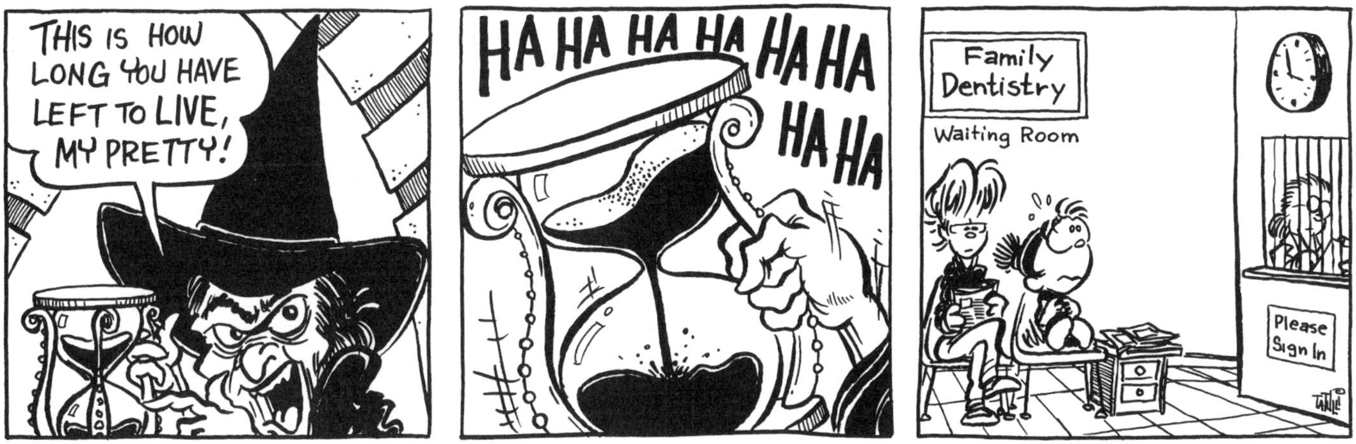
THIS IS HOW LONG YOU HAVE LEFT TO LIVE, MY PRETTY!
HA HA HA HA HA HA HA HA
Family Dentistry
Waiting Room
Please Sign In

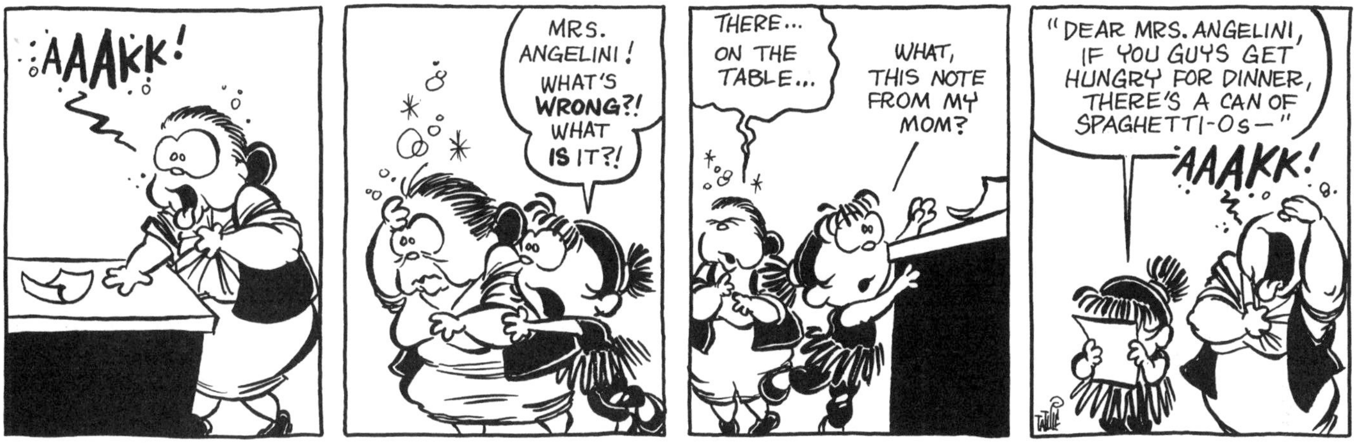
AAAKK!
MRS. ANGELINI! WHAT'S WRONG?! WHAT IS IT?!
THERE... ON THE TABLE...
WHAT, THIS NOTE FROM MY MOM?
"DEAR MRS. ANGELINI, IF YOU GUYS GET HUNGRY FOR DINNER, THERE'S A CAN OF SPAGHETTI-Os—"
AAAKK!

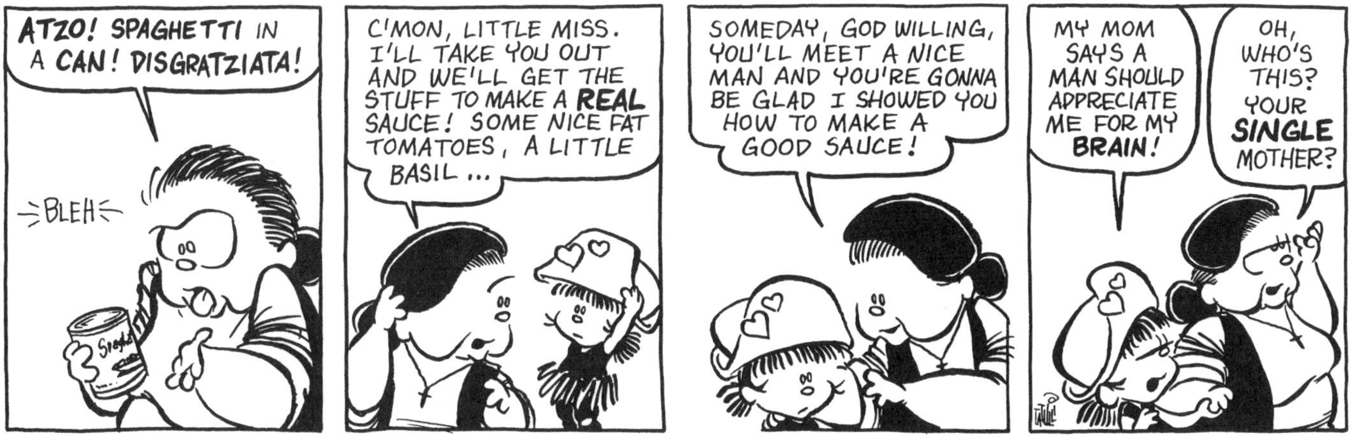
ATZO! SPAGHETTI IN A CAN! DISGRATZIATA!
BLEH
C'MON, LITTLE MISS. I'LL TAKE YOU OUT AND WE'LL GET THE STUFF TO MAKE A REAL SAUCE! SOME NICE FAT TOMATOES, A LITTLE BASIL...
SOMEDAY, GOD WILLING, YOU'LL MEET A NICE MAN AND YOU'RE GONNA BE GLAD I SHOWED YOU HOW TO MAKE A GOOD SAUCE!
MY MOM SAYS A MAN SHOULD APPRECIATE ME FOR MY BRAIN!
OH, WHO'S THIS? YOUR SINGLE MOTHER?

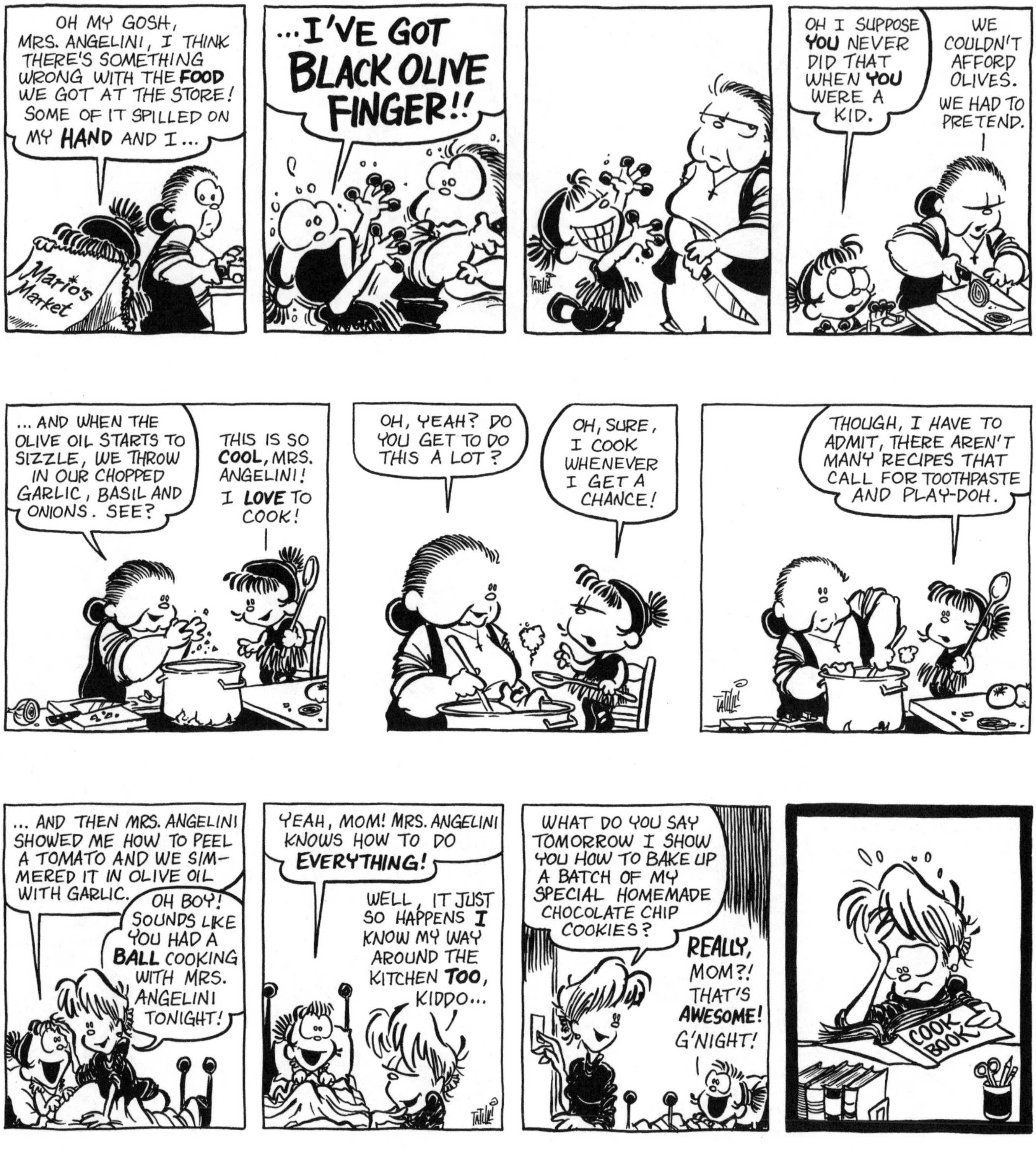
OH MY GOSH, MRS. ANGELINI, I THINK THERE'S SOMETHING WRONG WITH THE **FOOD** WE GOT AT THE STORE! SOME OF IT SPILLED ON MY **HAND** AND I...
Mario's Market
...I'VE GOT BLACK OLIVE FINGER!!
OH I SUPPOSE **YOU** NEVER DID THAT WHEN **YOU** WERE A KID.
WE COULDN'T AFFORD OLIVES. WE HAD TO PRETEND.
...AND WHEN THE OLIVE OIL STARTS TO SIZZLE, WE THROW IN OUR CHOPPED GARLIC, BASIL AND ONIONS. SEE?
THIS IS SO **COOL**, MRS. ANGELINI! I **LOVE** TO COOK!
OH, YEAH? DO YOU GET TO DO THIS A LOT?
OH, SURE, I COOK WHENEVER I GET A CHANCE!
THOUGH, I HAVE TO ADMIT, THERE AREN'T MANY RECIPES THAT CALL FOR TOOTHPASTE AND PLAY-DOH.
...AND THEN MRS. ANGELINI SHOWED ME HOW TO PEEL A TOMATO AND WE SIM-MERED IT IN OLIVE OIL WITH GARLIC.
OH BOY! SOUNDS LIKE YOU HAD A **BALL** COOKING WITH MRS. ANGELINI TONIGHT!
YEAH, MOM! MRS. ANGELINI KNOWS HOW TO DO **EVERYTHING!**
WELL, IT JUST SO HAPPENS **I** KNOW MY WAY AROUND THE KITCHEN **TOO**, KIDDO...
WHAT DO YOU SAY TOMORROW I SHOW YOU HOW TO BAKE UP A BATCH OF MY SPECIAL HOMEMADE CHOCOLATE CHIP COOKIES?
REALLY, MOM?! THAT'S **AWESOME!** G'NIGHT!
COOK BOOK

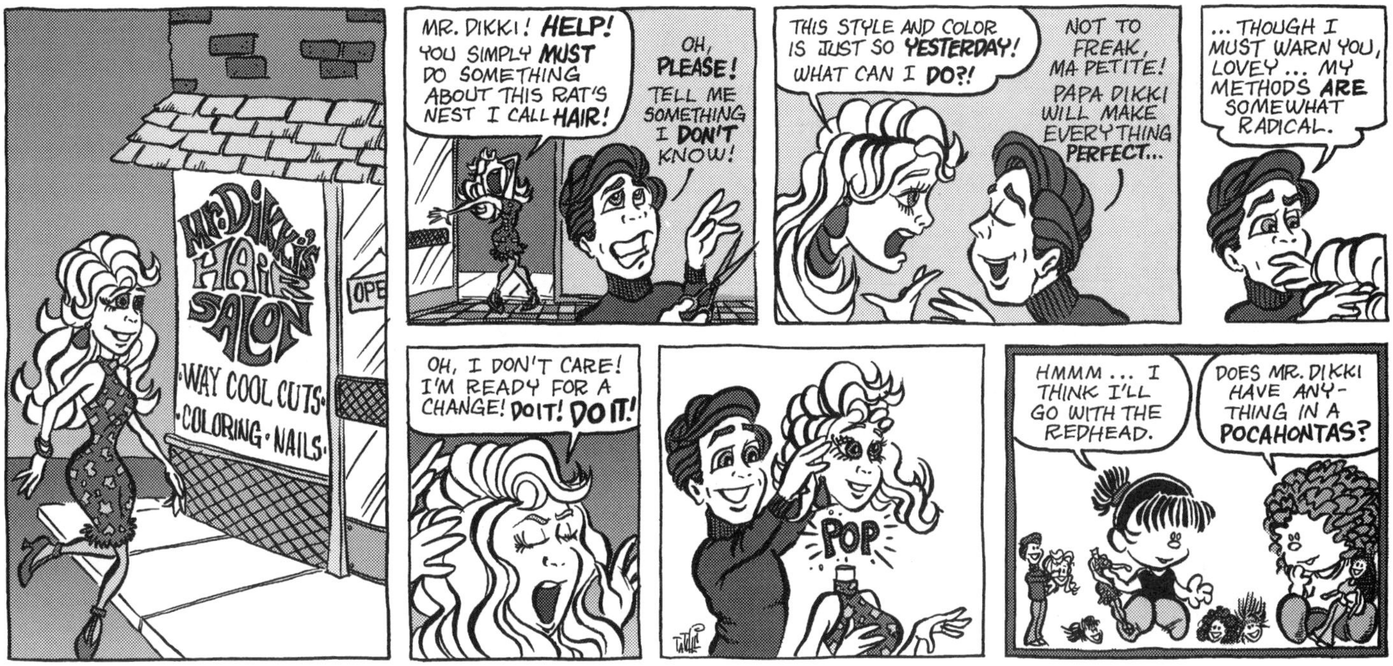
Mr. Dikki's Hair Salon
• Way Cool Cuts •
• Coloring • Nails •
OPE
MR. DIKKI! **HELP!** YOU SIMPLY **MUST** DO SOMETHING ABOUT THIS RAT'S NEST I CALL **HAIR!**
OH, **PLEASE!** TELL ME SOMETHING I **DON'T** KNOW!
THIS STYLE AND COLOR IS JUST SO **YESTERDAY!** WHAT CAN I **DO?!**
NOT TO FREAK, MA PETITE! PAPA DIKKI WILL MAKE EVERYTHING **PERFECT...**
... THOUGH I MUST WARN YOU, LOVEY ... MY METHODS **ARE** SOMEWHAT RADICAL.
OH, I DON'T CARE! I'M READY FOR A CHANGE! **DO IT! DO IT!**
POP
HMMM ... I THINK I'LL GO WITH THE REDHEAD.
DOES MR. DIKKI HAVE ANYTHING IN A **POCAHONTAS?**

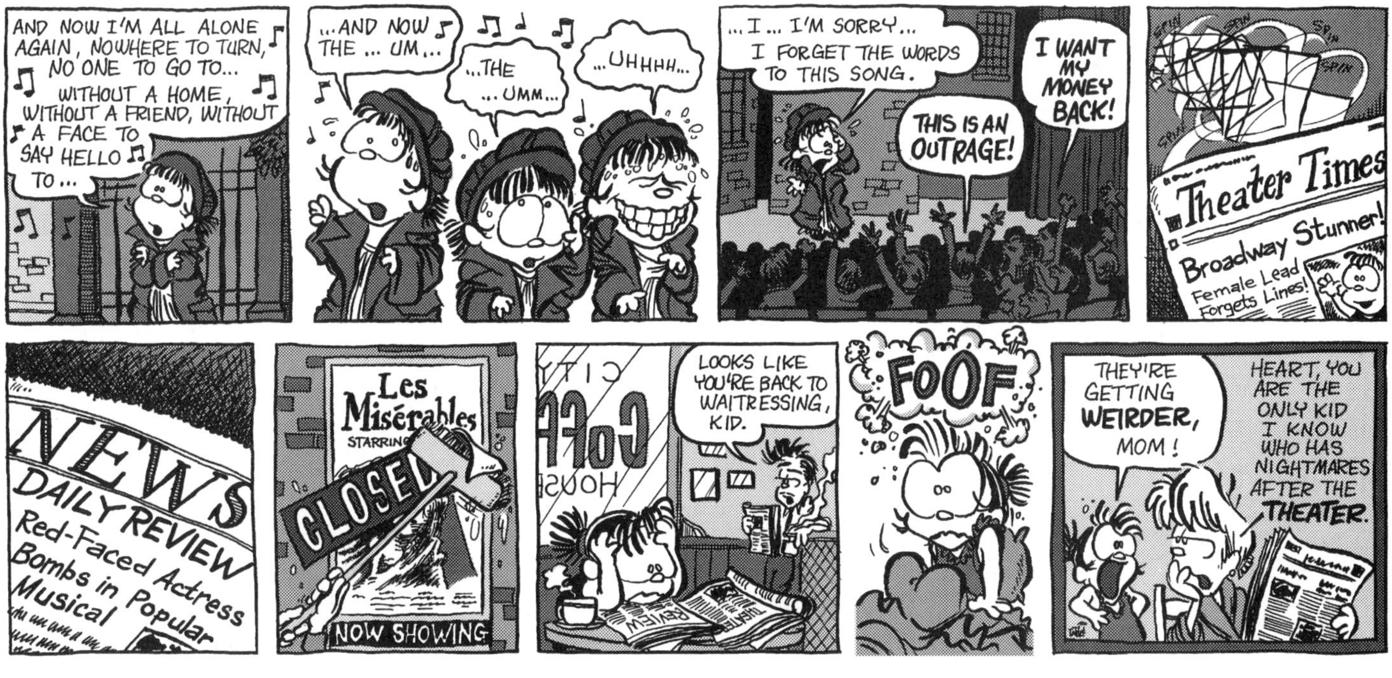
AND NOW I'M ALL ALONE AGAIN, NOWHERE TO TURN, NO ONE TO GO TO... WITHOUT A HOME, WITHOUT A FRIEND, WITHOUT A FACE TO SAY HELLO TO...
...AND NOW THE ... UM...
...THE ... UMM...
...UHHHH...
... I ... I'M SORRY... I FORGET THE WORDS TO THIS SONG.
THIS IS AN OUTRAGE!
I WANT MY MONEY BACK!
SPIN
SPIN
SPIN
SPIN
SPIN
Theater Times
Broadway Stunner!
Female Lead Forgets Lines!
NEWS
DAILY REVIEW
Red-Faced Actress Bombs in Popular Musical
Les Misérables
STARRING
CLOSED
NOW SHOWING
LOOKS LIKE YOU'RE BACK TO WAITRESSING, KID.
FOOF
THEY'RE GETTING **WEIRDER,** MOM!
HEART, YOU ARE THE ONLY KID I KNOW WHO HAS NIGHTMARES AFTER THE **THEATER.**

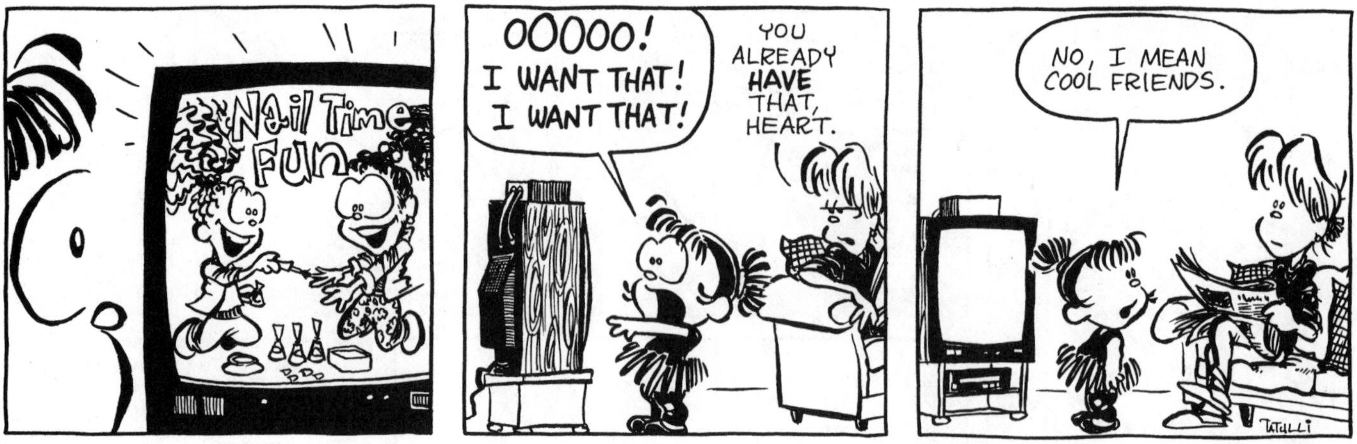
Nail Time Fun
OOOOO! I WANT THAT! I WANT THAT!
YOU ALREADY **HAVE** THAT, HEART.
NO, I MEAN COOL FRIENDS.
TATULLI

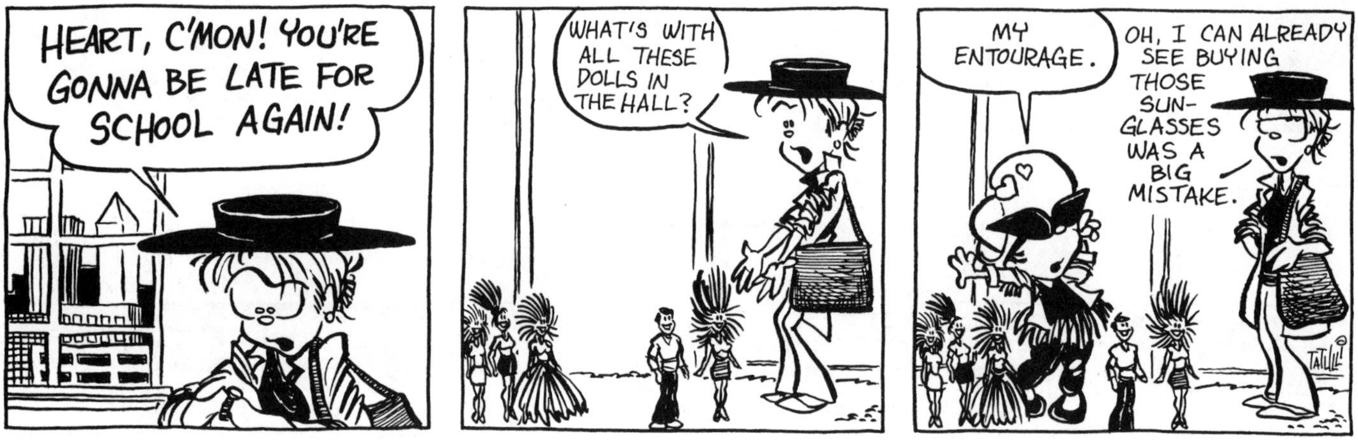
HEART, C'MON! YOU'RE GONNA BE LATE FOR SCHOOL AGAIN!
WHAT'S WITH ALL THESE DOLLS IN THE HALL?
MY ENTOURAGE.
OH, I CAN ALREADY SEE BUYING THOSE SUN-GLASSES WAS A BIG MISTAKE.
TATULLI

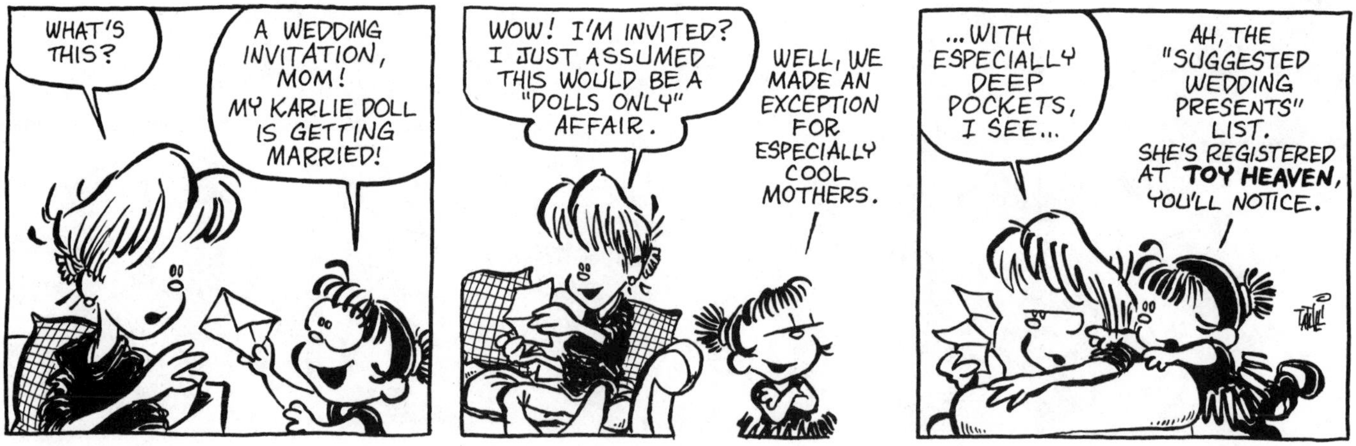
WHAT'S THIS?
A WEDDING INVITATION, MOM! MY KARLIE DOLL IS GETTING MARRIED!
WOW! I'M INVITED? I JUST ASSUMED THIS WOULD BE A "DOLLS ONLY" AFFAIR.
WELL, WE MADE AN EXCEPTION FOR ESPECIALLY COOL MOTHERS.
...WITH ESPECIALLY DEEP POCKETS, I SEE...
AH, THE "SUGGESTED WEDDING PRESENTS" LIST. SHE'S REGISTERED AT **TOY HEAVEN**, YOU'LL NOTICE.
TATULLI

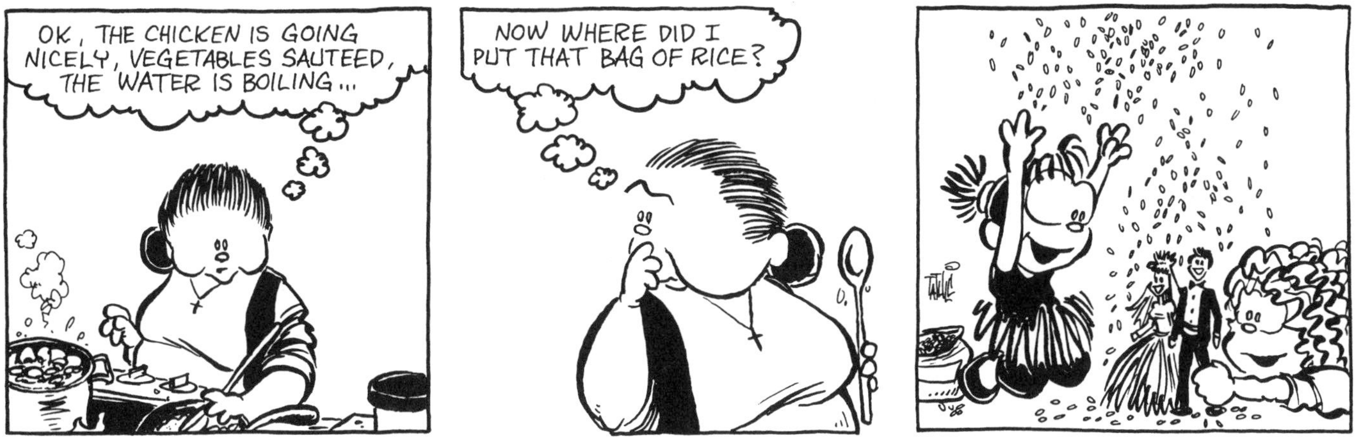
OK, THE CHICKEN IS GOING NICELY, VEGETABLES SAUTEED, THE WATER IS BOILING...
NOW WHERE DID I PUT THAT BAG OF RICE?

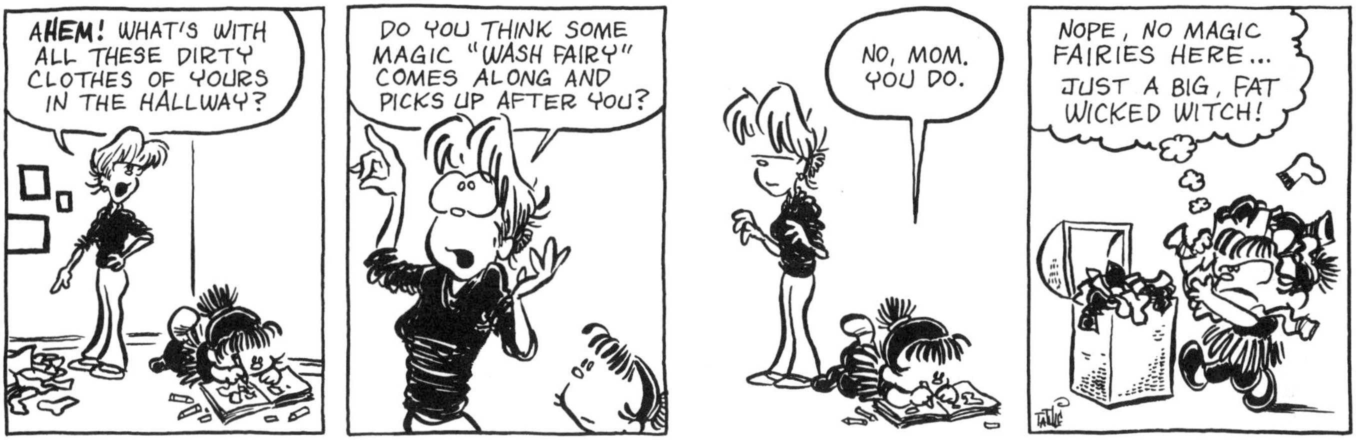
AHEM! WHAT'S WITH ALL THESE DIRTY CLOTHES OF YOURS IN THE HALLWAY?
DO YOU THINK SOME MAGIC "WASH FAIRY" COMES ALONG AND PICKS UP AFTER YOU?
NO, MOM. YOU DO.
NOPE, NO MAGIC FAIRIES HERE... JUST A BIG, FAT WICKED WITCH!

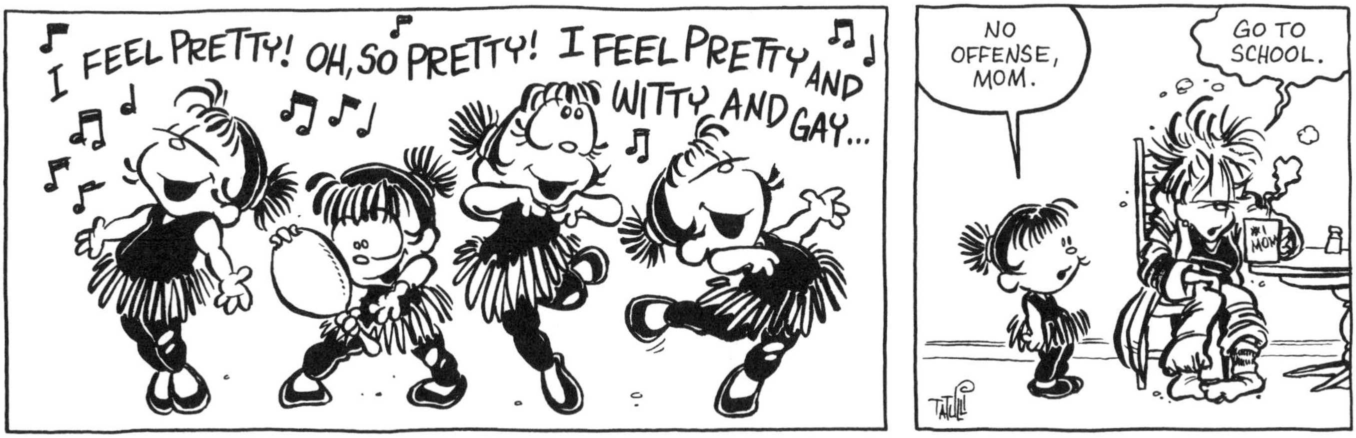
I FEEL PRETTY! OH, SO PRETTY! I FEEL PRETTY AND WITTY AND GAY...
NO OFFENSE, MOM.
GO TO SCHOOL.

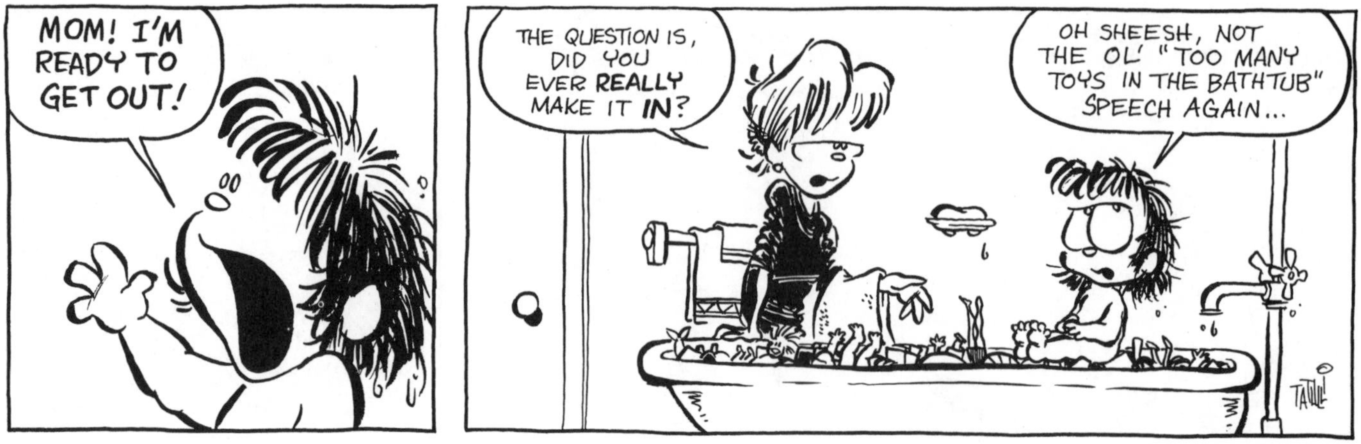
MOM! I'M READY TO GET OUT!
THE QUESTION IS, DID YOU EVER REALLY MAKE IT IN?
OH SHEESH, NOT THE OL' "TOO MANY TOYS IN THE BATHTUB" SPEECH AGAIN...

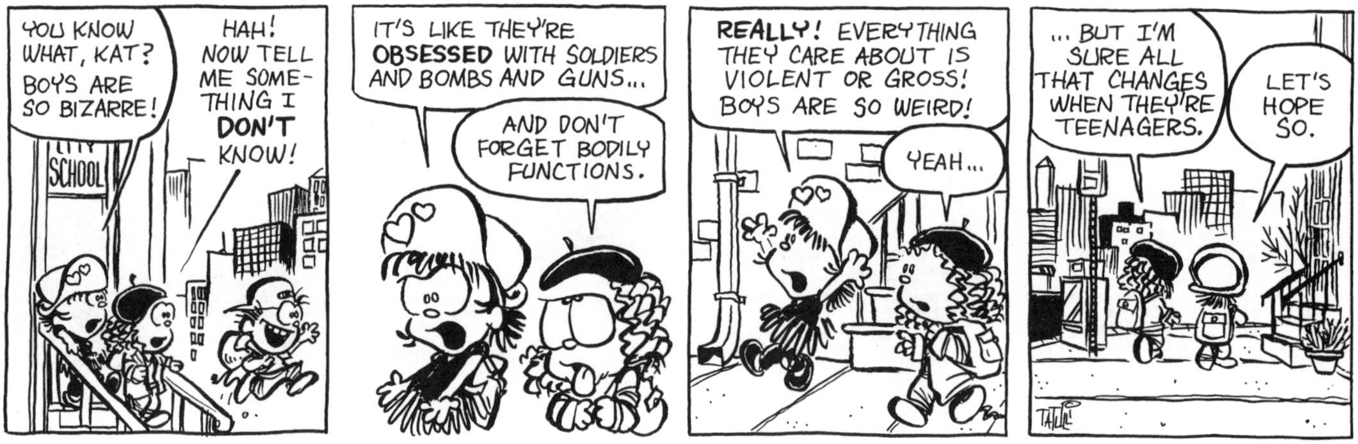
YOU KNOW WHAT, KAT? BOYS ARE SO BIZARRE!
HAH! NOW TELL ME SOMETHING I DON'T KNOW!
SCHOOL
IT'S LIKE THEY'RE OBSESSED WITH SOLDIERS AND BOMBS AND GUNS...
AND DON'T FORGET BODILY FUNCTIONS.
REALLY! EVERYTHING THEY CARE ABOUT IS VIOLENT OR GROSS! BOYS ARE SO WEIRD!
YEAH...
... BUT I'M SURE ALL THAT CHANGES WHEN THEY'RE TEENAGERS.
LET'S HOPE SO.

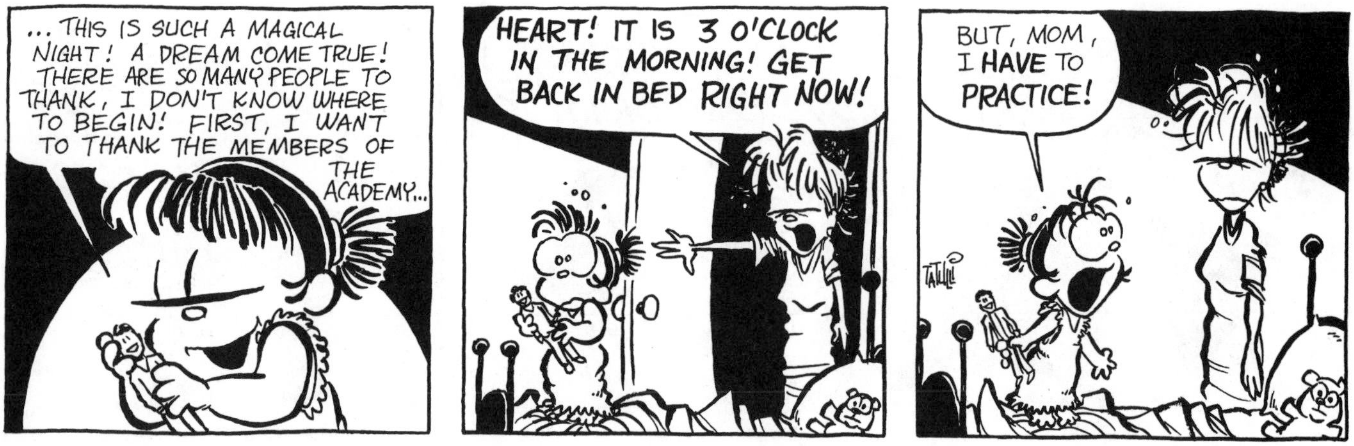
... THIS IS SUCH A MAGICAL NIGHT! A DREAM COME TRUE! THERE ARE SO MANY PEOPLE TO THANK, I DON'T KNOW WHERE TO BEGIN! FIRST, I WANT TO THANK THE MEMBERS OF THE ACADEMY...
HEART! IT IS 3 O'CLOCK IN THE MORNING! GET BACK IN BED RIGHT NOW!
BUT, MOM, I HAVE TO PRACTICE!

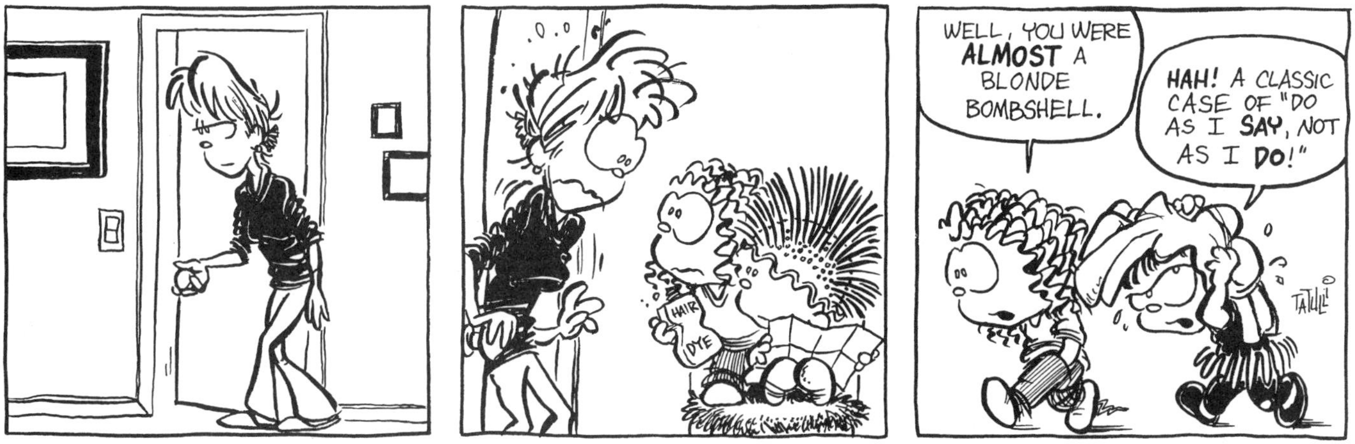
HAIR DYE
WELL, YOU WERE ALMOST A BLONDE BOMBSHELL.
HAH! A CLASSIC CASE OF "DO AS I SAY, NOT AS I DO!"

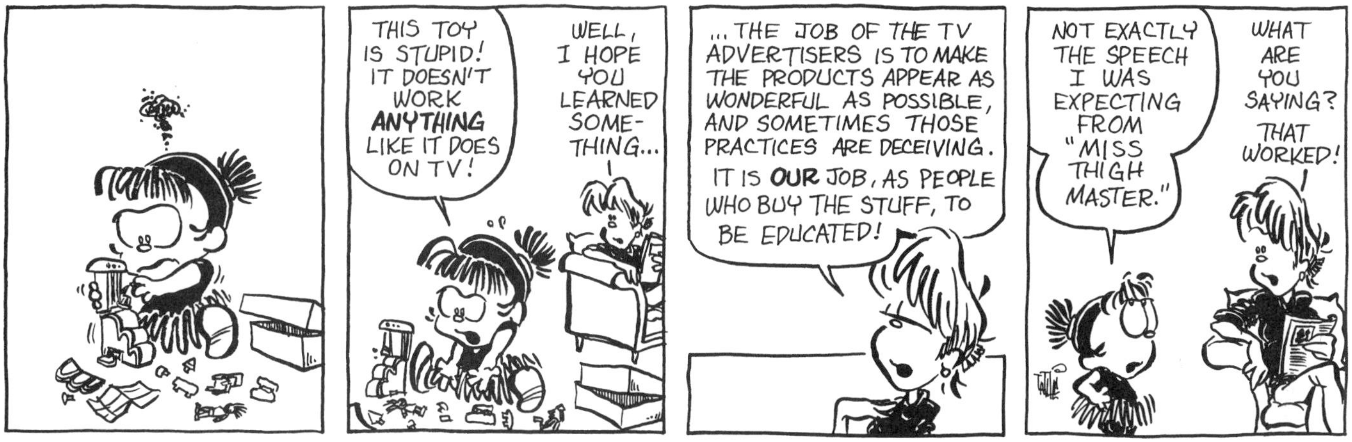
THIS TOY IS STUPID! IT DOESN'T WORK ANYTHING LIKE IT DOES ON TV!
WELL, I HOPE YOU LEARNED SOME-THING...
...THE JOB OF THE TV ADVERTISERS IS TO MAKE THE PRODUCTS APPEAR AS WONDERFUL AS POSSIBLE, AND SOMETIMES THOSE PRACTICES ARE DECEIVING.
IT IS OUR JOB, AS PEOPLE WHO BUY THE STUFF, TO BE EDUCATED!
NOT EXACTLY THE SPEECH I WAS EXPECTING FROM "MISS THIGH MASTER."
WHAT ARE YOU SAYING?
THAT WORKED!

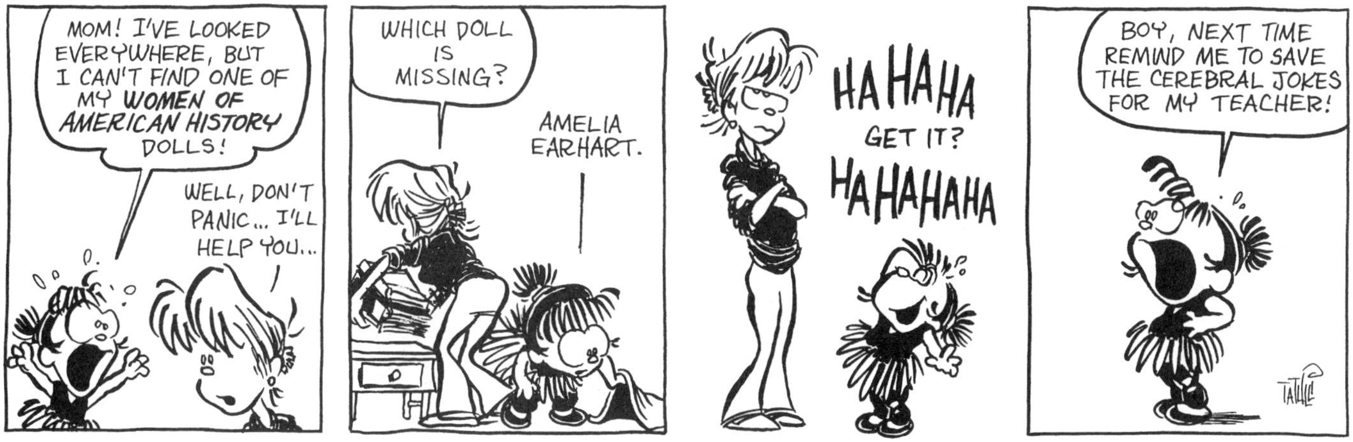
MOM! I'VE LOOKED EVERYWHERE, BUT I CAN'T FIND ONE OF MY WOMEN OF AMERICAN HISTORY DOLLS!
WELL, DON'T PANIC... I'LL HELP YOU...
WHICH DOLL IS MISSING?
AMELIA EARHART.
HAHAHA
GET IT?
HAHAHAHA
BOY, NEXT TIME REMIND ME TO SAVE THE CEREBRAL JOKES FOR MY TEACHER!

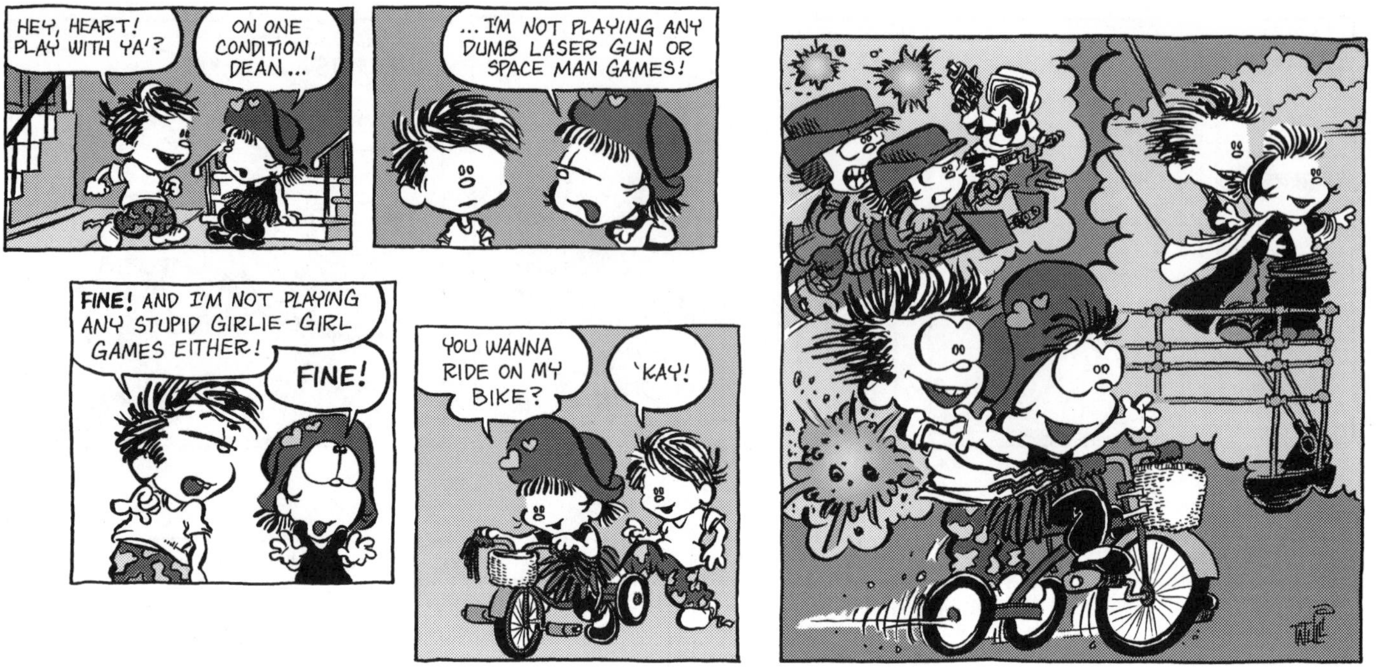
HEY, HEART! PLAY WITH YA'?
ON ONE CONDITION, DEAN...
...I'M NOT PLAYING ANY DUMB LASER GUN OR SPACE MAN GAMES!
FINE! AND I'M NOT PLAYING ANY STUPID GIRLIE-GIRL GAMES EITHER!
FINE!
YOU WANNA RIDE ON MY BIKE?
'KAY!

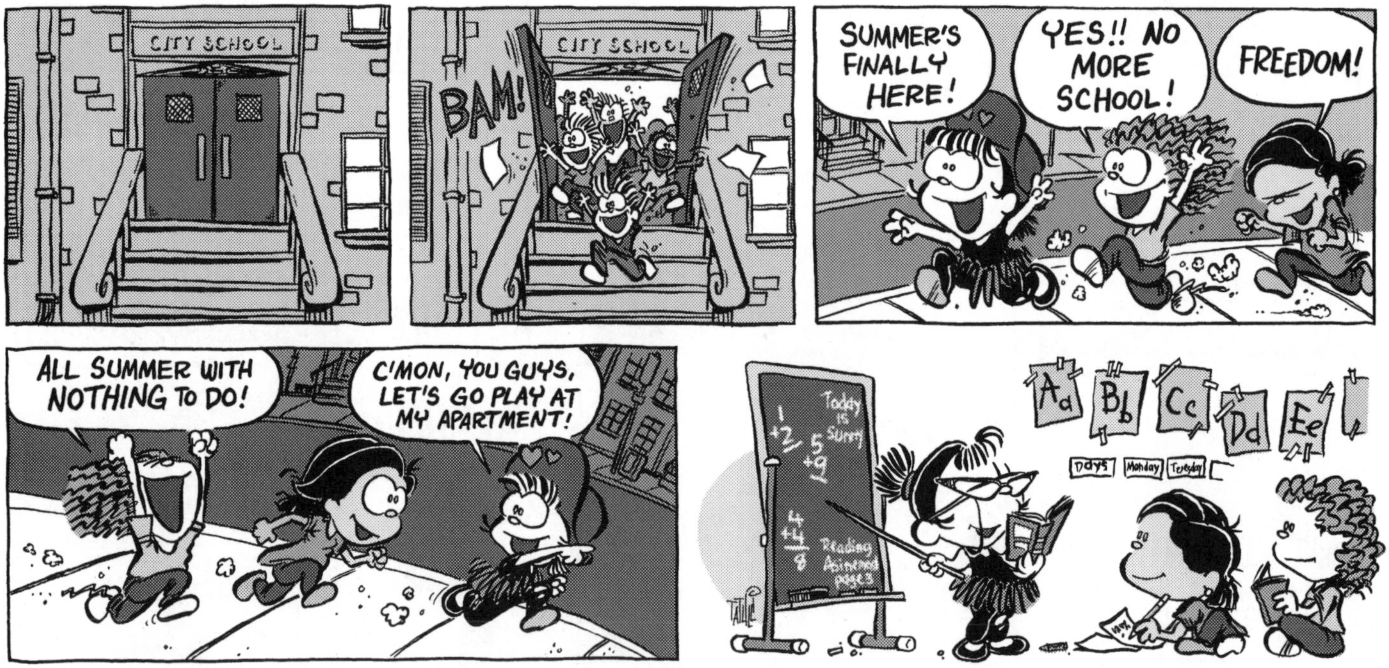
CITY SCHOOL
CITY SCHOOL
BAM!
SUMMER'S FINALLY HERE!
YES!! NO MORE SCHOOL!
FREEDOM!
ALL SUMMER WITH NOTHING TO DO!
C'MON, YOU GUYS, LET'S GO PLAY AT MY APARTMENT!
Aa Bb Cc Dd Ee
Monday Tuesday

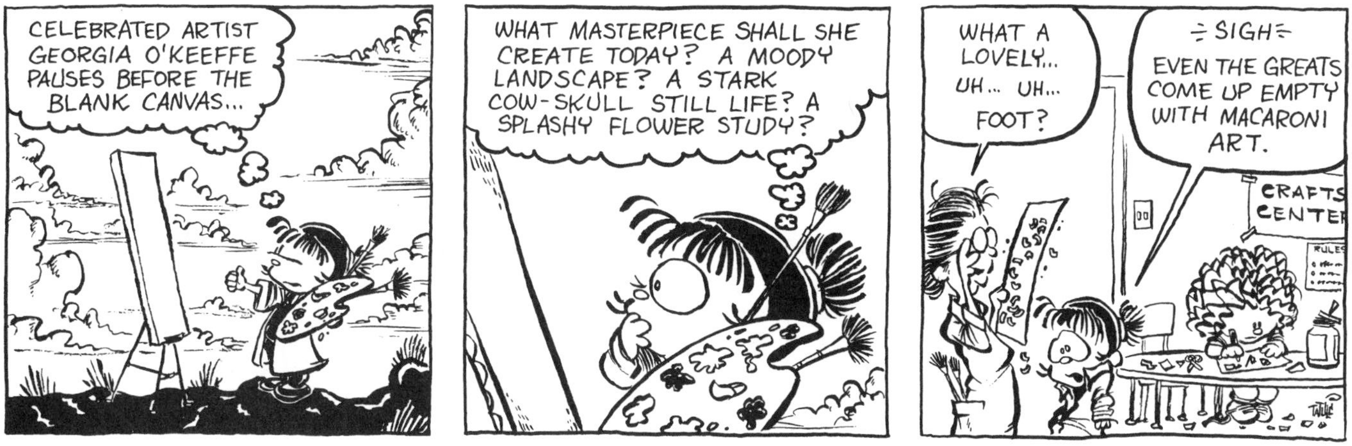
CELEBRATED ARTIST GEORGIA O'KEEFFE PAUSES BEFORE THE BLANK CANVAS...
WHAT MASTERPIECE SHALL SHE CREATE TODAY? A MOODY LANDSCAPE? A STARK COW-SKULL STILL LIFE? A SPLASHY FLOWER STUDY?
WHAT A LOVELY... UH... UH... FOOT?
SIGH
EVEN THE GREATS COME UP EMPTY WITH MACARONI ART.
CRAFTS CENTER
RULES

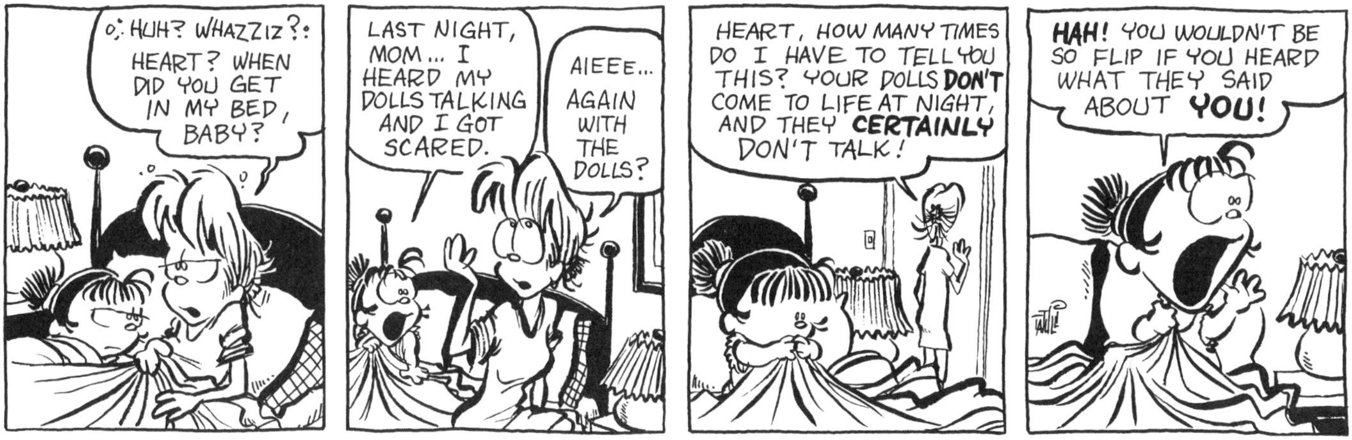
HUH? WHAZZIZ?
HEART? WHEN DID YOU GET IN MY BED, BABY?
LAST NIGHT, MOM... I HEARD MY DOLLS TALKING AND I GOT SCARED.
AIEEE... AGAIN WITH THE DOLLS?
HEART, HOW MANY TIMES DO I HAVE TO TELL YOU THIS? YOUR DOLLS **DON'T** COME TO LIFE AT NIGHT, AND THEY **CERTAINLY** DON'T TALK!
HAH! YOU WOULDN'T BE SO FLIP IF YOU HEARD WHAT THEY SAID ABOUT **YOU!**

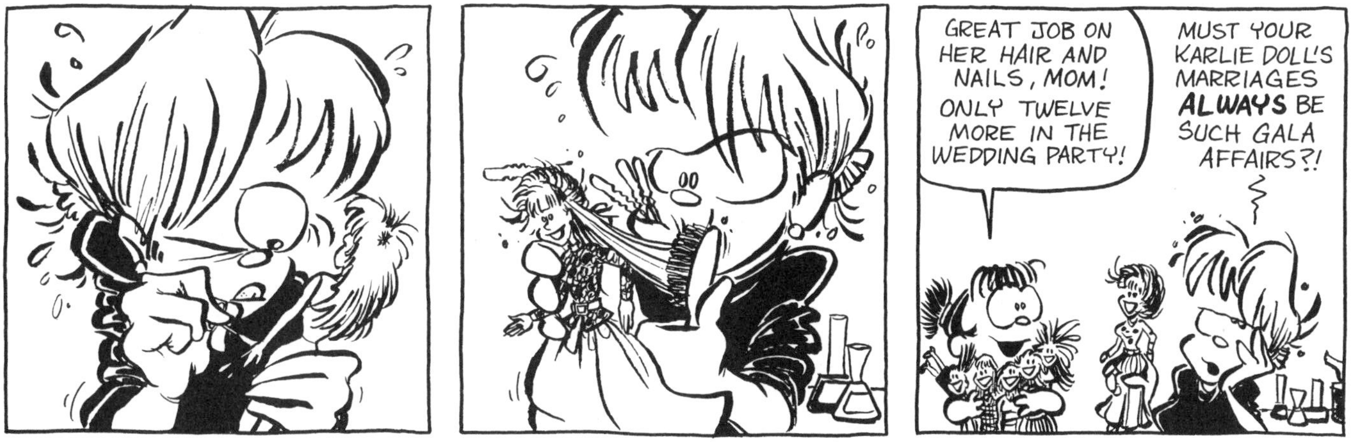
GREAT JOB ON HER HAIR AND NAILS, MOM! ONLY TWELVE MORE IN THE WEDDING PARTY!
MUST YOUR KARLIE DOLL'S MARRIAGES **ALWAYS** BE SUCH GALA AFFAIRS?!

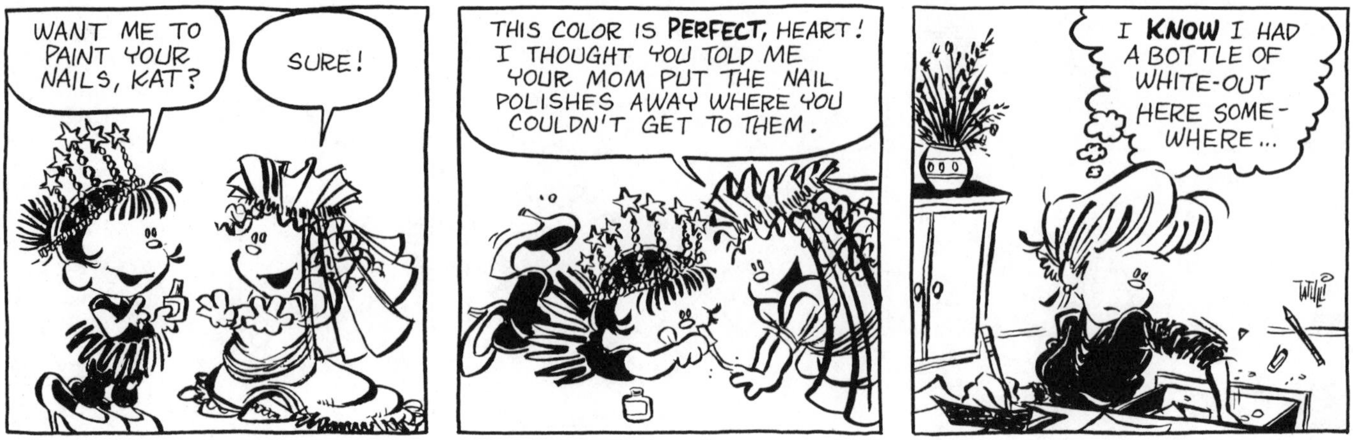
WANT ME TO PAINT YOUR NAILS, KAT?
SURE!
THIS COLOR IS **PERFECT**, HEART! I THOUGHT YOU TOLD ME YOUR MOM PUT THE NAIL POLISHES AWAY WHERE YOU COULDN'T GET TO THEM.
I **KNOW** I HAD A BOTTLE OF WHITE-OUT HERE SOMEWHERE...

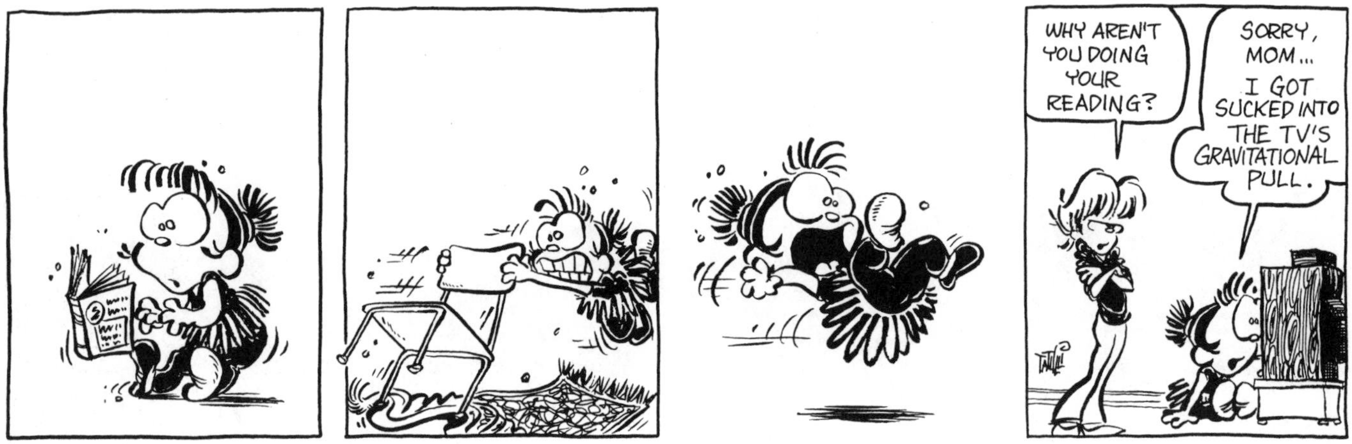
WHY AREN'T YOU DOING YOUR READING?
SORRY, MOM... I GOT SUCKED INTO THE TV'S GRAVITATIONAL PULL.

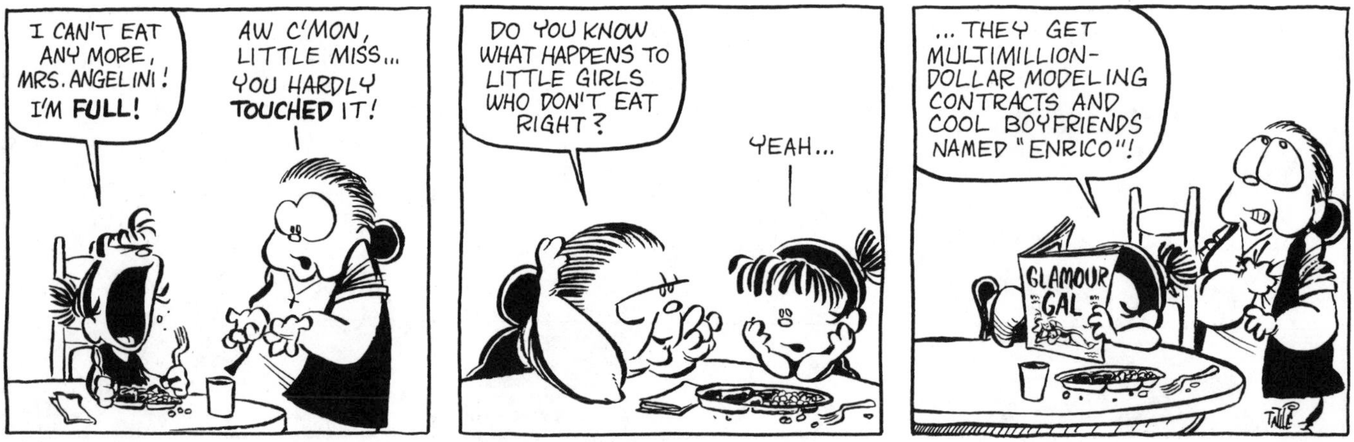
I CAN'T EAT ANY MORE, MRS. ANGELINI! I'M **FULL**!
AW C'MON, LITTLE MISS... YOU HARDLY **TOUCHED** IT!
DO YOU KNOW WHAT HAPPENS TO LITTLE GIRLS WHO DON'T EAT RIGHT?
YEAH...
...THEY GET MULTIMILLION-DOLLAR MODELING CONTRACTS AND COOL BOYFRIENDS NAMED "ENRICO"!
GLAMOUR GAL

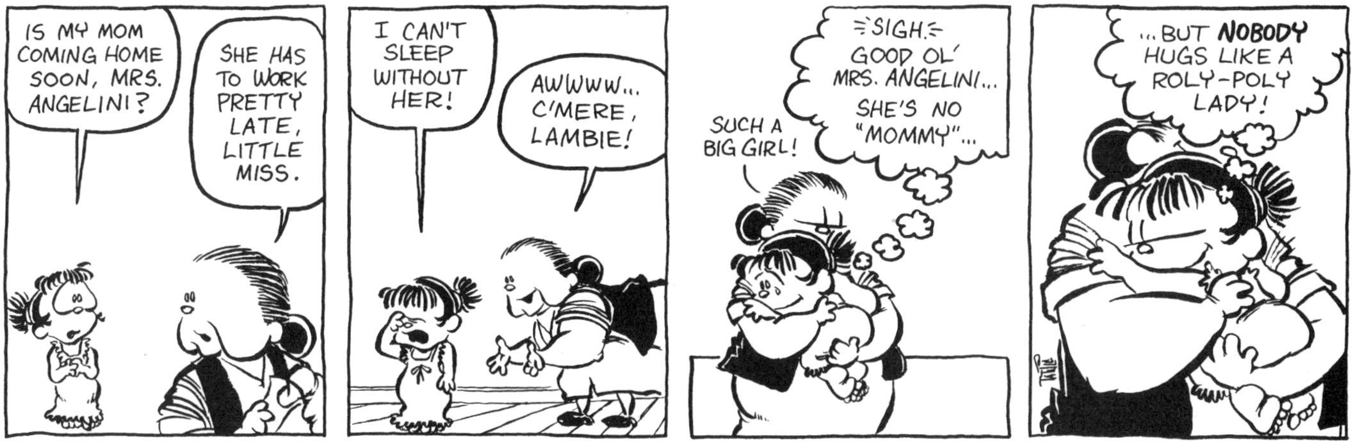
IS MY MOM COMING HOME SOON, MRS. ANGELINI?
SHE HAS TO WORK PRETTY LATE, LITTLE MISS.
I CAN'T SLEEP WITHOUT HER!
AWWWW... C'MERE, LAMBIE!
SUCH A BIG GIRL!
SIGH. GOOD OL' MRS. ANGELINI... SHE'S NO "MOMMY"...
...BUT NOBODY HUGS LIKE A ROLY-POLY LADY!

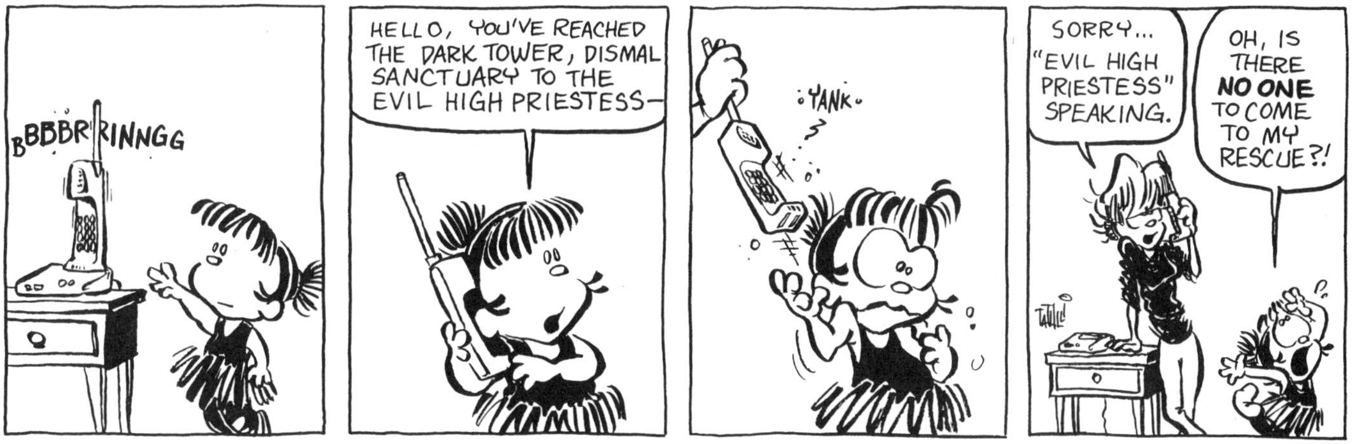
BBBBRRINNGG
HELLO, YOU'VE REACHED THE DARK TOWER, DISMAL SANCTUARY TO THE EVIL HIGH PRIESTESS—
YANK
SORRY... "EVIL HIGH PRIESTESS" SPEAKING.
OH, IS THERE NO ONE TO COME TO MY RESCUE?!

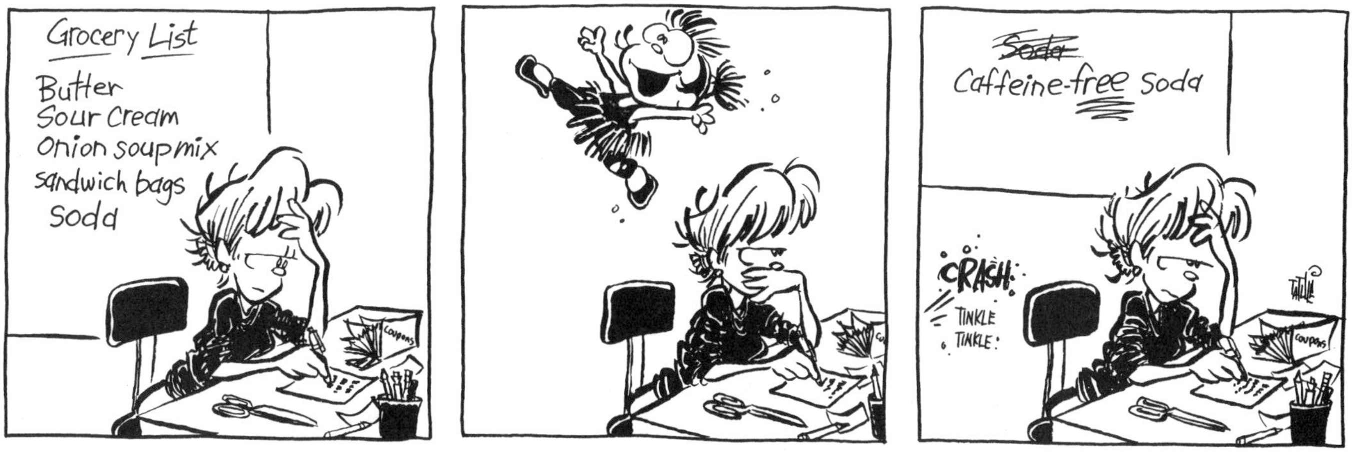
Grocery List
Butter
Sour Cream
Onion soupmix
sandwich bags
Soda
Soda
Caffeine-free Soda
CRASH
TINKLE
TINKLE

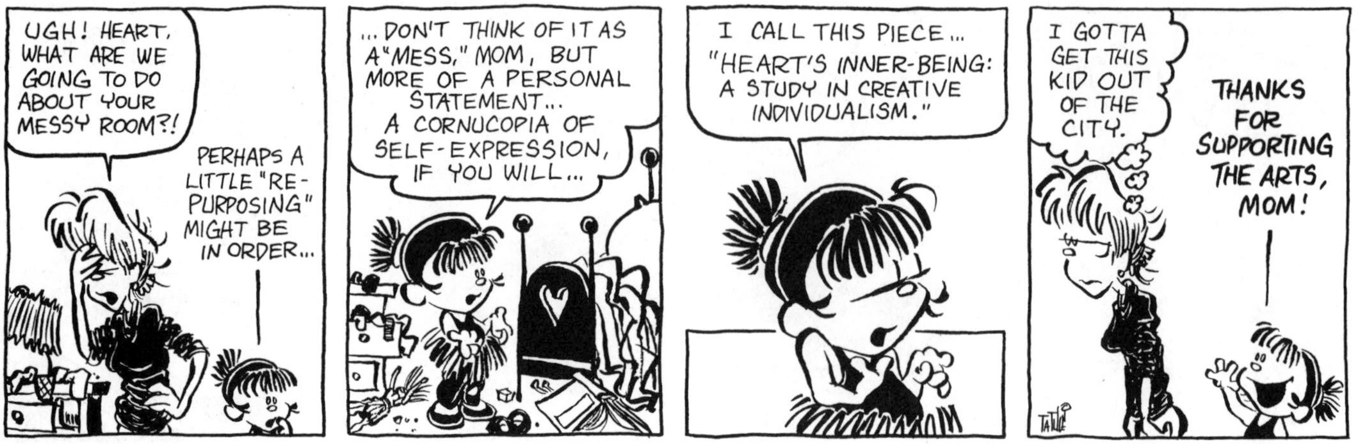
UGH! HEART, WHAT ARE WE GOING TO DO ABOUT YOUR MESSY ROOM?!
PERHAPS A LITTLE "RE-PURPOSING" MIGHT BE IN ORDER...
...DON'T THINK OF IT AS A "MESS," MOM, BUT MORE OF A PERSONAL STATEMENT... A CORNUCOPIA OF SELF-EXPRESSION, IF YOU WILL...
I CALL THIS PIECE... "HEART'S INNER-BEING: A STUDY IN CREATIVE INDIVIDUALISM."
I GOTTA GET THIS KID OUT OF THE CITY.
THANKS FOR SUPPORTING THE ARTS, MOM!

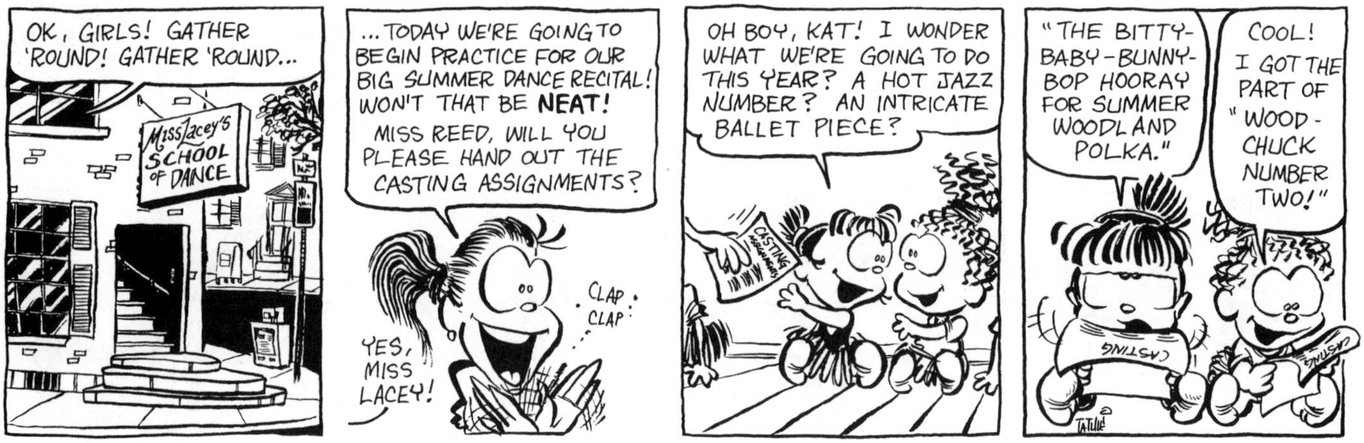
OK, GIRLS! GATHER 'ROUND! GATHER 'ROUND...
Miss Lacey's SCHOOL of DANCE
...TODAY WE'RE GOING TO BEGIN PRACTICE FOR OUR BIG SUMMER DANCE RECITAL! WON'T THAT BE NEAT!
MISS REED, WILL YOU PLEASE HAND OUT THE CASTING ASSIGNMENTS?
YES, MISS LACEY!
CLAP CLAP
OH BOY, KAT! I WONDER WHAT WE'RE GOING TO DO THIS YEAR? A HOT JAZZ NUMBER? AN INTRICATE BALLET PIECE?
"THE BITTY-BABY-BUNNY-BOP HOORAY FOR SUMMER WOODLAND POLKA."
COOL! I GOT THE PART OF "WOODCHUCK NUMBER TWO!"

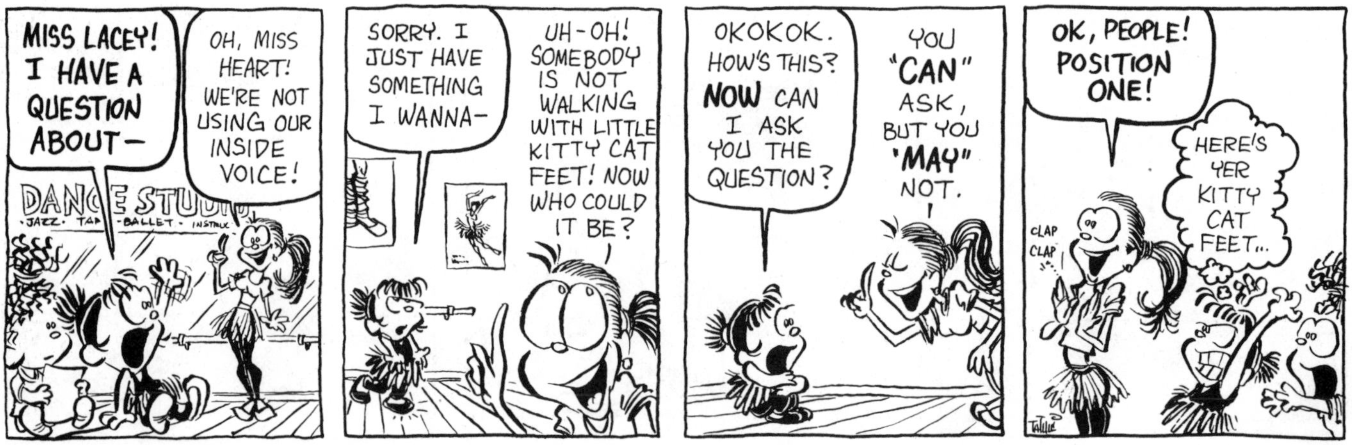
MISS LACEY! I HAVE A QUESTION ABOUT—
OH, MISS HEART! WE'RE NOT USING OUR INSIDE VOICE!
DANCE STUDIO
SORRY. I JUST HAVE SOMETHING I WANNA—
UH-OH! SOMEBODY IS NOT WALKING WITH LITTLE KITTY CAT FEET! NOW WHO COULD IT BE?
OKOKOK. HOW'S THIS? NOW CAN I ASK YOU THE QUESTION?
YOU "CAN" ASK, BUT YOU "MAY" NOT.
OK, PEOPLE! POSITION ONE!
HERE'S YER KITTY CAT FEET...
CLAP CLAP

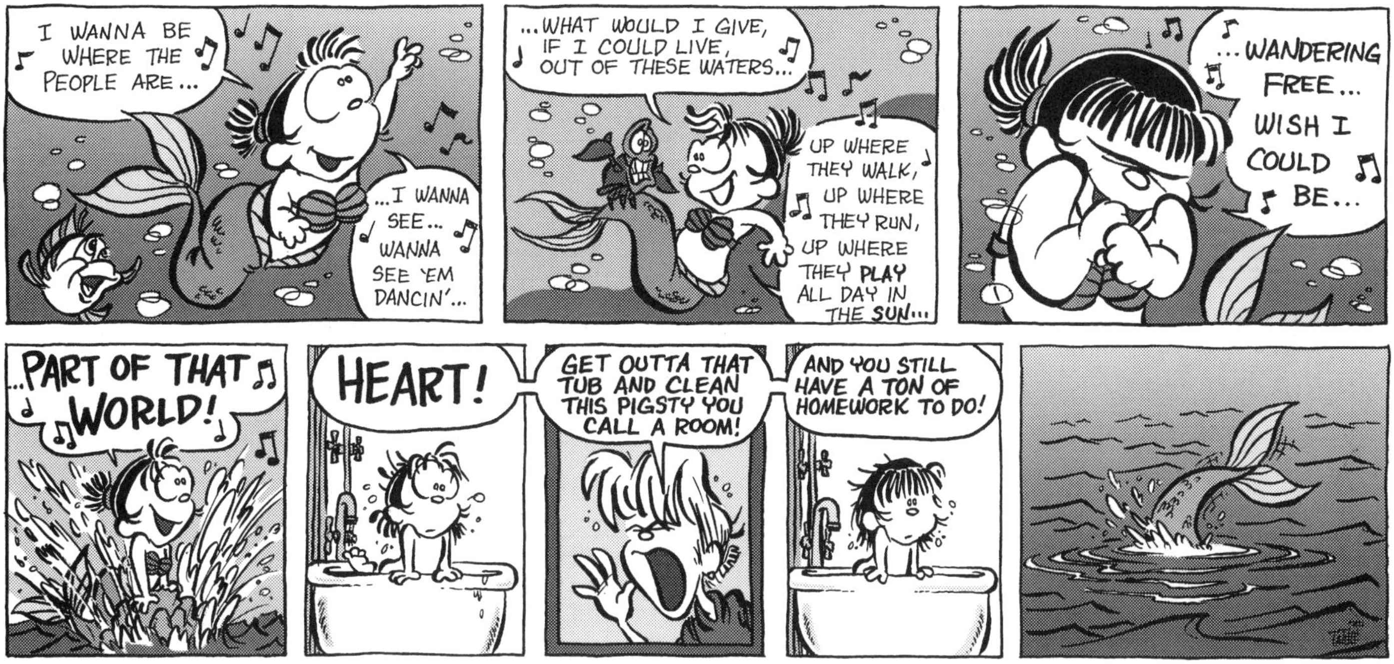
I WANNA BE WHERE THE PEOPLE ARE...
...I WANNA SEE... WANNA SEE 'EM DANCIN'...
...WHAT WOULD I GIVE, IF I COULD LIVE, OUT OF THESE WATERS...
UP WHERE THEY WALK, UP WHERE THEY RUN, UP WHERE THEY PLAY ALL DAY IN THE SUN...
...WANDERING FREE... WISH I COULD BE...
...PART OF THAT WORLD!
HEART!
GET OUTTA THAT TUB AND CLEAN THIS PIGSTY YOU CALL A ROOM!
AND YOU STILL HAVE A TON OF HOMEWORK TO DO!

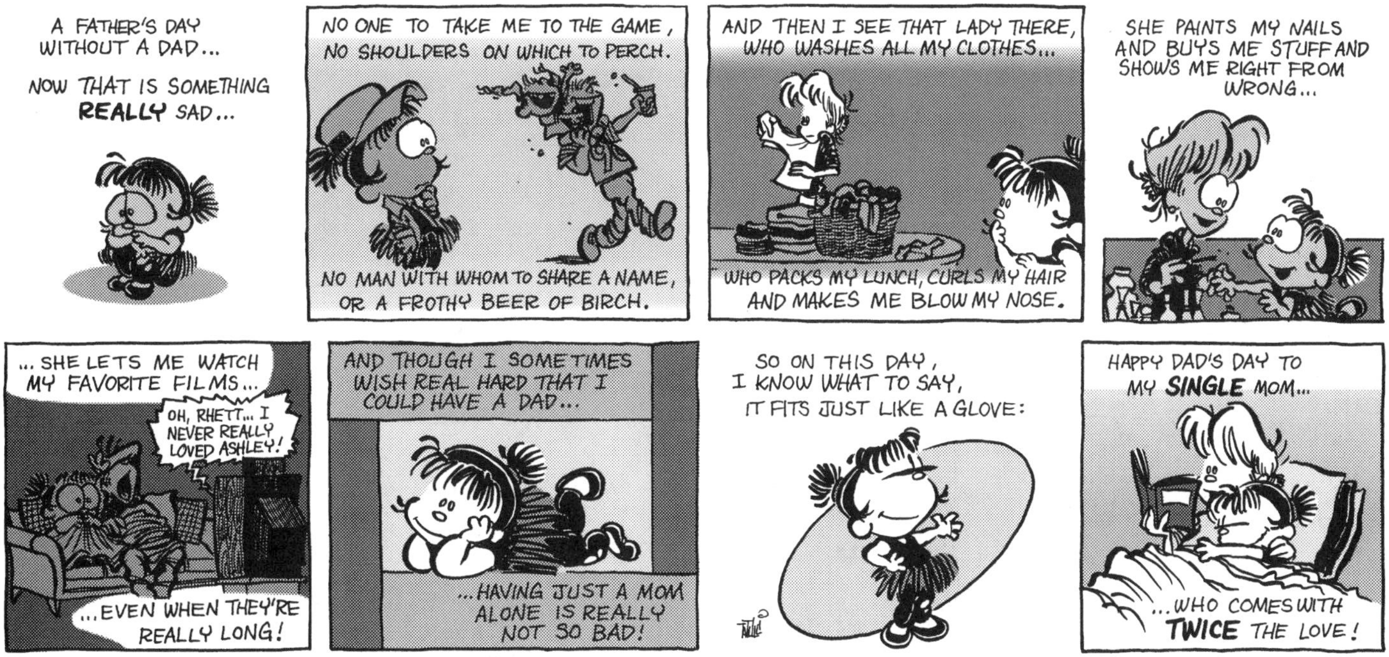
A FATHER'S DAY WITHOUT A DAD...
NOW THAT IS SOMETHING REALLY SAD...
NO ONE TO TAKE ME TO THE GAME, NO SHOULDERS ON WHICH TO PERCH.
NO MAN WITH WHOM TO SHARE A NAME, OR A FROTHY BEER OF BIRCH.
AND THEN I SEE THAT LADY THERE, WHO WASHES ALL MY CLOTHES...
WHO PACKS MY LUNCH, CURLS MY HAIR AND MAKES ME BLOW MY NOSE.
SHE PAINTS MY NAILS AND BUYS ME STUFF AND SHOWS ME RIGHT FROM WRONG...
... SHE LETS ME WATCH MY FAVORITE FILMS...
OH, RHETT... I NEVER REALLY LOVED ASHLEY!
...EVEN WHEN THEY'RE REALLY LONG!
AND THOUGH I SOMETIMES WISH REAL HARD THAT I COULD HAVE A DAD...
...HAVING JUST A MOM ALONE IS REALLY NOT SO BAD!
SO ON THIS DAY, I KNOW WHAT TO SAY, IT FITS JUST LIKE A GLOVE:
HAPPY DAD'S DAY TO MY SINGLE MOM...
...WHO COMES WITH TWICE THE LOVE!

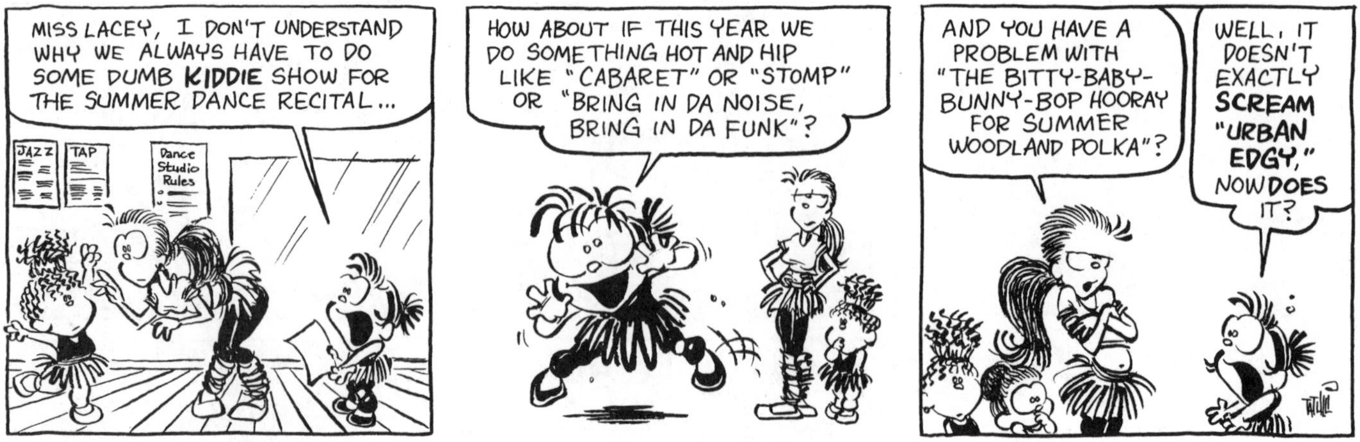
MISS LACEY, I DON'T UNDERSTAND WHY WE ALWAYS HAVE TO DO SOME DUMB KIDDIE SHOW FOR THE SUMMER DANCE RECITAL...
JAZZ
TAP
Dance Studio Rules
HOW ABOUT IF THIS YEAR WE DO SOMETHING HOT AND HIP LIKE "CABARET" OR "STOMP" OR "BRING IN DA NOISE, BRING IN DA FUNK"?
AND YOU HAVE A PROBLEM WITH "THE BITTY-BABY-BUNNY-BOP HOORAY FOR SUMMER WOODLAND POLKA"?
WELL, IT DOESN'T EXACTLY SCREAM "URBAN EDGY," NOW DOES IT?

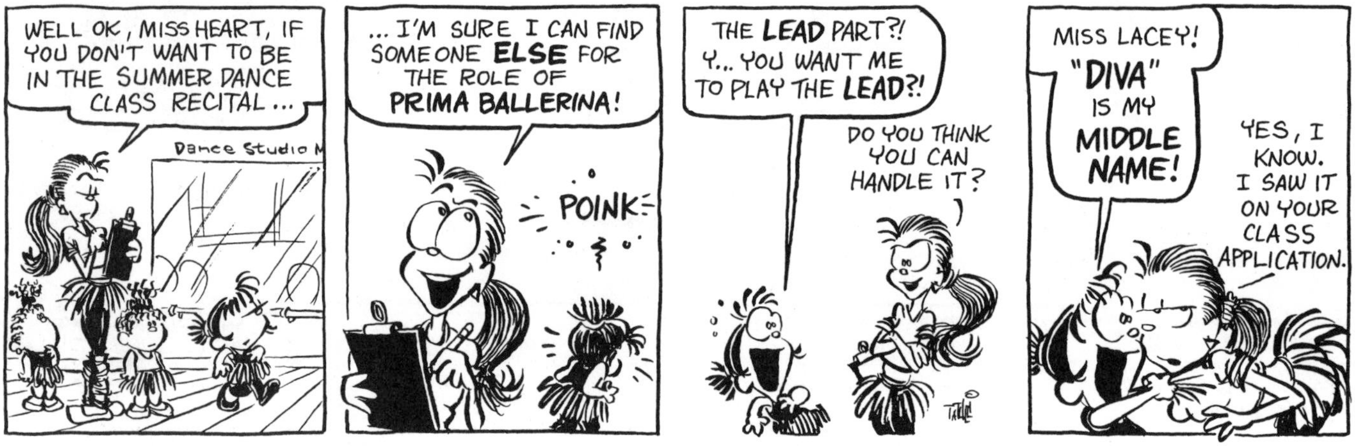
WELL OK, MISS HEART, IF YOU DON'T WANT TO BE IN THE SUMMER DANCE CLASS RECITAL...
Dance Studio M
...I'M SURE I CAN FIND SOMEONE ELSE FOR THE ROLE OF PRIMA BALLERINA!
POINK
THE LEAD PART?! Y... YOU WANT ME TO PLAY THE LEAD?!
DO YOU THINK YOU CAN HANDLE IT?
MISS LACEY! "DIVA" IS MY MIDDLE NAME!
YES, I KNOW. I SAW IT ON YOUR CLASS APPLICATION.

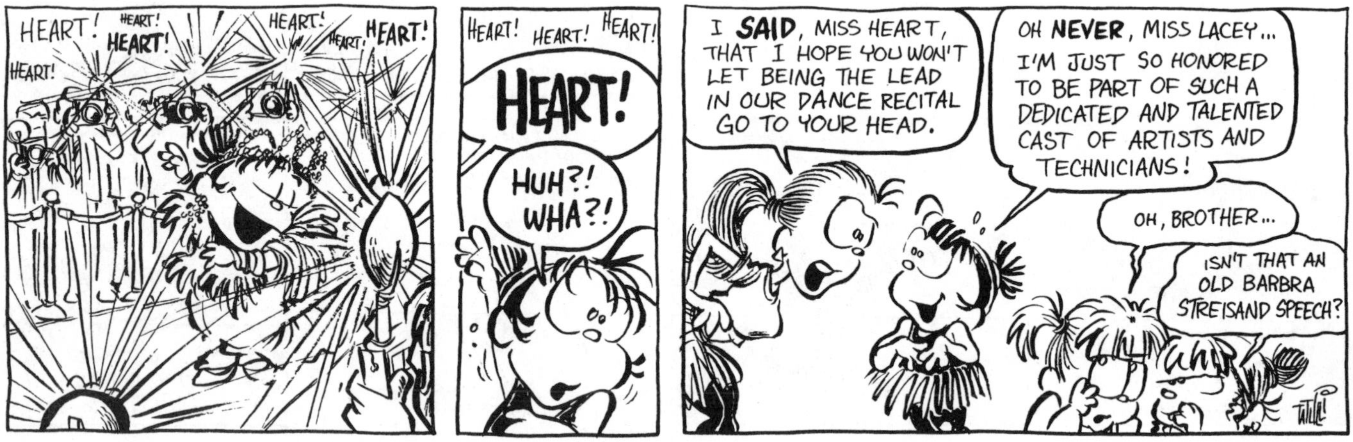
HEART! HEART! HEART! HEART! HEART! HEART! HEART!
HEART! HEART! HEART!
HEART!
HUH?! WHA?!
I SAID, MISS HEART, THAT I HOPE YOU WON'T LET BEING THE LEAD IN OUR DANCE RECITAL GO TO YOUR HEAD.
OH NEVER, MISS LACEY... I'M JUST SO HONORED TO BE PART OF SUCH A DEDICATED AND TALENTED CAST OF ARTISTS AND TECHNICIANS!
OH, BROTHER...
ISN'T THAT AN OLD BARBRA STREISAND SPEECH?

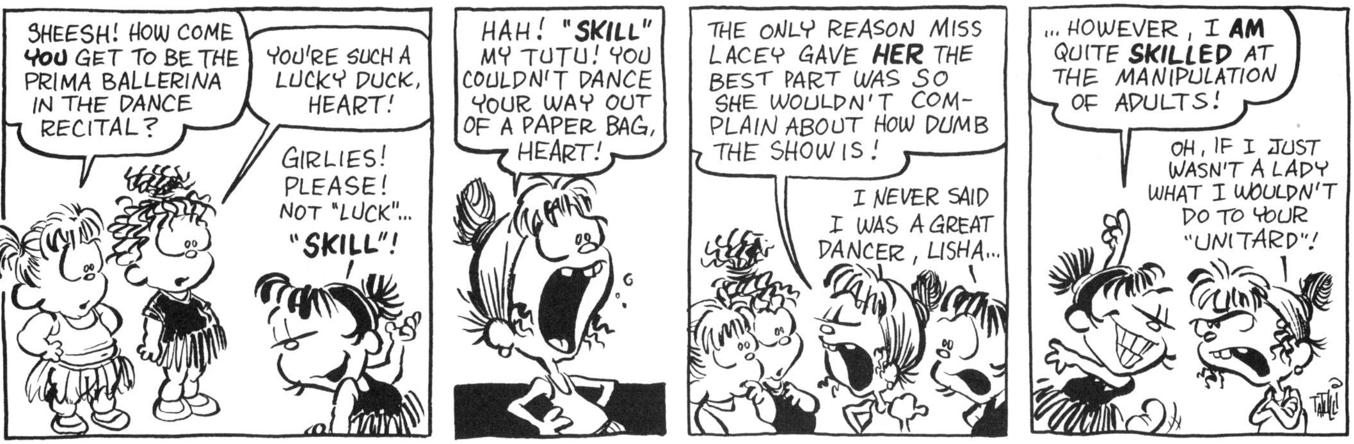
SHEESH! HOW COME **YOU** GET TO BE THE PRIMA BALLERINA IN THE DANCE RECITAL?
YOU'RE SUCH A LUCKY DUCK, HEART!
GIRLIES! PLEASE! NOT "LUCK"... "**SKILL**"!
HAH! "**SKILL**" MY TUTU! YOU COULDN'T DANCE YOUR WAY OUT OF A PAPER BAG, HEART!
THE ONLY REASON MISS LACEY GAVE **HER** THE BEST PART WAS SO SHE WOULDN'T COMPLAIN ABOUT HOW DUMB THE SHOW IS!
I NEVER SAID I WAS A GREAT DANCER, LISHA...
... HOWEVER, I **AM** QUITE **SKILLED** AT THE MANIPULATION OF ADULTS!
OH, IF I JUST WASN'T A LADY WHAT I WOULDN'T DO TO YOUR "UNITARD"!

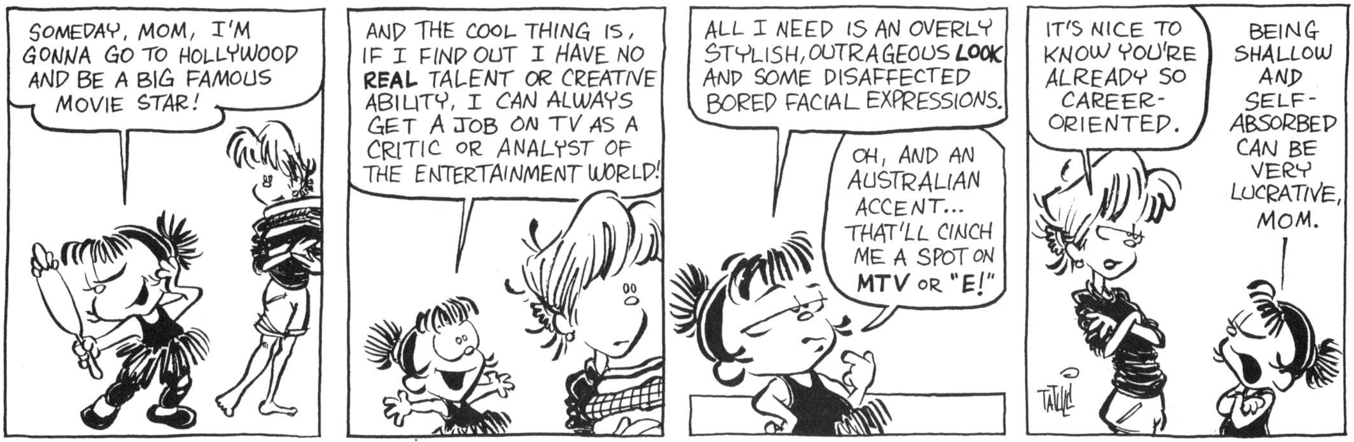
SOMEDAY, MOM, I'M GONNA GO TO HOLLYWOOD AND BE A BIG FAMOUS MOVIE STAR!
AND THE COOL THING IS, IF I FIND OUT I HAVE NO **REAL** TALENT OR CREATIVE ABILITY, I CAN ALWAYS GET A JOB ON TV AS A CRITIC OR ANALYST OF THE ENTERTAINMENT WORLD!
ALL I NEED IS AN OVERLY STYLISH, OUTRAGEOUS **LOOK** AND SOME DISAFFECTED BORED FACIAL EXPRESSIONS.
OH, AND AN AUSTRALIAN ACCENT... THAT'LL CINCH ME A SPOT ON **MTV** OR **"E!"**
IT'S NICE TO KNOW YOU'RE ALREADY SO CAREER-ORIENTED.
BEING SHALLOW AND SELF-ABSORBED CAN BE VERY LUCRATIVE, MOM.

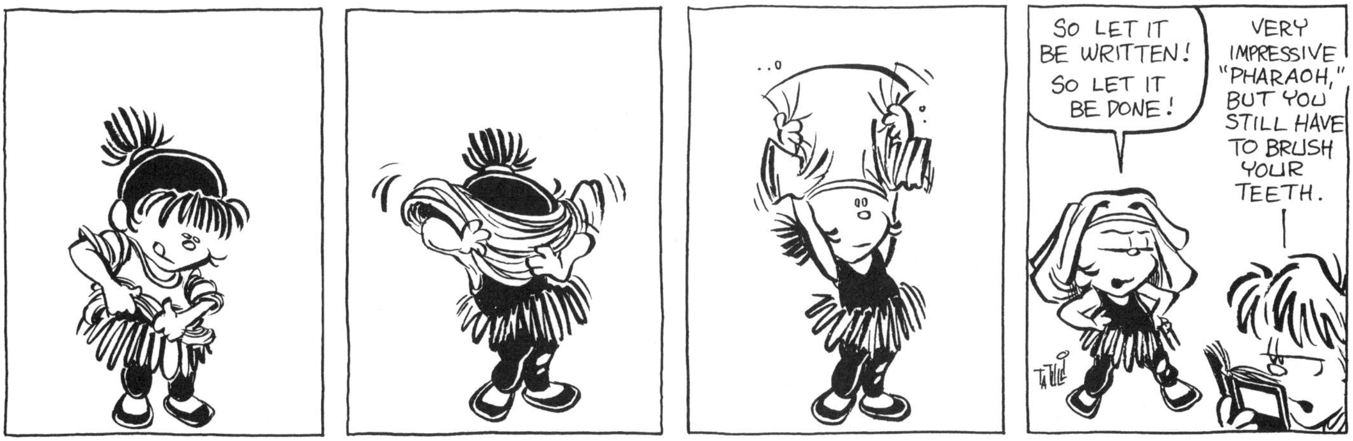
SO LET IT BE WRITTEN! SO LET IT BE DONE!
VERY IMPRESSIVE "PHARAOH," BUT YOU STILL HAVE TO BRUSH YOUR TEETH.

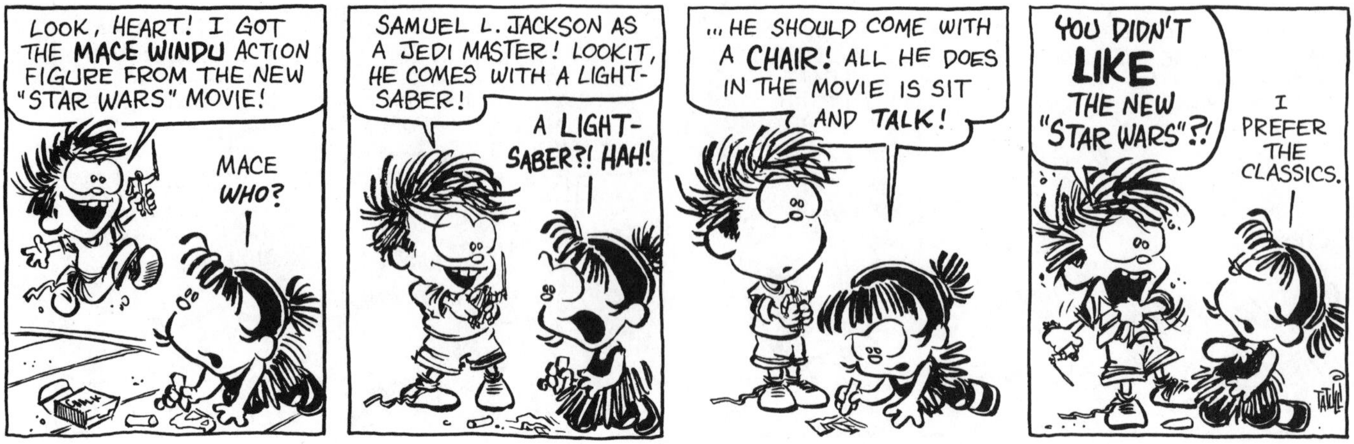
LOOK, HEART! I GOT THE **MACE WINDU** ACTION FIGURE FROM THE NEW "STAR WARS" MOVIE!
MACE *WHO?*
SAMUEL L. JACKSON AS A JEDI MASTER! LOOKIT, HE COMES WITH A LIGHT-SABER!
A **LIGHT-SABER?! HAH!**
...HE SHOULD COME WITH A **CHAIR!** ALL HE DOES IN THE MOVIE IS SIT AND **TALK!**
YOU DIDN'T **LIKE** THE NEW "STAR WARS"?!
I PREFER THE CLASSICS.

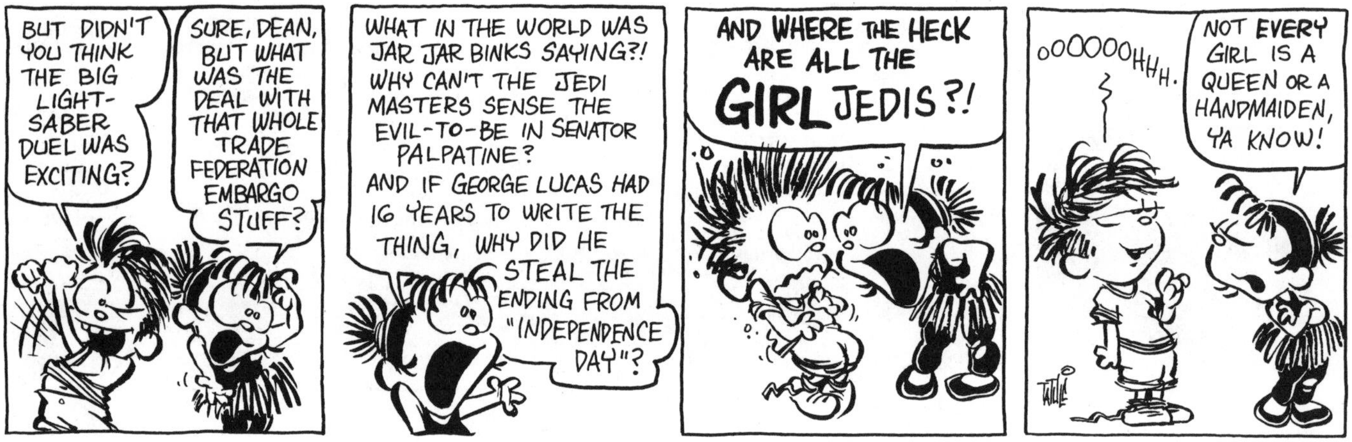
BUT DIDN'T YOU THINK THE BIG LIGHT-SABER DUEL WAS EXCITING?
SURE, DEAN, BUT WHAT WAS THE DEAL WITH THAT WHOLE TRADE FEDERATION EMBARGO STUFF?
WHAT IN THE WORLD WAS JAR JAR BINKS SAYING?! WHY CAN'T THE JEDI MASTERS SENSE THE EVIL-TO-BE IN SENATOR PALPATINE?
AND IF GEORGE LUCAS HAD 16 YEARS TO WRITE THE THING, WHY DID HE STEAL THE ENDING FROM "INDEPENDENCE DAY"?
AND WHERE THE HECK ARE ALL THE GIRL JEDIS?!
oOOOOOHHH.
NOT **EVERY** GIRL IS A QUEEN OR A HANDMAIDEN, YA KNOW!

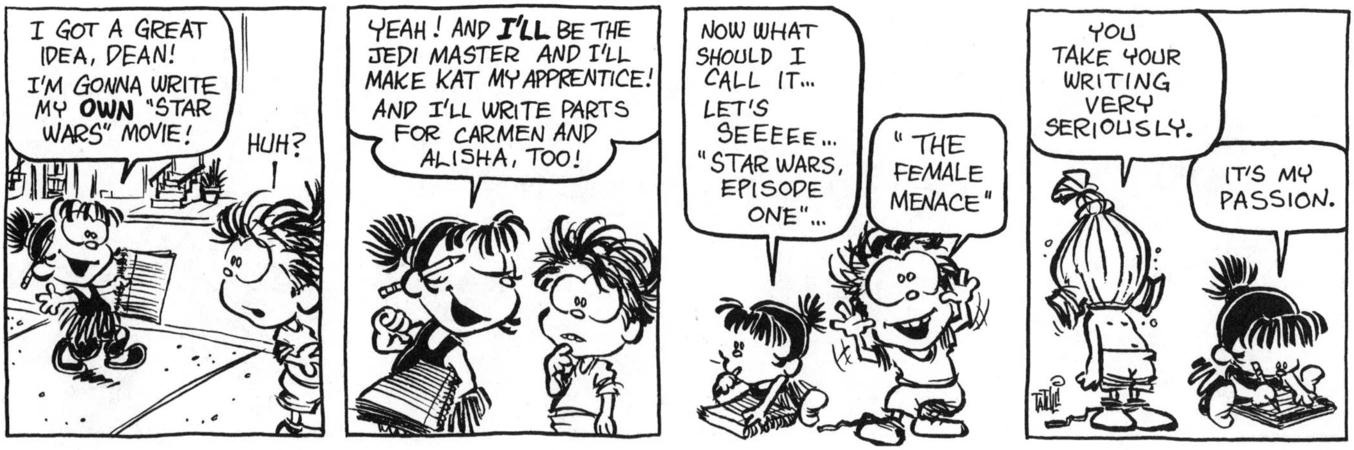
I GOT A GREAT IDEA, DEAN! I'M GONNA WRITE MY **OWN** "STAR WARS" MOVIE!
HUH?
YEAH! AND **I'LL** BE THE JEDI MASTER AND I'LL MAKE KAT MY APPRENTICE! AND I'LL WRITE PARTS FOR CARMEN AND ALISHA, TOO!
NOW WHAT SHOULD I CALL IT... LET'S SEEEEE... "STAR WARS, EPISODE ONE"...
"THE FEMALE MENACE"
YOU TAKE YOUR WRITING VERY SERIOUSLY.
IT'S MY PASSION.

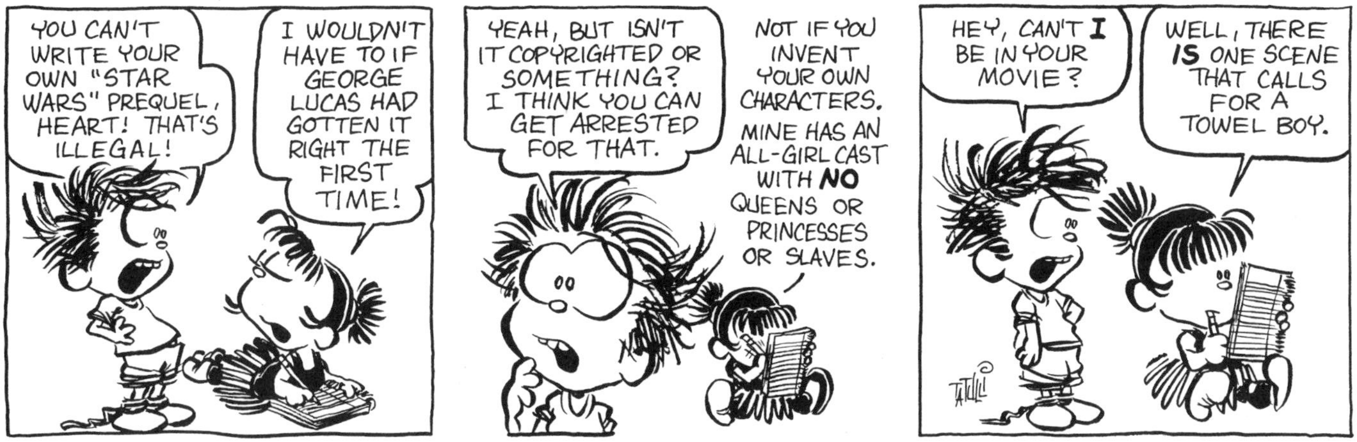
YOU CAN'T WRITE YOUR OWN "STAR WARS" PREQUEL, HEART! THAT'S ILLEGAL!
I WOULDN'T HAVE TO IF GEORGE LUCAS HAD GOTTEN IT RIGHT THE FIRST TIME!
YEAH, BUT ISN'T IT COPYRIGHTED OR SOMETHING? I THINK YOU CAN GET ARRESTED FOR THAT.
NOT IF YOU INVENT YOUR OWN CHARACTERS.
MINE HAS AN ALL-GIRL CAST WITH **NO** QUEENS OR PRINCESSES OR SLAVES.
HEY, CAN'T **I** BE IN YOUR MOVIE?
WELL, THERE **IS** ONE SCENE THAT CALLS FOR A TOWEL BOY.
TATULLI

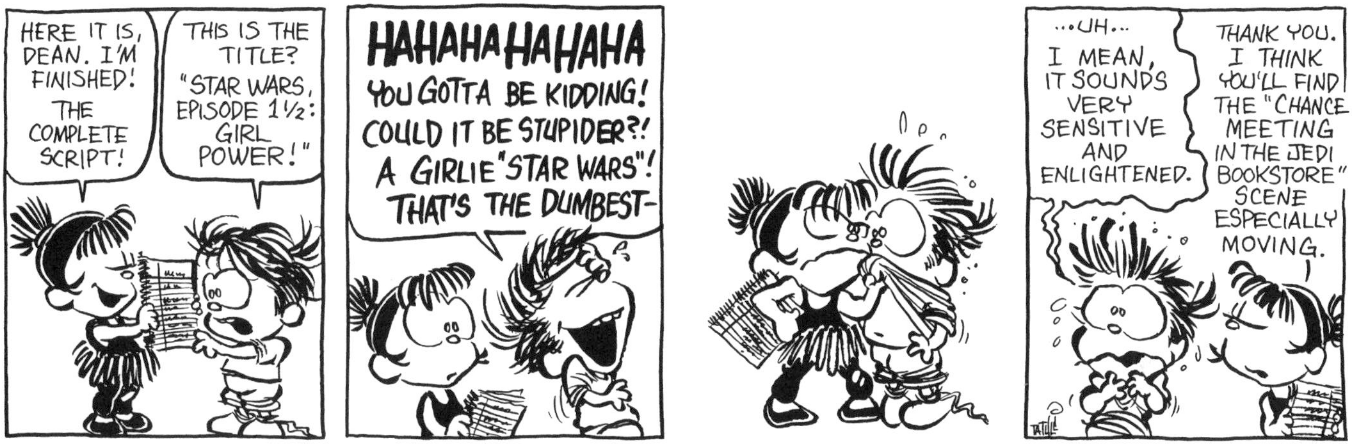
HERE IT IS, DEAN. I'M FINISHED! THE COMPLETE SCRIPT!
THIS IS THE TITLE? "STAR WARS, EPISODE 1½: GIRL POWER!"
HAHAHAHAHAHA
YOU GOTTA BE KIDDING! COULD IT BE STUPIDER?! A GIRLIE "STAR WARS"! THAT'S THE DUMBEST-
...UH... I MEAN, IT SOUNDS VERY SENSITIVE AND ENLIGHTENED.
THANK YOU. I THINK YOU'LL FIND THE "CHANCE MEETING IN THE JEDI BOOKSTORE" SCENE ESPECIALLY MOVING.
TATULLI

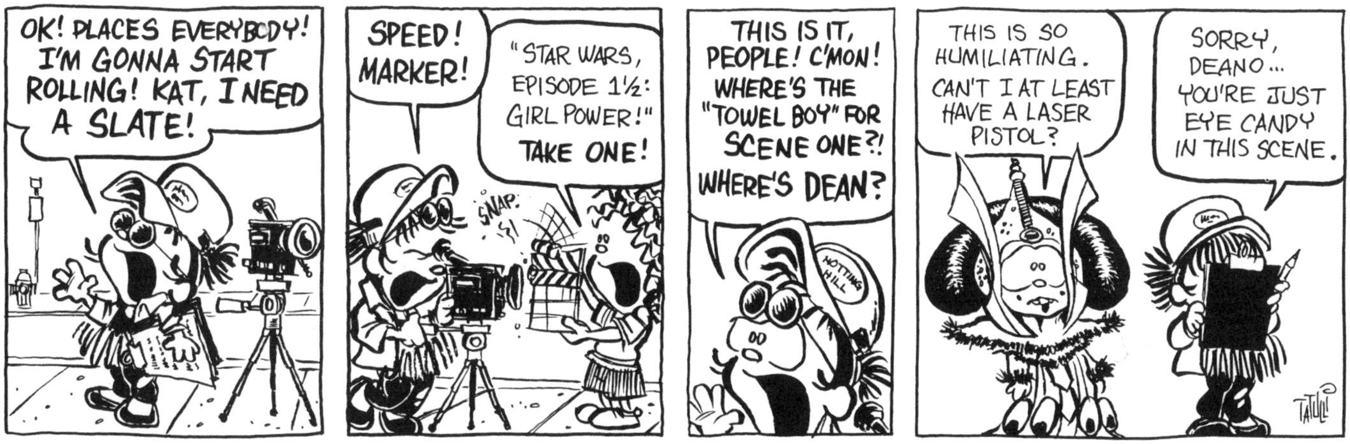
OK! PLACES EVERYBODY! I'M GONNA START ROLLING! KAT, I NEED A SLATE!
SPEED! MARKER!
"STAR WARS, EPISODE 1½: GIRL POWER!" TAKE ONE!
THIS IS IT, PEOPLE! C'MON! WHERE'S THE "TOWEL BOY" FOR SCENE ONE?! WHERE'S DEAN?
NOTTING HILL
THIS IS SO HUMILIATING. CAN'T I AT LEAST HAVE A LASER PISTOL?
SORRY, DEANO... YOU'RE JUST EYE CANDY IN THIS SCENE.
TATULLI

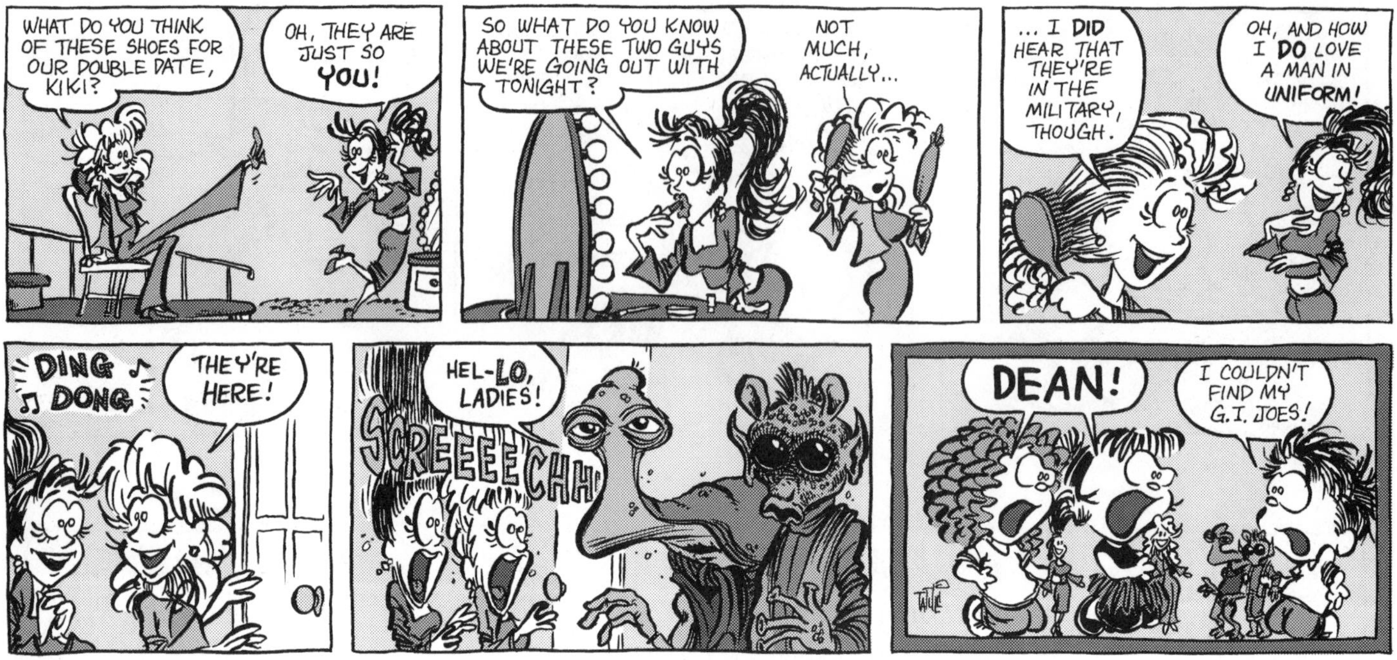
WHAT DO YOU THINK OF THESE SHOES FOR OUR DOUBLE DATE, KIKI?
OH, THEY ARE JUST SO **YOU!**
SO WHAT DO YOU KNOW ABOUT THESE TWO GUYS WE'RE GOING OUT WITH TONIGHT?
NOT MUCH, ACTUALLY...
... I **DID** HEAR THAT THEY'RE IN THE MILITARY, THOUGH.
OH, AND HOW I **DO** LOVE A MAN IN **UNIFORM!**
DING DONG
THEY'RE HERE!
SCREEEEECHH
HEL-**LO**, LADIES!
DEAN!
I COULDN'T FIND MY G.I. JOES!

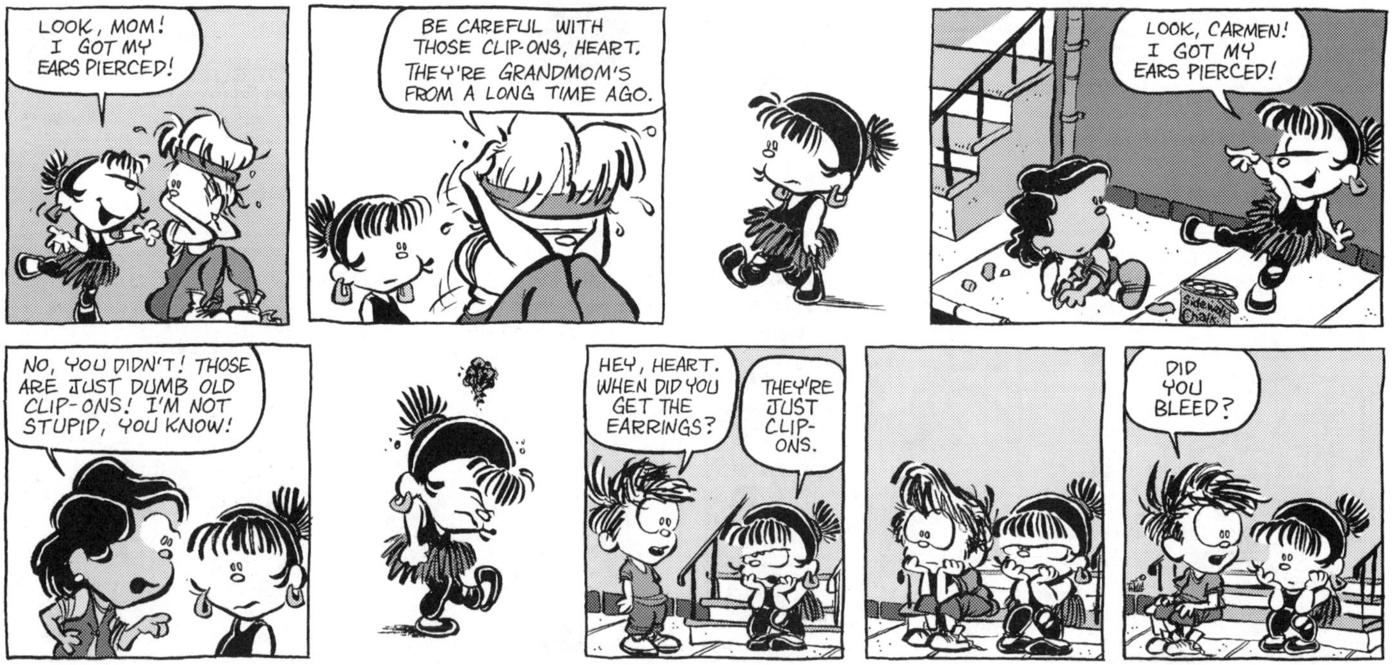
LOOK, MOM! I GOT MY EARS PIERCED!
BE CAREFUL WITH THOSE CLIP-ONS, HEART. THEY'RE GRANDMOM'S FROM A LONG TIME AGO.
LOOK, CARMEN! I GOT MY EARS PIERCED!
NO, YOU DIDN'T! THOSE ARE JUST DUMB OLD CLIP-ONS! I'M NOT STUPID, YOU KNOW!
HEY, HEART. WHEN DID YOU GET THE EARRINGS?
THEY'RE JUST CLIP-ONS.
DID YOU BLEED?

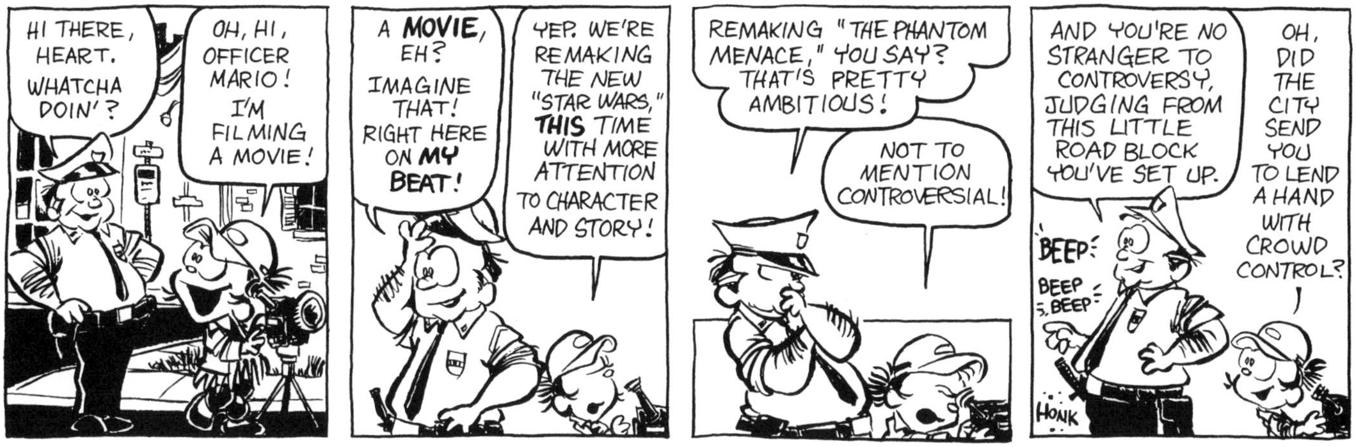
HI THERE, HEART. WHATCHA DOIN'?
OH, HI, OFFICER MARIO! I'M FILMING A MOVIE!
A **MOVIE**, EH? IMAGINE THAT! RIGHT HERE ON **MY** BEAT!
YEP. WE'RE REMAKING THE NEW "STAR WARS," **THIS** TIME WITH MORE ATTENTION TO CHARACTER AND STORY!
REMAKING "THE PHANTOM MENACE," YOU SAY? THAT'S PRETTY AMBITIOUS!
NOT TO MENTION CONTROVERSIAL!
AND YOU'RE NO STRANGER TO CONTROVERSY, JUDGING FROM THIS LITTLE ROAD BLOCK YOU'VE SET UP.
BEEP
BEEP BEEP
HONK
OH, DID THE CITY SEND YOU TO LEND A HAND WITH CROWD CONTROL?

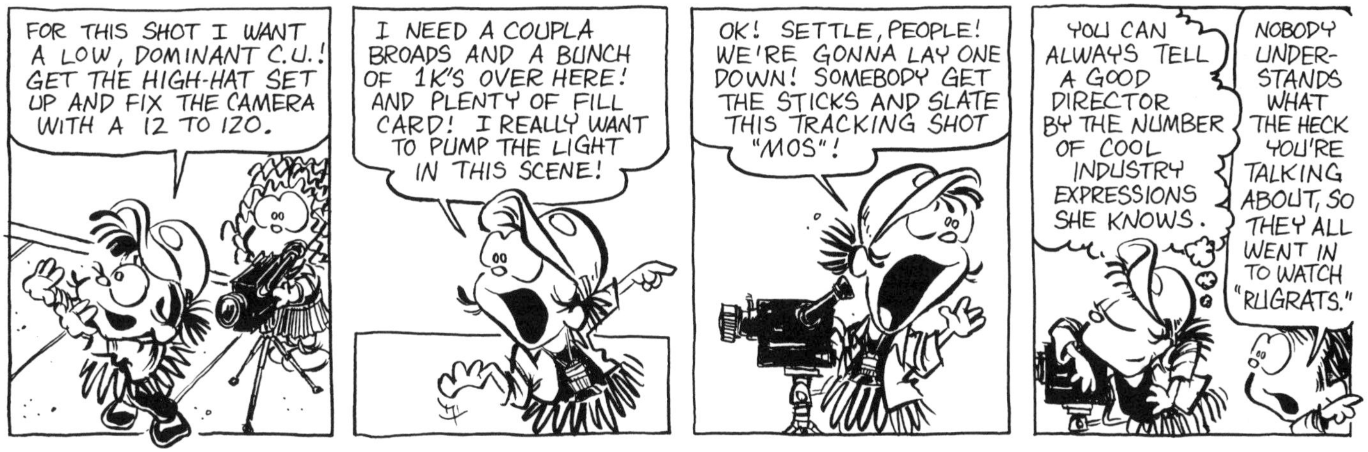
FOR THIS SHOT I WANT A LOW, DOMINANT C.U.! GET THE HIGH-HAT SET UP AND FIX THE CAMERA WITH A 12 TO 120.
I NEED A COUPLA BROADS AND A BUNCH OF 1K'S OVER HERE! AND PLENTY OF FILL CARD! I REALLY WANT TO PUMP THE LIGHT IN THIS SCENE!
OK! SETTLE, PEOPLE! WE'RE GONNA LAY ONE DOWN! SOMEBODY GET THE STICKS AND SLATE THIS TRACKING SHOT "MOS"!
YOU CAN ALWAYS TELL A GOOD DIRECTOR BY THE NUMBER OF COOL INDUSTRY EXPRESSIONS SHE KNOWS.
NOBODY UNDER-STANDS WHAT THE HECK YOU'RE TALKING ABOUT, SO THEY ALL WENT IN TO WATCH "RUGRATS."

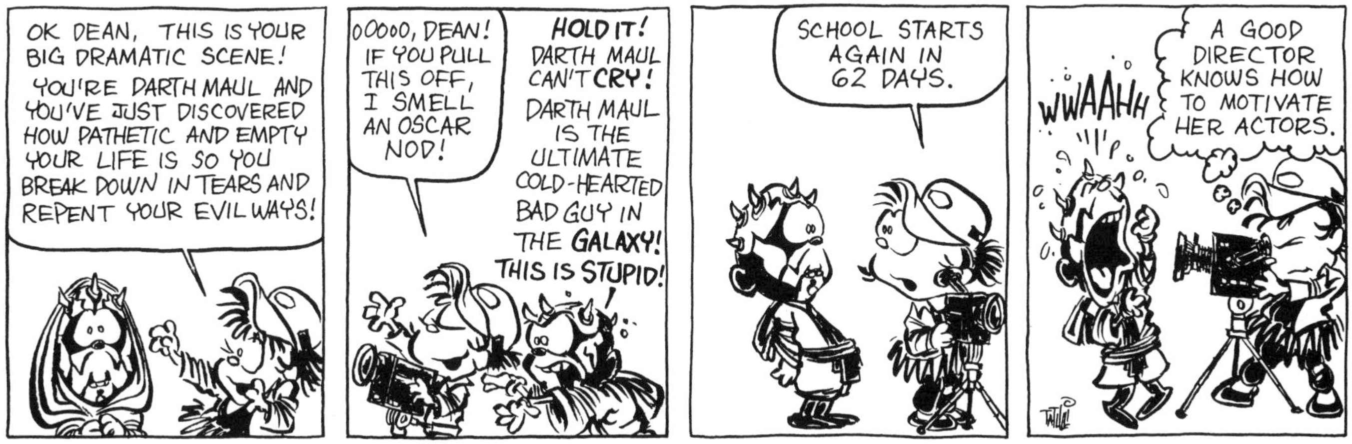
OK DEAN, THIS IS YOUR BIG DRAMATIC SCENE! YOU'RE DARTH MAUL AND YOU'VE JUST DISCOVERED HOW PATHETIC AND EMPTY YOUR LIFE IS SO YOU BREAK DOWN IN TEARS AND REPENT YOUR EVIL WAYS!
OOOOO, DEAN! IF YOU PULL THIS OFF, I SMELL AN OSCAR NOD!
HOLD IT! DARTH MAUL CAN'T **CRY**! DARTH MAUL IS THE ULTIMATE COLD-HEARTED BAD GUY IN THE **GALAXY**! THIS IS **STUPID**!
SCHOOL STARTS AGAIN IN 62 DAYS.
WWAAHH
A GOOD DIRECTOR KNOWS HOW TO MOTIVATE HER ACTORS.

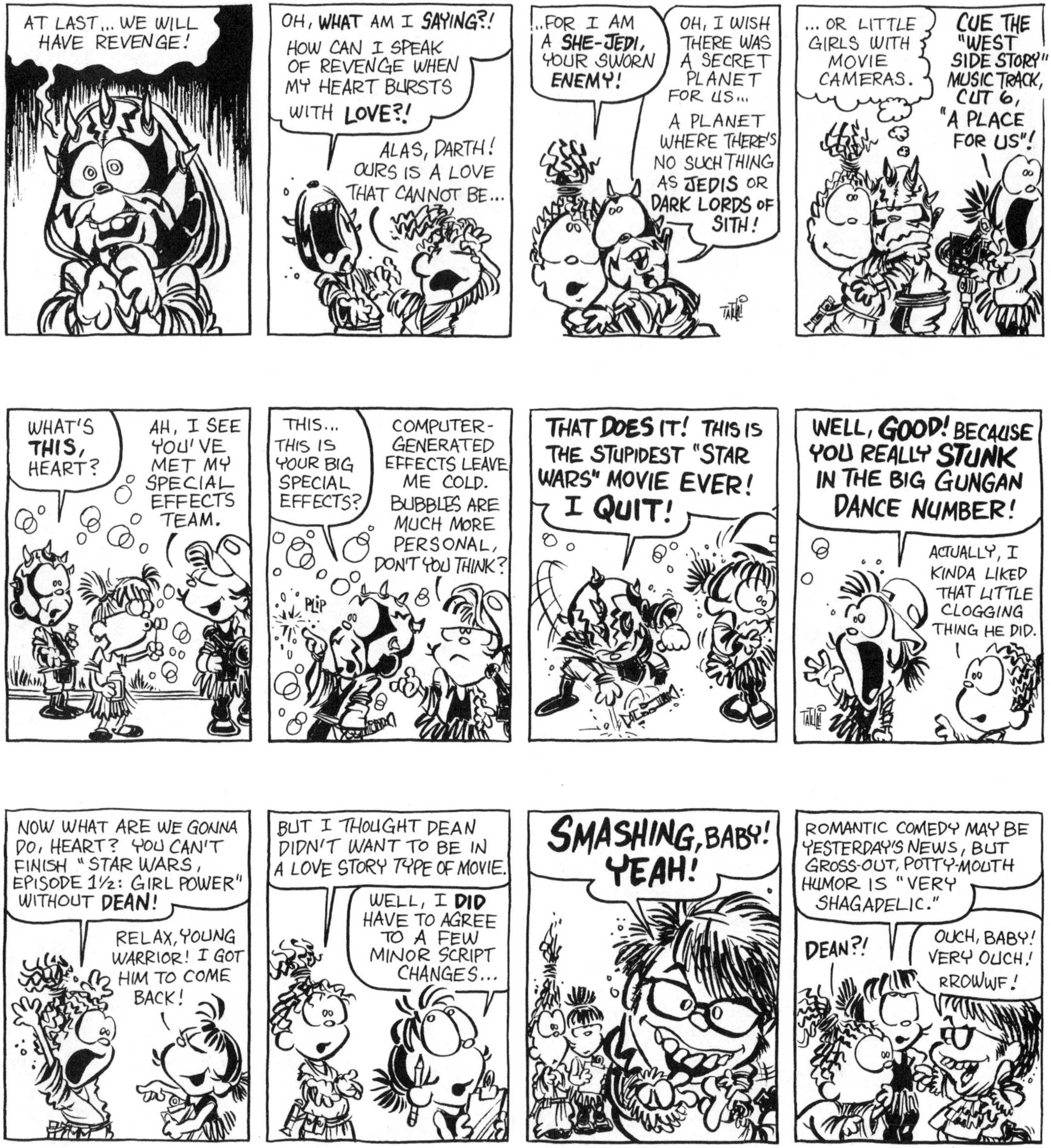
AT LAST... WE WILL HAVE REVENGE!
OH, WHAT AM I SAYING?! HOW CAN I SPEAK OF REVENGE WHEN MY HEART BURSTS WITH LOVE?!
ALAS, DARTH! OURS IS A LOVE THAT CANNOT BE...
...FOR I AM A SHE-JEDI, YOUR SWORN ENEMY!
OH, I WISH THERE WAS A SECRET PLANET FOR US...
A PLANET WHERE THERE'S NO SUCH THING AS JEDIS OR DARK LORDS OF SITH!
... OR LITTLE GIRLS WITH MOVIE CAMERAS.
CUE THE "WEST SIDE STORY" MUSIC TRACK, CUT 6, "A PLACE FOR US"!
WHAT'S THIS, HEART?
AH, I SEE YOU'VE MET MY SPECIAL EFFECTS TEAM.
THIS... THIS IS YOUR BIG SPECIAL EFFECTS?
COMPUTER-GENERATED EFFECTS LEAVE ME COLD. BUBBLES ARE MUCH MORE PERSONAL, DON'T YOU THINK?
PLIP
THAT DOES IT! THIS IS THE STUPIDEST "STAR WARS" MOVIE EVER! I QUIT!
WELL, GOOD! BECAUSE YOU REALLY STUNK IN THE BIG GUNGAN DANCE NUMBER!
ACTUALLY, I KINDA LIKED THAT LITTLE CLOGGING THING HE DID.
NOW WHAT ARE WE GONNA DO, HEART? YOU CAN'T FINISH "STAR WARS, EPISODE 1½: GIRL POWER" WITHOUT DEAN!
RELAX, YOUNG WARRIOR! I GOT HIM TO COME BACK!
BUT I THOUGHT DEAN DIDN'T WANT TO BE IN A LOVE STORY TYPE OF MOVIE.
WELL, I DID HAVE TO AGREE TO A FEW MINOR SCRIPT CHANGES...
SMASHING, BABY! YEAH!
ROMANTIC COMEDY MAY BE YESTERDAY'S NEWS, BUT GROSS-OUT, POTTY-MOUTH HUMOR IS "VERY SHAGADELIC."
DEAN?!
OUCH, BABY! VERY OUCH! RROWWF!

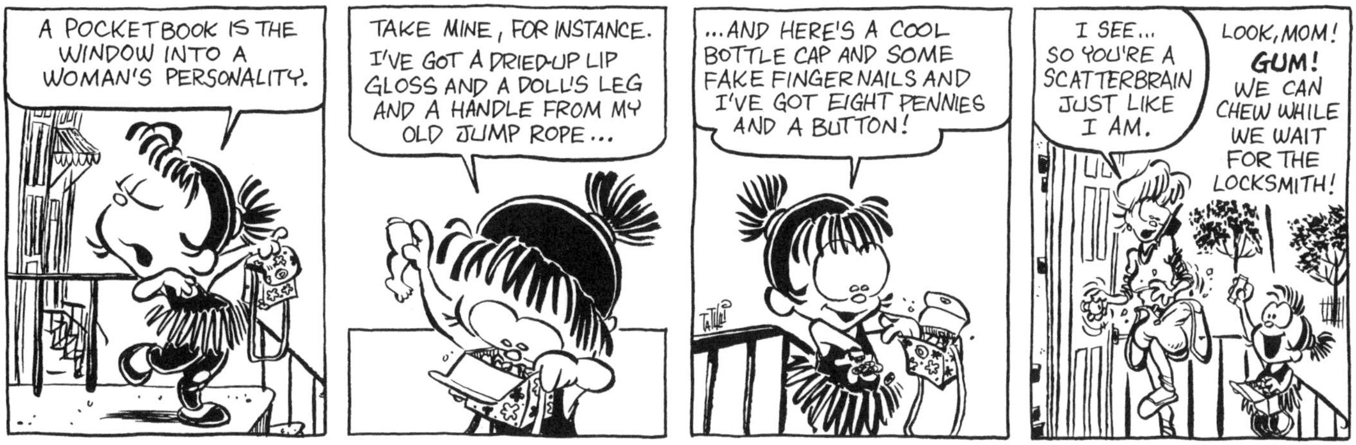
A POCKETBOOK IS THE WINDOW INTO A WOMAN'S PERSONALITY.
TAKE MINE, FOR INSTANCE. I'VE GOT A DRIED-UP LIP GLOSS AND A DOLL'S LEG AND A HANDLE FROM MY OLD JUMP ROPE...
...AND HERE'S A COOL BOTTLE CAP AND SOME FAKE FINGERNAILS AND I'VE GOT EIGHT PENNIES AND A BUTTON!
I SEE... SO YOU'RE A SCATTERBRAIN JUST LIKE I AM.
LOOK, MOM! **GUM!** WE CAN CHEW WHILE WE WAIT FOR THE LOCKSMITH!

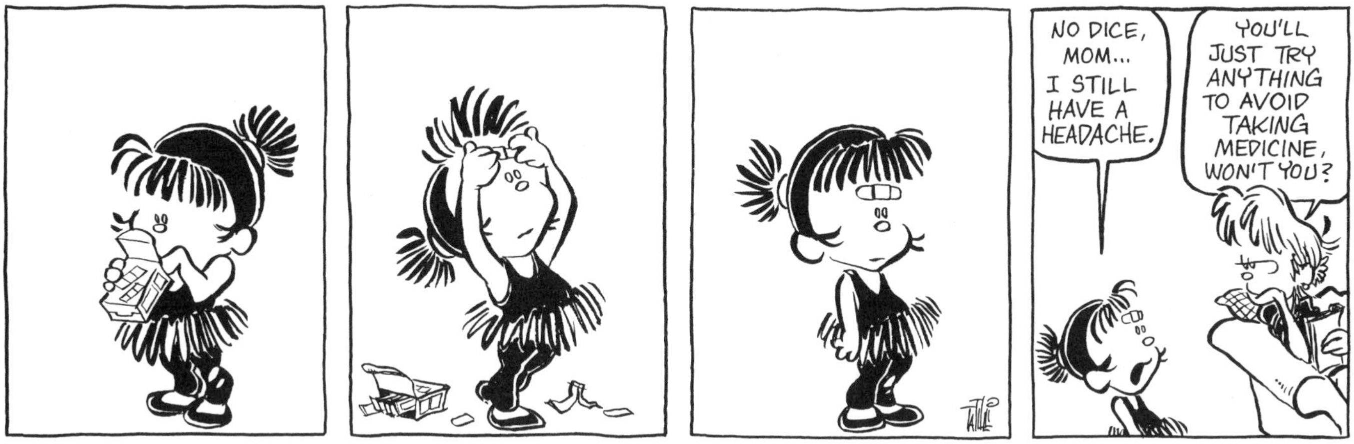
NO DICE, MOM... I STILL HAVE A HEADACHE.
YOU'LL JUST TRY ANYTHING TO AVOID TAKING MEDICINE, WON'T YOU?

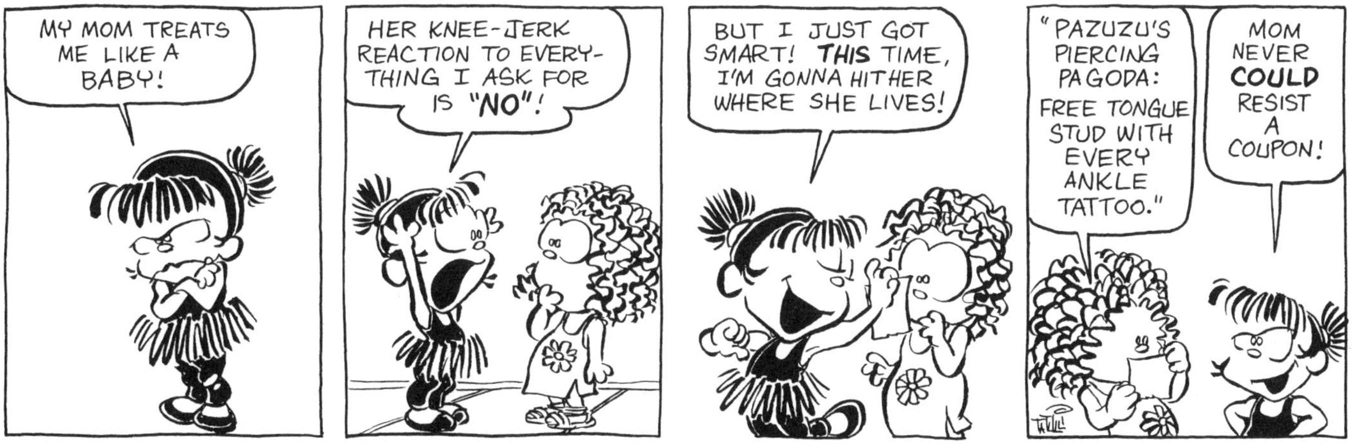
MY MOM TREATS ME LIKE A BABY!
HER KNEE-JERK REACTION TO EVERYTHING I ASK FOR IS "**NO**"!
BUT I JUST GOT SMART! **THIS** TIME, I'M GONNA HIT HER WHERE SHE LIVES!
"PAZUZU'S PIERCING PAGODA: FREE TONGUE STUD WITH EVERY ANKLE TATTOO."
MOM NEVER **COULD** RESIST A COUPON!

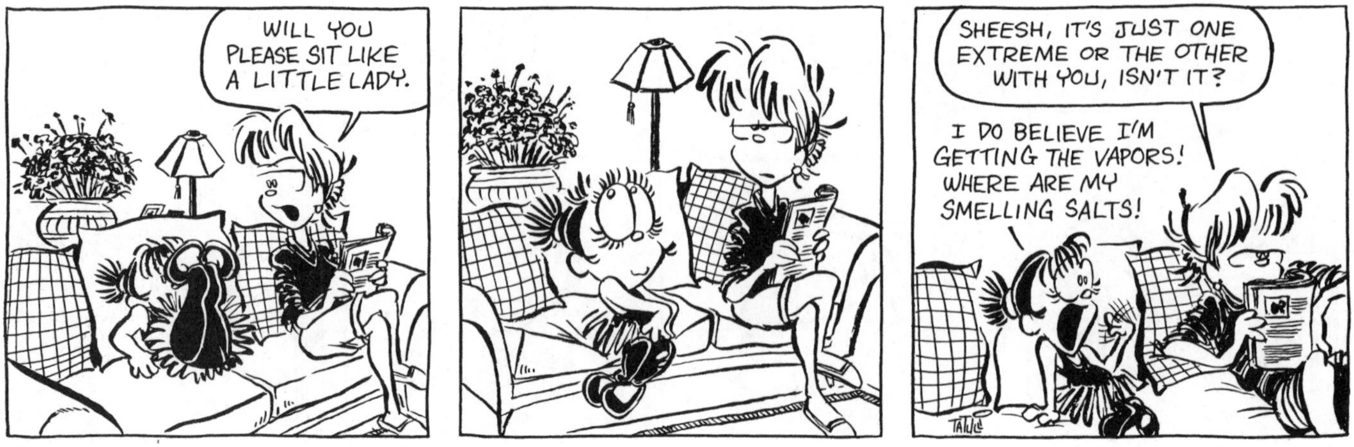
WILL YOU PLEASE SIT LIKE A LITTLE LADY.
I DO BELIEVE I'M GETTING THE VAPORS! WHERE ARE MY SMELLING SALTS!
SHEESH, IT'S JUST ONE EXTREME OR THE OTHER WITH YOU, ISN'T IT?

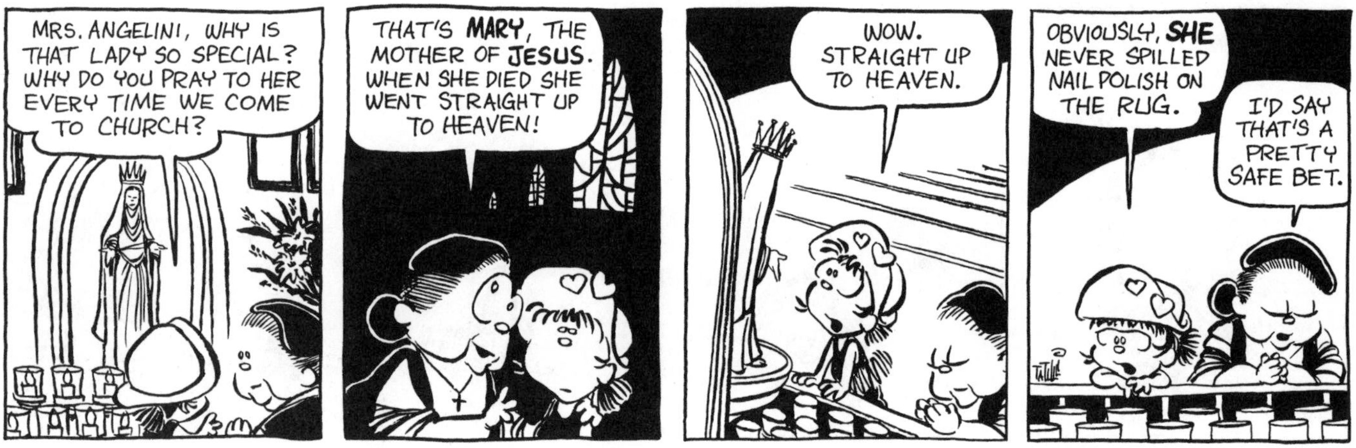
MRS. ANGELINI, WHY IS THAT LADY SO SPECIAL? WHY DO YOU PRAY TO HER EVERY TIME WE COME TO CHURCH?
THAT'S **MARY**, THE MOTHER OF **JESUS**. WHEN SHE DIED SHE WENT STRAIGHT UP TO HEAVEN!
WOW. STRAIGHT UP TO HEAVEN.
OBVIOUSLY, **SHE** NEVER SPILLED NAIL POLISH ON THE RUG.
I'D SAY THAT'S A PRETTY SAFE BET.

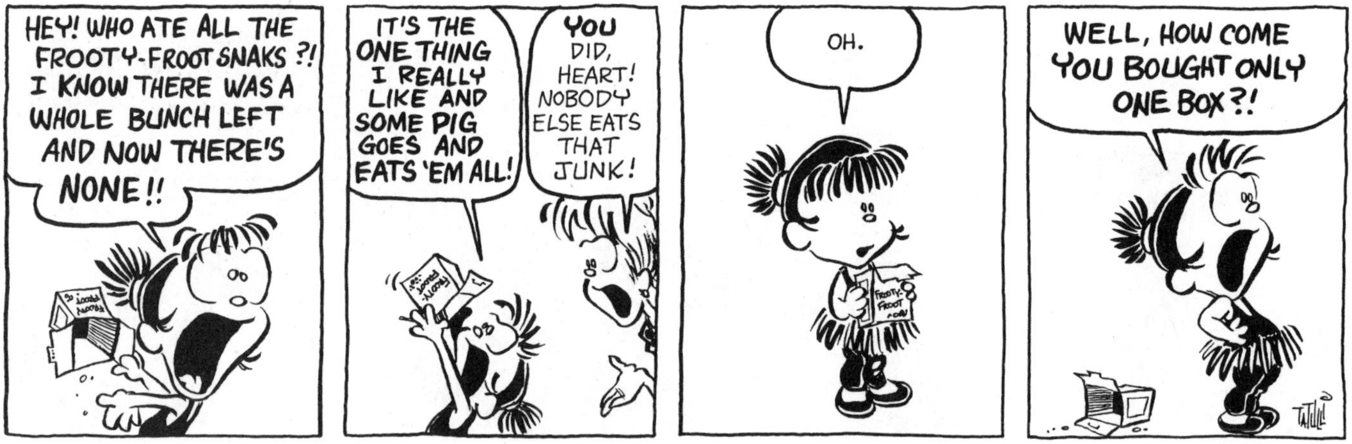
HEY! WHO ATE ALL THE FROOTY-FROOT SNAKS ?! I KNOW THERE WAS A WHOLE BUNCH LEFT AND NOW THERE'S NONE!!
IT'S THE ONE THING I REALLY LIKE AND SOME PIG GOES AND EATS 'EM ALL!
YOU DID, HEART! NOBODY ELSE EATS THAT JUNK!
OH.
WELL, HOW COME YOU BOUGHT ONLY ONE BOX ?!

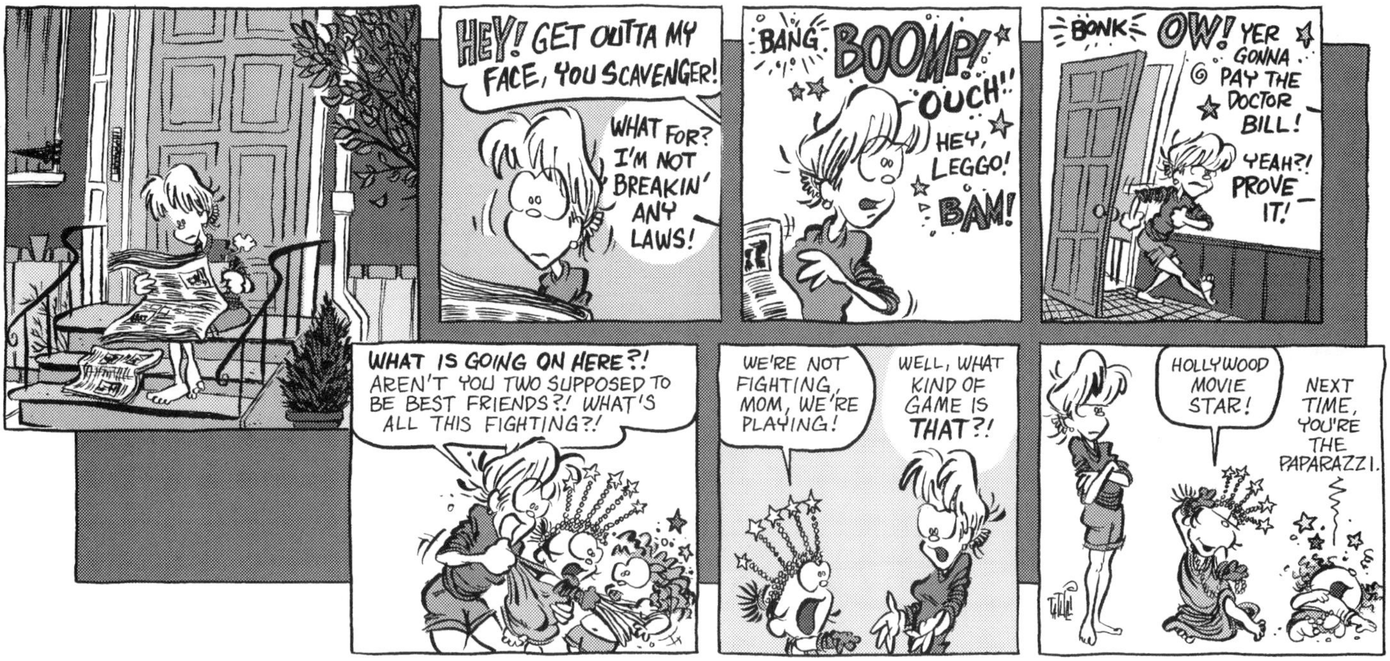

HEY! GET OUTTA MY FACE, YOU SCAVENGER!
WHAT FOR? I'M NOT BREAKIN' ANY LAWS!
BANG
BOOMP!
OUCH!!
HEY, LEGGO!
BAM!
BONK
OW!
YER GONNA PAY THE DOCTOR BILL!
YEAH?! PROVE IT!
WHAT IS GOING ON HERE?! AREN'T YOU TWO SUPPOSED TO BE BEST FRIENDS?! WHAT'S ALL THIS FIGHTING?!
WE'RE NOT FIGHTING, MOM, WE'RE PLAYING!
WELL, WHAT KIND OF GAME IS THAT?!
HOLLYWOOD MOVIE STAR!
NEXT TIME, YOU'RE THE PAPARAZZI.

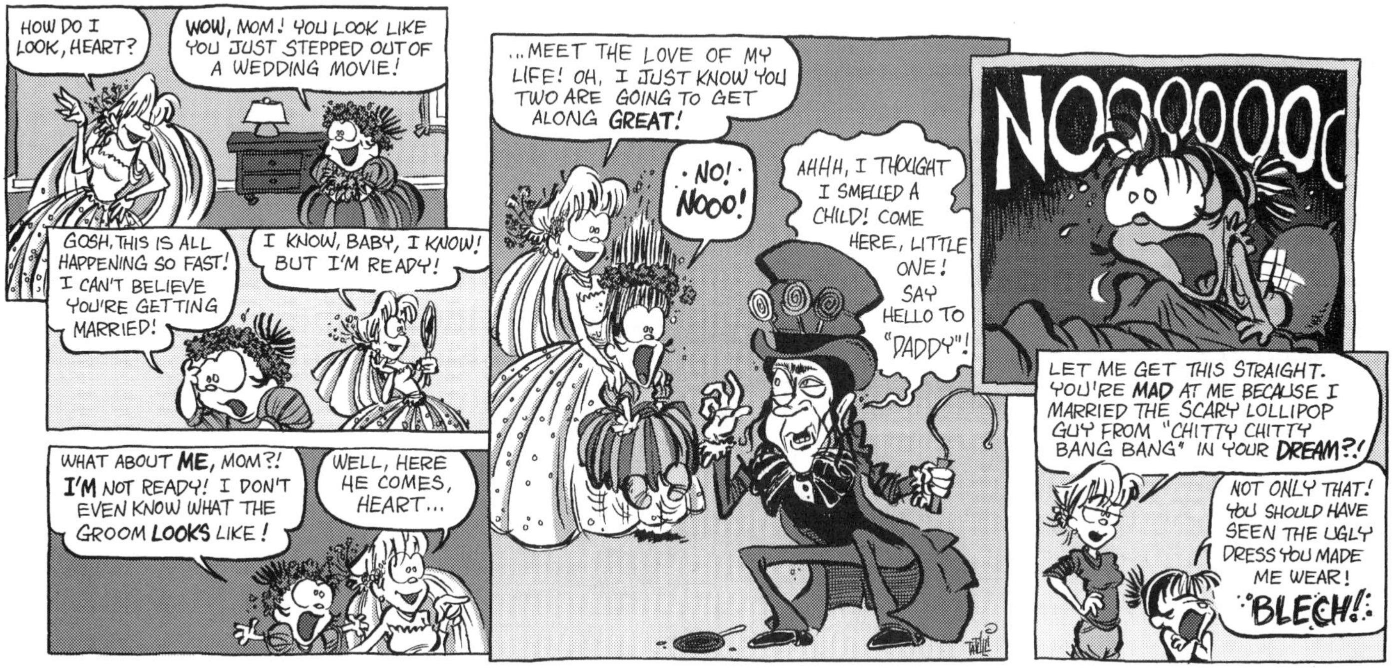

HOW DO I LOOK, HEART?
WOW, MOM! YOU LOOK LIKE YOU JUST STEPPED OUT OF A WEDDING MOVIE!
GOSH, THIS IS ALL HAPPENING SO FAST! I CAN'T BELIEVE YOU'RE GETTING MARRIED!
I KNOW, BABY, I KNOW! BUT I'M READY!
WHAT ABOUT ME, MOM?! I'M NOT READY! I DON'T EVEN KNOW WHAT THE GROOM LOOKS LIKE!
WELL, HERE HE COMES, HEART...
...MEET THE LOVE OF MY LIFE! OH, I JUST KNOW YOU TWO ARE GOING TO GET ALONG GREAT!
NO! NOOO!
AHHH, I THOUGHT I SMELLED A CHILD! COME HERE, LITTLE ONE! SAY HELLO TO "DADDY"!
NOOOOOOO
LET ME GET THIS STRAIGHT. YOU'RE MAD AT ME BECAUSE I MARRIED THE SCARY LOLLIPOP GUY FROM "CHITTY CHITTY BANG BANG" IN YOUR DREAM?!
NOT ONLY THAT! YOU SHOULD HAVE SEEN THE UGLY DRESS YOU MADE ME WEAR! BLECH!

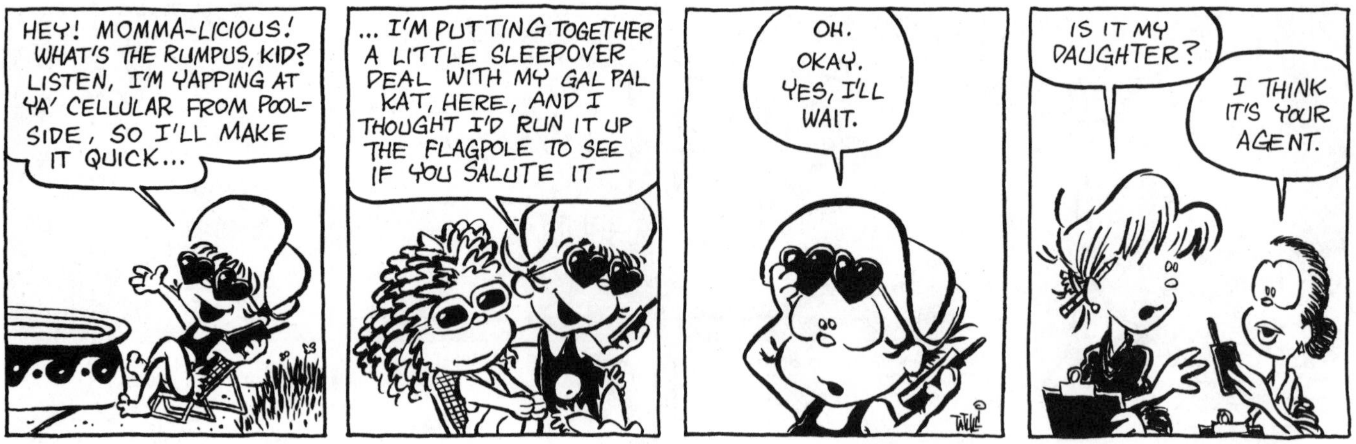
HEY! MOMMA-LICIOUS! WHAT'S THE RUMPUS, KID? LISTEN, I'M YAPPING AT YA' CELLULAR FROM POOL-SIDE, SO I'LL MAKE IT QUICK...
... I'M PUTTING TOGETHER A LITTLE SLEEPOVER DEAL WITH MY GAL PAL KAT, HERE, AND I THOUGHT I'D RUN IT UP THE FLAGPOLE TO SEE IF YOU SALUTE IT—
OH. OKAY. YES, I'LL WAIT.
IS IT MY DAUGHTER?
I THINK IT'S YOUR AGENT.

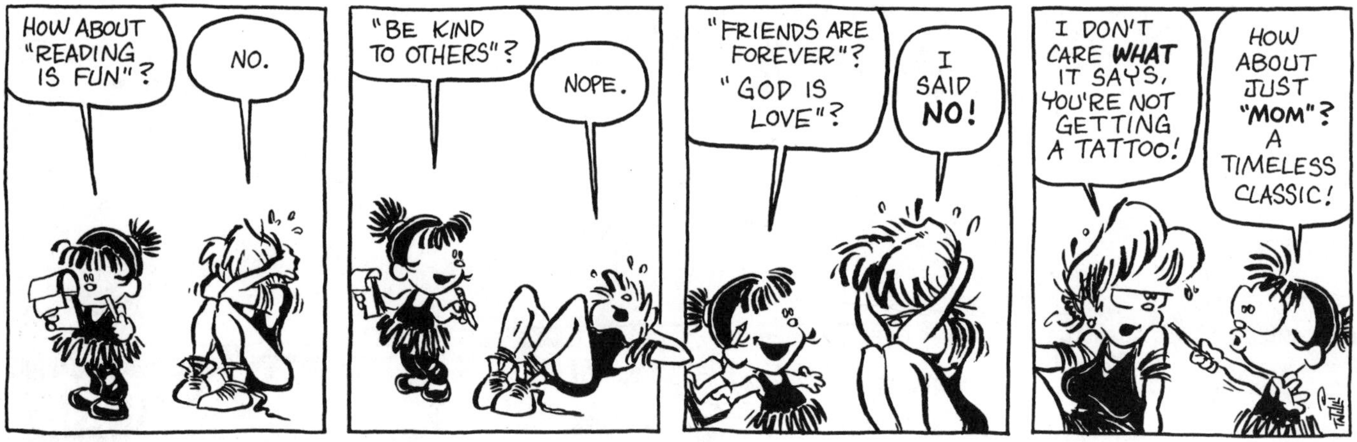
HOW ABOUT "READING IS FUN"?
NO.
"BE KIND TO OTHERS"?
NOPE.
"FRIENDS ARE FOREVER"? "GOD IS LOVE"?
I SAID NO!
I DON'T CARE WHAT IT SAYS, YOU'RE NOT GETTING A TATTOO!
HOW ABOUT JUST "MOM"? A TIMELESS CLASSIC!

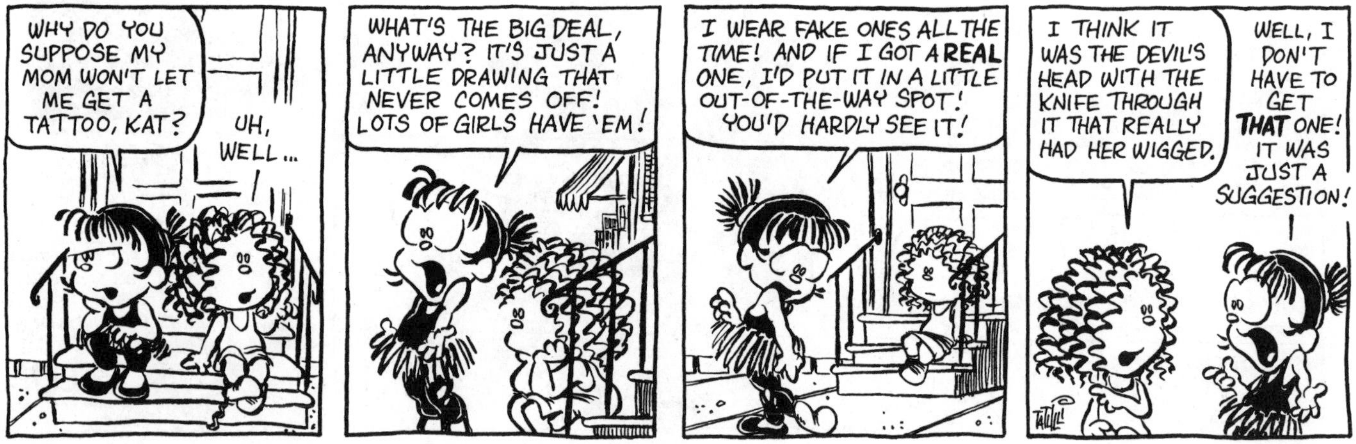
WHY DO YOU SUPPOSE MY MOM WON'T LET ME GET A TATTOO, KAT?
UH, WELL...
WHAT'S THE BIG DEAL, ANYWAY? IT'S JUST A LITTLE DRAWING THAT NEVER COMES OFF! LOTS OF GIRLS HAVE 'EM!
I WEAR FAKE ONES ALL THE TIME! AND IF I GOT A REAL ONE, I'D PUT IT IN A LITTLE OUT-OF-THE-WAY SPOT! YOU'D HARDLY SEE IT!
I THINK IT WAS THE DEVIL'S HEAD WITH THE KNIFE THROUGH IT THAT REALLY HAD HER WIGGED.
WELL, I DON'T HAVE TO GET THAT ONE! IT WAS JUST A SUGGESTION!

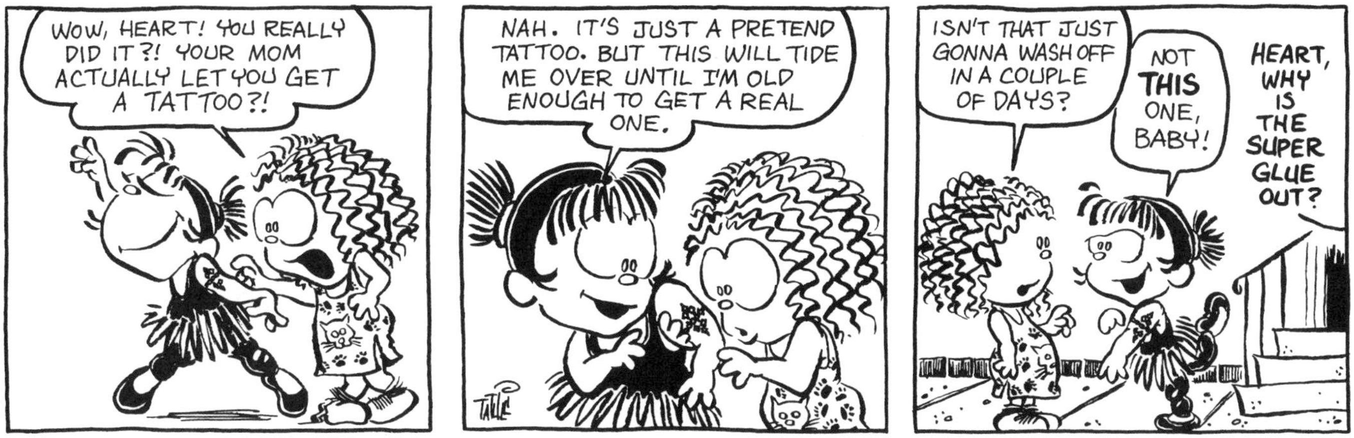
WOW, HEART! YOU REALLY DID IT?! YOUR MOM ACTUALLY LET YOU GET A TATTOO?!
NAH. IT'S JUST A PRETEND TATTOO. BUT THIS WILL TIDE ME OVER UNTIL I'M OLD ENOUGH TO GET A REAL ONE.
ISN'T THAT JUST GONNA WASH OFF IN A COUPLE OF DAYS?
NOT **THIS** ONE, BABY!
HEART, WHY IS THE SUPER GLUE OUT?

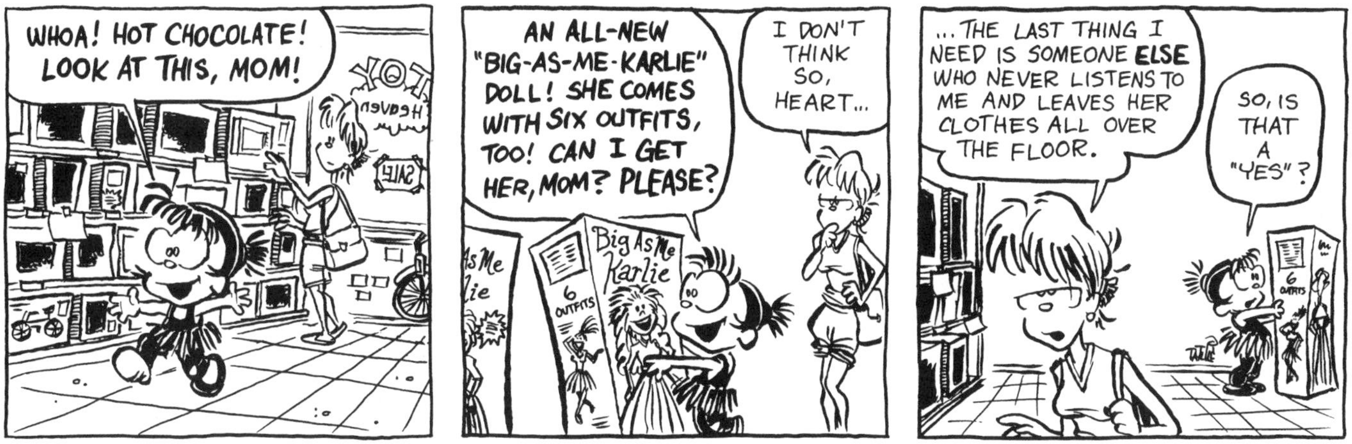
WHOA! HOT CHOCOLATE! LOOK AT THIS, MOM!
AN ALL-NEW "BIG-AS-ME-KARLIE" DOLL! SHE COMES WITH SIX OUTFITS, TOO! CAN I GET HER, MOM? PLEASE?
Big As Me Karlie
6 OUTFITS
I DON'T THINK SO, HEART...
...THE LAST THING I NEED IS SOMEONE **ELSE** WHO NEVER LISTENS TO ME AND LEAVES HER CLOTHES ALL OVER THE FLOOR.
SO, IS THAT A "YES"?

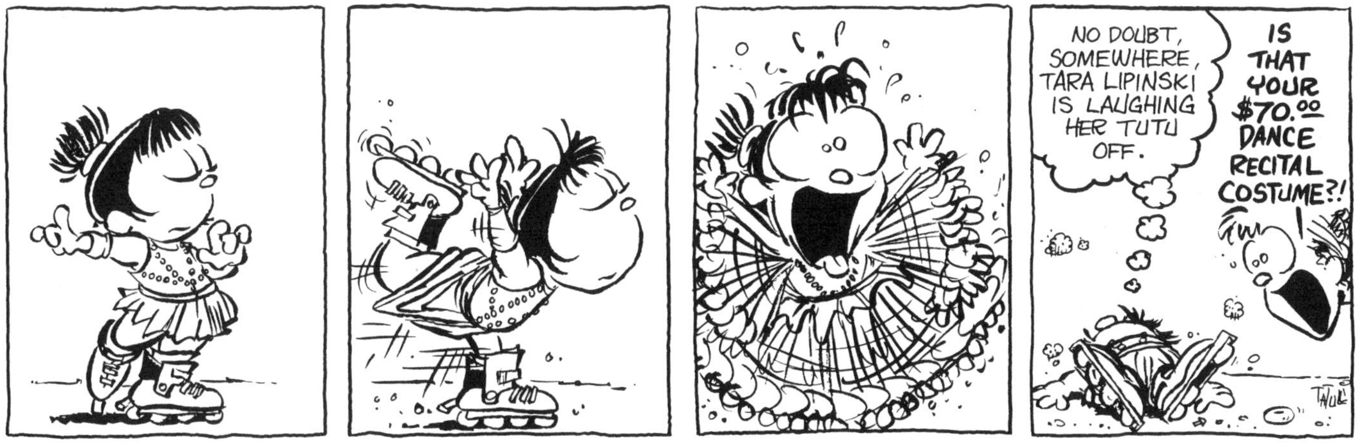
NO DOUBT, SOMEWHERE, TARA LIPINSKI IS LAUGHING HER TUTU OFF.
IS THAT YOUR $70.00 DANCE RECITAL COSTUME?!

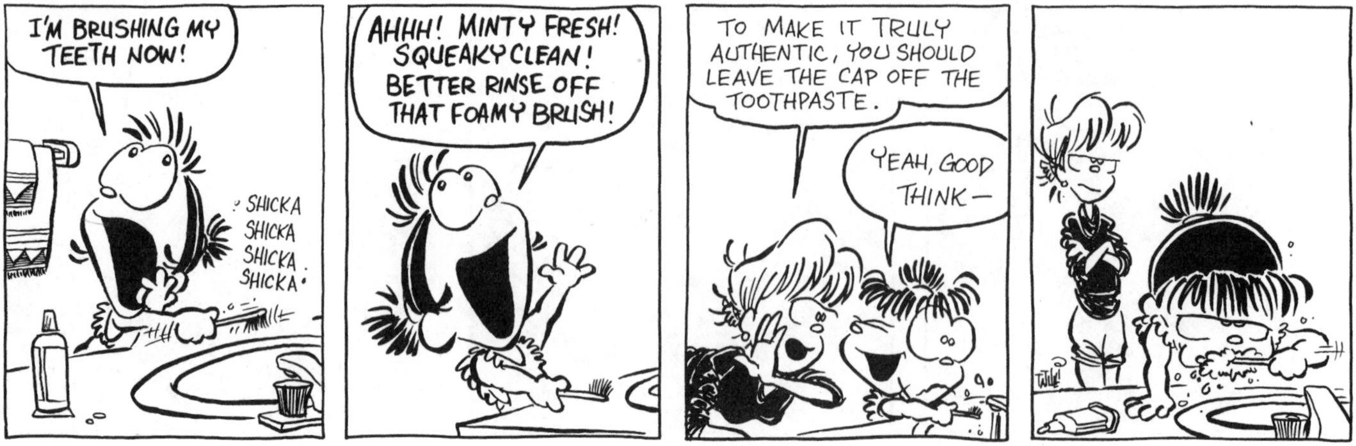
I'M BRUSHING MY TEETH NOW!
SHICKA SHICKA SHICKA SHICKA
AHHH! MINTY FRESH! SQUEAKY CLEAN! BETTER RINSE OFF THAT FOAMY BRUSH!
TO MAKE IT TRULY AUTHENTIC, YOU SHOULD LEAVE THE CAP OFF THE TOOTHPASTE.
YEAH, GOOD THINK—

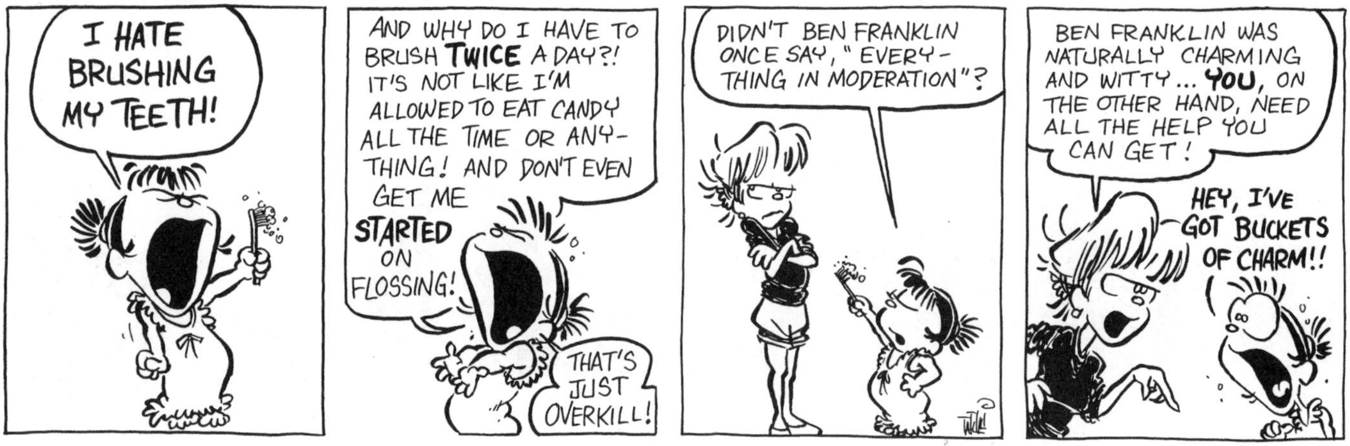
I HATE BRUSHING MY TEETH!
AND WHY DO I HAVE TO BRUSH TWICE A DAY?! IT'S NOT LIKE I'M ALLOWED TO EAT CANDY ALL THE TIME OR ANYTHING! AND DON'T EVEN GET ME STARTED ON FLOSSING!
THAT'S JUST OVERKILL!
DIDN'T BEN FRANKLIN ONCE SAY, "EVERYTHING IN MODERATION"?
BEN FRANKLIN WAS NATURALLY CHARMING AND WITTY... YOU, ON THE OTHER HAND, NEED ALL THE HELP YOU CAN GET!
HEY, I'VE GOT BUCKETS OF CHARM!!

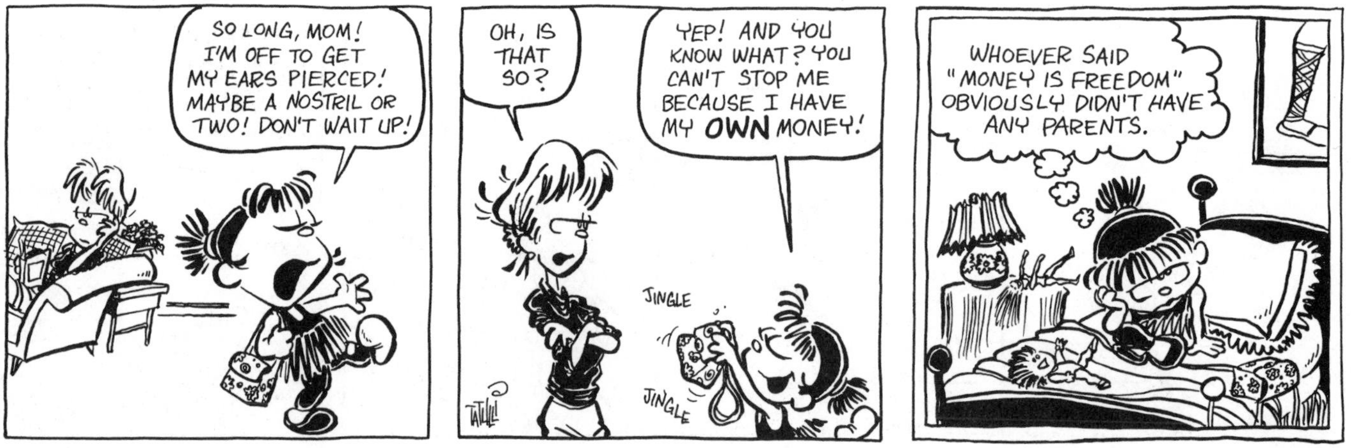
SO LONG, MOM! I'M OFF TO GET MY EARS PIERCED! MAYBE A NOSTRIL OR TWO! DON'T WAIT UP!
OH, IS THAT SO?
YEP! AND YOU KNOW WHAT? YOU CAN'T STOP ME BECAUSE I HAVE MY OWN MONEY!
JINGLE
JINGLE
WHOEVER SAID "MONEY IS FREEDOM" OBVIOUSLY DIDN'T HAVE ANY PARENTS.

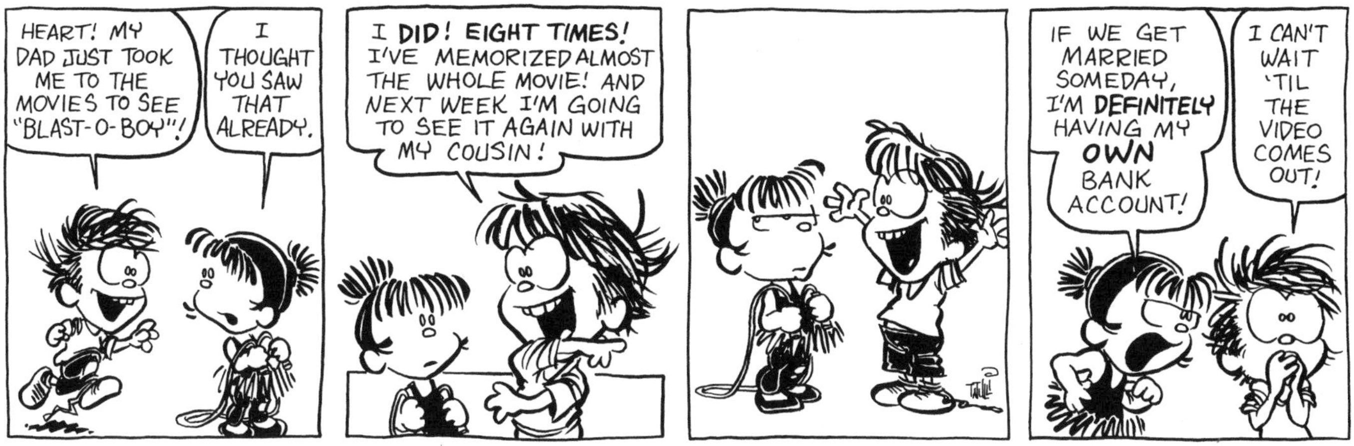
HEART! MY DAD JUST TOOK ME TO THE MOVIES TO SEE "BLAST-O-BOY"!
I THOUGHT YOU SAW THAT ALREADY.
I **DID**! **EIGHT TIMES!** I'VE MEMORIZED ALMOST THE WHOLE MOVIE! AND NEXT WEEK I'M GOING TO SEE IT AGAIN WITH MY COUSIN!
IF WE GET MARRIED SOMEDAY, I'M **DEFINITELY** HAVING MY **OWN** BANK ACCOUNT!
I CAN'T WAIT 'TIL THE VIDEO COMES OUT!

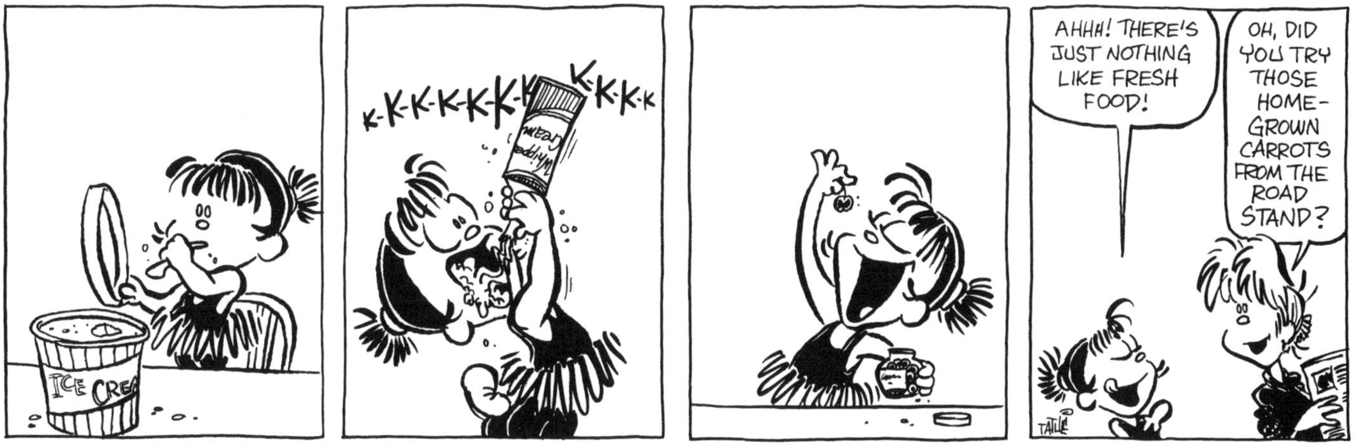
ICE CREA
K-K-K-K-K-K-K K-K-K-K
AHHH! THERE'S JUST NOTHING LIKE FRESH FOOD!
OH, DID YOU TRY THOSE HOME-GROWN CARROTS FROM THE ROAD STAND?

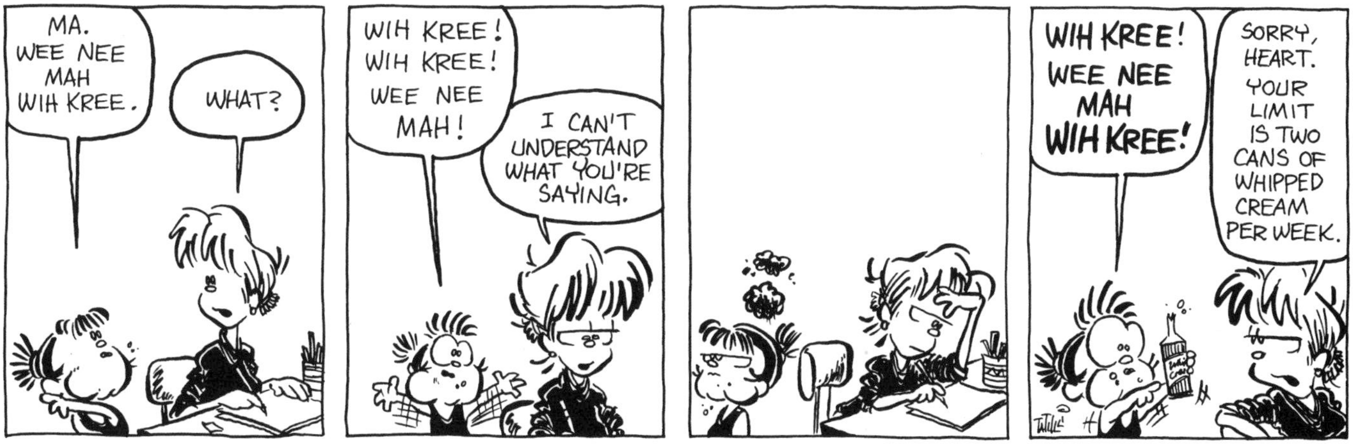
MA. WEE NEE MAH WIH KREE.
WHAT?
WIH KREE! WIH KREE! WEE NEE MAH!
I CAN'T UNDERSTAND WHAT YOU'RE SAYING.
WIH KREE! WEE NEE MAH WIH KREE!
SORRY, HEART. YOUR LIMIT IS TWO CANS OF WHIPPED CREAM PER WEEK.

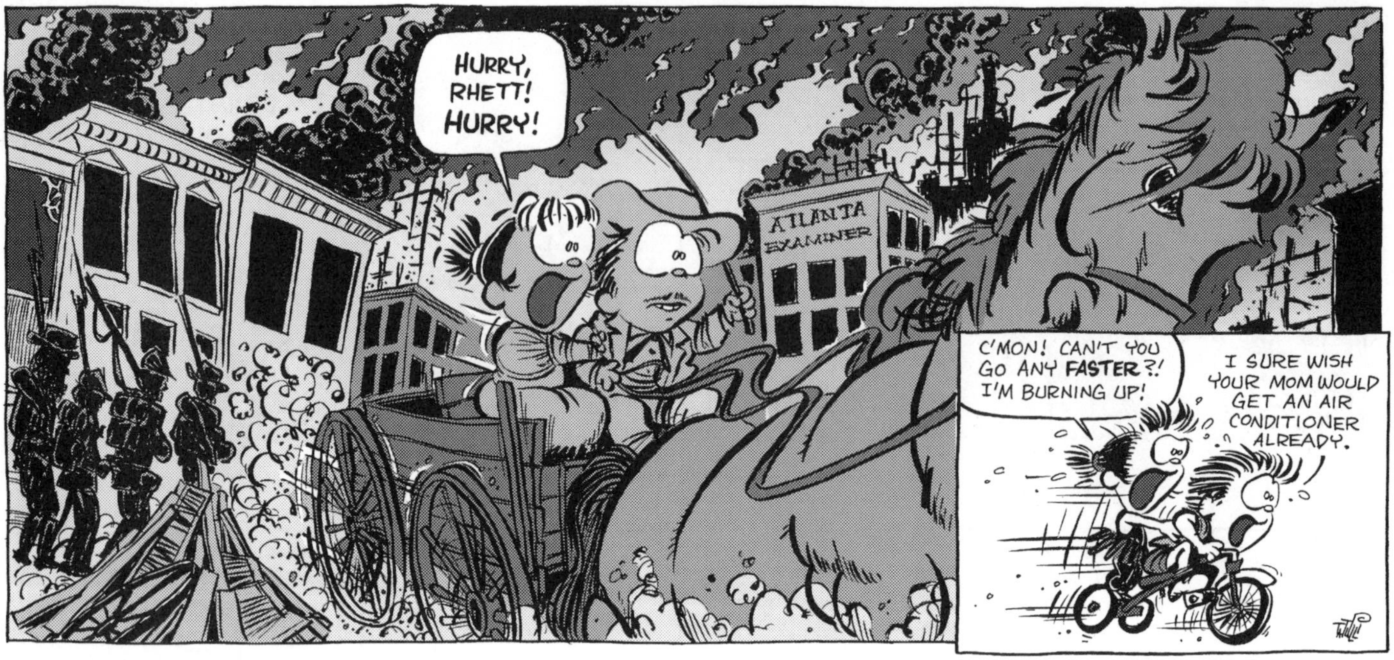
HURRY, RHETT! HURRY!
ATLANTA EXAMINER
C'MON! CAN'T YOU GO ANY **FASTER**?! I'M BURNING UP!
I SURE WISH YOUR MOM WOULD GET AN AIR CONDITIONER ALREADY.

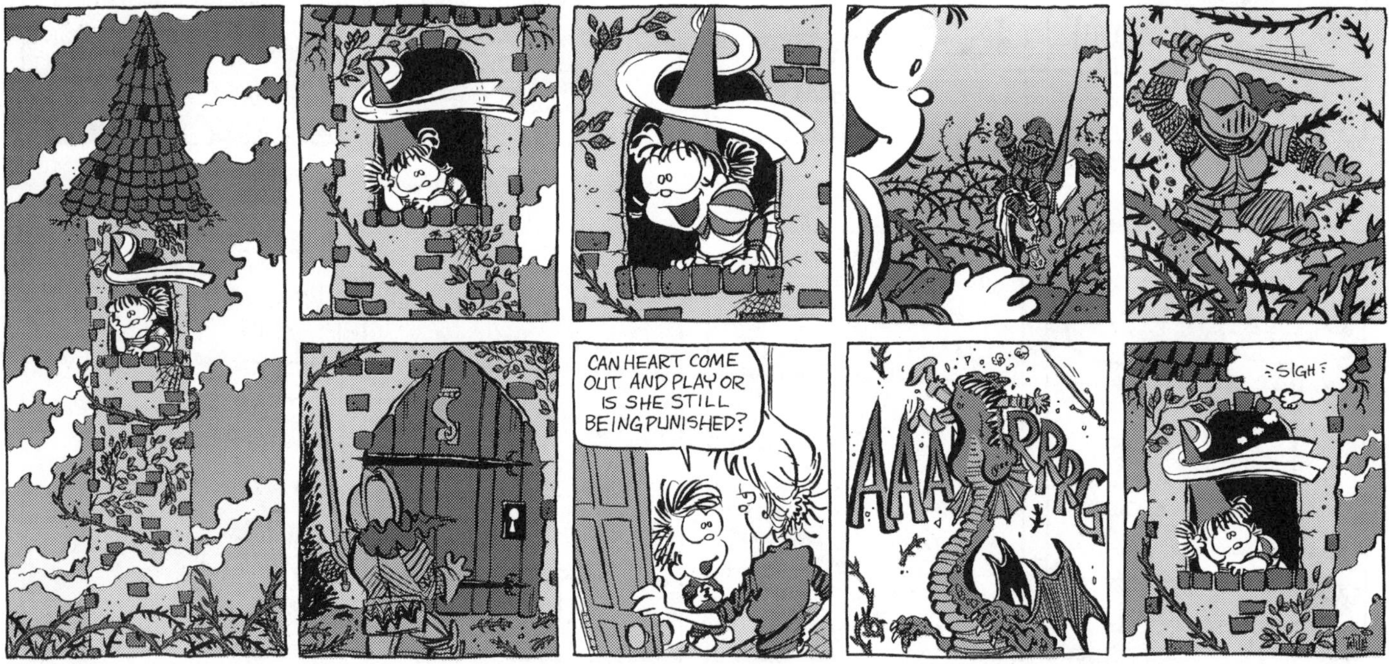
CAN HEART COME OUT AND PLAY OR IS SHE STILL BEING PUNISHED?
AAA
RRRG
SIGH

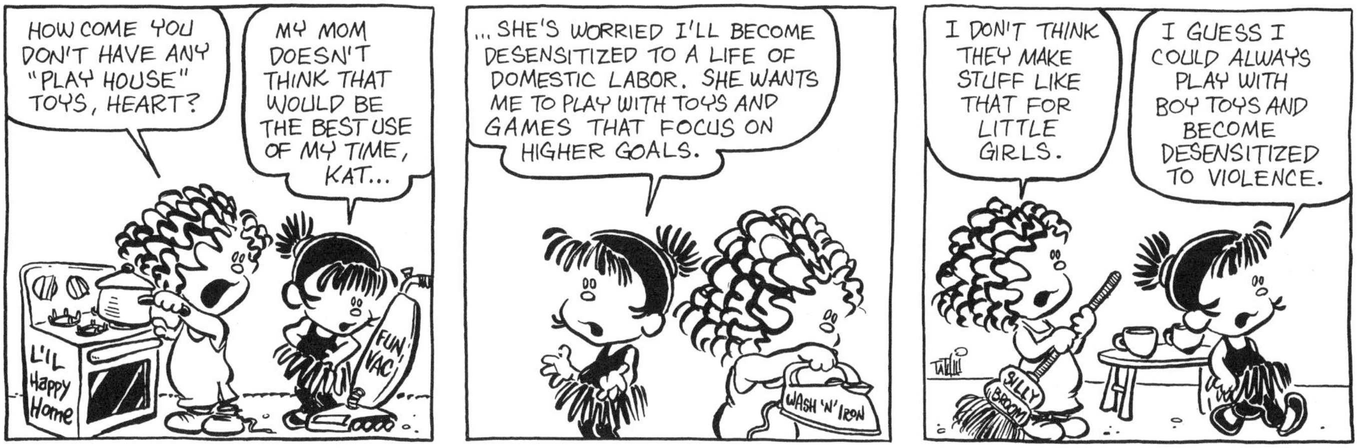
HOW COME YOU DON'T HAVE ANY "PLAY HOUSE" TOYS, HEART?
MY MOM DOESN'T THINK THAT WOULD BE THE BEST USE OF MY TIME, KAT...
L'IL Happy Home
FUN VAC
...SHE'S WORRIED I'LL BECOME DESENSITIZED TO A LIFE OF DOMESTIC LABOR. SHE WANTS ME TO PLAY WITH TOYS AND GAMES THAT FOCUS ON HIGHER GOALS.
WASH 'N' IRON
I DON'T THINK THEY MAKE STUFF LIKE THAT FOR LITTLE GIRLS.
I GUESS I COULD ALWAYS PLAY WITH BOY TOYS AND BECOME DESENSITIZED TO VIOLENCE.
SILLY BROOM

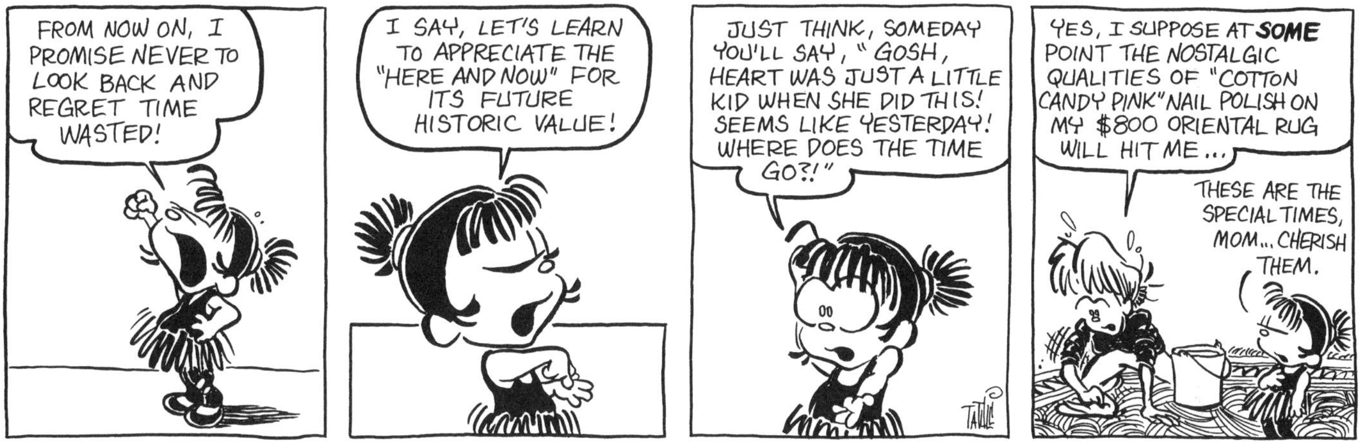
FROM NOW ON, I PROMISE NEVER TO LOOK BACK AND REGRET TIME WASTED!
I SAY, LET'S LEARN TO APPRECIATE THE "HERE AND NOW" FOR ITS FUTURE HISTORIC VALUE!
JUST THINK, SOMEDAY YOU'LL SAY, "GOSH, HEART WAS JUST A LITTLE KID WHEN SHE DID THIS! SEEMS LIKE YESTERDAY! WHERE DOES THE TIME GO?!"
YES, I SUPPOSE AT **SOME** POINT THE NOSTALGIC QUALITIES OF "COTTON CANDY PINK" NAIL POLISH ON MY $800 ORIENTAL RUG WILL HIT ME...
THESE ARE THE SPECIAL TIMES, MOM... CHERISH THEM.

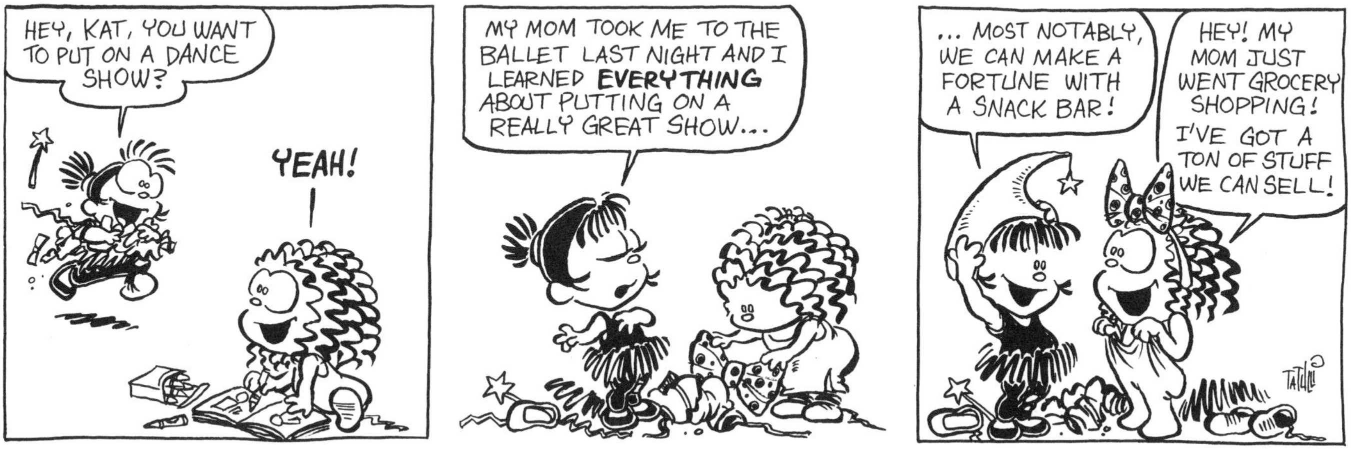
HEY, KAT, YOU WANT TO PUT ON A DANCE SHOW?
YEAH!
MY MOM TOOK ME TO THE BALLET LAST NIGHT AND I LEARNED **EVERYTHING** ABOUT PUTTING ON A REALLY GREAT SHOW...
... MOST NOTABLY, WE CAN MAKE A FORTUNE WITH A SNACK BAR!
HEY! MY MOM JUST WENT GROCERY SHOPPING!
I'VE GOT A TON OF STUFF WE CAN SELL!

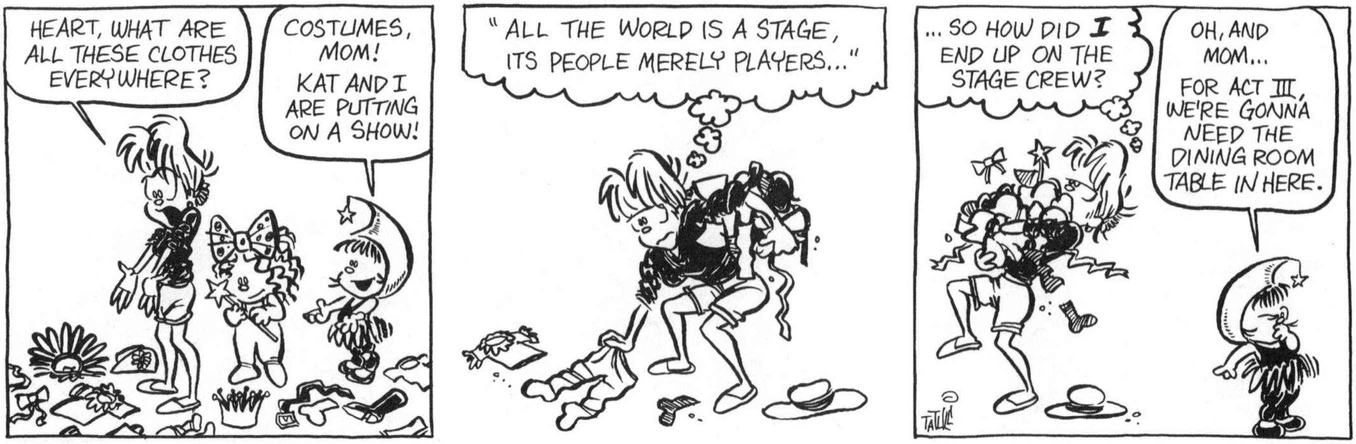
HEART, WHAT ARE ALL THESE CLOTHES EVERYWHERE?
COSTUMES, MOM! KAT AND I ARE PUTTING ON A SHOW!
"ALL THE WORLD IS A STAGE, ITS PEOPLE MERELY PLAYERS..."
...SO HOW DID I END UP ON THE STAGE CREW?
OH, AND MOM... FOR ACT III, WE'RE GONNA NEED THE DINING ROOM TABLE IN HERE.

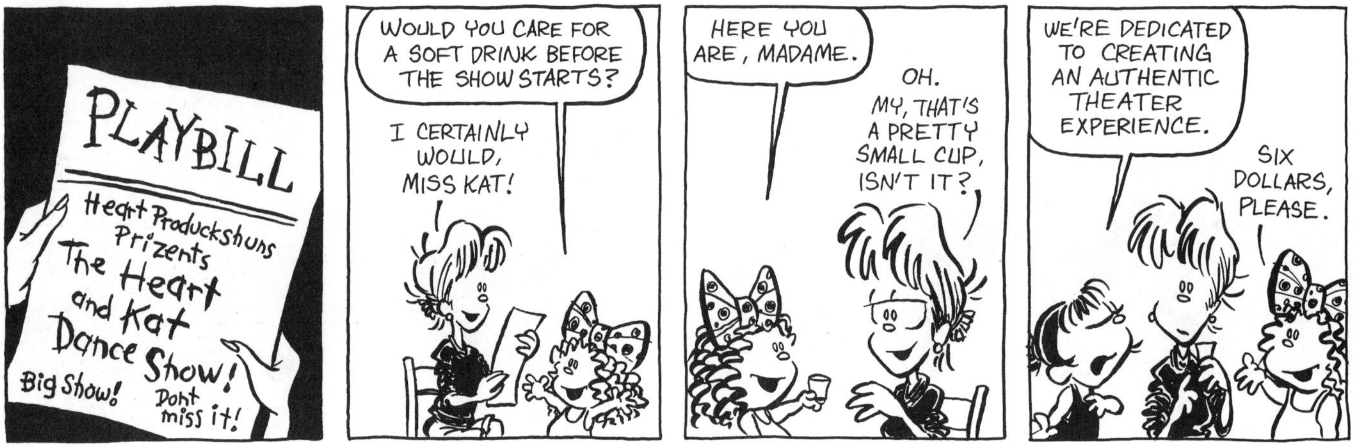
PLAYBILL
Heart Produckshuns Prizents The Heart and Kat Dance Show!
Big Show!
Dont miss it!
WOULD YOU CARE FOR A SOFT DRINK BEFORE THE SHOW STARTS?
I CERTAINLY WOULD, MISS KAT!
HERE YOU ARE, MADAME.
OH. MY, THAT'S A PRETTY SMALL CUP, ISN'T IT?
WE'RE DEDICATED TO CREATING AN AUTHENTIC THEATER EXPERIENCE.
SIX DOLLARS, PLEASE.

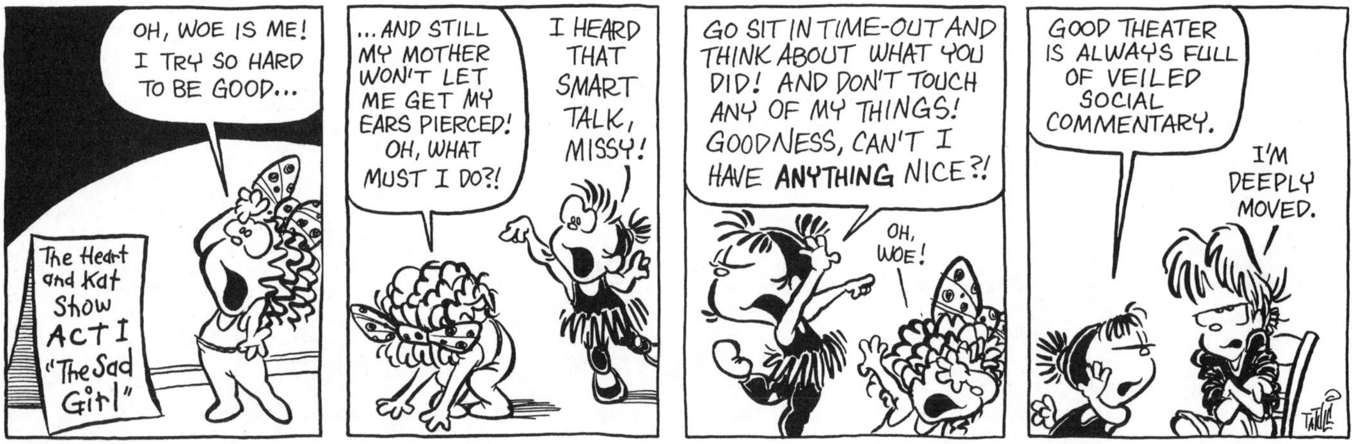
OH, WOE IS ME! I TRY SO HARD TO BE GOOD...
The Heart and Kat Show ACT I "The Sad Girl"
...AND STILL MY MOTHER WON'T LET ME GET MY EARS PIERCED! OH, WHAT MUST I DO?!
I HEARD THAT SMART TALK, MISSY!
GO SIT IN TIME-OUT AND THINK ABOUT WHAT YOU DID! AND DON'T TOUCH ANY OF MY THINGS! GOODNESS, CAN'T I HAVE ANYTHING NICE?!
OH, WOE!
GOOD THEATER IS ALWAYS FULL OF VEILED SOCIAL COMMENTARY.
I'M DEEPLY MOVED.

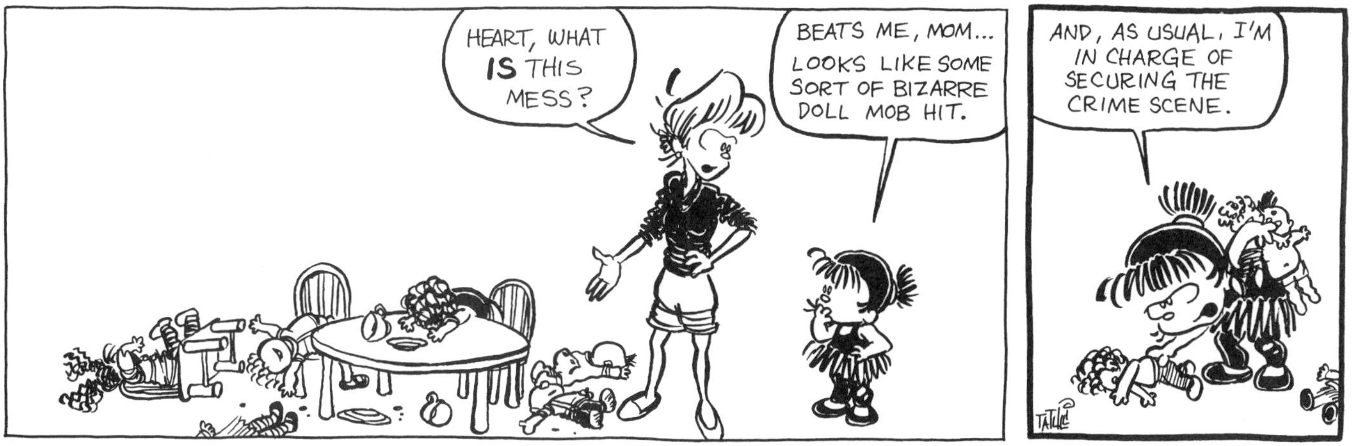
HEART, WHAT **IS** THIS MESS?
BEATS ME, MOM... LOOKS LIKE SOME SORT OF BIZARRE DOLL MOB HIT.
AND, AS USUAL, I'M IN CHARGE OF SECURING THE CRIME SCENE.

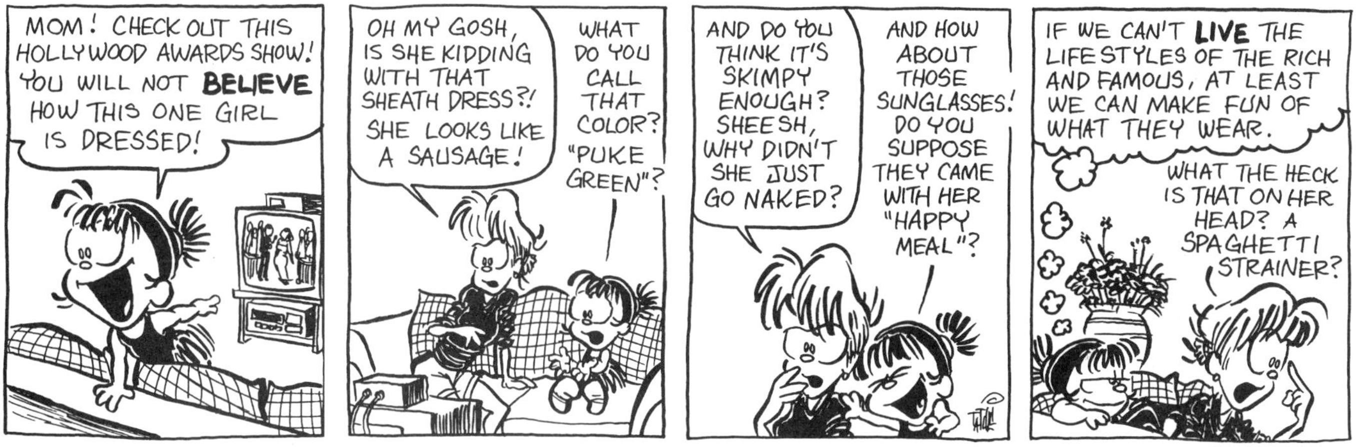
MOM! CHECK OUT THIS HOLLYWOOD AWARDS SHOW! YOU WILL NOT **BELIEVE** HOW THIS ONE GIRL IS DRESSED!
OH MY GOSH, IS SHE KIDDING WITH THAT SHEATH DRESS?! SHE LOOKS LIKE A SAUSAGE!
WHAT DO YOU CALL THAT COLOR? "PUKE GREEN"?
AND DO YOU THINK IT'S SKIMPY ENOUGH? SHEESH, WHY DIDN'T SHE JUST GO NAKED?
AND HOW ABOUT THOSE SUNGLASSES! DO YOU SUPPOSE THEY CAME WITH HER "HAPPY MEAL"?
IF WE CAN'T **LIVE** THE LIFESTYLES OF THE RICH AND FAMOUS, AT LEAST WE CAN MAKE FUN OF WHAT THEY WEAR.
WHAT THE HECK IS THAT ON HER HEAD? A SPAGHETTI STRAINER?

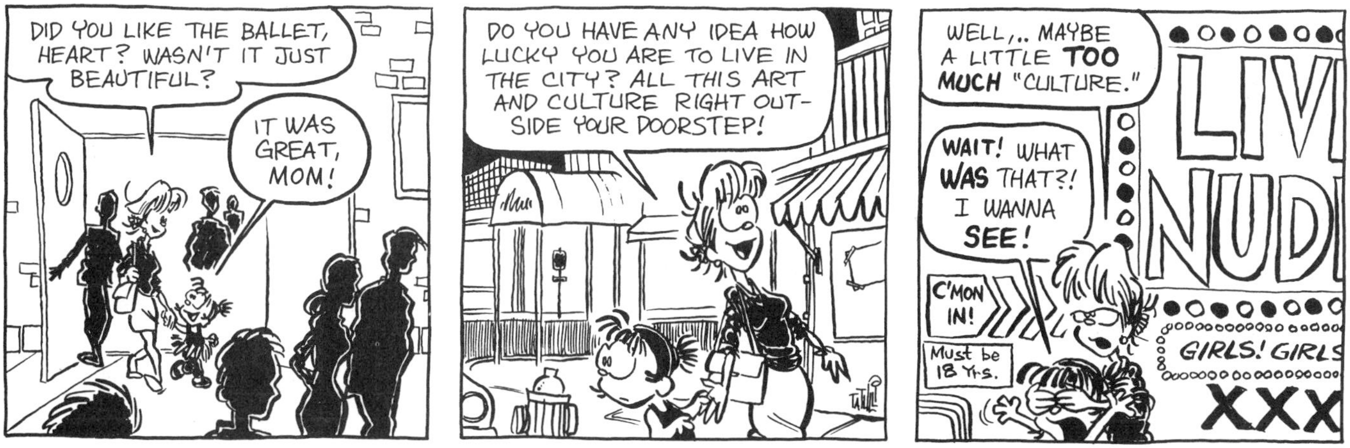
DID YOU LIKE THE BALLET, HEART? WASN'T IT JUST BEAUTIFUL?
IT WAS GREAT, MOM!
DO YOU HAVE ANY IDEA HOW LUCKY YOU ARE TO LIVE IN THE CITY? ALL THIS ART AND CULTURE RIGHT OUTSIDE YOUR DOORSTEP!
WELL,.. MAYBE A LITTLE **TOO MUCH** "CULTURE."
WAIT! WHAT **WAS** THAT?! I WANNA **SEE!**
LIV
NUD
C'MON IN!
Must be 18 Yrs.
GIRLS! GIRLS
XXX

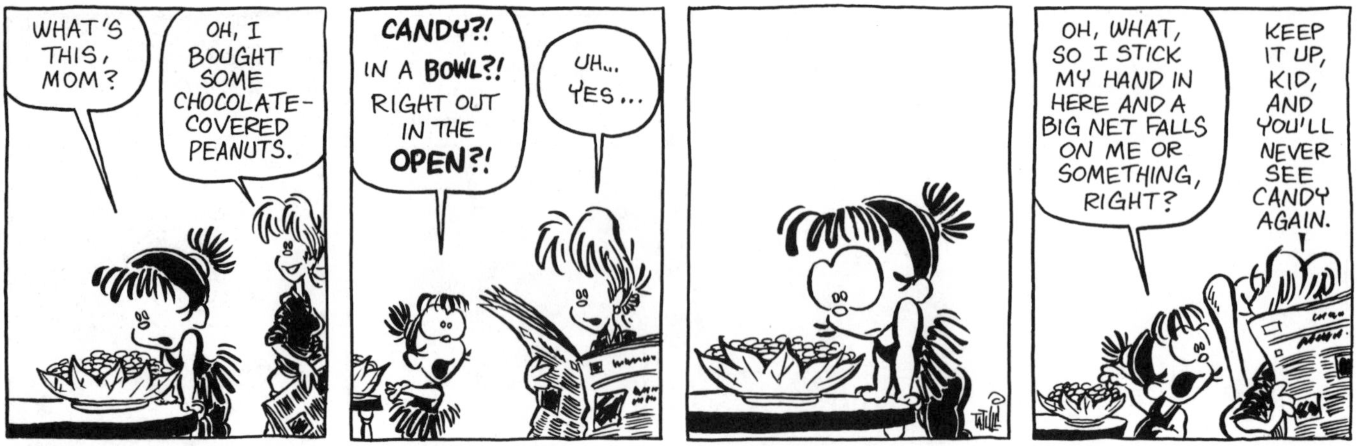
WHAT'S THIS, MOM?
OH, I BOUGHT SOME CHOCOLATE-COVERED PEANUTS.
CANDY?! IN A BOWL?! RIGHT OUT IN THE OPEN?!
UH... YES...
OH, WHAT, SO I STICK MY HAND IN HERE AND A BIG NET FALLS ON ME OR SOMETHING, RIGHT?
KEEP IT UP, KID, AND YOU'LL NEVER SEE CANDY AGAIN.

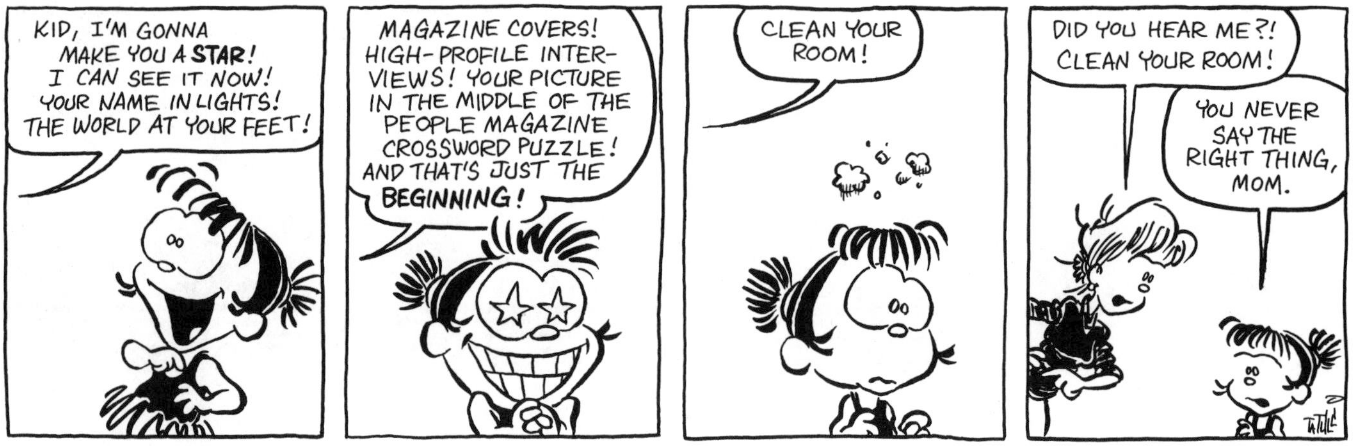
KID, I'M GONNA MAKE YOU A STAR! I CAN SEE IT NOW! YOUR NAME IN LIGHTS! THE WORLD AT YOUR FEET!
MAGAZINE COVERS! HIGH-PROFILE INTERVIEWS! YOUR PICTURE IN THE MIDDLE OF THE PEOPLE MAGAZINE CROSSWORD PUZZLE! AND THAT'S JUST THE BEGINNING!
CLEAN YOUR ROOM!
DID YOU HEAR ME?! CLEAN YOUR ROOM!
YOU NEVER SAY THE RIGHT THING, MOM.

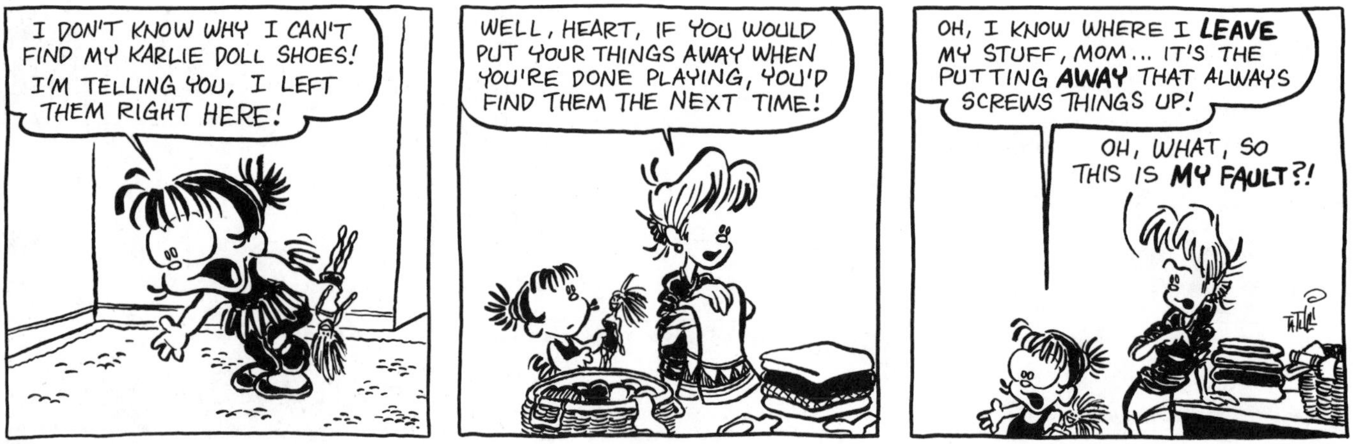
I DON'T KNOW WHY I CAN'T FIND MY KARLIE DOLL SHOES! I'M TELLING YOU, I LEFT THEM RIGHT HERE!
WELL, HEART, IF YOU WOULD PUT YOUR THINGS AWAY WHEN YOU'RE DONE PLAYING, YOU'D FIND THEM THE NEXT TIME!
OH, I KNOW WHERE I LEAVE MY STUFF, MOM... IT'S THE PUTTING AWAY THAT ALWAYS SCREWS THINGS UP!
OH, WHAT, SO THIS IS MY FAULT?!

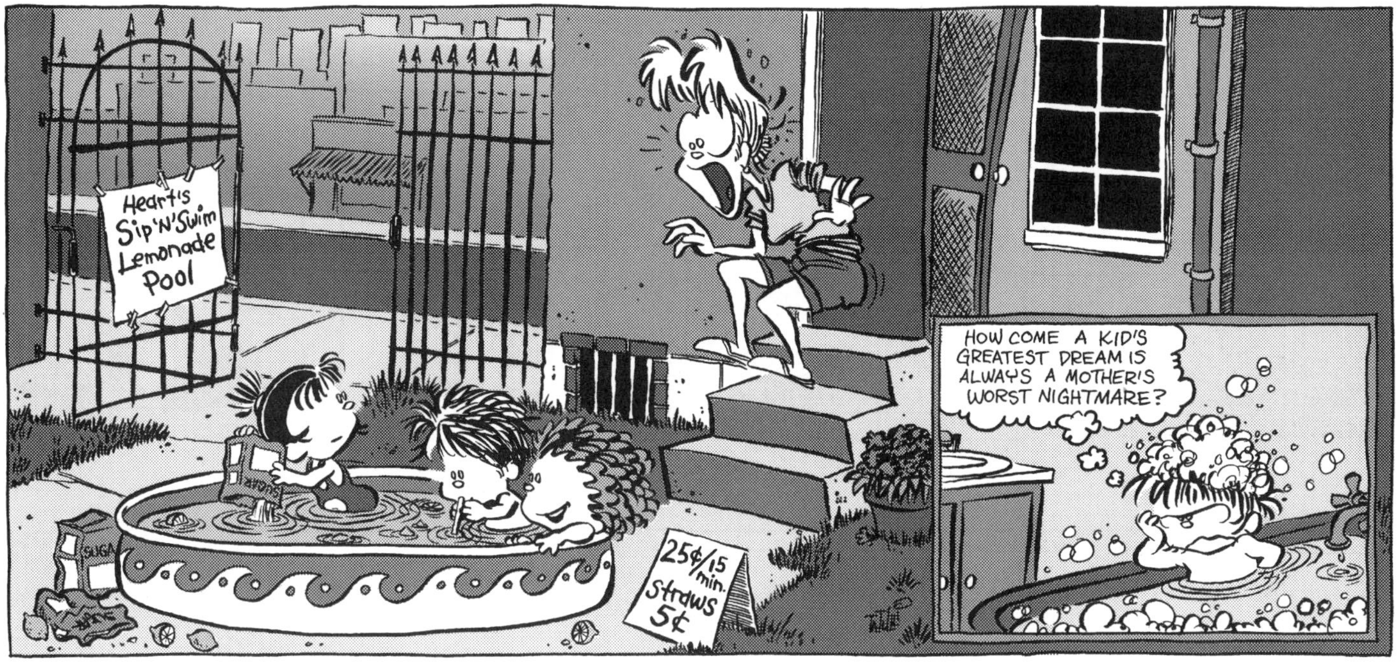
Heart's Sip'N'Swim Lemonade Pool
25¢/15 min. Straws 5¢
HOW COME A KID'S GREATEST DREAM IS ALWAYS A MOTHER'S WORST NIGHTMARE?

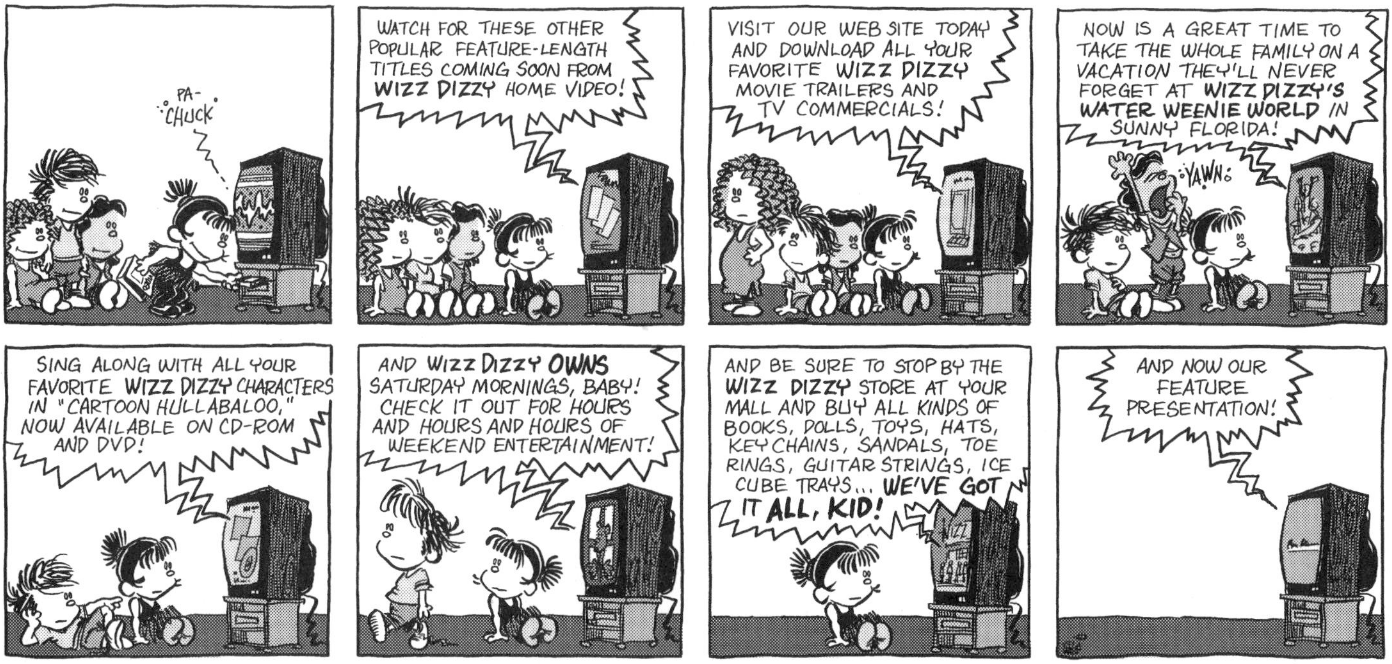
PA-CHUCK
WATCH FOR THESE OTHER POPULAR FEATURE-LENGTH TITLES COMING SOON FROM WIZZ DIZZY HOME VIDEO!
VISIT OUR WEB SITE TODAY AND DOWNLOAD ALL YOUR FAVORITE WIZZ DIZZY MOVIE TRAILERS AND TV COMMERCIALS!
NOW IS A GREAT TIME TO TAKE THE WHOLE FAMILY ON A VACATION THEY'LL NEVER FORGET AT WIZZ DIZZY'S WATER WEENIE WORLD IN SUNNY FLORIDA!
YAWN
SING ALONG WITH ALL YOUR FAVORITE WIZZ DIZZY CHARACTERS IN "CARTOON HULLABALOO," NOW AVAILABLE ON CD-ROM AND DVD!
AND WIZZ DIZZY OWNS SATURDAY MORNINGS, BABY! CHECK IT OUT FOR HOURS AND HOURS AND HOURS OF WEEKEND ENTERTAINMENT!
AND BE SURE TO STOP BY THE WIZZ DIZZY STORE AT YOUR MALL AND BUY ALL KINDS OF BOOKS, DOLLS, TOYS, HATS, KEY CHAINS, SANDALS, TOE RINGS, GUITAR STRINGS, ICE CUBE TRAYS... WE'VE GOT IT ALL, KID!
AND NOW OUR FEATURE PRESENTATION!

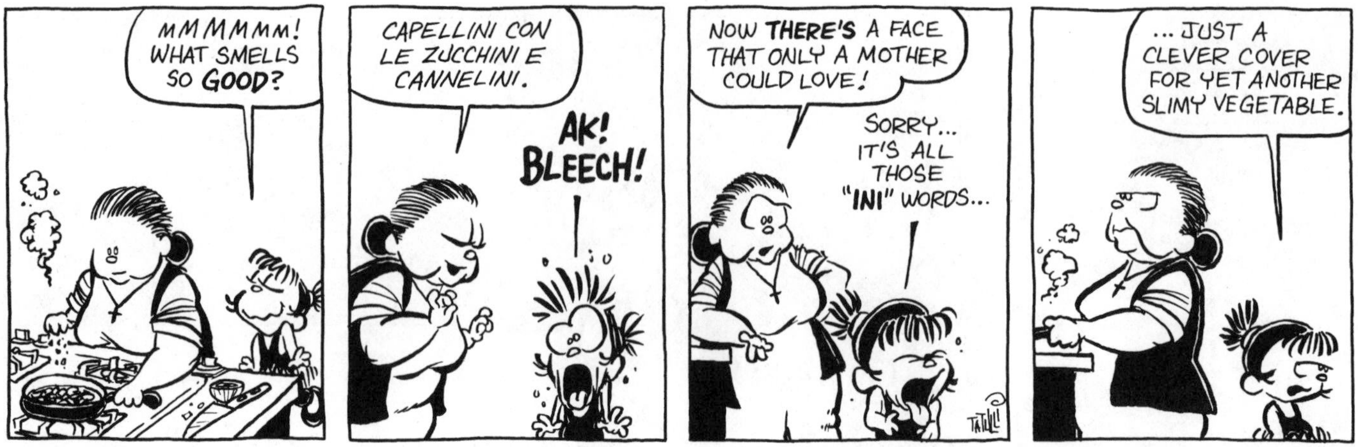
MMMMMM! WHAT SMELLS SO GOOD?
CAPELLINI CON LE ZUCCHINI E CANNELINI.
AK! BLEECH!
NOW THERE'S A FACE THAT ONLY A MOTHER COULD LOVE!
SORRY... IT'S ALL THOSE "INI" WORDS...
... JUST A CLEVER COVER FOR YET ANOTHER SLIMY VEGETABLE.

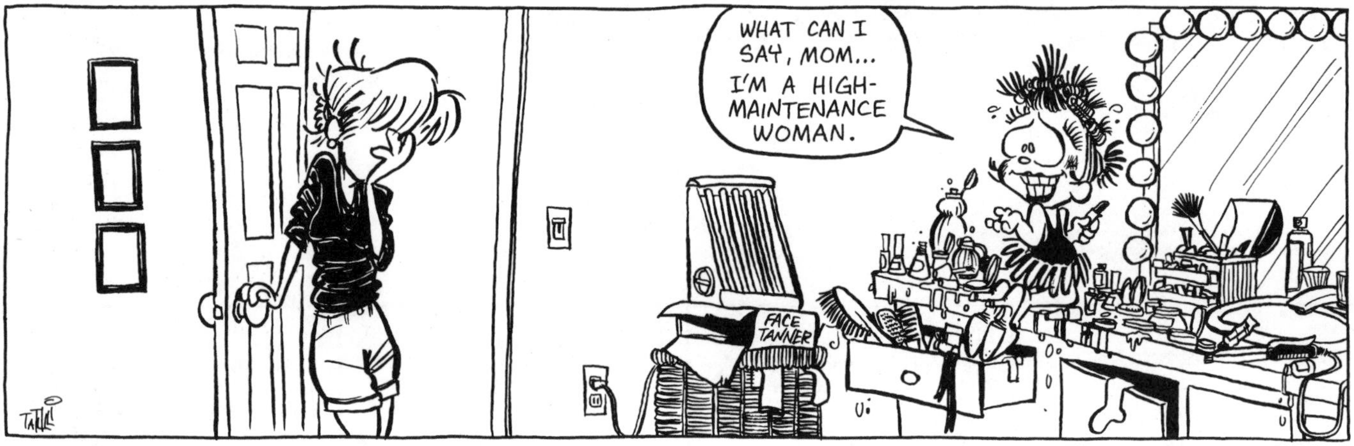
WHAT CAN I SAY, MOM... I'M A HIGH-MAINTENANCE WOMAN.
FACE TANNER

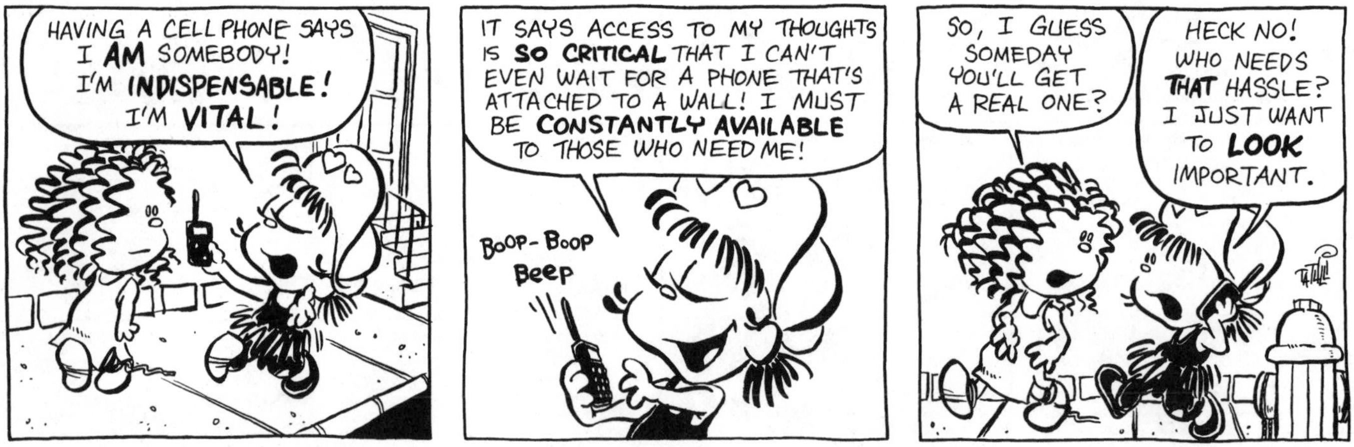
HAVING A CELLPHONE SAYS I AM SOMEBODY! I'M INDISPENSABLE! I'M VITAL!
IT SAYS ACCESS TO MY THOUGHTS IS SO CRITICAL THAT I CAN'T EVEN WAIT FOR A PHONE THAT'S ATTACHED TO A WALL! I MUST BE CONSTANTLY AVAILABLE TO THOSE WHO NEED ME!
BOOP-BOOP BEEP
SO, I GUESS SOMEDAY YOU'LL GET A REAL ONE?
HECK NO! WHO NEEDS THAT HASSLE? I JUST WANT TO LOOK IMPORTANT.

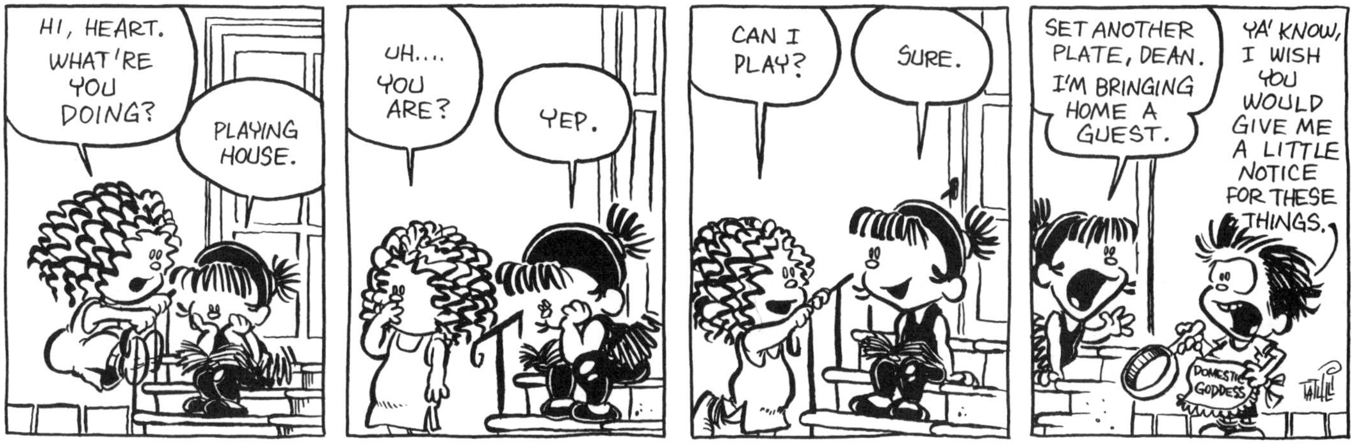
HI, HEART. WHAT'RE YOU DOING?
PLAYING HOUSE.
UH.... YOU ARE?
YEP.
CAN I PLAY?
SURE.
SET ANOTHER PLATE, DEAN. I'M BRINGING HOME A GUEST.
YA' KNOW, I WISH YOU WOULD GIVE ME A LITTLE NOTICE FOR THESE THINGS.
DOMESTIC GODDESS

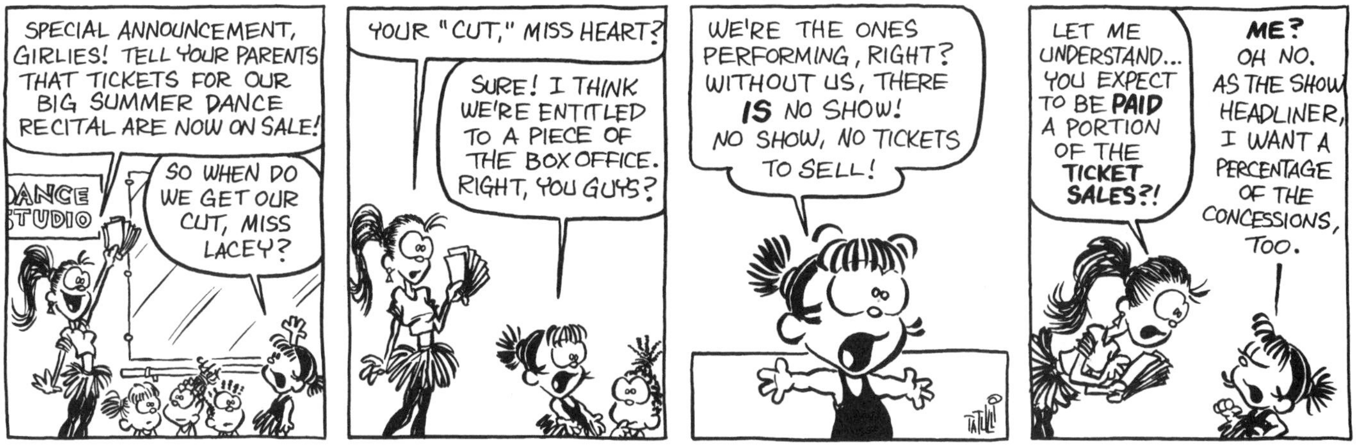
SPECIAL ANNOUNCEMENT, GIRLIES! TELL YOUR PARENTS THAT TICKETS FOR OUR BIG SUMMER DANCE RECITAL ARE NOW ON SALE!
DANCE STUDIO
SO WHEN DO WE GET OUR CUT, MISS LACEY?
YOUR "CUT," MISS HEART?
SURE! I THINK WE'RE ENTITLED TO A PIECE OF THE BOX OFFICE. RIGHT, YOU GUYS?
WE'RE THE ONES PERFORMING, RIGHT? WITHOUT US, THERE **IS** NO SHOW! NO SHOW, NO TICKETS TO SELL!
LET ME UNDERSTAND... YOU EXPECT TO BE **PAID** A PORTION OF THE **TICKET SALES?!**
ME? OH NO. AS THE SHOW HEADLINER, I WANT A PERCENTAGE OF THE CONCESSIONS, TOO.

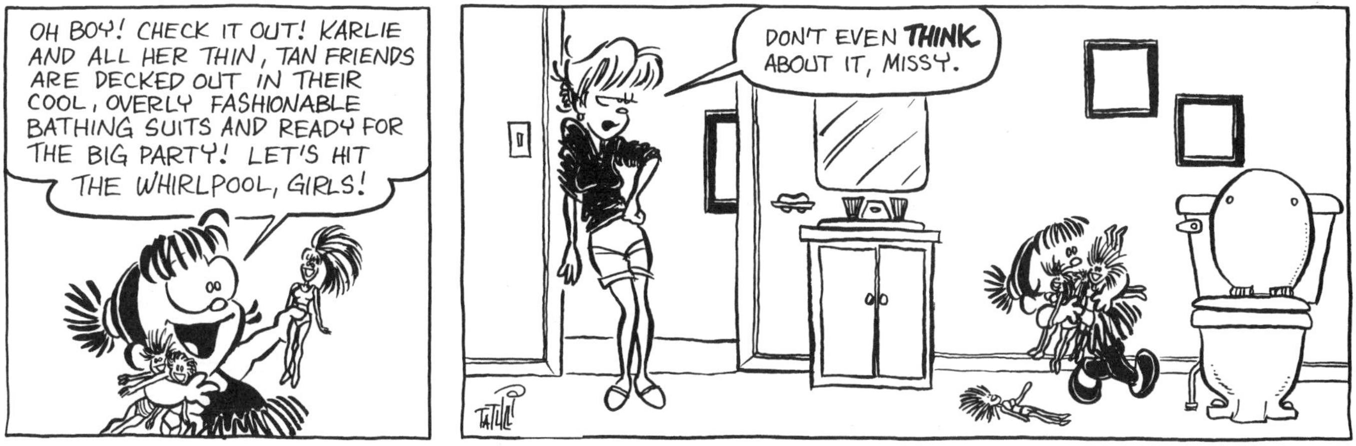
OH BOY! CHECK IT OUT! KARLIE AND ALL HER THIN, TAN FRIENDS ARE DECKED OUT IN THEIR COOL, OVERLY FASHIONABLE BATHING SUITS AND READY FOR THE BIG PARTY! LET'S HIT THE WHIRLPOOL, GIRLS!
DON'T EVEN **THINK** ABOUT IT, MISSY.

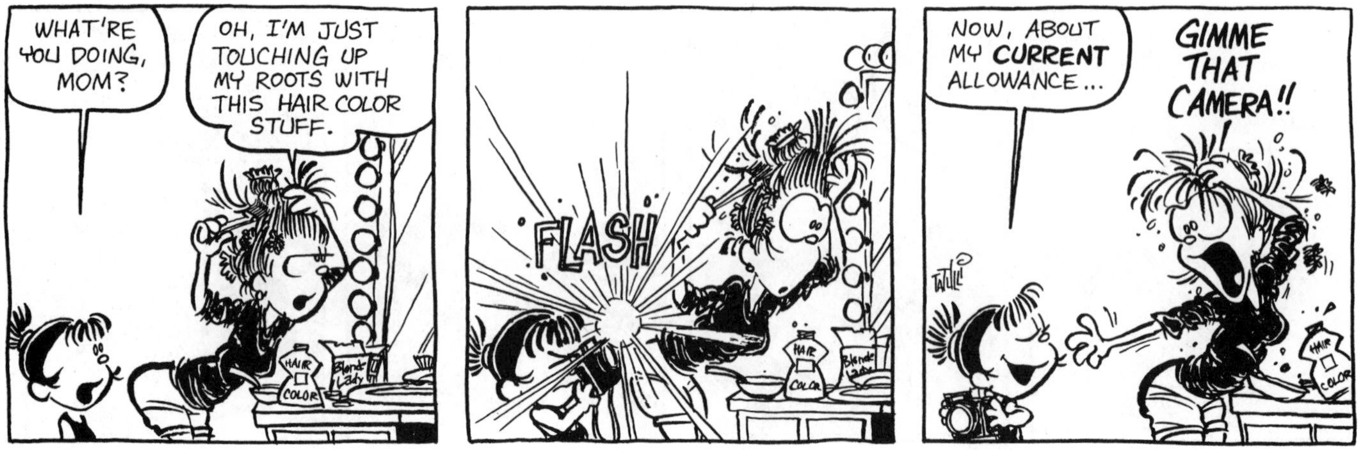
WHAT'RE YOU DOING, MOM?
OH, I'M JUST TOUCHING UP MY ROOTS WITH THIS HAIR COLOR STUFF.
FLASH
NOW, ABOUT MY **CURRENT** ALLOWANCE...
GIMME THAT CAMERA!!

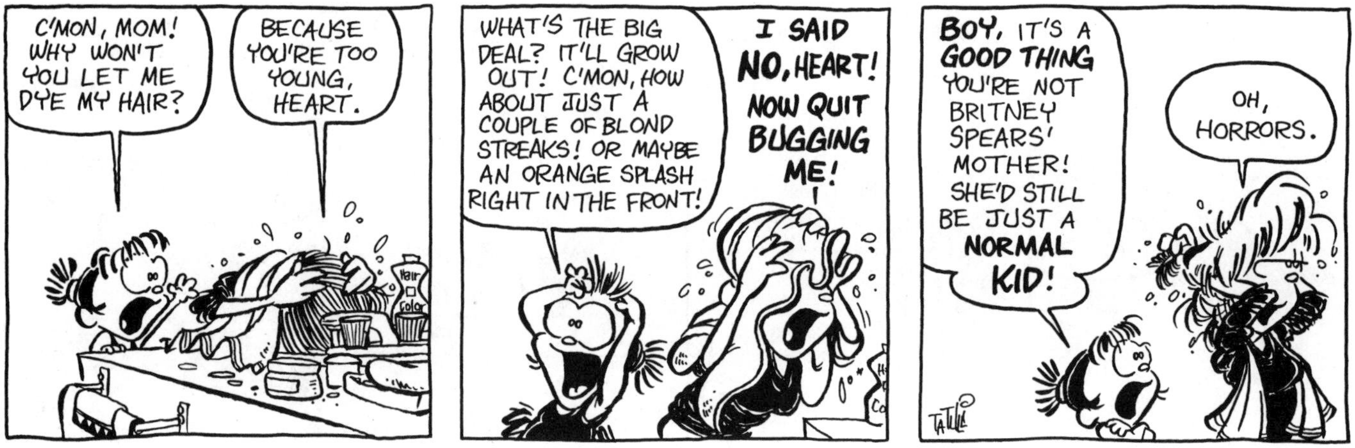
C'MON, MOM! WHY WON'T YOU LET ME DYE MY HAIR?
BECAUSE YOU'RE TOO YOUNG, HEART.
WHAT'S THE BIG DEAL? IT'LL GROW OUT! C'MON, HOW ABOUT JUST A COUPLE OF BLOND STREAKS! OR MAYBE AN ORANGE SPLASH RIGHT IN THE FRONT!
I SAID NO, HEART! NOW QUIT BUGGING ME!
BOY, IT'S A **GOOD THING** YOU'RE NOT BRITNEY SPEARS' MOTHER! SHE'D STILL BE JUST A **NORMAL KID!**
OH, HORRORS.

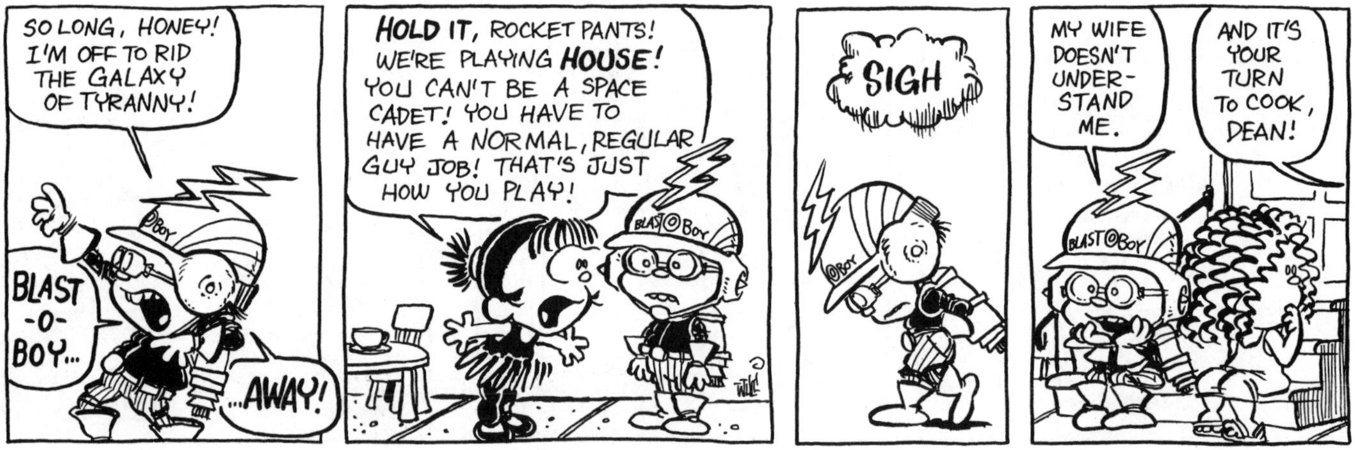
SO LONG, HONEY! I'M OFF TO RID THE GALAXY OF TYRANNY!
BLAST -O- BOY...
...AWAY!
HOLD IT, ROCKET PANTS! WE'RE PLAYING **HOUSE**! YOU CAN'T BE A SPACE CADET! YOU HAVE TO HAVE A NORMAL, REGULAR GUY JOB! THAT'S JUST HOW YOU PLAY!
SIGH
MY WIFE DOESN'T UNDER- STAND ME.
AND IT'S YOUR TURN TO COOK, DEAN!

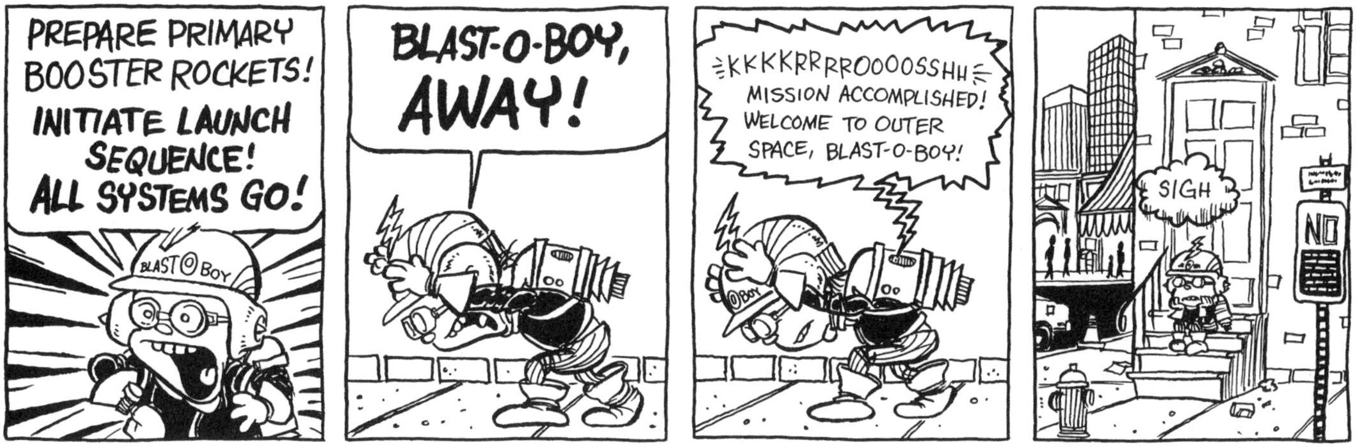
PREPARE PRIMARY BOOSTER ROCKETS! INITIATE LAUNCH SEQUENCE! ALL SYSTEMS GO!
BLAST O BOY
BLAST-O-BOY, AWAY!
KKKKRRRROOOOOSSHH MISSION ACCOMPLISHED! WELCOME TO OUTER SPACE, BLAST-O-BOY!
SIGH
NO

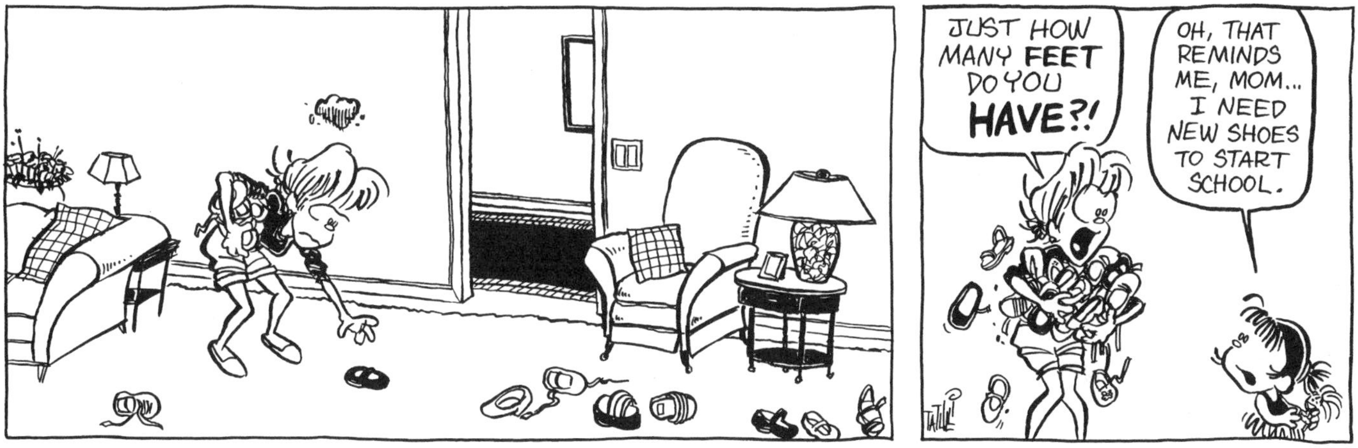
JUST HOW MANY FEET DO YOU HAVE?!
OH, THAT REMINDS ME, MOM... I NEED NEW SHOES TO START SCHOOL.
TATULLI

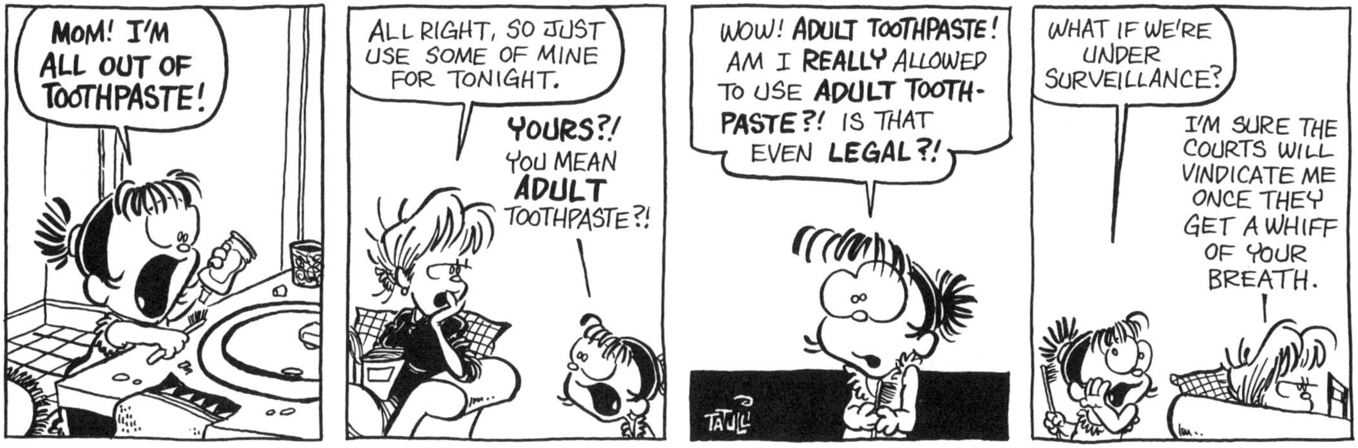
MOM! I'M ALL OUT OF TOOTHPASTE!
ALL RIGHT, SO JUST USE SOME OF MINE FOR TONIGHT.
YOURS?! YOU MEAN ADULT TOOTHPASTE?!
WOW! ADULT TOOTHPASTE! AM I REALLY ALLOWED TO USE ADULT TOOTH-PASTE?! IS THAT EVEN LEGAL?!
TATULLI
WHAT IF WE'RE UNDER SURVEILLANCE?
I'M SURE THE COURTS WILL VINDICATE ME ONCE THEY GET A WHIFF OF YOUR BREATH.

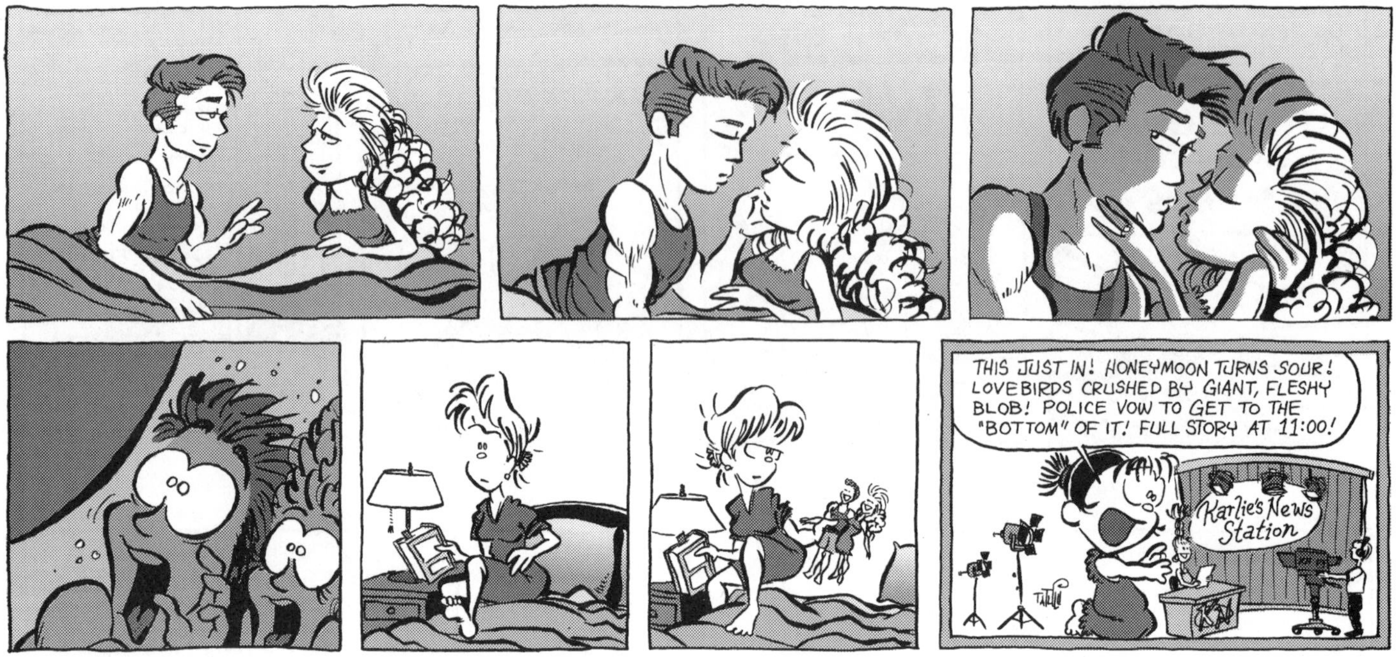
THIS JUST IN! HONEYMOON TURNS SOUR! LOVEBIRDS CRUSHED BY GIANT, FLESHY BLOB! POLICE VOW TO GET TO THE "BOTTOM" OF IT! FULL STORY AT 11:00!
Karlie's News Station

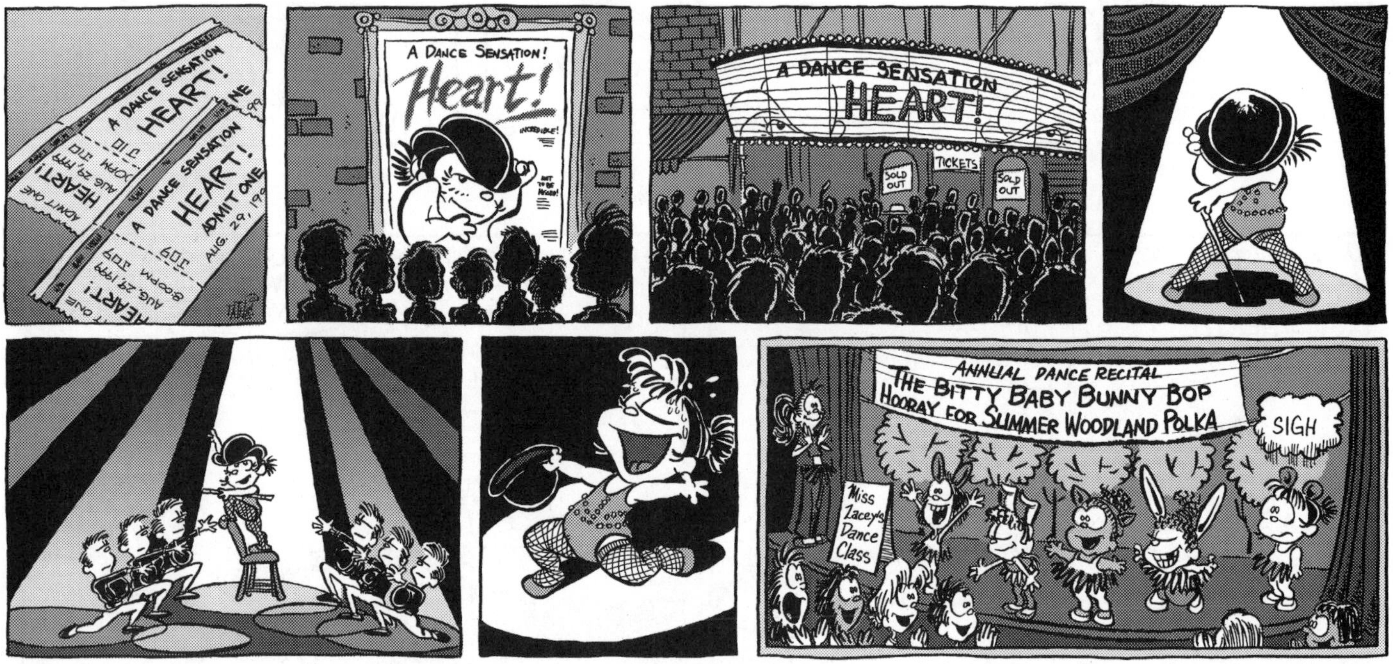
A DANCE SENSATION
HEART!
A DANCE SENSATION
HEART!
ADMIT ONE
A DANCE SENSATION!
Heart!
INCREDIBLE!
A DANCE SENSATION
HEART!
TICKETS
SOLD OUT
SOLD OUT
ANNUAL DANCE RECITAL
THE BITTY BABY BUNNY BOP
HOORAY FOR SUMMER WOODLAND POLKA
SIGH
Miss Lacey's Dance Class

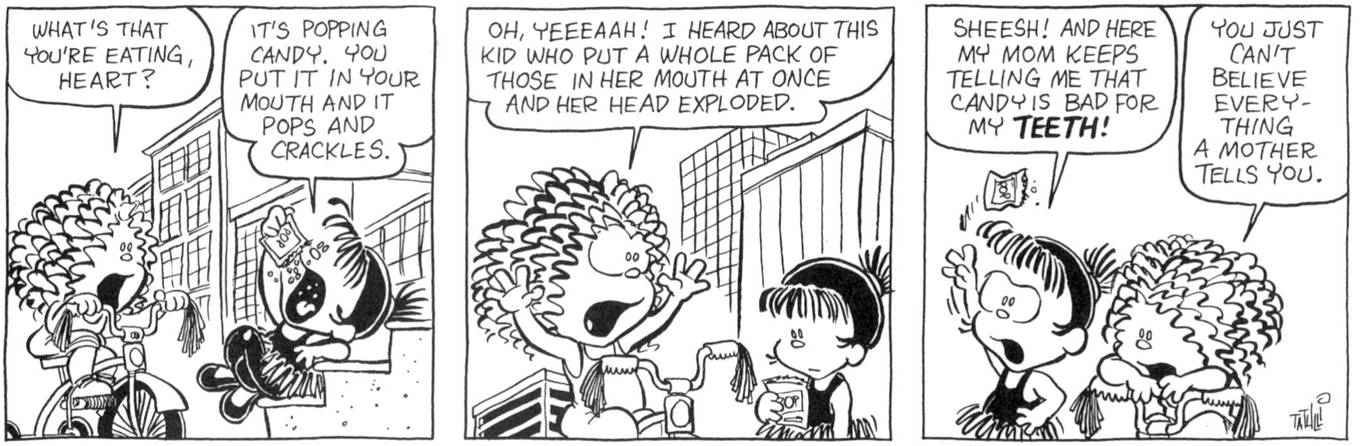
WHAT'S THAT YOU'RE EATING, HEART?
IT'S POPPING CANDY. YOU PUT IT IN YOUR MOUTH AND IT POPS AND CRACKLES.
OH, YEEEAAH! I HEARD ABOUT THIS KID WHO PUT A WHOLE PACK OF THOSE IN HER MOUTH AT ONCE AND HER HEAD EXPLODED.
SHEESH! AND HERE MY MOM KEEPS TELLING ME THAT CANDY IS BAD FOR MY **TEETH!**
YOU JUST CAN'T BELIEVE EVERYTHING A MOTHER TELLS YOU.

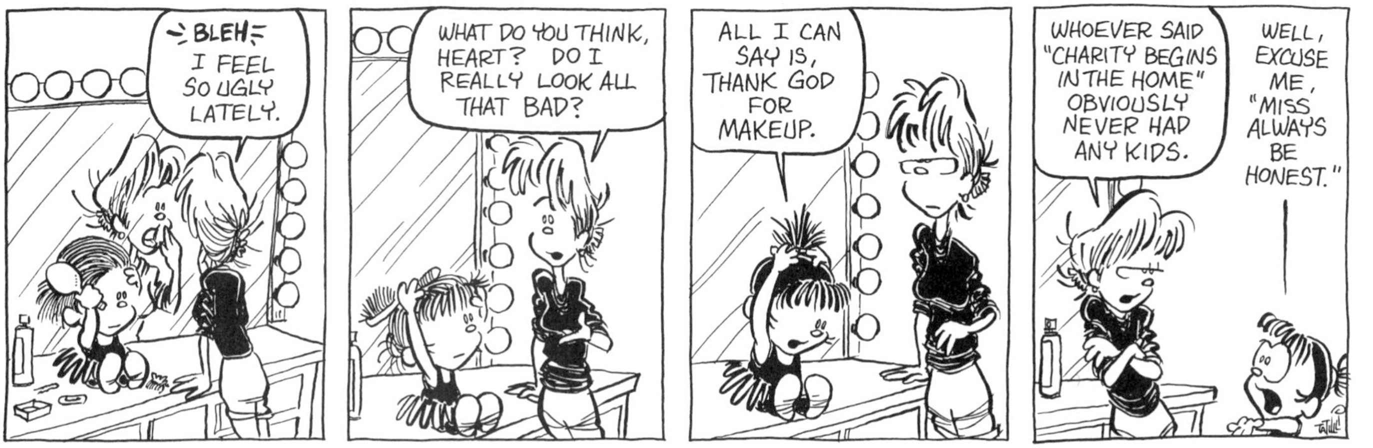
BLEH
I FEEL SO UGLY LATELY.
WHAT DO YOU THINK, HEART? DO I REALLY LOOK ALL THAT BAD?
ALL I CAN SAY IS, THANK GOD FOR MAKEUP.
WHOEVER SAID "CHARITY BEGINS IN THE HOME" OBVIOUSLY NEVER HAD ANY KIDS.
WELL, EXCUSE ME, "MISS ALWAYS BE HONEST."

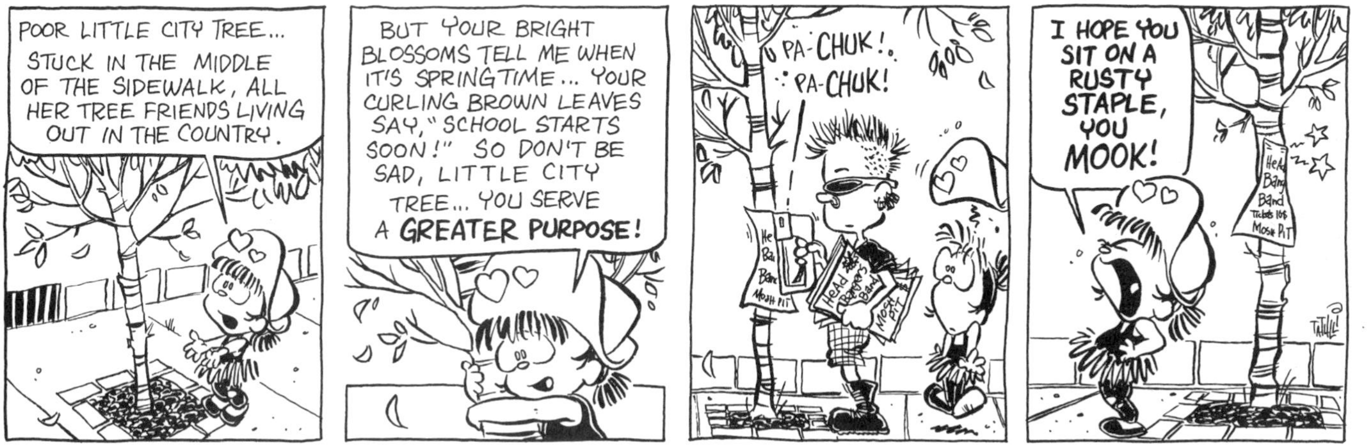
POOR LITTLE CITY TREE... STUCK IN THE MIDDLE OF THE SIDEWALK, ALL HER TREE FRIENDS LIVING OUT IN THE COUNTRY.
BUT YOUR BRIGHT BLOSSOMS TELL ME WHEN IT'S SPRINGTIME... YOUR CURLING BROWN LEAVES SAY, "SCHOOL STARTS SOON!" SO DON'T BE SAD, LITTLE CITY TREE... YOU SERVE A **GREATER PURPOSE!**
PA-CHUK!
PA-CHUK!
I HOPE YOU SIT ON A RUSTY STAPLE, YOU MOOK!

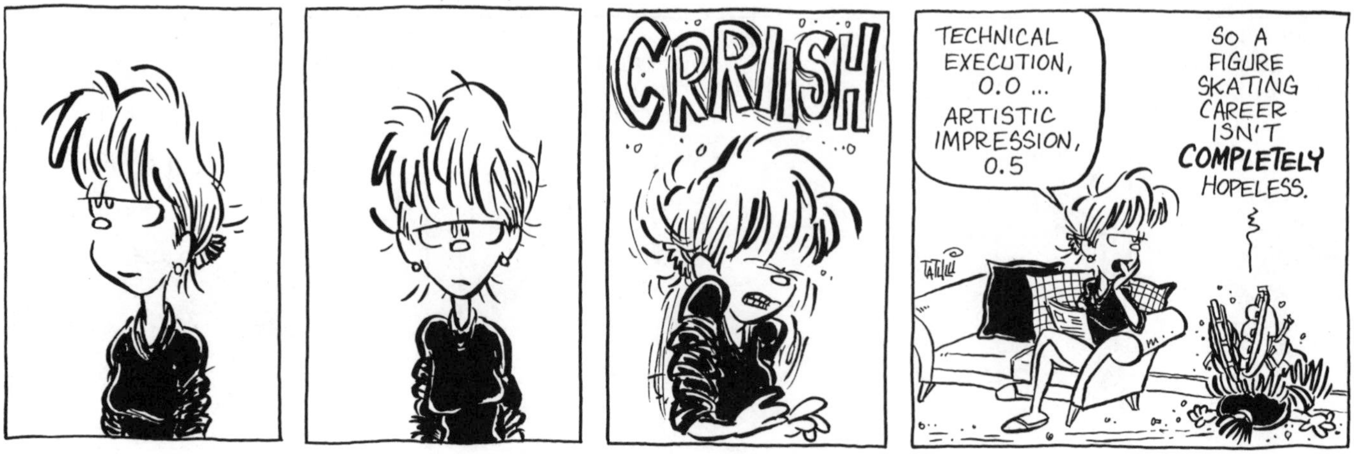
CRRUSH
TECHNICAL EXECUTION, 0.0 ... ARTISTIC IMPRESSION, 0.5
SO A FIGURE SKATING CAREER ISN'T **COMPLETELY** HOPELESS.

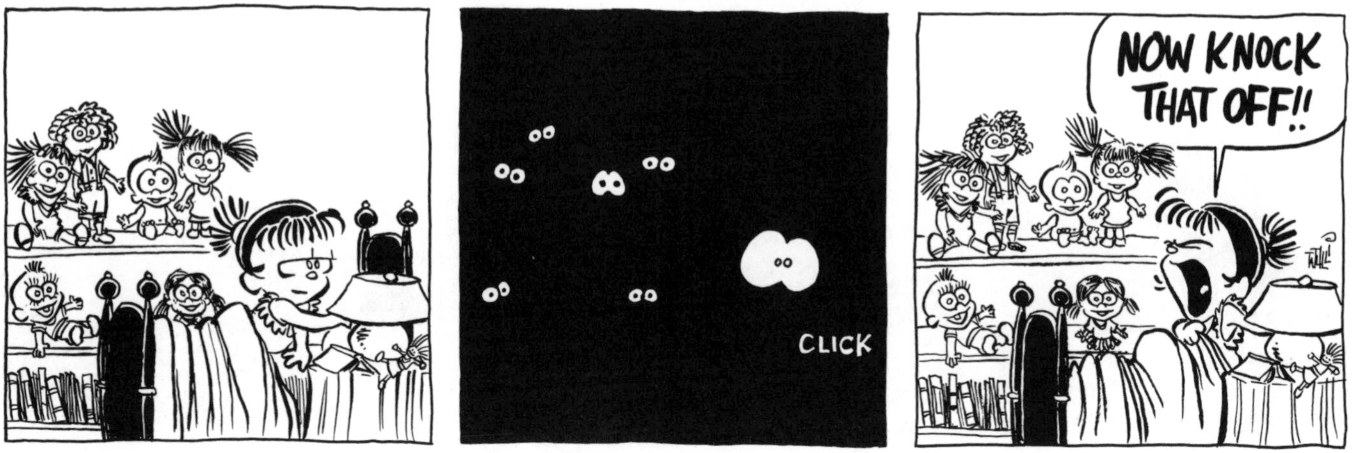
CLICK
NOW KNOCK THAT OFF!!

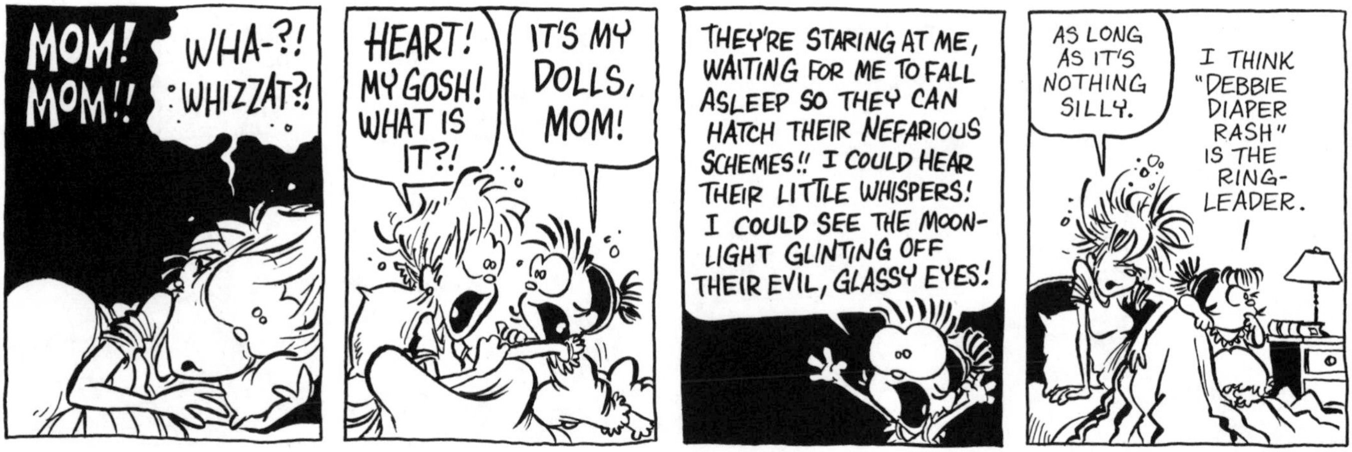
MOM! MOM!!
WHA-?! WHIZZAT?!
HEART! MY GOSH! WHAT IS IT?!
IT'S MY DOLLS, MOM!
THEY'RE STARING AT ME, WAITING FOR ME TO FALL ASLEEP SO THEY CAN HATCH THEIR NEFARIOUS SCHEMES!! I COULD HEAR THEIR LITTLE WHISPERS! I COULD SEE THE MOONLIGHT GLINTING OFF THEIR EVIL, GLASSY EYES!
AS LONG AS IT'S NOTHING SILLY.
I THINK "DEBBIE DIAPER RASH" IS THE RINGLEADER.

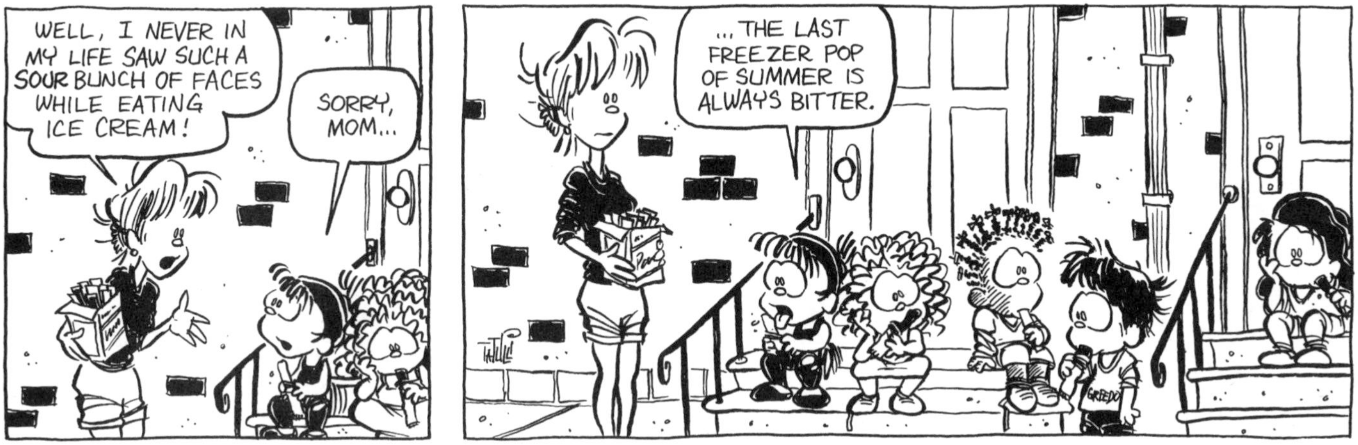
WELL, I NEVER IN MY LIFE SAW SUCH A SOUR BUNCH OF FACES WHILE EATING ICE CREAM!
SORRY, MOM...
...THE LAST FREEZER POP OF SUMMER IS ALWAYS BITTER.

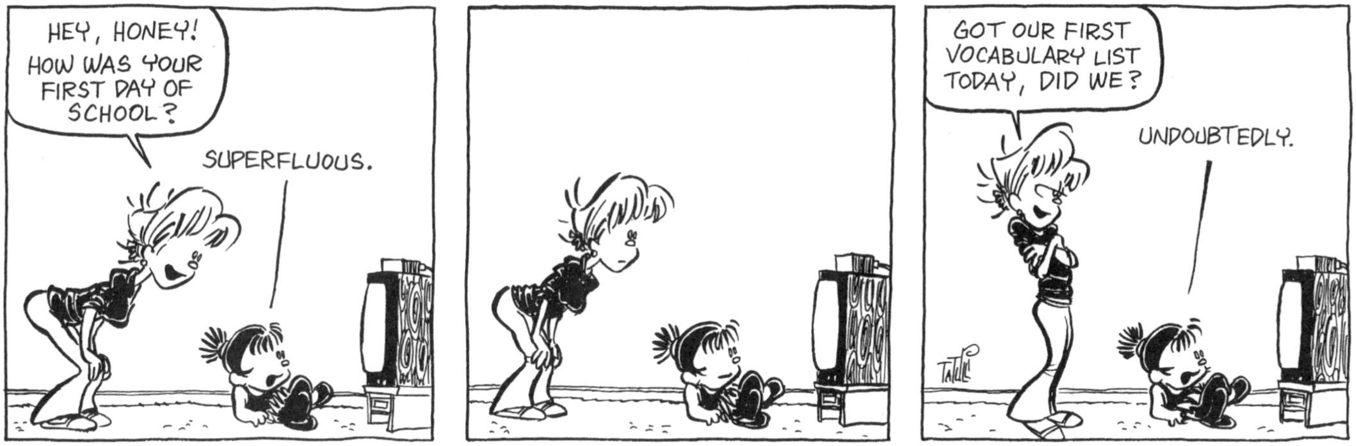
HEY, HONEY! HOW WAS YOUR FIRST DAY OF SCHOOL?
SUPERFLUOUS.
GOT OUR FIRST VOCABULARY LIST TODAY, DID WE?
UNDOUBTEDLY.

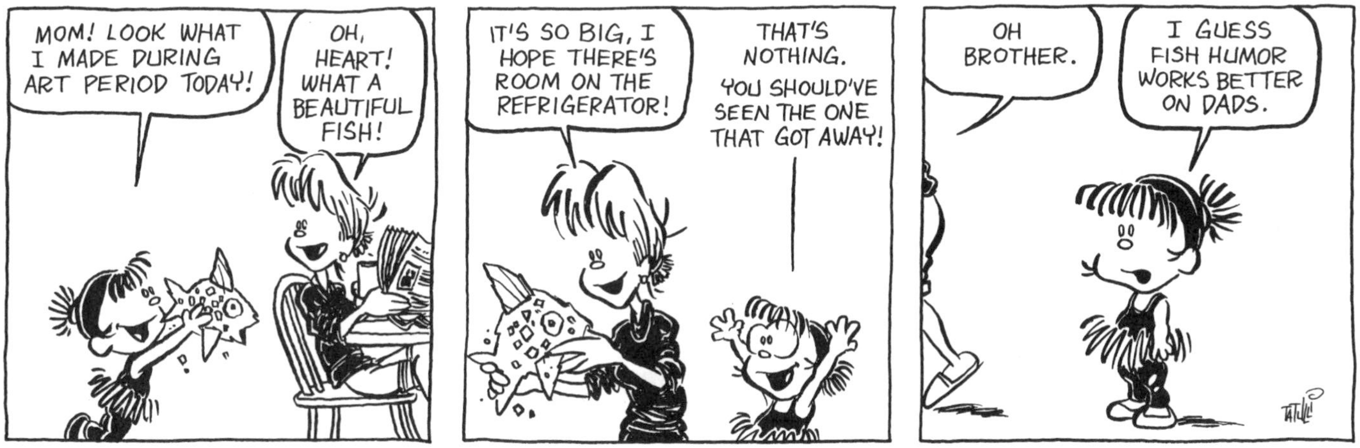
MOM! LOOK WHAT I MADE DURING ART PERIOD TODAY!
OH, HEART! WHAT A BEAUTIFUL FISH!
IT'S SO BIG, I HOPE THERE'S ROOM ON THE REFRIGERATOR!
THAT'S NOTHING. YOU SHOULD'VE SEEN THE ONE THAT GOT AWAY!
OH BROTHER.
I GUESS FISH HUMOR WORKS BETTER ON DADS.

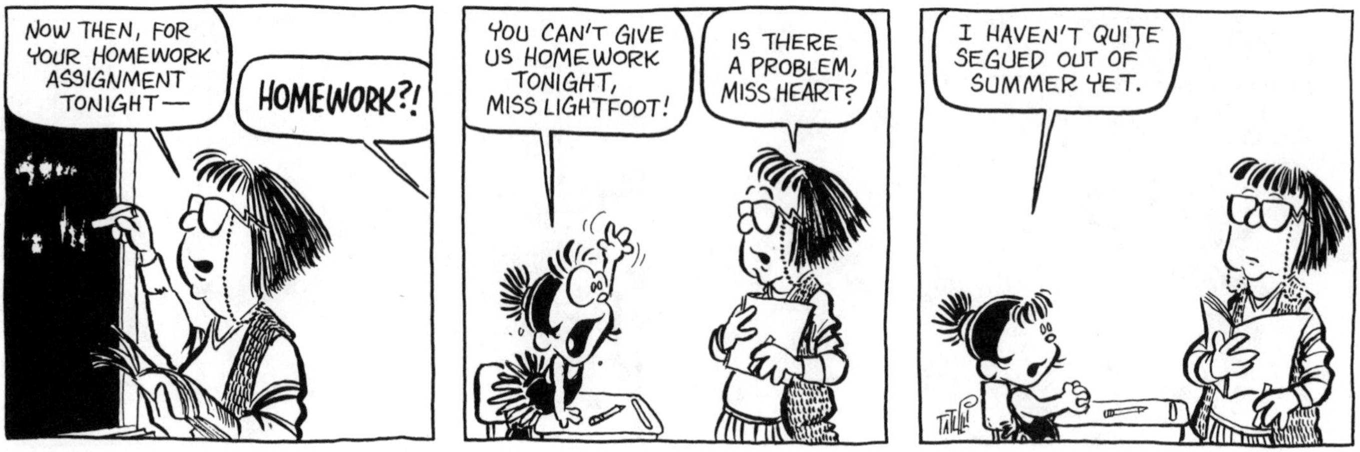
NOW THEN, FOR YOUR HOMEWORK ASSIGNMENT TONIGHT—
HOMEWORK?!
YOU CAN'T GIVE US HOMEWORK TONIGHT, MISS LIGHTFOOT!
IS THERE A PROBLEM, MISS HEART?
I HAVEN'T QUITE SEGUED OUT OF SUMMER YET.
TATULLI

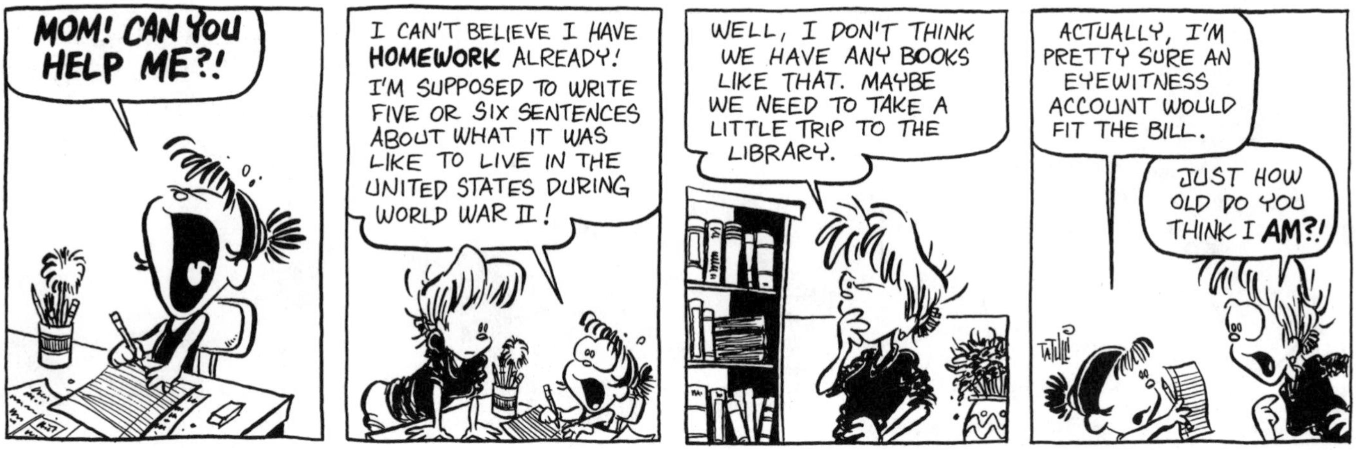
MOM! CAN YOU HELP ME?!
I CAN'T BELIEVE I HAVE **HOMEWORK** ALREADY! I'M SUPPOSED TO WRITE FIVE OR SIX SENTENCES ABOUT WHAT IT WAS LIKE TO LIVE IN THE UNITED STATES DURING WORLD WAR II!
WELL, I DON'T THINK WE HAVE ANY BOOKS LIKE THAT. MAYBE WE NEED TO TAKE A LITTLE TRIP TO THE LIBRARY.
ACTUALLY, I'M PRETTY SURE AN EYEWITNESS ACCOUNT WOULD FIT THE BILL.
JUST HOW OLD DO YOU THINK I **AM**?!
TATULLI

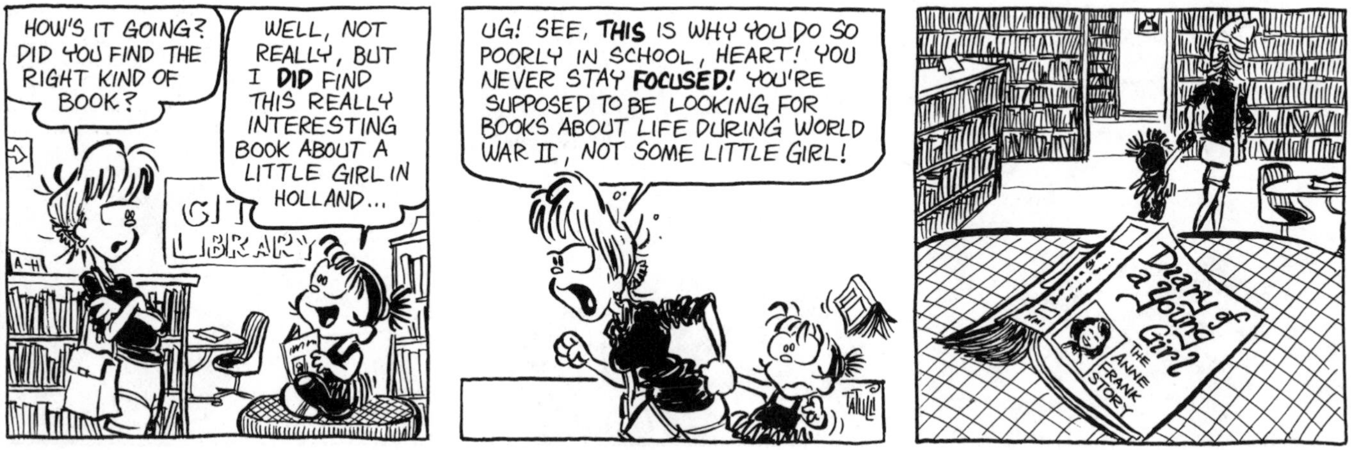
HOW'S IT GOING? DID YOU FIND THE RIGHT KIND OF BOOK?
WELL, NOT REALLY, BUT I **DID** FIND THIS REALLY INTERESTING BOOK ABOUT A LITTLE GIRL IN HOLLAND...
A-H
LIBRARY
UG! SEE, **THIS** IS WHY YOU DO SO POORLY IN SCHOOL, HEART! YOU NEVER STAY **FOCUSED**! YOU'RE SUPPOSED TO BE LOOKING FOR BOOKS ABOUT LIFE DURING WORLD WAR II, NOT SOME LITTLE GIRL!
TATULLI
Diary of a Young Girl
THE ANNE FRANK STORY

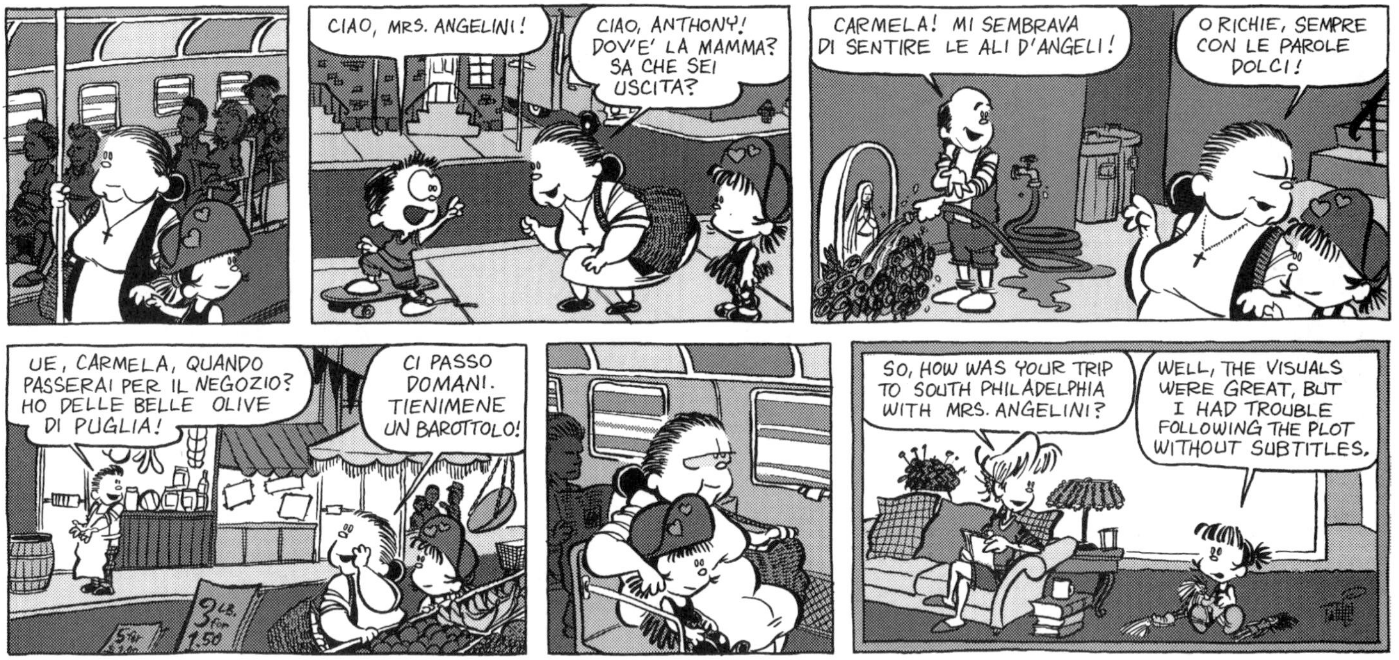
CIAO, MRS. ANGELINI!
CIAO, ANTHONY! DOV'E' LA MAMMA? SA CHE SEI USCITA?
CARMELA! MI SEMBRAVA DI SENTIRE LE ALI D'ANGELI!
O RICHIE, SEMPRE CON LE PAROLE DOLCI!
UE, CARMELA, QUANDO PASSERAI PER IL NEGOZIO? HO DELLE BELLE OLIVE DI PUGLIA!
CI PASSO DOMANI. TIENIMENE UN BAROTTOLO!
SO, HOW WAS YOUR TRIP TO SOUTH PHILADELPHIA WITH MRS. ANGELINI?
WELL, THE VISUALS WERE GREAT, BUT I HAD TROUBLE FOLLOWING THE PLOT WITHOUT SUBTITLES.

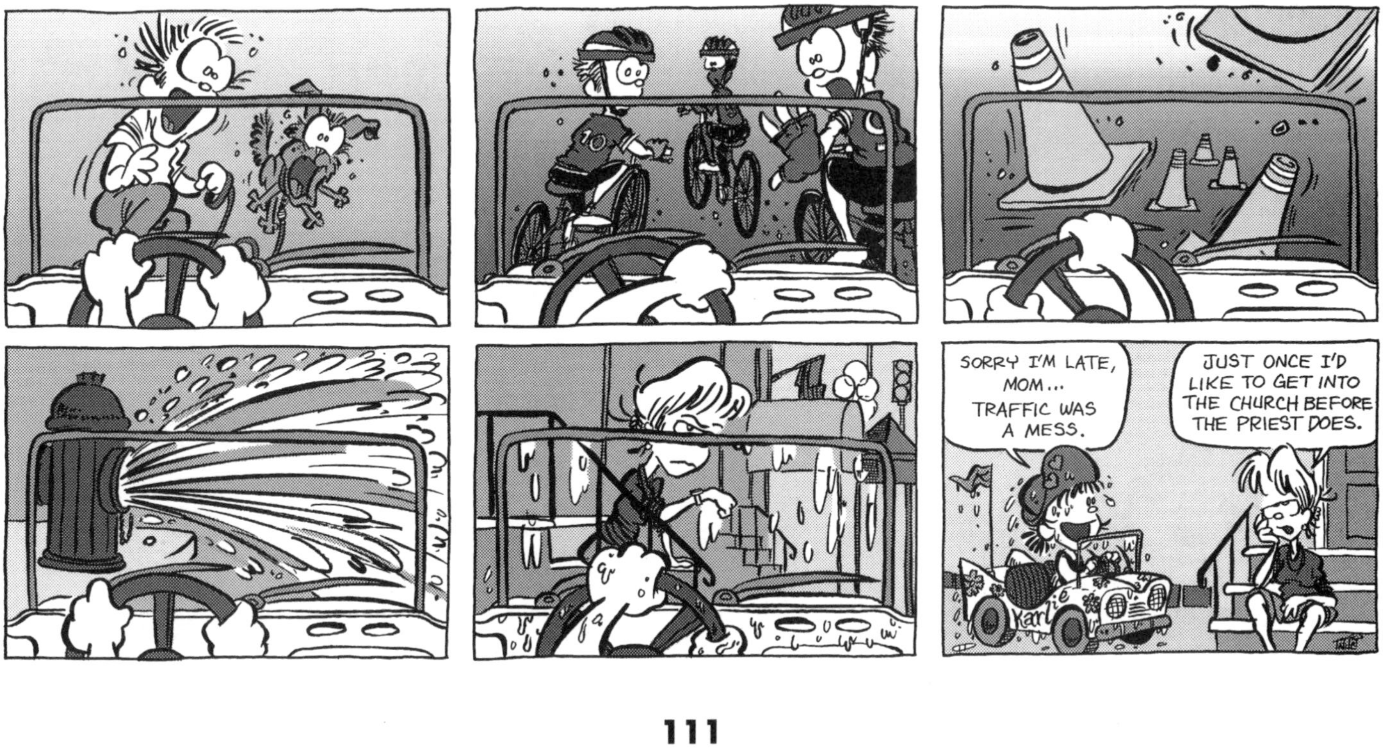
SORRY I'M LATE, MOM... TRAFFIC WAS A MESS.
JUST ONCE I'D LIKE TO GET INTO THE CHURCH BEFORE THE PRIEST DOES.
Karlie

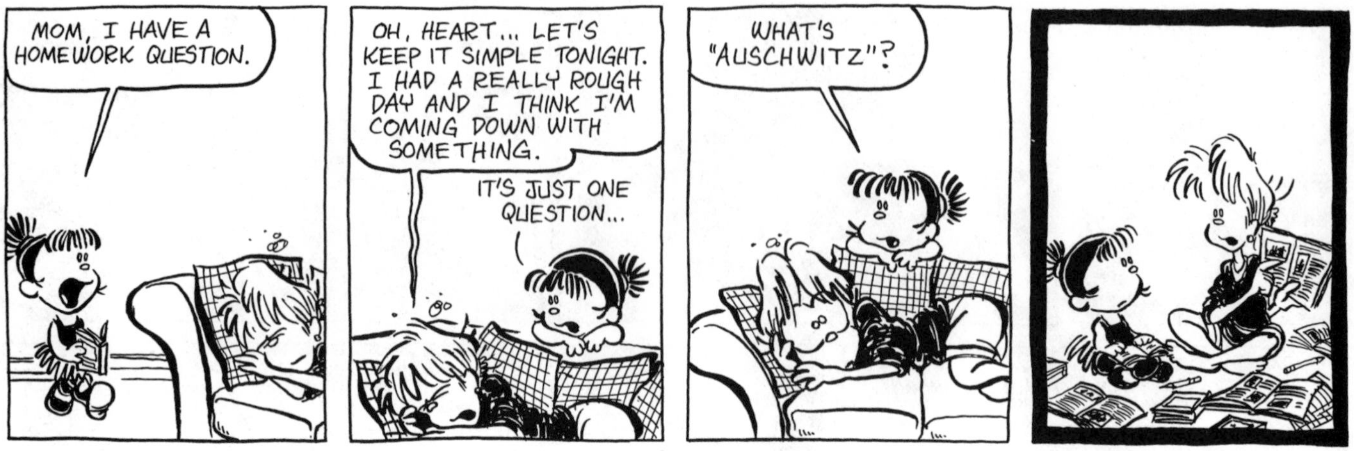
MOM, I HAVE A HOMEWORK QUESTION.
OH, HEART... LET'S KEEP IT SIMPLE TONIGHT. I HAD A REALLY ROUGH DAY AND I THINK I'M COMING DOWN WITH SOMETHING.
IT'S JUST ONE QUESTION...
WHAT'S "AUSCHWITZ"?

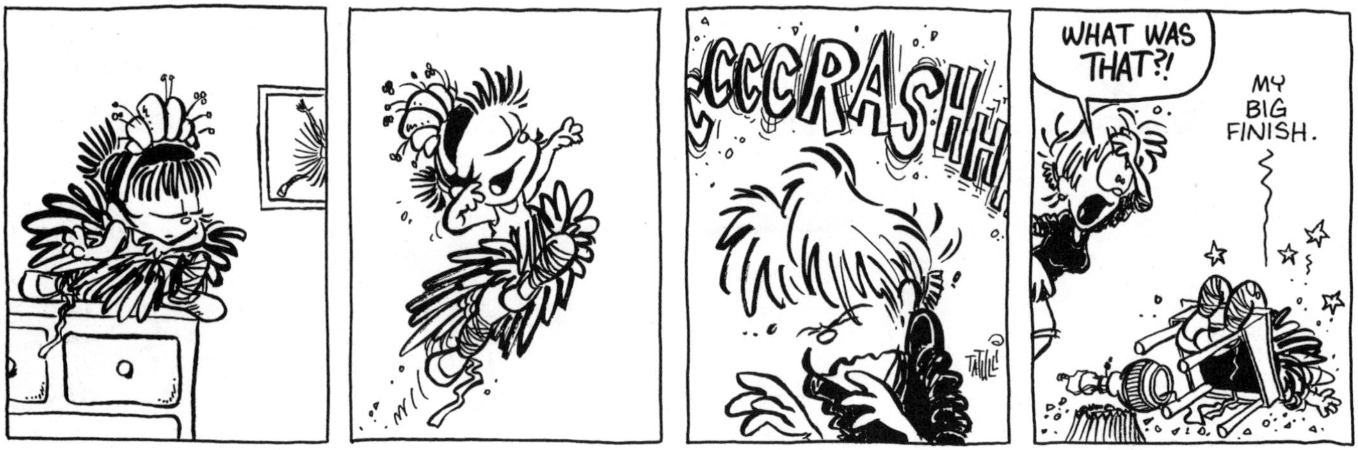
CCCCRASHH!
WHAT WAS THAT?!
MY BIG FINISH.

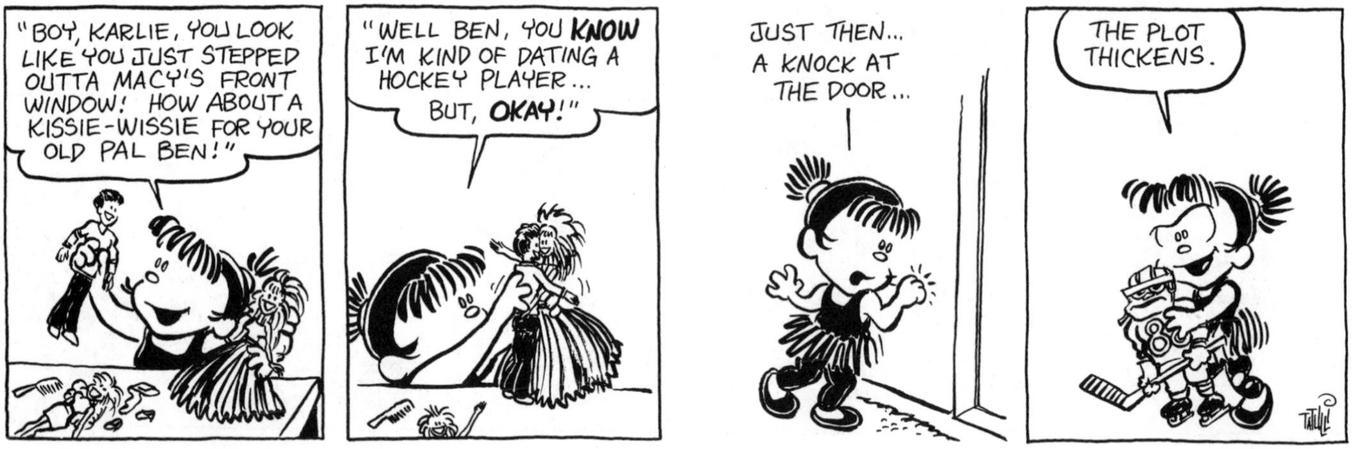
"BOY, KARLIE, YOU LOOK LIKE YOU JUST STEPPED OUTTA MACY'S FRONT WINDOW! HOW ABOUT A KISSIE-WISSIE FOR YOUR OLD PAL BEN!"
"WELL BEN, YOU KNOW I'M KIND OF DATING A HOCKEY PLAYER... BUT, OKAY!"
JUST THEN... A KNOCK AT THE DOOR...
THE PLOT THICKENS.

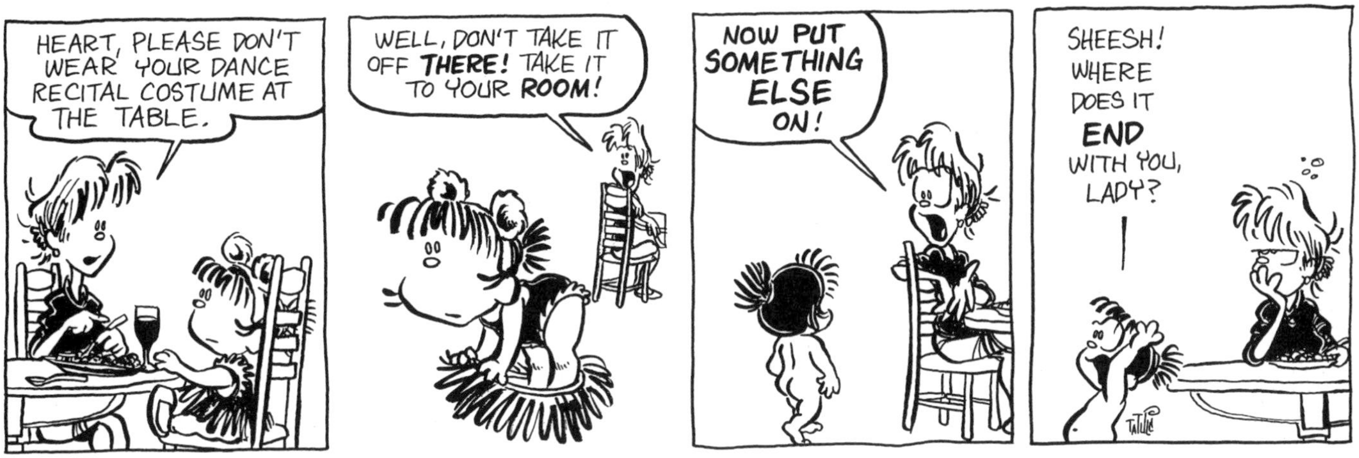
HEART, PLEASE DON'T WEAR YOUR DANCE RECITAL COSTUME AT THE TABLE.
WELL, DON'T TAKE IT OFF THERE! TAKE IT TO YOUR ROOM!
NOW PUT SOMETHING ELSE ON!
SHEESH! WHERE DOES IT END WITH YOU, LADY?

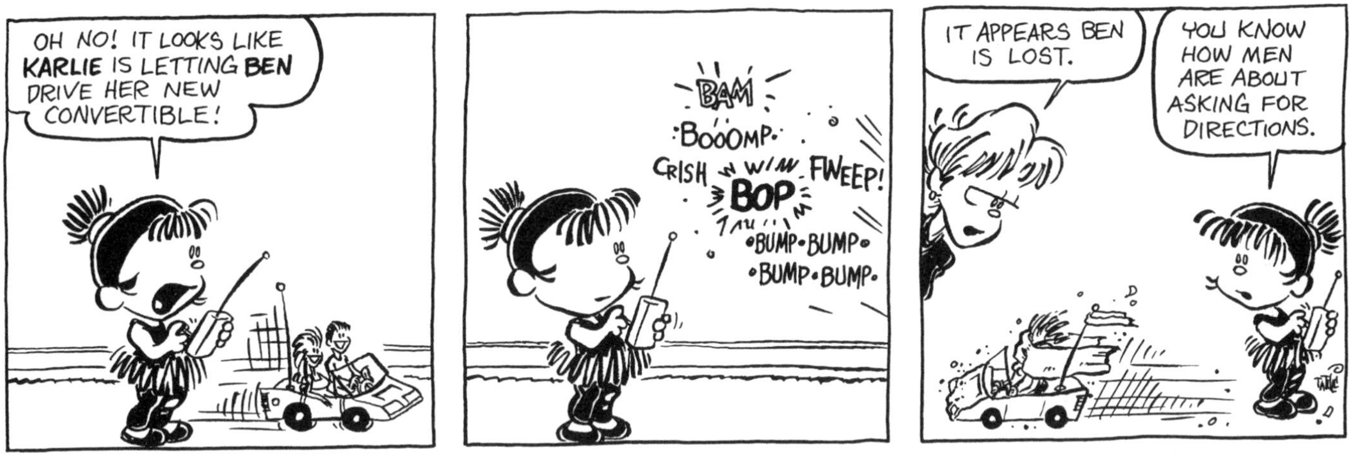
OH NO! IT LOOKS LIKE KARLIE IS LETTING BEN DRIVE HER NEW CONVERTIBLE!
BAM
BOOOMP
CRISH
BOP
FWEEP!
BUMP BUMP
BUMP BUMP
IT APPEARS BEN IS LOST.
YOU KNOW HOW MEN ARE ABOUT ASKING FOR DIRECTIONS.

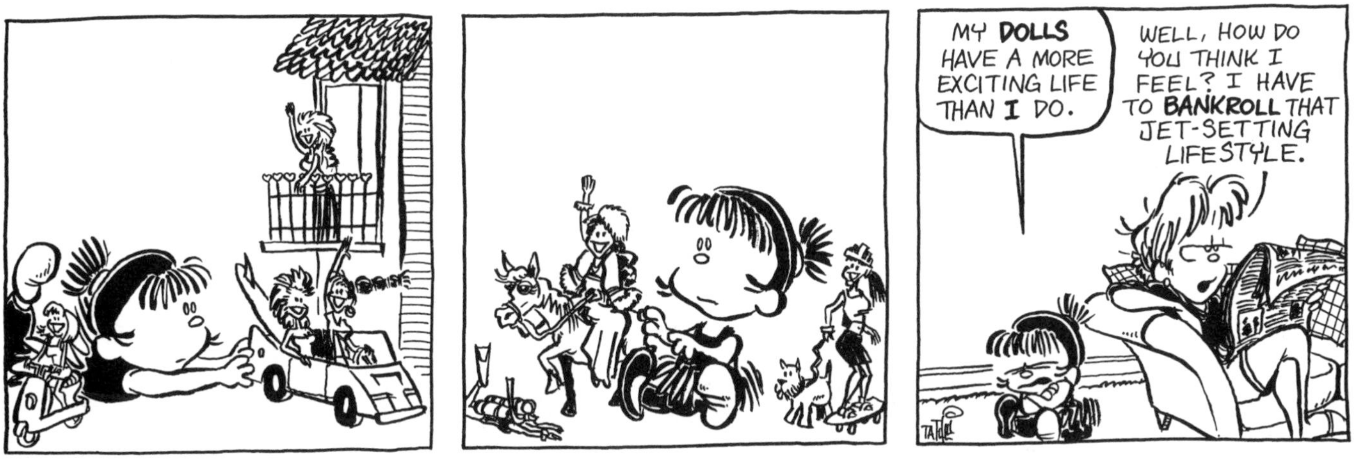
MY DOLLS HAVE A MORE EXCITING LIFE THAN I DO.
WELL, HOW DO YOU THINK I FEEL? I HAVE TO BANKROLL THAT JET-SETTING LIFESTYLE.

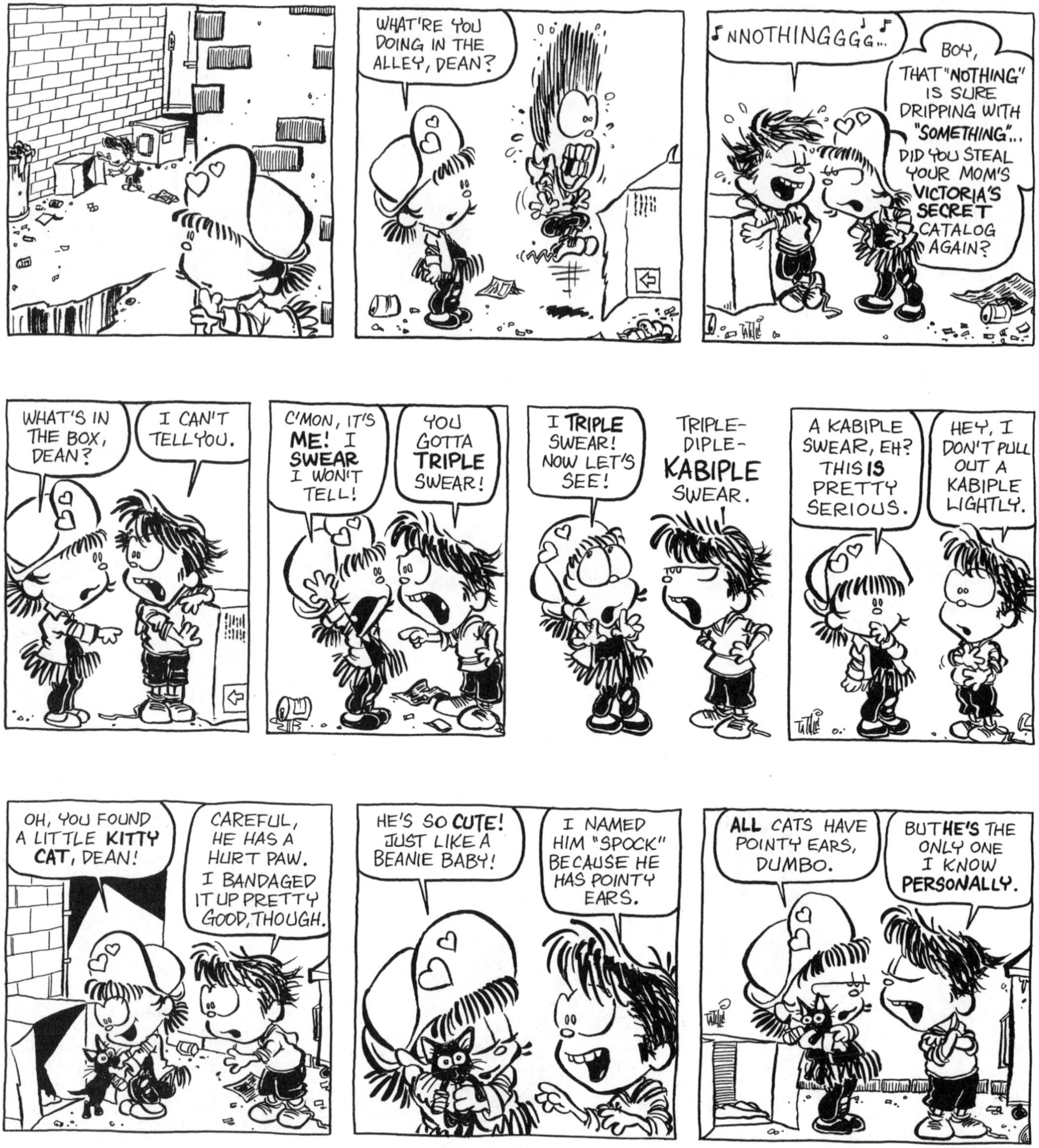
WHAT'RE YOU DOING IN THE ALLEY, DEAN?
♪ NNOTHINGGGG... ♪
BOY, THAT "NOTHING" IS SURE DRIPPING WITH "SOMETHING"... DID YOU STEAL YOUR MOM'S VICTORIA'S SECRET CATALOG AGAIN?
WHAT'S IN THE BOX, DEAN?
I CAN'T TELL YOU.
C'MON, IT'S ME! I SWEAR I WON'T TELL!
YOU GOTTA TRIPLE SWEAR!
I TRIPLE SWEAR! NOW LET'S SEE!
TRIPLE-DIPLE-KABIPLE SWEAR.
A KABIPLE SWEAR, EH? THIS IS PRETTY SERIOUS.
HEY, I DON'T PULL OUT A KABIPLE LIGHTLY.
OH, YOU FOUND A LITTLE KITTY CAT, DEAN!
CAREFUL, HE HAS A HURT PAW. I BANDAGED IT UP PRETTY GOOD, THOUGH.
HE'S SO CUTE! JUST LIKE A BEANIE BABY!
I NAMED HIM "SPOCK" BECAUSE HE HAS POINTY EARS.
ALL CATS HAVE POINTY EARS, DUMBO.
BUT HE'S THE ONLY ONE I KNOW PERSONALLY.

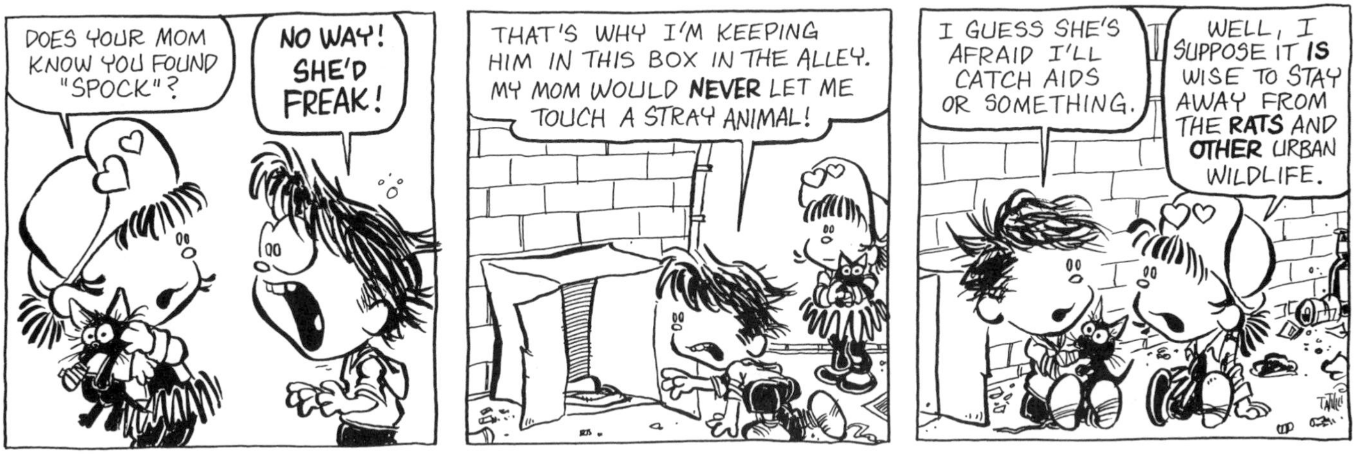
DOES YOUR MOM KNOW YOU FOUND "SPOCK"?
NO WAY! SHE'D FREAK!
THAT'S WHY I'M KEEPING HIM IN THIS BOX IN THE ALLEY. MY MOM WOULD NEVER LET ME TOUCH A STRAY ANIMAL!
I GUESS SHE'S AFRAID I'LL CATCH AIDS OR SOMETHING.
WELL, I SUPPOSE IT IS WISE TO STAY AWAY FROM THE RATS AND OTHER URBAN WILDLIFE.

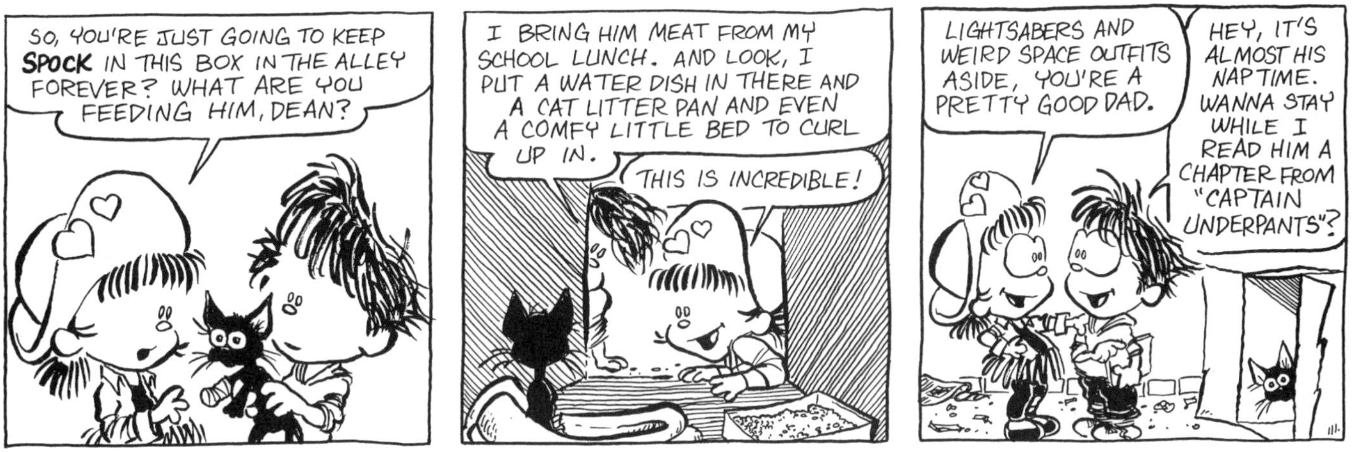
SO, YOU'RE JUST GOING TO KEEP SPOCK IN THIS BOX IN THE ALLEY FOREVER? WHAT ARE YOU FEEDING HIM, DEAN?
I BRING HIM MEAT FROM MY SCHOOL LUNCH. AND LOOK, I PUT A WATER DISH IN THERE AND A CAT LITTER PAN AND EVEN A COMFY LITTLE BED TO CURL UP IN.
THIS IS INCREDIBLE!
LIGHTSABERS AND WEIRD SPACE OUTFITS ASIDE, YOU'RE A PRETTY GOOD DAD.
HEY, IT'S ALMOST HIS NAP TIME. WANNA STAY WHILE I READ HIM A CHAPTER FROM "CAPTAIN UNDERPANTS"?

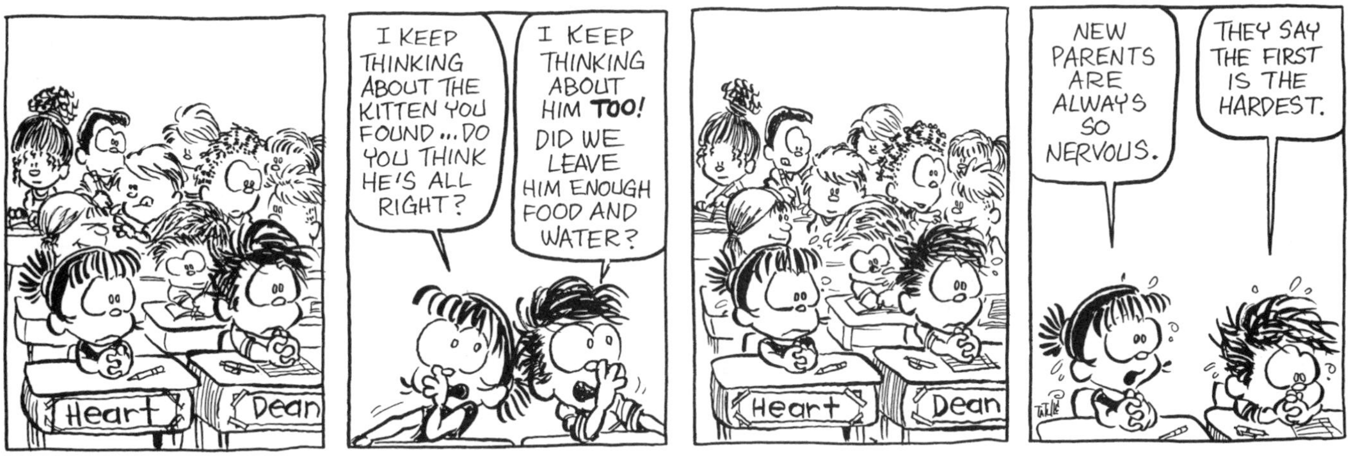
Heart
Dean
I KEEP THINKING ABOUT THE KITTEN YOU FOUND... DO YOU THINK HE'S ALL RIGHT?
I KEEP THINKING ABOUT HIM TOO! DID WE LEAVE HIM ENOUGH FOOD AND WATER?
Heart
Dean
NEW PARENTS ARE ALWAYS SO NERVOUS.
THEY SAY THE FIRST IS THE HARDEST.

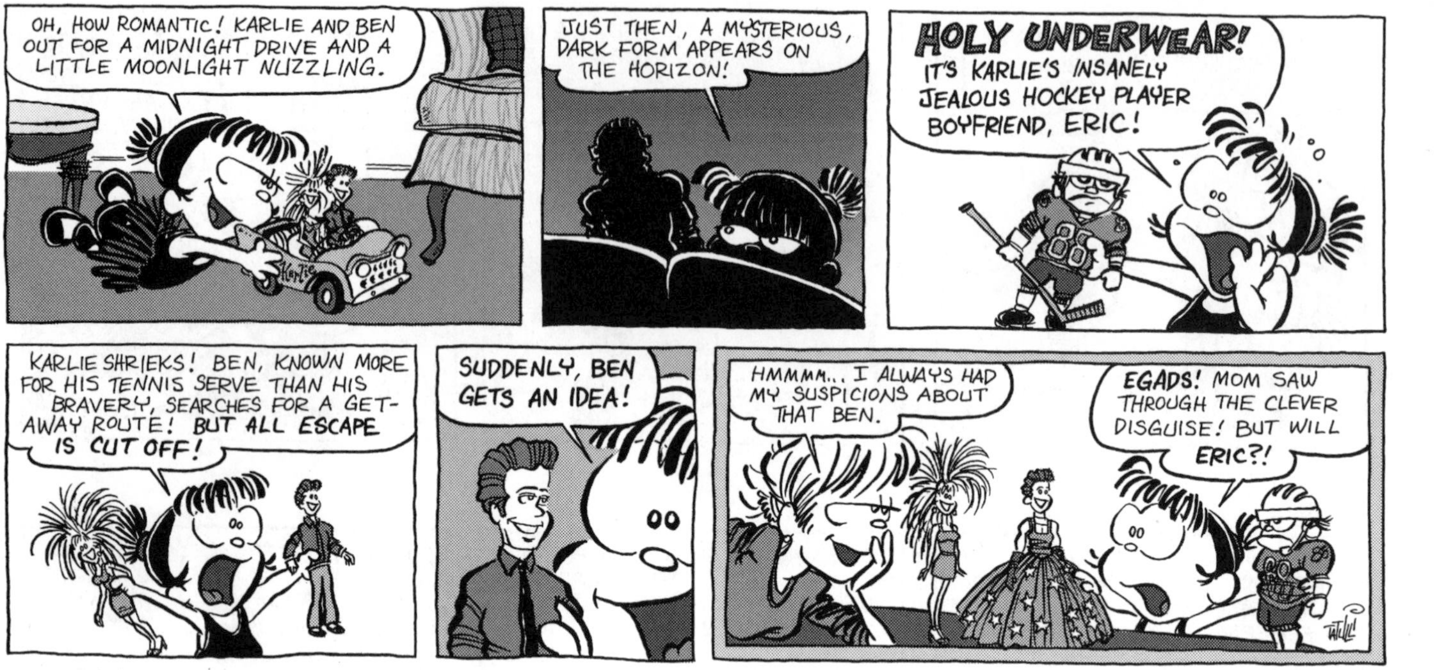
OH, HOW ROMANTIC! KARLIE AND BEN OUT FOR A MIDNIGHT DRIVE AND A LITTLE MOONLIGHT NUZZLING.
JUST THEN, A MYSTERIOUS, DARK FORM APPEARS ON THE HORIZON!
HOLY UNDERWEAR! IT'S KARLIE'S INSANELY JEALOUS HOCKEY PLAYER BOYFRIEND, ERIC!
KARLIE SHRIEKS! BEN, KNOWN MORE FOR HIS TENNIS SERVE THAN HIS BRAVERY, SEARCHES FOR A GET-AWAY ROUTE! BUT ALL ESCAPE IS CUT OFF!
SUDDENLY, BEN GETS AN IDEA!
HMMMM... I ALWAYS HAD MY SUSPICIONS ABOUT THAT BEN.
EGADS! MOM SAW THROUGH THE CLEVER DISGUISE! BUT WILL ERIC?!

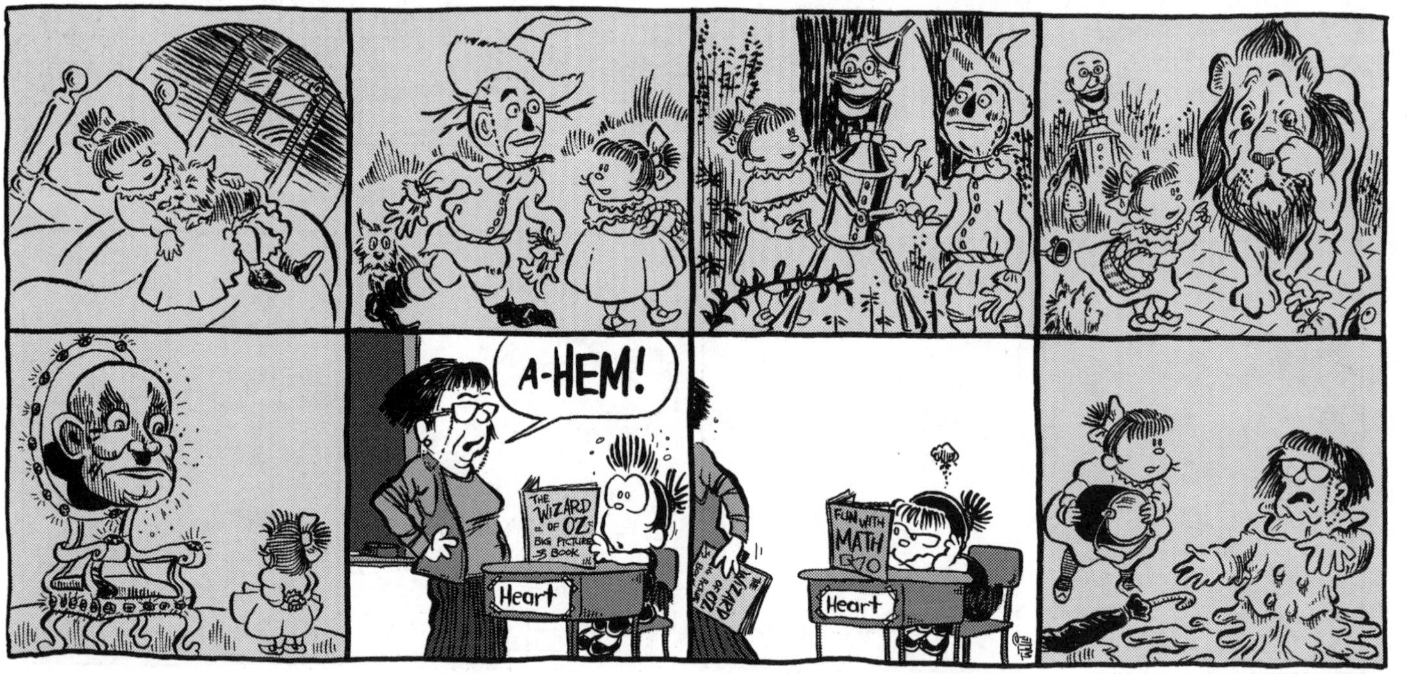
A-HEM!
THE WIZARD OF OZ BIG PICTURE BOOK
Heart
FUN WITH MATH
Heart

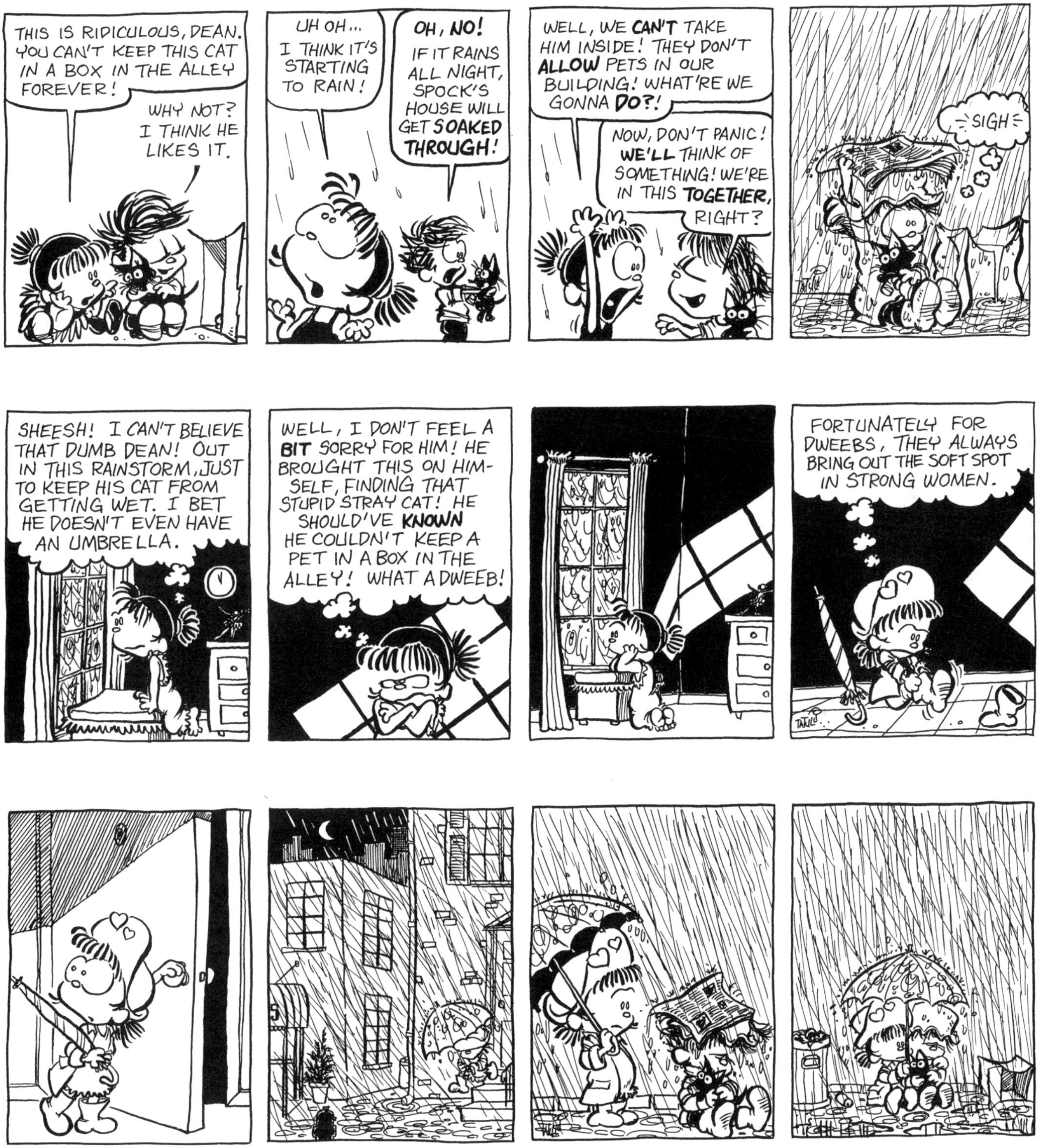

THIS IS RIDICULOUS, DEAN. YOU CAN'T KEEP THIS CAT IN A BOX IN THE ALLEY FOREVER!
WHY NOT? I THINK HE LIKES IT.
UH OH... I THINK IT'S STARTING TO RAIN!
OH, NO! IF IT RAINS ALL NIGHT, SPOCK'S HOUSE WILL GET SOAKED THROUGH!
WELL, WE CAN'T TAKE HIM INSIDE! THEY DON'T ALLOW PETS IN OUR BUILDING! WHAT'RE WE GONNA DO?!
NOW, DON'T PANIC! WE'LL THINK OF SOMETHING! WE'RE IN THIS TOGETHER, RIGHT?
SIGH
SHEESH! I CAN'T BELIEVE THAT DUMB DEAN! OUT IN THIS RAINSTORM, JUST TO KEEP HIS CAT FROM GETTING WET. I BET HE DOESN'T EVEN HAVE AN UMBRELLA.
WELL, I DON'T FEEL A BIT SORRY FOR HIM! HE BROUGHT THIS ON HIMSELF, FINDING THAT STUPID STRAY CAT! HE SHOULD'VE KNOWN HE COULDN'T KEEP A PET IN A BOX IN THE ALLEY! WHAT A DWEEB!
FORTUNATELY FOR DWEEBS, THEY ALWAYS BRING OUT THE SOFT SPOT IN STRONG WOMEN.

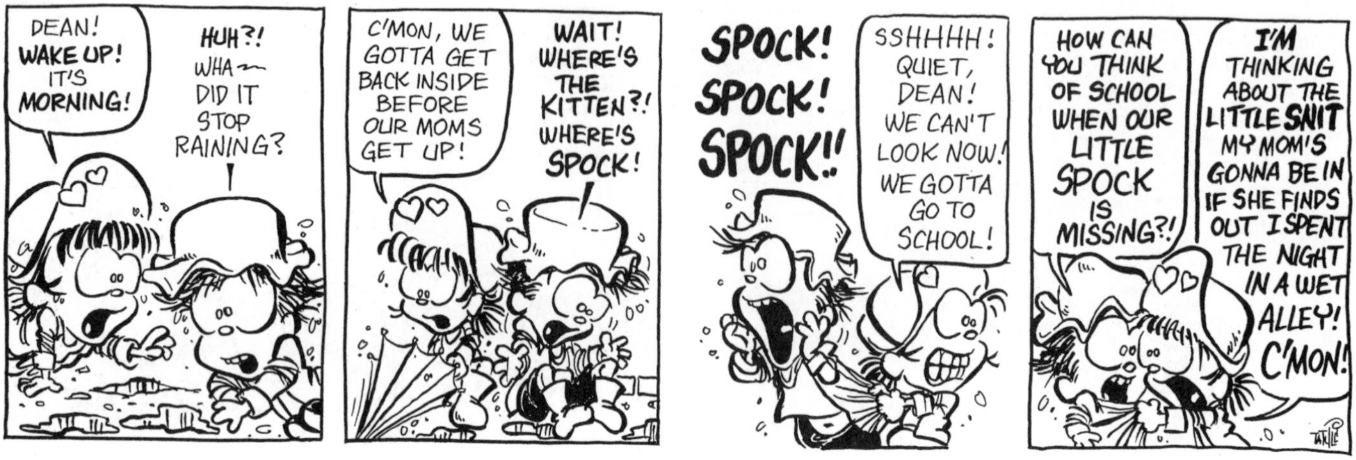
DEAN! WAKE UP! IT'S MORNING!
HUH?! WHA— DID IT STOP RAINING?
C'MON, WE GOTTA GET BACK INSIDE BEFORE OUR MOMS GET UP!
WAIT! WHERE'S THE KITTEN?! WHERE'S SPOCK!
SPOCK! SPOCK! SPOCK!!
SSHHHH! QUIET, DEAN! WE CAN'T LOOK NOW! WE GOTTA GO TO SCHOOL!
HOW CAN YOU THINK OF SCHOOL WHEN OUR LITTLE SPOCK IS MISSING?!
I'M THINKING ABOUT THE LITTLE SNIT MY MOM'S GONNA BE IN IF SHE FINDS OUT I SPENT THE NIGHT IN A WET ALLEY! C'MON!
TATULLI

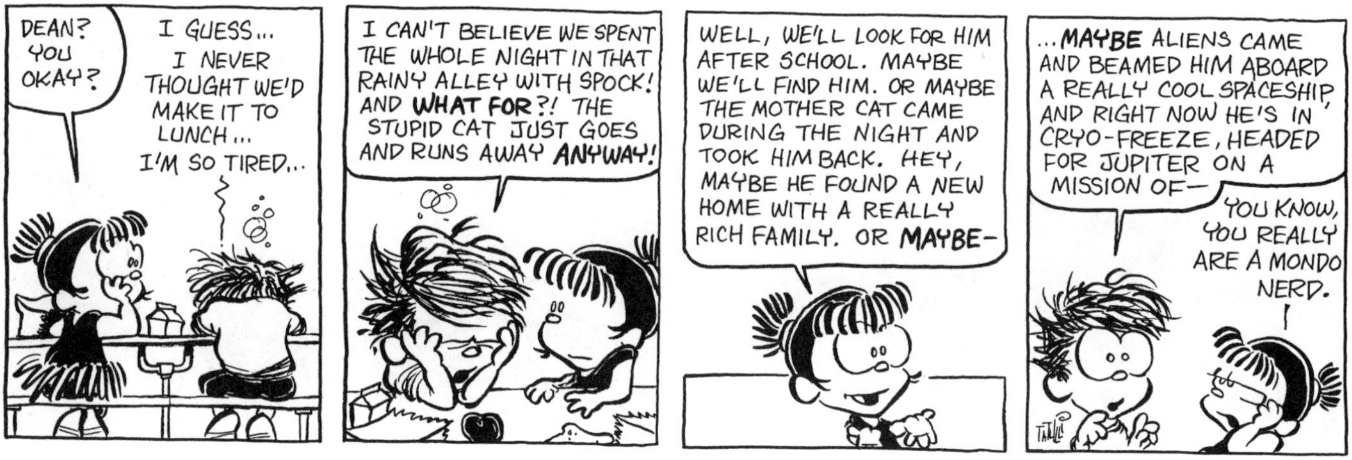
DEAN? YOU OKAY?
I GUESS... I NEVER THOUGHT WE'D MAKE IT TO LUNCH... I'M SO TIRED...
I CAN'T BELIEVE WE SPENT THE WHOLE NIGHT IN THAT RAINY ALLEY WITH SPOCK! AND WHAT FOR?! THE STUPID CAT JUST GOES AND RUNS AWAY ANYWAY!
WELL, WE'LL LOOK FOR HIM AFTER SCHOOL. MAYBE WE'LL FIND HIM. OR MAYBE THE MOTHER CAT CAME DURING THE NIGHT AND TOOK HIM BACK. HEY, MAYBE HE FOUND A NEW HOME WITH A REALLY RICH FAMILY. OR MAYBE-
...MAYBE ALIENS CAME AND BEAMED HIM ABOARD A REALLY COOL SPACESHIP, AND RIGHT NOW HE'S IN CRYO-FREEZE, HEADED FOR JUPITER ON A MISSION OF—
YOU KNOW, YOU REALLY ARE A MONDO NERD.
TATULLI

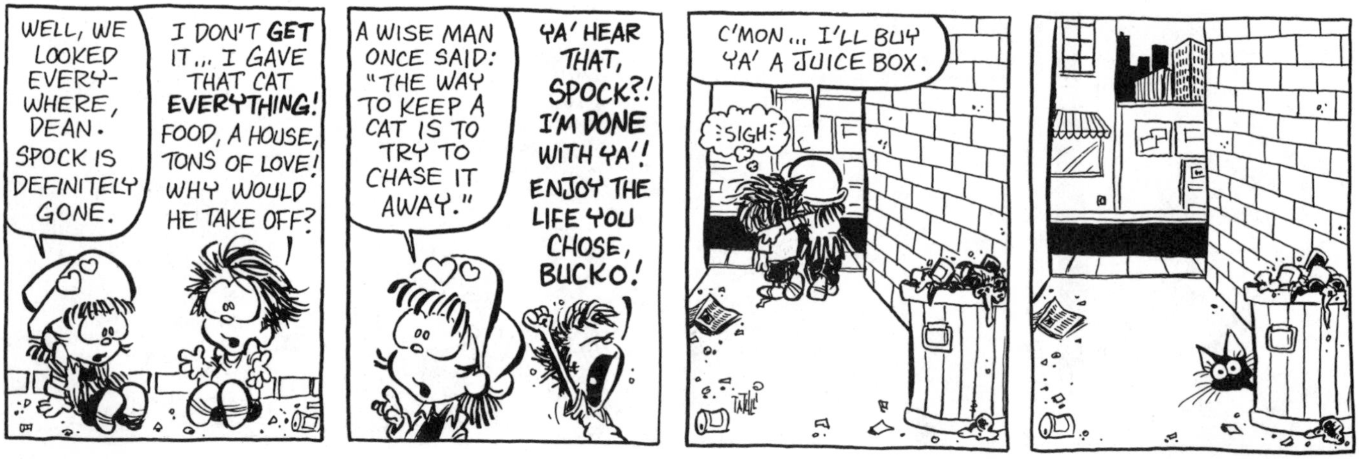
WELL, WE LOOKED EVERY-WHERE, DEAN. SPOCK IS DEFINITELY GONE.
I DON'T GET IT... I GAVE THAT CAT EVERYTHING! FOOD, A HOUSE, TONS OF LOVE! WHY WOULD HE TAKE OFF?
A WISE MAN ONCE SAID: "THE WAY TO KEEP A CAT IS TO TRY TO CHASE IT AWAY."
YA' HEAR THAT, SPOCK?! I'M DONE WITH YA'! ENJOY THE LIFE YOU CHOSE, BUCKO!
C'MON... I'LL BUY YA' A JUICE BOX.
SIGH
TATULLI

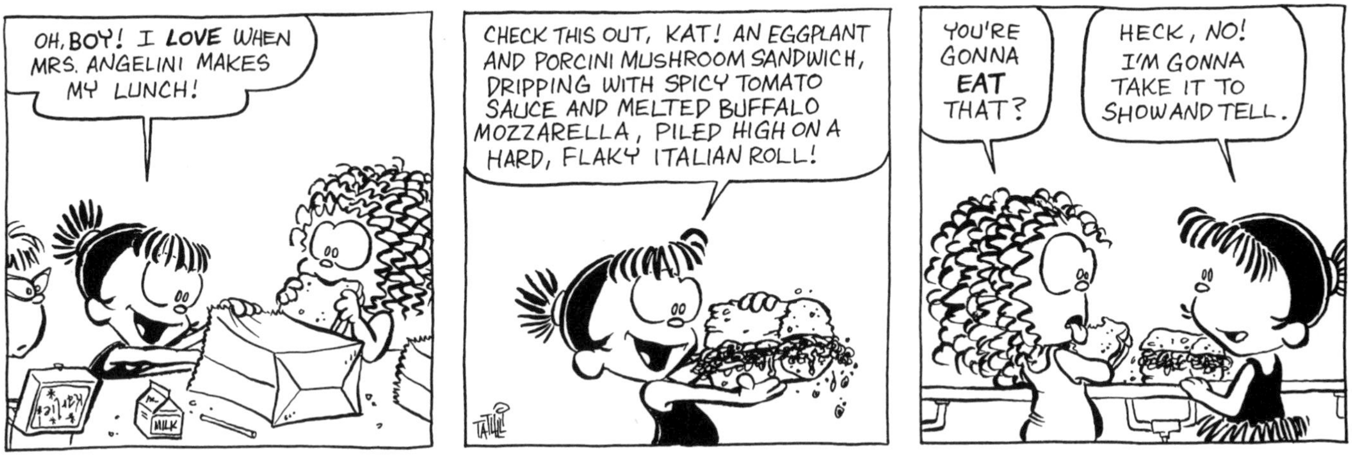

OH, BOY! I **LOVE** WHEN MRS. ANGELINI MAKES MY LUNCH!
CHECK THIS OUT, KAT! AN EGGPLANT AND PORCINI MUSHROOM SANDWICH, DRIPPING WITH SPICY TOMATO SAUCE AND MELTED BUFFALO MOZZARELLA, PILED HIGH ON A HARD, FLAKY ITALIAN ROLL!
YOU'RE GONNA **EAT** THAT?
HECK, NO! I'M GONNA TAKE IT TO SHOW AND TELL.

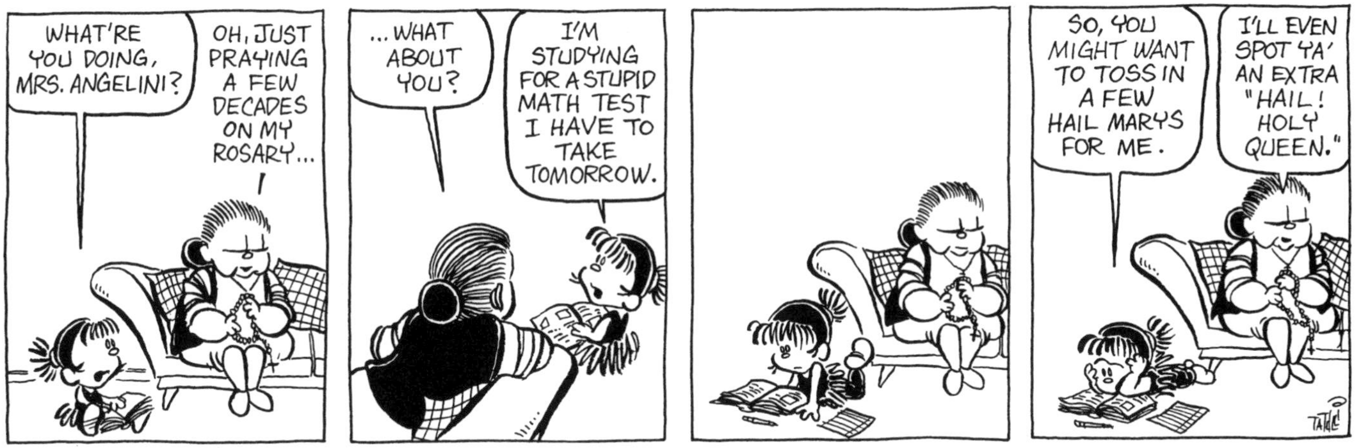

WHAT'RE YOU DOING, MRS. ANGELINI?
OH, JUST PRAYING A FEW DECADES ON MY ROSARY...
...WHAT ABOUT YOU?
I'M STUDYING FOR A STUPID MATH TEST I HAVE TO TAKE TOMORROW.
SO, YOU MIGHT WANT TO TOSS IN A FEW HAIL MARYS FOR ME.
I'LL EVEN SPOT YA' AN EXTRA "HAIL! HOLY QUEEN."

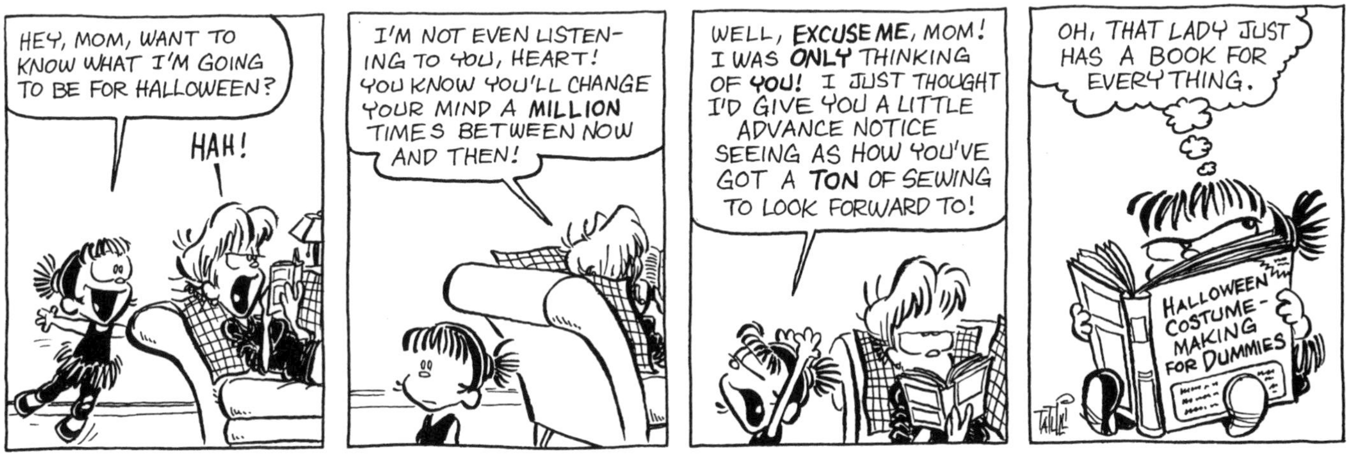

HEY, MOM, WANT TO KNOW WHAT I'M GOING TO BE FOR HALLOWEEN?
HAH!
I'M NOT EVEN LISTENING TO YOU, HEART! YOU KNOW YOU'LL CHANGE YOUR MIND A **MILLION** TIMES BETWEEN NOW AND THEN!
WELL, **EXCUSE ME**, MOM! I WAS **ONLY** THINKING OF **YOU**! I JUST THOUGHT I'D GIVE YOU A LITTLE ADVANCE NOTICE SEEING AS HOW YOU'VE GOT A **TON** OF SEWING TO LOOK FORWARD TO!
OH, THAT LADY JUST HAS A BOOK FOR EVERYTHING.
HALLOWEEN COSTUME-MAKING FOR DUMMIES

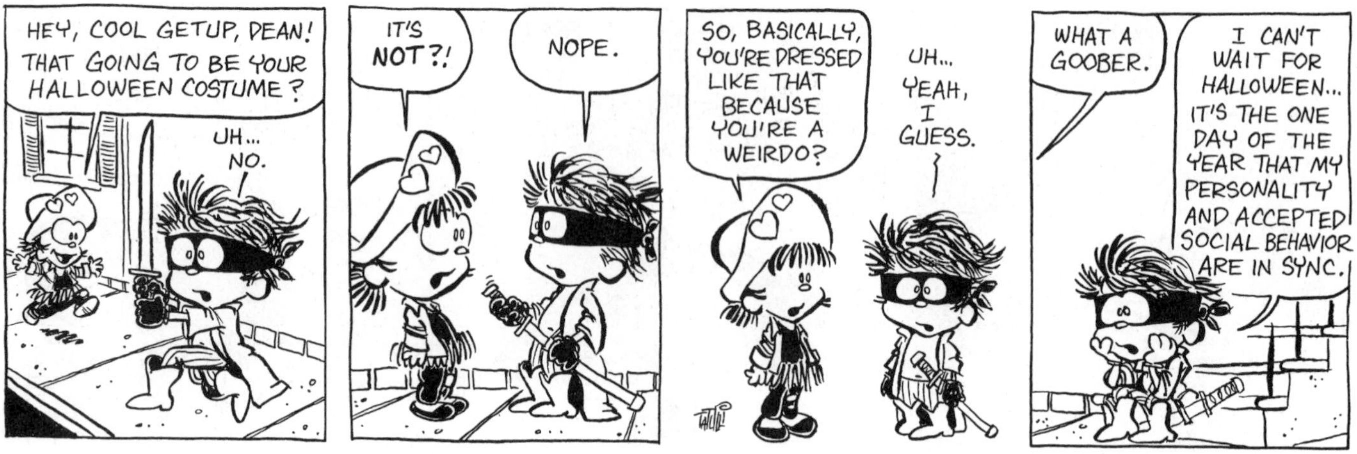
HEY, COOL GETUP, DEAN! THAT GOING TO BE YOUR HALLOWEEN COSTUME?
UH... NO.
IT'S NOT?!
NOPE.
SO, BASICALLY, YOU'RE DRESSED LIKE THAT BECAUSE YOU'RE A WEIRDO?
UH... YEAH, I GUESS.
WHAT A GOOBER.
I CAN'T WAIT FOR HALLOWEEN... IT'S THE ONE DAY OF THE YEAR THAT MY PERSONALITY AND ACCEPTED SOCIAL BEHAVIOR ARE IN SYNC.

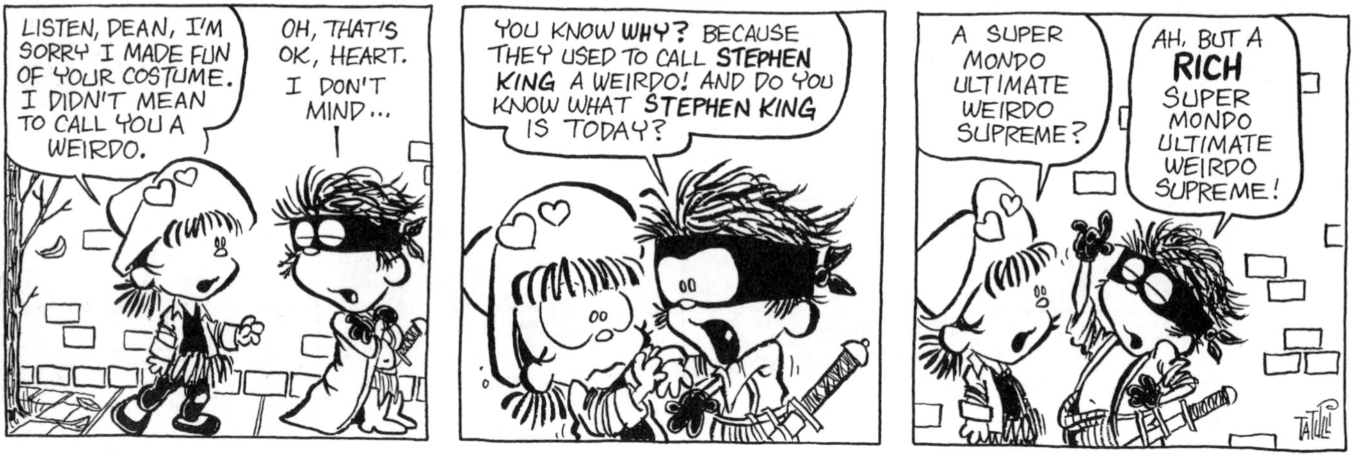
LISTEN, DEAN, I'M SORRY I MADE FUN OF YOUR COSTUME. I DIDN'T MEAN TO CALL YOU A WEIRDO.
OH, THAT'S OK, HEART. I DON'T MIND...
YOU KNOW WHY? BECAUSE THEY USED TO CALL STEPHEN KING A WEIRDO! AND DO YOU KNOW WHAT STEPHEN KING IS TODAY?
A SUPER MONDO ULTIMATE WEIRDO SUPREME?
AH, BUT A RICH SUPER MONDO ULTIMATE WEIRDO SUPREME!

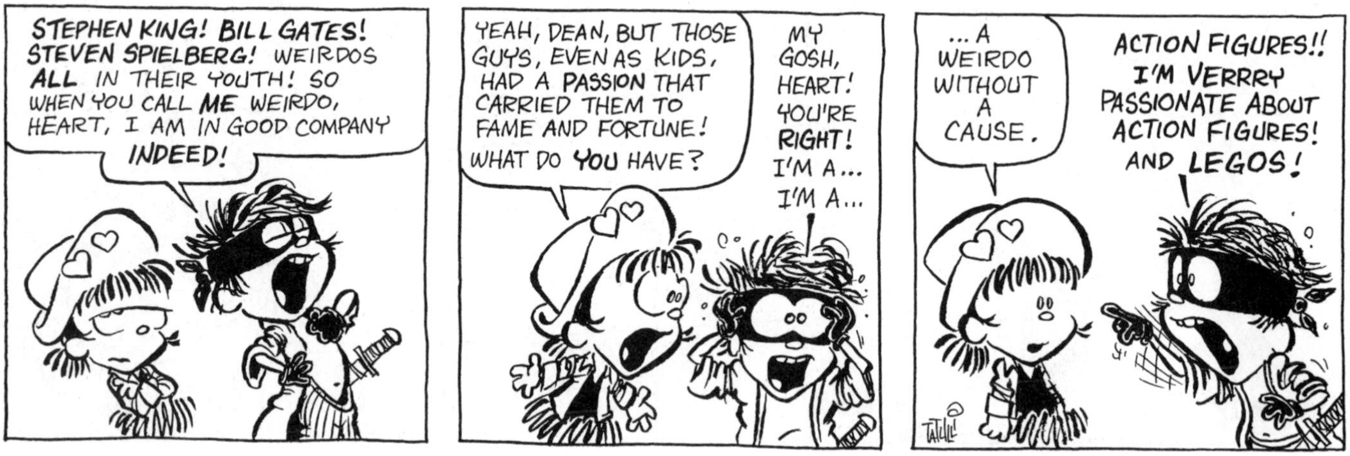
STEPHEN KING! BILL GATES! STEVEN SPIELBERG! WEIRDOS ALL IN THEIR YOUTH! SO WHEN YOU CALL ME WEIRDO, HEART, I AM IN GOOD COMPANY INDEED!
YEAH, DEAN, BUT THOSE GUYS, EVEN AS KIDS, HAD A PASSION THAT CARRIED THEM TO FAME AND FORTUNE! WHAT DO YOU HAVE?
MY GOSH, HEART! YOU'RE RIGHT! I'M A... I'M A...
... A WEIRDO WITHOUT A CAUSE.
ACTION FIGURES!! I'M VERRRY PASSIONATE ABOUT ACTION FIGURES! AND LEGOS!

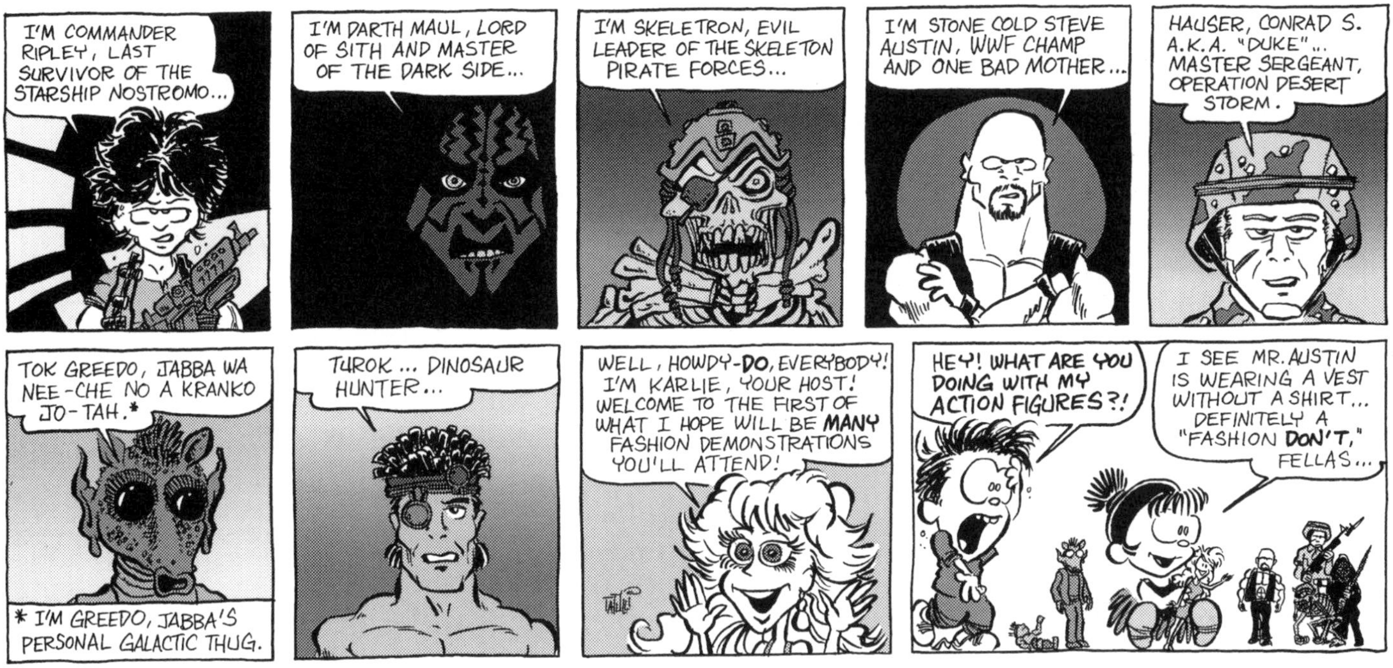
I'M COMMANDER RIPLEY, LAST SURVIVOR OF THE STARSHIP NOSTROMO...
I'M DARTH MAUL, LORD OF SITH AND MASTER OF THE DARK SIDE...
I'M SKELETRON, EVIL LEADER OF THE SKELETON PIRATE FORCES...
I'M STONE COLD STEVE AUSTIN, WWF CHAMP AND ONE BAD MOTHER...
HAUSER, CONRAD S. A.K.A. "DUKE"... MASTER SERGEANT, OPERATION DESERT STORM.
TOK GREEDO, JABBA WA NEE-CHE NO A KRANKO JO-TAH.*
* I'M GREEDO, JABBA'S PERSONAL GALACTIC THUG.
TUROK... DINOSAUR HUNTER...
WELL, HOWDY-DO, EVERYBODY! I'M KARLIE, YOUR HOST! WELCOME TO THE FIRST OF WHAT I HOPE WILL BE MANY FASHION DEMONSTRATIONS YOU'LL ATTEND!
HEY! WHAT ARE YOU DOING WITH MY ACTION FIGURES?!
I SEE MR. AUSTIN IS WEARING A VEST WITHOUT A SHIRT... DEFINITELY A "FASHION DON'T," FELLAS...

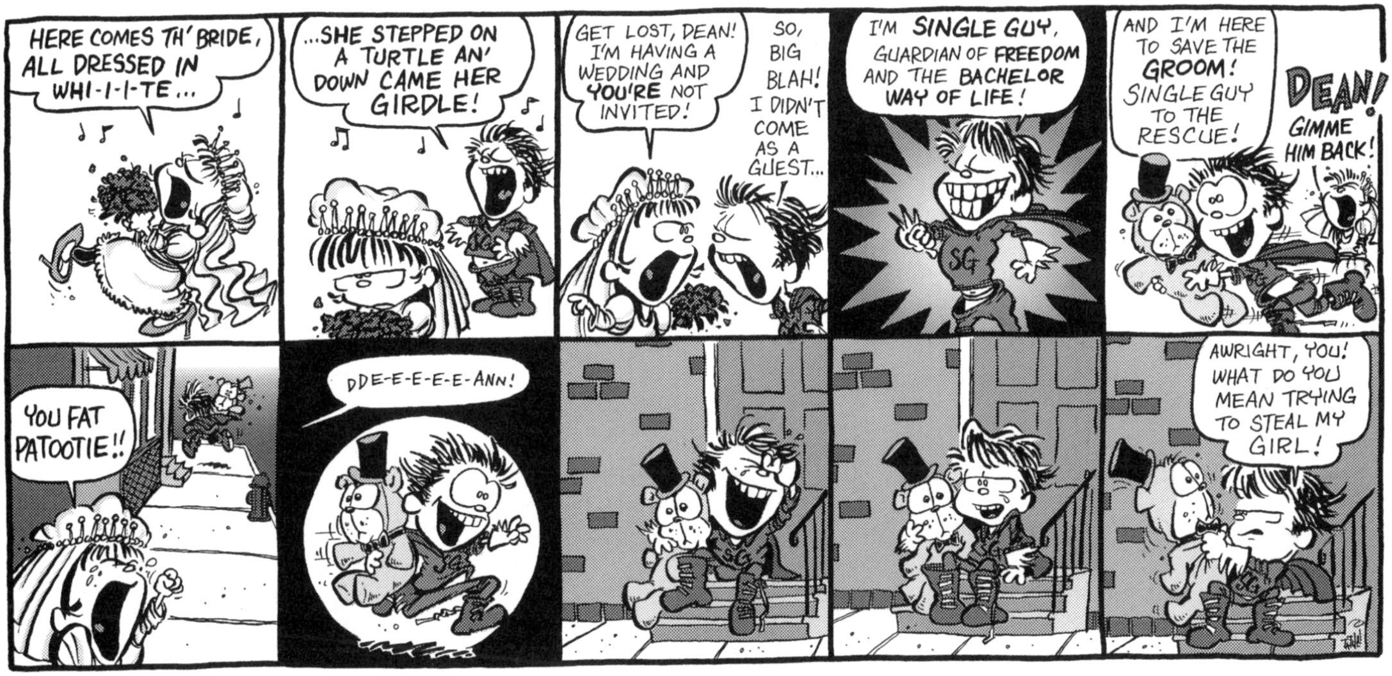
HERE COMES TH' BRIDE, ALL DRESSED IN WHI-I-I-TE...
...SHE STEPPED ON A TURTLE AN' DOWN CAME HER GIRDLE!
GET LOST, DEAN! I'M HAVING A WEDDING AND YOU'RE NOT INVITED!
SO, BIG BLAH! I DIDN'T COME AS A GUEST...
I'M SINGLE GUY, GUARDIAN OF FREEDOM AND THE BACHELOR WAY OF LIFE!
AND I'M HERE TO SAVE THE GROOM! SINGLE GUY TO THE RESCUE!
DEAN! GIMME HIM BACK!
YOU FAT PATOOTIE!!
DDE-E-E-E-E-ANN!
AWRIGHT, YOU! WHAT DO YOU MEAN TRYING TO STEAL MY GIRL!

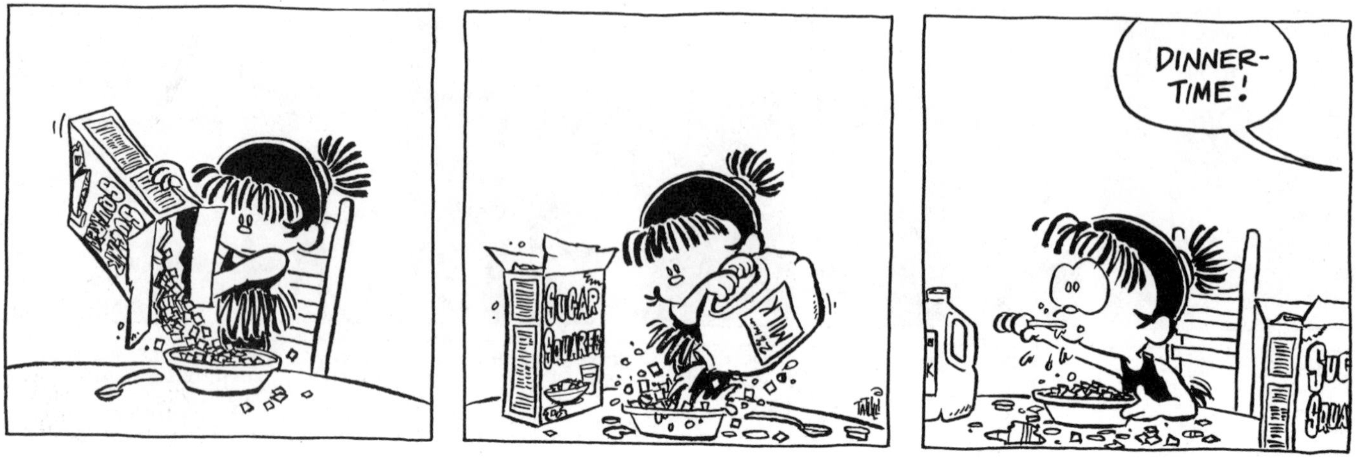
SUGAR SQUARES
DINNER-TIME!

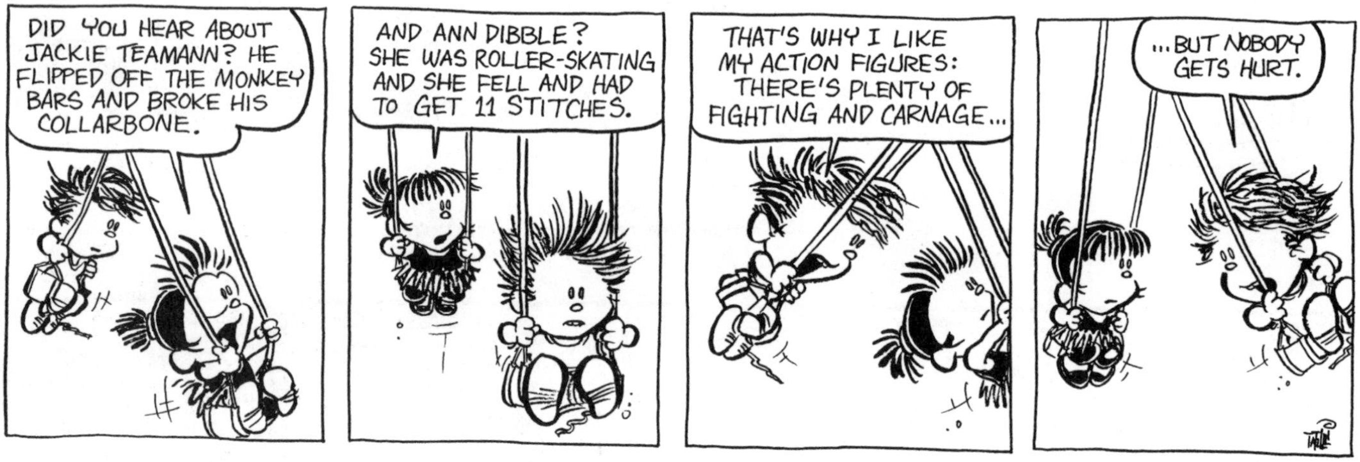
DID YOU HEAR ABOUT JACKIE TEAMANN? HE FLIPPED OFF THE MONKEY BARS AND BROKE HIS COLLARBONE.
AND ANN DIBBLE? SHE WAS ROLLER-SKATING AND SHE FELL AND HAD TO GET 11 STITCHES.
THAT'S WHY I LIKE MY ACTION FIGURES: THERE'S PLENTY OF FIGHTING AND CARNAGE...
...BUT NOBODY GETS HURT.

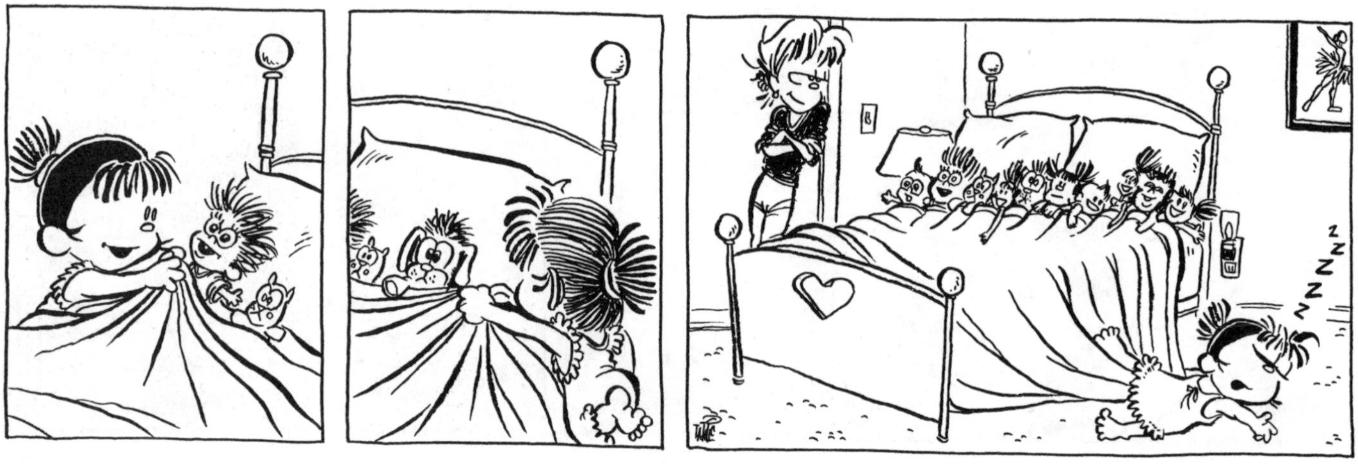
Z
Z
Z
Z

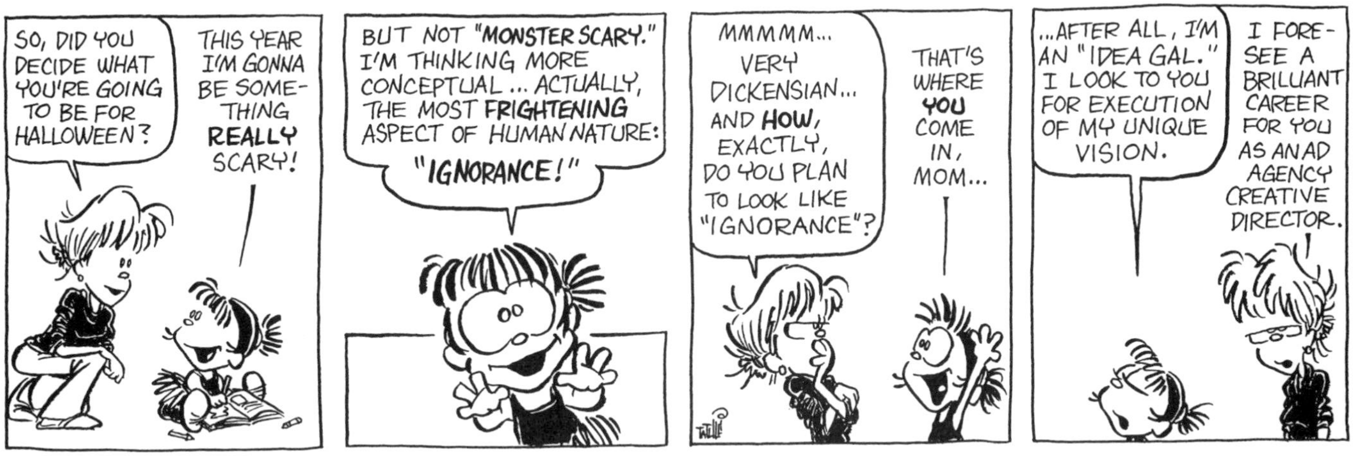
SO, DID YOU DECIDE WHAT YOU'RE GOING TO BE FOR HALLOWEEN?
THIS YEAR I'M GONNA BE SOMETHING REALLY SCARY!
BUT NOT "MONSTER SCARY." I'M THINKING MORE CONCEPTUAL ... ACTUALLY, THE MOST FRIGHTENING ASPECT OF HUMAN NATURE:
"IGNORANCE!"
MMMMM... VERY DICKENSIAN... AND HOW, EXACTLY, DO YOU PLAN TO LOOK LIKE "IGNORANCE"?
THAT'S WHERE YOU COME IN, MOM...
...AFTER ALL, I'M AN "IDEA GAL." I LOOK TO YOU FOR EXECUTION OF MY UNIQUE VISION.
I FORESEE A BRILLIANT CAREER FOR YOU AS AN AD AGENCY CREATIVE DIRECTOR.

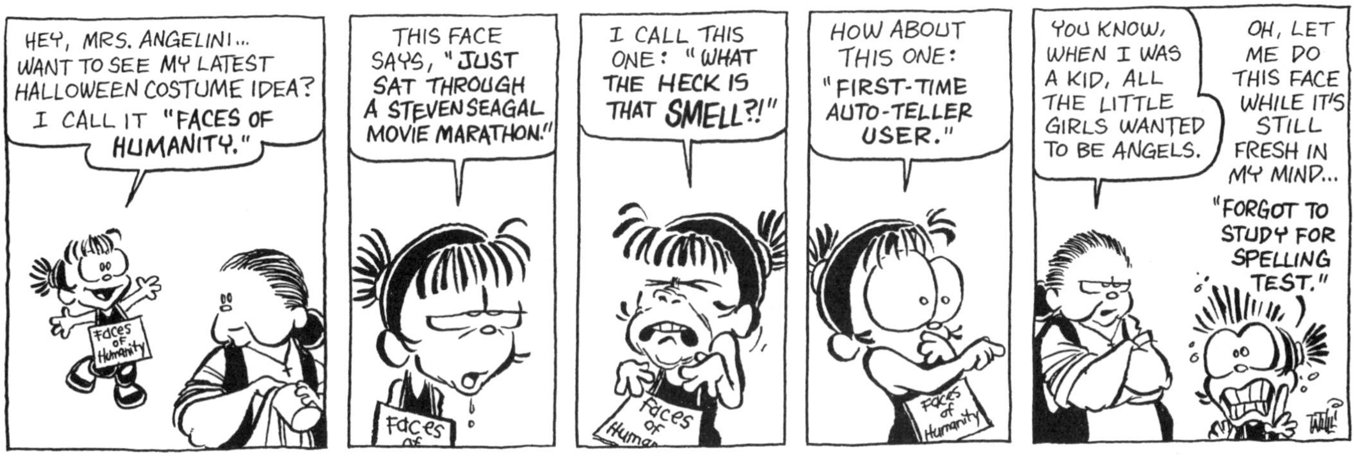
HEY, MRS. ANGELINI... WANT TO SEE MY LATEST HALLOWEEN COSTUME IDEA? I CALL IT "FACES OF HUMANITY."
Faces of Humanity
THIS FACE SAYS, "JUST SAT THROUGH A STEVEN SEAGAL MOVIE MARATHON."
I CALL THIS ONE: "WHAT THE HECK IS THAT SMELL?!"
HOW ABOUT THIS ONE: "FIRST-TIME AUTO-TELLER USER."
YOU KNOW, WHEN I WAS A KID, ALL THE LITTLE GIRLS WANTED TO BE ANGELS.
OH, LET ME DO THIS FACE WHILE IT'S STILL FRESH IN MY MIND...
"FORGOT TO STUDY FOR SPELLING TEST."

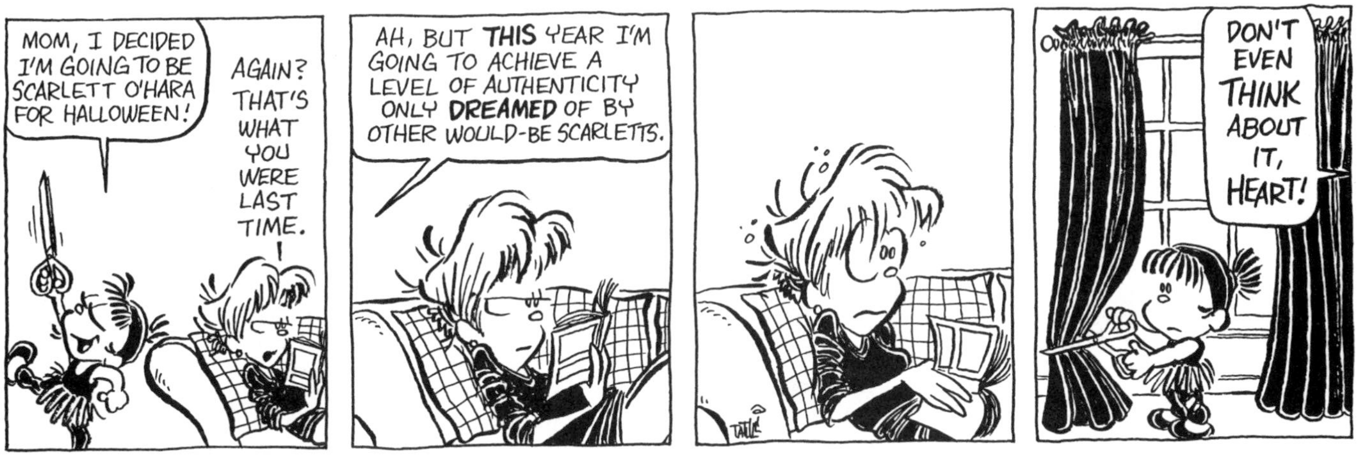
MOM, I DECIDED I'M GOING TO BE SCARLETT O'HARA FOR HALLOWEEN!
AGAIN? THAT'S WHAT YOU WERE LAST TIME.
AH, BUT THIS YEAR I'M GOING TO ACHIEVE A LEVEL OF AUTHENTICITY ONLY DREAMED OF BY OTHER WOULD-BE SCARLETTS.
DON'T EVEN THINK ABOUT IT, HEART!

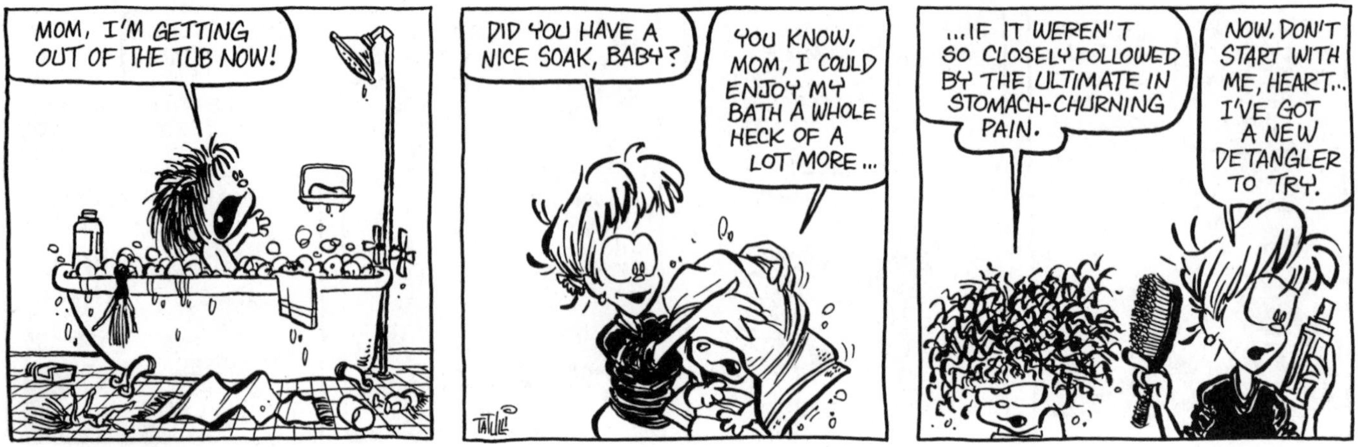
MOM, I'M GETTING OUT OF THE TUB NOW!
DID YOU HAVE A NICE SOAK, BABY?
YOU KNOW, MOM, I COULD ENJOY MY BATH A WHOLE HECK OF A LOT MORE...
...IF IT WEREN'T SO CLOSELY FOLLOWED BY THE ULTIMATE IN STOMACH-CHURNING PAIN.
NOW, DON'T START WITH ME, HEART... I'VE GOT A NEW DETANGLER TO TRY.

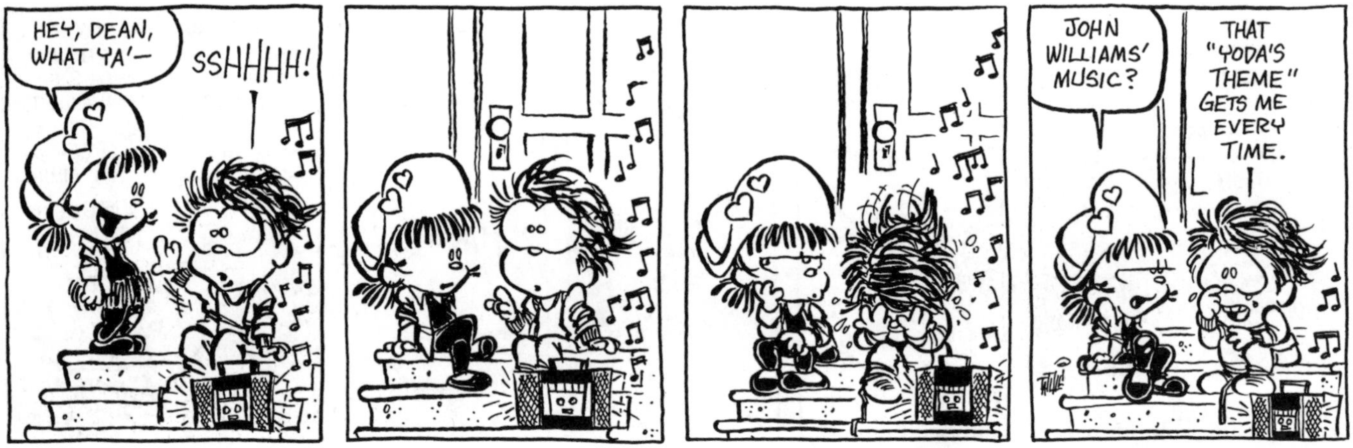
HEY, DEAN, WHAT YA'—
SSHHHH!
JOHN WILLIAMS' MUSIC?
THAT "YODA'S THEME" GETS ME EVERY TIME.

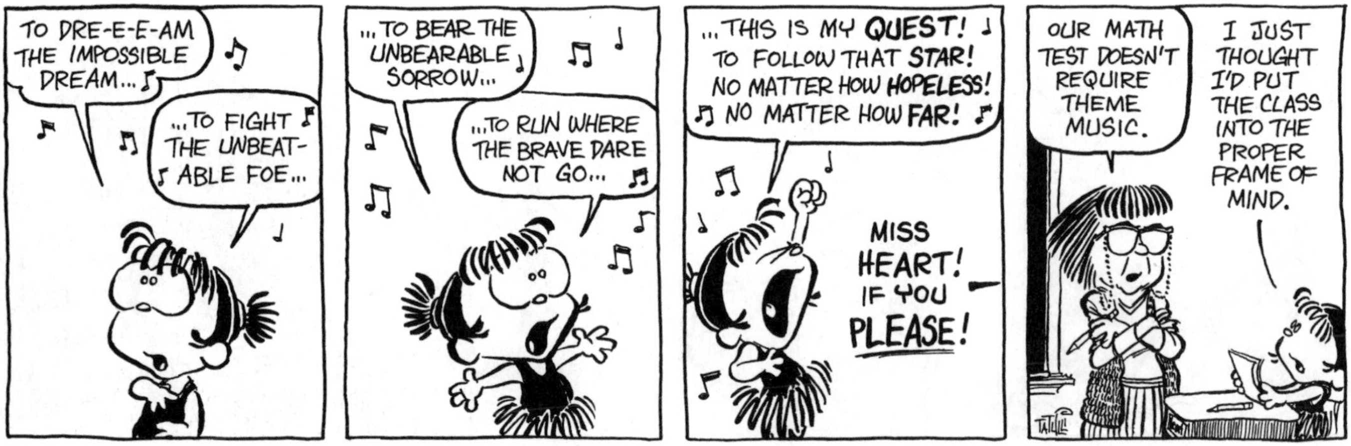
TO DRE-E-E-AM THE IMPOSSIBLE DREAM...
...TO FIGHT THE UNBEAT-ABLE FOE...
...TO BEAR THE UNBEARABLE SORROW...
...TO RUN WHERE THE BRAVE DARE NOT GO...
...THIS IS MY QUEST! TO FOLLOW THAT STAR! NO MATTER HOW HOPELESS! NO MATTER HOW FAR!
MISS HEART! IF YOU PLEASE!
OUR MATH TEST DOESN'T REQUIRE THEME MUSIC.
I JUST THOUGHT I'D PUT THE CLASS INTO THE PROPER FRAME OF MIND.

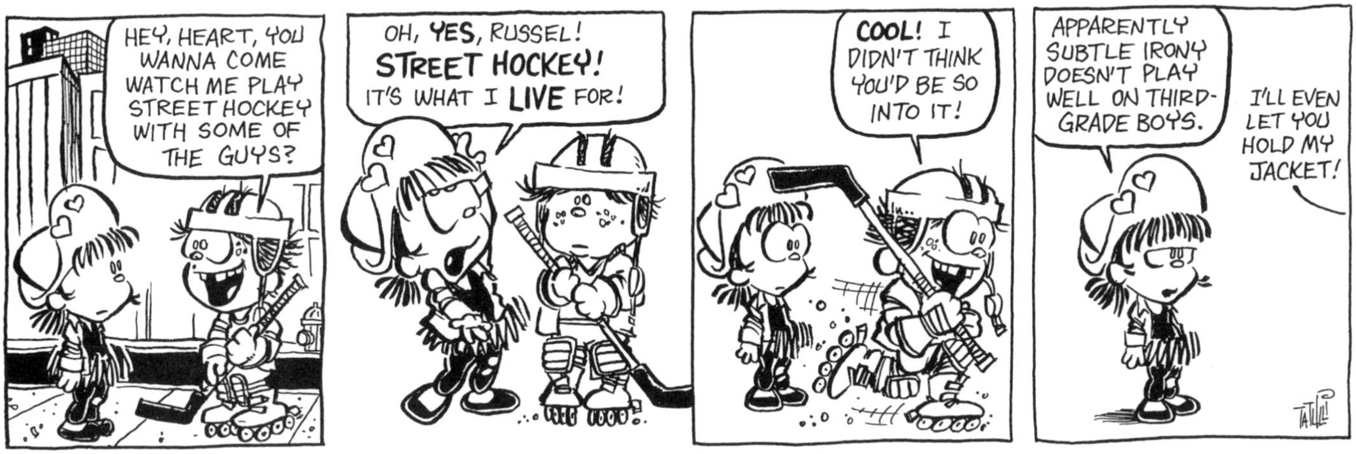
HEY, HEART, YOU WANNA COME WATCH ME PLAY STREET HOCKEY WITH SOME OF THE GUYS?
OH, YES, RUSSEL! STREET HOCKEY! IT'S WHAT I LIVE FOR!
COOL! I DIDN'T THINK YOU'D BE SO INTO IT!
APPARENTLY SUBTLE IRONY DOESN'T PLAY WELL ON THIRD-GRADE BOYS.
I'LL EVEN LET YOU HOLD MY JACKET!

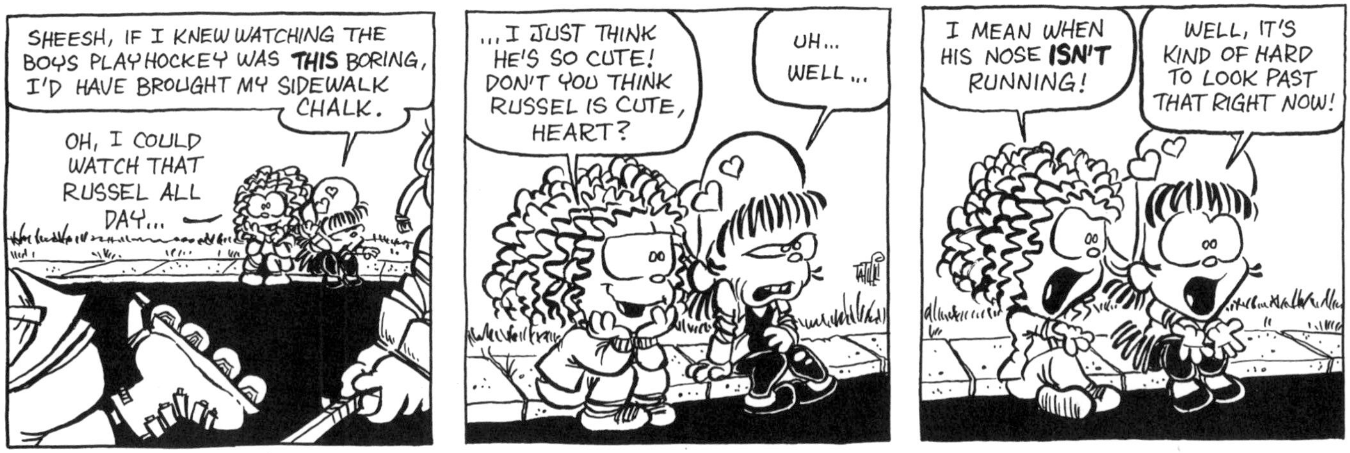
SHEESH, IF I KNEW WATCHING THE BOYS PLAY HOCKEY WAS THIS BORING, I'D HAVE BROUGHT MY SIDEWALK CHALK.
OH, I COULD WATCH THAT RUSSEL ALL DAY...
...I JUST THINK HE'S SO CUTE! DON'T YOU THINK RUSSEL IS CUTE, HEART?
UH... WELL...
I MEAN WHEN HIS NOSE ISN'T RUNNING!
WELL, IT'S KIND OF HARD TO LOOK PAST THAT RIGHT NOW!

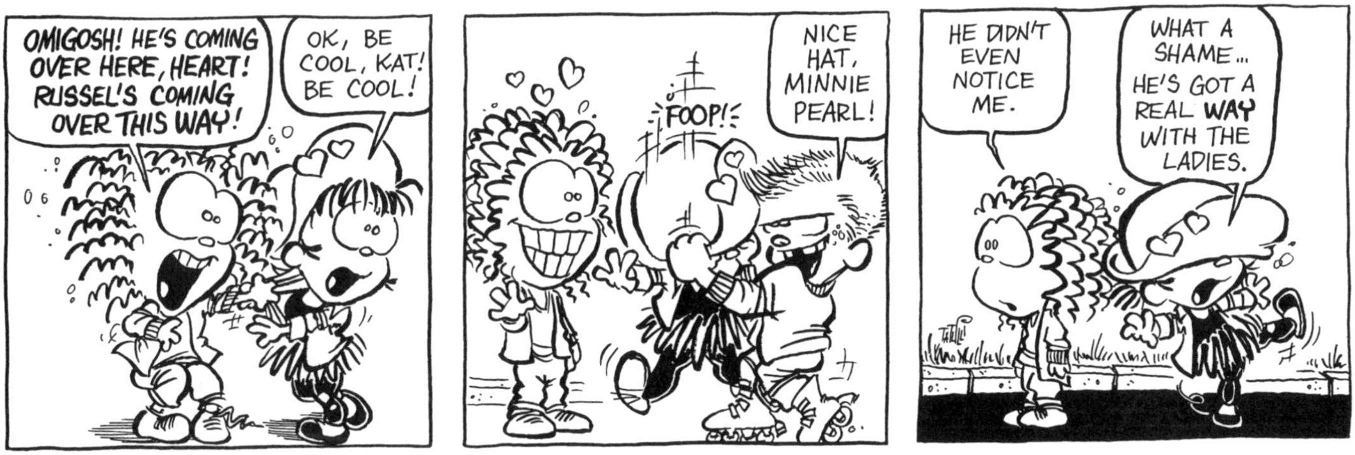
OMIGOSH! HE'S COMING OVER HERE, HEART! RUSSEL'S COMING OVER THIS WAY!
OK, BE COOL, KAT! BE COOL!
FOOP!
NICE HAT, MINNIE PEARL!
HE DIDN'T EVEN NOTICE ME.
WHAT A SHAME... HE'S GOT A REAL WAY WITH THE LADIES.

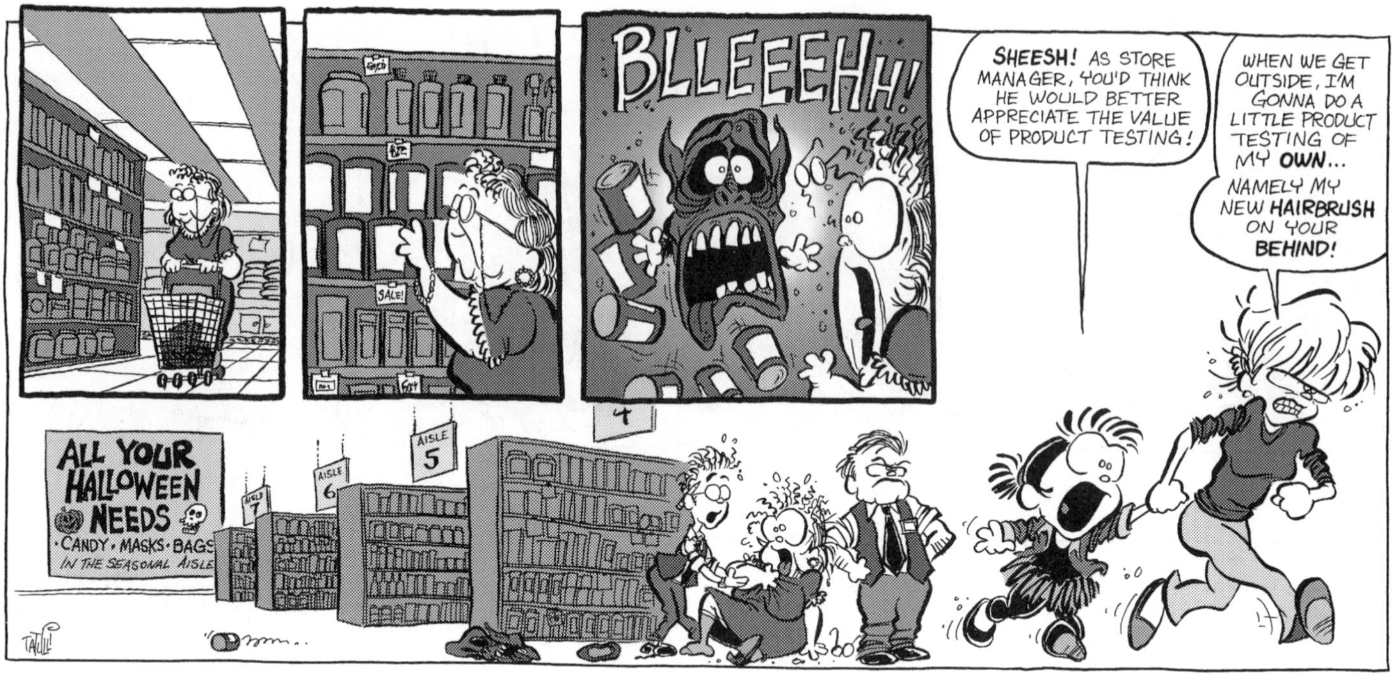
BLLEEEHH!
SHEESH! AS STORE MANAGER, YOU'D THINK HE WOULD BETTER APPRECIATE THE VALUE OF PRODUCT TESTING!
WHEN WE GET OUTSIDE, I'M GONNA DO A LITTLE PRODUCT TESTING OF MY OWN... NAMELY MY NEW HAIRBRUSH ON YOUR BEHIND!
ALL YOUR HALLOWEEN NEEDS
·CANDY·MASKS·BAGS
IN THE SEASONAL AISLE
AISLE 5
AISLE 6
AISLE 7
SALE!

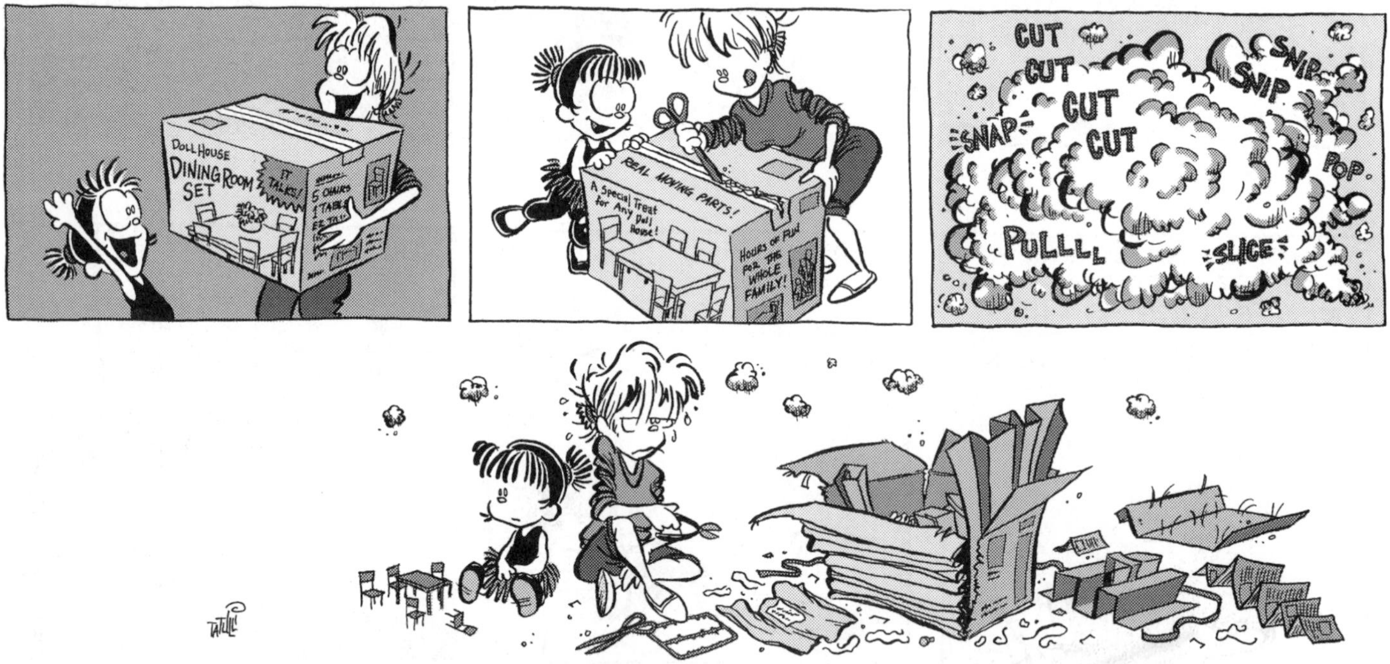
DOLL HOUSE DINING ROOM SET
IT TALKS!
REAL MOVING PARTS!
A Special Treat for Any Doll House!
HOURS OF FUN FOR THE WHOLE FAMILY!
CUT
CUT
CUT
CUT
SNIP
SNIP
SNAP
POP
PULLLL
SLICE

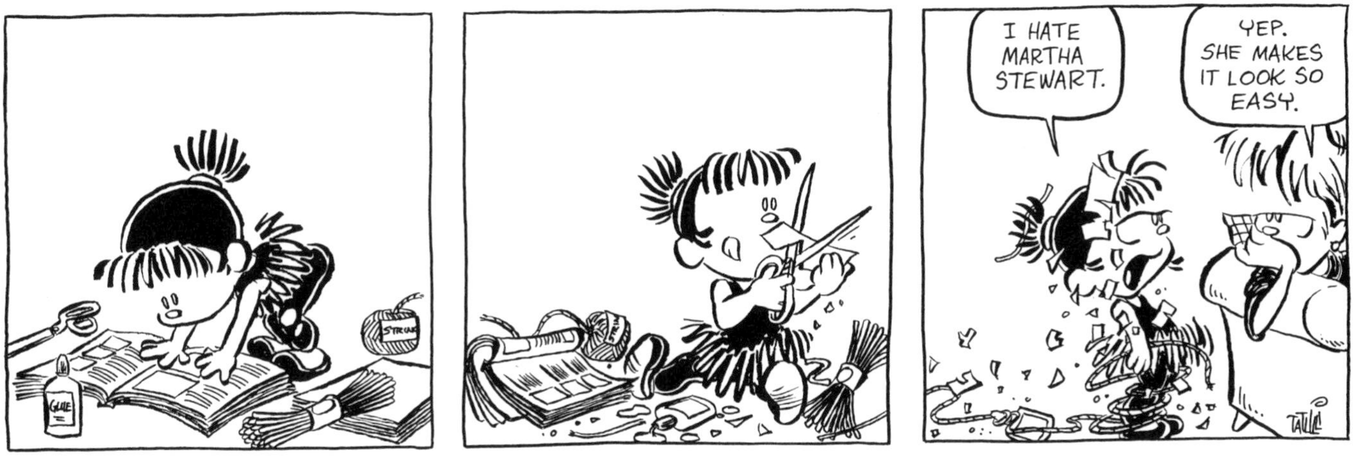
GLUE
STRING
I HATE MARTHA STEWART.
YEP. SHE MAKES IT LOOK SO EASY.

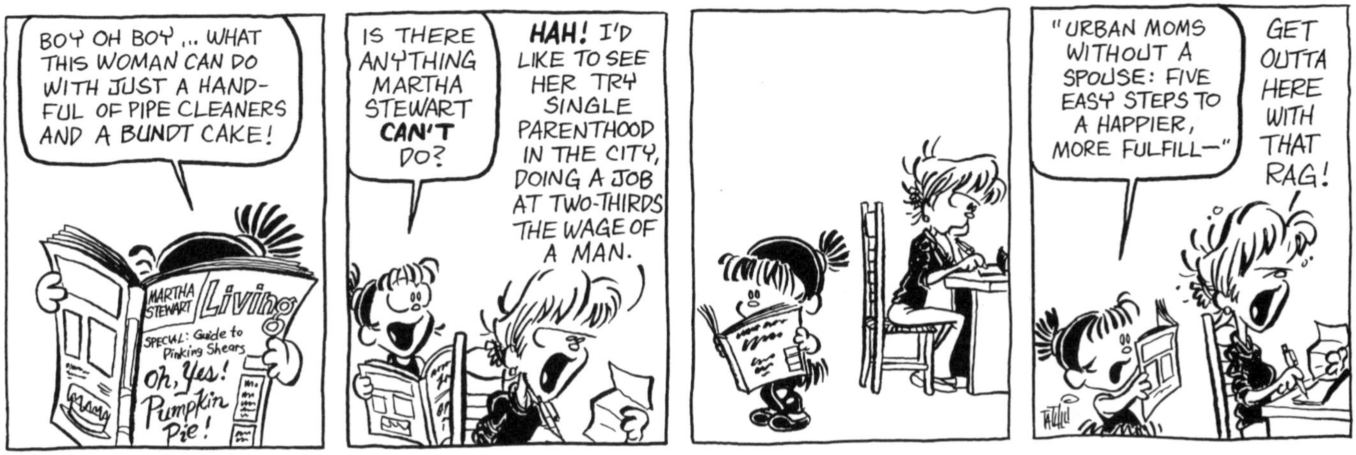
BOY OH BOY ... WHAT THIS WOMAN CAN DO WITH JUST A HAND-FUL OF PIPE CLEANERS AND A BUNDT CAKE!
MARTHA STEWART Living
SPECIAL: Guide to Pinking Shears
Oh, Yes! Pumpkin Pie!
IS THERE ANYTHING MARTHA STEWART **CAN'T** DO?
HAH! I'D LIKE TO SEE HER TRY SINGLE PARENTHOOD IN THE CITY, DOING A JOB AT TWO-THIRDS THE WAGE OF A MAN.
"URBAN MOMS WITHOUT A SPOUSE: FIVE EASY STEPS TO A HAPPIER, MORE FULFILL—"
GET OUTTA HERE WITH THAT RAG!

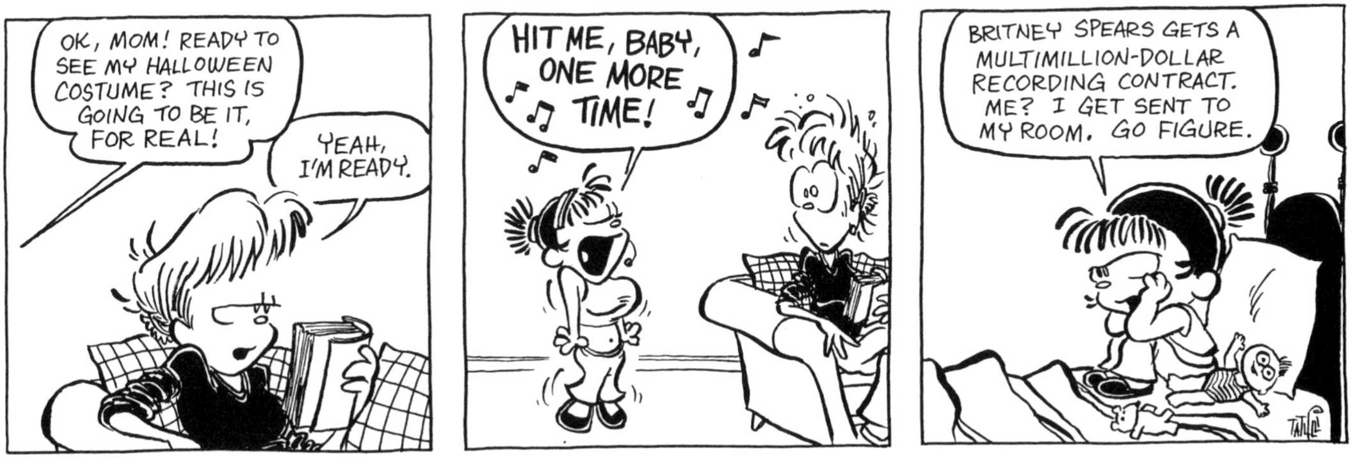
OK, MOM! READY TO SEE MY HALLOWEEN COSTUME? THIS IS GOING TO BE IT, FOR REAL!
YEAH, I'M READY.
HIT ME, BABY, ONE MORE TIME!
BRITNEY SPEARS GETS A MULTIMILLION-DOLLAR RECORDING CONTRACT. ME? I GET SENT TO MY ROOM. GO FIGURE.

The End

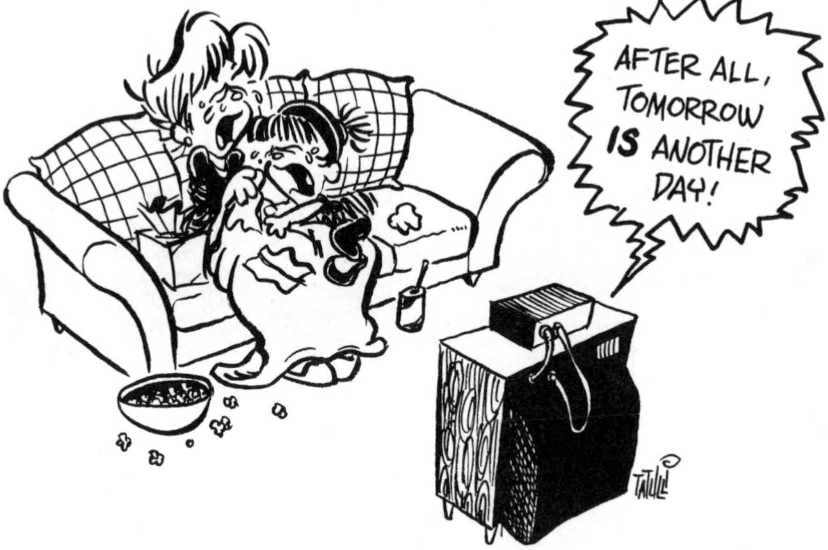
AFTER ALL, TOMORROW **IS** ANOTHER DAY!

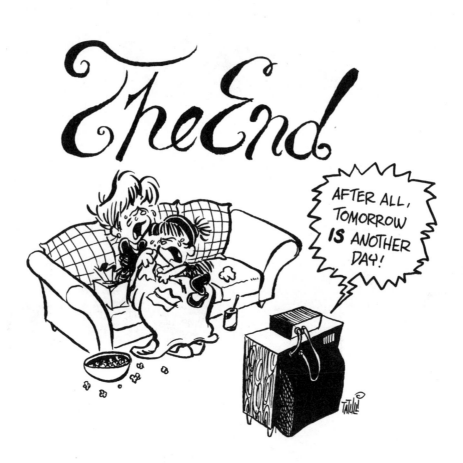